UNEQUAL PARTNERS
IN PEACE AND WAR

UNEQUAL PARTNERS IN PEACE AND WAR

*The Republic of Korea and the
United States, 1948–1953*

Jongsuk Chay

Westport, Connecticut
London

Library of Congress Cataloging-in-Publication Data

Chay, Jongsuk.
    Unequal partners in peace and war : the Republic of Korea and the United States,
    1948-1953 / Jongsuk Chay.
        p.   cm.
    Includes bibliographical references and index.
    ISBN 0-275-97125-2 (alk. paper)
    1. United States—Foreign relations—Korea (South).   2. Korea (South)—Foreign
relations—United States.   3. United States—Foreign relations—1945-1953.   4. Korean
War, 1950-1953—Diplomatic history.   I. Title.
    E183.8.K6C446   2002
    327.5195073′09′044—dc21   2001045836

British Library Cataloguing in Publication Data is available.

Library of Congress Catalog Card Number: 2001045836
ISBN: 0-275-97125-2

First published in 2002

Praeger Publishers, 88 Post Road West, Westport, CT 06881
An imprint of Greenwood Publishing Group, Inc.
www.praeger.com

Printed in the United States of America

The paper used in this book complies with the
Permanent Paper Standard issued by the National
Information Standards Organization (Z39.48–1984).

10 9 8 7 6 5 4 3 2 1

To my parents
Chay Konglin and Myung Ju
and all others who suffered because of the 38th parallel
and the war in Korea

Contents

Preface

This study is the second part of my three-part study of a century of Korean–American relations between 1860 and 1961. The first volume, *Diplomacy of Asymmetry*, covered the early years of the two-nation relationship to 1910. This study treats the following forty-three-year, two-nation relationship, with an emphasis on the seven critical years of the formal diplomatic relationship of the two republics between 1948 and 1953.

A great number of U.S. and other government documents and other writings of contemporaries and later authors have been produced concerning the Korean War (even though it is often called "the forgotten war"), and an examination of the archival and published materials for the subject has been an enormous task. I hope I have not made too many hasty or unfair judgments in analyzing these materials. The paucity of Korean archival materials is regrettable, but nothing much can be done about the lost materials. The presently available Chinese and Russian materials regarding the Korean War are certainly interesting and valuable for viewing the other side of the story, but the story based on these materials is only probable and tentative because of their limited and selective nature.

I am grateful to a number of institutions for their financial support for my research: the University of North Carolina at Pembroke, the Harry S. Truman Library, the American Philosophical Society, the Korean Foundation, and the Far Eastern Institute of the Kyŏngnam University. Staff members of the archives and the libraries I have used have been very generous in providing efficient services for my research: the UNC Pembroke Library, the National Archives, the Harry S. Truman Library, the Dwight D. Eisenhower

Library, the Princeton University Library, the Library of Congress, UNC Chapel Hill Library, the St. Andrews Presbyterian College Library, the Seoul National University Library, and the National Central Library and the National Assembly Library, both in Seoul. I am very heavily indebted to a number of individuals for their selfless assistance for my project. Youngnok Koo and Ki-moon Lee have given me very precious encouragement and assistance for years of my research; Grace Gibson, Robert Brown, William Stueck, and Robert Swartout read the whole manuscript and gave me numerous valuable suggestions and comments. Of course, all decisions and shortcomings in the book are mine. Shirley Deese gave me her usual, generous staff support. My wife June has also given me many years of dedicated support for this project.

Introduction

The special relationship between Korea and the United States began in the late nineteenth century with the opening of the "Hermit Kingdom" by an American naval officer, Commodore Robert W. Schufeldt. This relationship continued through the following century, with a lengthy break of three and a half decades from 1910 to 1945 when Korea was under Japanese imperial control. After three years of military occupation by the United States following the end of the Second World War, the diplomatic relationship between the two nations resumed in 1948. The following five-year period from 1948 to 1953, which included two years of relatively quiet but fierce ideological conflict between democracy and communism followed by three years of war on the Korean peninsula, is the major period covered by this study. The Korean–American relationship during this critical five-year period may be characterized as a relationship between two strikingly different nations—a weak, poor, and underdeveloped East Asian nation and a powerful, rich, and developed Western nation. To a large extent, the difficulties in the two nations' relationship stemmed from the contradictory general nature of modern diplomacy, which is based on legal equality and power differences.

A number of factors play an important role in international relations, and national interest is one of those. One of the concerns in dealing with national interest is the existence of different kinds of interests—common, complementary, and in conflict—which influences nation-to-nation relations but tug in conflicting directions and with varying strength from situation to situation. Another concern in dealing with national interests is the length of time involved, whether short, middle, or long term. Often a problem for a nation is its loss of a proper balance among the different lengths of interests, for governments tend to become preoccupied with short-term interests while neglecting middle- and long-term interests. Also we must consider whether the matter of national interest has received too much emphasis in the study of modern international relations. Despite the fact that the nation-state system dominates human life in the modern era, other interests, ranging from individual to universal, should not be neglected. These concerns will provide a guide for this study.[1]

Power, another important factor in international relations, played a key role for Korean–American relations as the United States stood atop the global hierarchy in the post–World War II era and Korea stood near the bottom. Although South Korea had a military force of considerable size, because of the antagonistic relationship with North Korea, the net military strength in South Korea was almost negligible. Perhaps the most important element to a real understanding of the relationship between the Republic of Korea and the United States is its asymmetry. While not unique in bilateral relationships, this asymmetry became the defining matter of anxiety in the Korean–American relationship. The United States, very powerful and wealthy yet traditionally with little interest in Korean affairs, stood in stark contrast to Korea, very weak and poor but with great need for the assistance of the United States. Given this asymmetrical condition, the two-nation relationship was bound to have difficulties. The geopolitical factor, always significant for the Korean peninsula, one of the best examples of buffer states in the world, deserves special attention for the understanding of international relations surrounding the peninsula. As in most cases of international relationships, issues of mutual trust and threat became significant. Special attention is needed to see how these two factors worked through the years for Korean–American relations. Political leaders play a central role in relations between nations; they make a nation's policies and execute them, while the people follow their leaders and sometimes express their opinions on national policies. Understanding the nature and characteristics of Korean and American leaders becomes especially important for Korean–American relations because of their controversial personalities which were shaped by two different cultural traditions.

Illustrious leaders served on both sides: in Korea, there were Syngman Rhee and a number of lesser figures, while on the American side were Harry Truman, Dwight Eisenhower, Dean Acheson, and John Foster Dulles. Rhee's role is particularly important through the entire post–World War II period in Korea, but it is still very inadequately understood or perhaps misunderstood. Because of his crude and pernicious handling of domestic politics, he has been largely neglected or avoided by Korean scholars as a subject for study, and the treatment of him by foreign authors has been much colored by cultural bias. The Koreans have just begun to realize the need to properly understand the founder of their republic. To many foreign observers, Syngman Rhee is simply one of the worst Oriental despots, who was noted for his Machiavellian techniques and tolerance of corruption; on the other hand, when Rhee's actions were beyond easy comprehension, he was simply considered to be senile. It is necessary to avoid the trap of stereotyped views and to try to understand why he acted as he did. Because of his domination of the Korean scene, the roles of other Korean leaders have been neglected. The post–World War II years in Korea bear similarity to the latter part of the eighteenth century in North America; almost by necessity a number of heroes emerged in Korea. A group of very capable and patriotic Koreans like Kim Ku, Kim Kyusik, Yŏ Un-hyŏng, Song Chin-u, Chang Dŏk-su, and Chough Pyŏng-ok dedicated their lives to the nation in those critical years, although because of special circumstances, they could not play the roles comparable to those played by Thomas Jefferson, John Adams, Alexander Hamilton, and Benjamin Franklin.

The post–World War II years were crucial for the United States because of the Cold War. Truman and Acheson played key roles in making the policy decisions and executing them to fight the war. As head of the government and chief advisers for the nation's external policy, the two worked very closely and efficiently together. Their leadership role in decisions about national priorities and strategies in dealing with Korea had decisive impact on the matter of peace and war, and their capabilities and limitations shaped U.S. policy. Had others been in their positions, Korean–American relations in the 1940s would have been much different; further, if others had been in their positions in 1950, it is likely that not only the history of Korean–American diplomatic relations but also the whole history of the Cold War would have been different. Eisenhower and Dulles also played important roles in Korean–American relations; they inherited the war on the peninsula from their predecessors and had to manage it. Because of Eisenhower's unique background, he was able to handle more effectively the process of making peace. His background and personality had much importance for the Korean leaders; his warm personal outlook and an ability to understand some of Rhee's leadership qualities along with his shortcomings became a positive factor for the Korean leaders. Rhee had some definite warm personal feeling toward Dulles, which was reciprocated. The relationship between Rhee and General MacArthur is also an interesting case: Rhee had special feelings toward and a great sense of trust in MacArthur, but it is doubtful how much of it was returned by the general.

A cultural factor closely related to that of leadership and extremely important in international relationship has much to do with perception or image formation in the foreign policy-making process. The world of a policy maker is, in a sense, not a real world but a perceived world, created largely by his cultural background. The resulting problem of intercultural communication poses difficult, if not impossible, challenges in the process of diplomatic relations. Cultural diplomacy, or what a nation does to another nation to make itself better understood, plays a determining role in international relations. In a broader sense, international relations is a part of intercultural relations, and when two nations have political interactions, in a real sense two cultures collide. Hence, to understand international relations we must understand intercultural relations, and we need to understand the relations between Korean and American cultures to understand their diplomatic relations.[2]

Ideological conflict dominated the latter half of the twentieth century. After 1945 the world was gripped by the struggle between two ideologies—communism and liberal democracy. Since Korean–American relations in the post–World War II years developed within the context of this ideological conflict, the role of ideology in diplomatic relationship was significant. Both ideologies were strange to the Koreans at this time, even though a small segment of the Korean population had some understanding of them. Nevertheless, once this conflict was thrust upon the nation, the Koreans had no choice but to live through the 1940s and 1950s with the fear of the ideological conflict. This imposition happened not only to the Koreans, but also to the Americans. In a sense, the whole world was victimized by the seemingly unnecessary calamity of ideological struggle. In this ideological conflict, the idea of neutralization of the Korean peninsula was bound to fail, yet it entered into the process of Korean–American relations in the 1940s and the 1950s, and as a consequence deserves our attention.

The Korean War, the most important event of this study, lasted a little over three years between 1950 and 1953 and occupied the major portion of the two-nation relationship during the five years from 1948 to 1953. Hence, the war's origins and characteristics, the main strategies employed, the nature and problems of the peacemaking process, and the consequences of the war demand our careful attention. Scholarly controversies continue as to whether it was a civil war or an international war, a necessary or an unnecessary war, and an important war or a forgotten war. Obviously, the war was both Korean and international, and the question is whether it had more of a Korean or an international character. The question of origins of the war, which has occupied the center of many previous studies on the war, raises the causality question, a matter quite difficult to deal with. Considerations in trying to answer this question include a number of key factors: (1) the status of the two armies on the Korean peninsula in the spring of 1950; (2) U.S. perceptions, policies, and declarations regarding Korean security in the same period; (3) what the Koreans did or failed to do during a year and a half period from the summer of 1948 to the end of the following year; (4) the U.S. troop withdrawal and U.S. military and economic aid policies in South Korea during the same period; (5) the U.S. perception of the strategic value of the Korean peninsula, and the referral of the Korean case to the United Nations in 1947; (6) the U.S. decision in favor of military occupation and occupation policies; (7) Korean actions and failures during the occupation period; (8) the decision for the division of the Korean peninsula along the 38th parallel; and (9) the role or lack of the role played by the Koreans in the division and liberation. Finding causal linkages among these factors and weighing them according to relative importance is a difficult but important task.

The Korean War had many surprises: U.S. intervention, contrary to the expectations of North Koreans, Russians, Chinese, South Koreans, and many Americans; General MacArthur's successful resistance and the Inchŏn landing and the ensuing march to the Korean–Manchurian border; Chinese intervention, against the expectations of many, including MacArthur himself; the U.S. decision to limit the war and accept the end of the fighting without victory; and the Chinese acceptance of its failure to push the U.N. forces out of the peninsula. And, while all these events were underway, what were the Koreans doing?

The Korean peace was one of the most difficult made in modern time, mainly because of its negotiation at a time of stalemate on the battlefield and in the context of mutual distrust between the two ideologically and culturally different negotiating teams. The leadership, the strategies and tactics adopted, and the ideals and realities perceived in the peace negotiations accordingly need special attention. Also, the role played by the threat of nuclear weapons and roles played by the South and the North Koreans deserve due attention. Finally, the war as well as the peace had different meanings for the different nations involved: the war's great and long-lasting impact upon Korean politics and society, both in the North and the South; the Korean War's considerable impact upon the U.S. security posture and its relations with communist China and the Soviet Union; the war's impact upon both communist China and the Soviet Union; and the unavoidable impact of the U.N.'s participation in the war on the collective security system.

The war brought special diplomatic problems to the relationship between the Republic of Korea and the United States, including relief and rehabilitation. The Koreans paid a great price in the war. A key question arose as to how much relief the Korean population needed and how it would be delivered. The matter of relief and rehabilitation was also closely connected to the problem of reconstruction and the question of how to handle immediate as well as long-range needs. The collective approach through the United Nations added complexity to the question.

Another important concern arose during the war: the issue of American intervention in the domestic politics of the Republic of Korea. Americans faced the problem of how to reconcile the traditional policy of nonintervention in other nations' affairs with the need for an intervention dictated by wartime conditions on the Korean peninsula. Another important question was to find a conciliation point for the divergent national objectives of the two nations regarding the peacemaking process; the problem of finding the proper conversion point between the Korean effort to maximize American guarantees of security after the conclusion of the truce negotiation and the American effort to minimize its promises for future Korean security against the communist threat.

The key concern of this study is how the two different and unequal partners behaved in dealing with the other through times of peace and war. National interests, power, geopolitics, ideology, culture, and personality were some of the key factors which played decisive roles for this two-nation relationship. Although wartime and peacetime should receive equal attention in a study of history, most historical studies are event oriented, and this study is not an exception to this tradition. The two years preceeding the Korean War will be treated more as a part of the coming crisis. The two-nation diplomacy, including the outbreak of the war, war strategies and battles, and peacemaking, provide the focus of the war period. Fortunately, some Russian and Chinese archival materials have become available in recent years and have been helpful for the author to examine the line of thinking and series of actions on the other side of the war.

NOTES

1. For recent and comprehensive discussion on national interests, see Koo Youngnok, *Hankukŭi kukka iik: Oekyo chŏngch'iŭi hyŏnsilkwa isang* (National interests of Korea: The reality and the ideal in international politics) (Seoul: Pŏpmunsa, 1995).

2. See Samuel P. Huntington, "The Clash of Civilizations?" *Foreign Affairs* 72 (1993): 22–49; Chay Jongsuk, ed., *Culture and International Relations* (New York: Praeger, 1990). See also John Beate, "The Power of Culture in International Relations: The Spanish Conquest in the Americas and Its Theoretical Repercussions" (manuscript, 1996).

PART I

PRELUDE:
KOREAN–AMERICAN
RELATIONS TO 1948

CHAPTER 1

Korea and the United States before the Second World War

This study begins with a sketch of the thirty-eight-year gap in formal diplomatic relations between 1910, when Korean sovereignty was lost and diplomatic ties were broken, and 1948, when Korean sovereignty was restored and full diplomatic relations were resumed. The beginning of the Korean–American relationship can be traced back to the late eighteenth century, when the medicinal herb ginseng, which had been produced in Korea and the United States, began to compete in the Chinese market. As American trade with China grew during the following century, American ships occasionally wrecked on the Korean coast, with the result that contact between the Koreans and Americans became more frequent. Two significant events not long after the end of the American Civil War accelerated the development of relations between the two nations. The first event was the *General Sherman* incident of 1866, and the second was the 1871 American naval expedition to the Korean coast.

The *General Sherman*, an American schooner of about eighty tons loaded with cotton and other goods and with a crew of three Americans, two British, and nineteen Malays and Chinese, entered Korean waters in July 1866. Ignoring the local magistrate's warning, the vessel ascended the Taedong River toward P'yŏngyang. The *General Sherman* was heavily armed, and it appears that part of the purpose of the trip was piracy; be that as it may, the main objective of the voyage was trade, which violated both Korean law and policy. Violence soon broke out between the insolent intruders and the excited natives, and the ship as well as its crew were burned and destroyed.

This unfortunate incident drew the attention of the American government, and two fact-finding naval missions set out in the following two years. The affair also provided one of the reasons for the 1871 naval expedition.[1]

The Low-Rodgers expedition of 1871 was an even more unfortunate event. By dispatching this large-scale expedition, the American government indicated that its main objective was to open the "Hermit Kingdom." The resulting violence, however, delayed the opening of Korea by over a decade. In addition to this objective of opening the last closed East Asian kingdom, the expedition also was intended to obtain more information regarding the *General Sherman* incident. The expedition was a joint project of the State and Navy Departments, and Minister Frederick Low in China and Admiral John Rodgers, the commander of the American Asiatic Fleet, were charged with execution of the project. For a two-month expedition in May and June 1871, five naval ships with a total of over ten thousand tons and eighty-five guns and over one thousand men were mobilized. When the expeditionary forces arrived in the Korean waters near Chemulp'o, present-day Inch'ŏn, its commanders decided to explore the Han River up to the capital city of Seoul. After initial communications with minor local Korean officials about the purpose of a peaceful mission, including plans for surveys, two gunboats set out. But when American naval forces reached some Korean forts, they were fired upon unexpectedly, and an exchange of gunfire took place. Somewhat hastily the Americans decided to carry out a punitive action that would also demonstrate their power. A three-day amphibious operation, involving three gunboats and 759 men, was launched against the five forts on the Kanghwa Island. This miniature war ended in a great military victory for the American force, and all five forts were destroyed, at a cost of 350 Korean casualties, while only two Americans were killed and nine wounded. The mission, however, failed to achieve its main objective of opening the doors of the Korean kingdom.[2]

After the opening of the doors of China and Japan in the mid-nineteenth century, Korea remained the only East Asian nation still closed to the outside world. Motives behind the American determination to open Korea were similar to those which forced the opening of Japan, and they included better treatment for shipwrecked crews and trade. And, as with Japan, personal ambition was an important factor behind the opening of Korea. Commodore Robert W. Shufeldt's personal interest in Korea played a significant role in the American action. After seven American abortive attempts, including that of 1871, Shufeldt made his first attempt in 1880 during his *Ticonderoga* mission. The Koreans were not yet ready for a positive response, and Schufeldt's attempt failed, but he took the very important step of establishing contact with Li Hung-chang of China, who was in a powerful position in Chinese politics and able to influence the external policy of Korea. After an arduous ten-month period of waiting and indirect negotiations through Li, the Treaty of Peace, Amity and Navigation (the Inch'ŏn Treaty) was finally signed on May 22, 1882. The treaty was typical of the so-called nonequal treaties with provisions for extraterritoriality, a most-favored nation clause, and other such measures common to an unequal treaty, but it also had special features, like a more lenient tariff rate and a good offices clause. As it turned out, the Korean–American treaty of 1882 was beneficial for all the nations involved. Even though some thought that the treaty hurt Korea by opening the nation to international intrigues, this opening would have come sooner or later, and sooner was better for the Koreans in the long run. The treaty with the United States also became a model for later treaties with other nations. The treaty did not bring any immediate tangible benefit to the United States, but it must have added some weight to the nation's long-term world leadership role. Despite Li's failure to put the dependency clause into the treaty, China at least achieved the objective of enhancing its relative influence in Korea against the Japanese ascendancy. For Korea, the treaty marked an important turning point on her road toward modernization.[3]

The twelve years between 1882 and 1894 provided important opportunities for the Koreans. Had they used these years wisely and courageously, they might have been able to make up for losses during the three past decades and lay the groundwork for the building of a modern nation during the following three decades. Their major problem during this period was how to maintain their independence against a vigorous Chinese policy of intervention and to move quickly to modernize the nation by learning from nations like the United States and Japan. For the Americans, these twelve years were the period in which they established diplomatic relations with the newly opened nation and determined the basic policy lines toward the East Asian kingdom. Through the first minister Lucius H. Foote and succeeding representatives in Seoul, the American government gave small but thoughtful assistance to the Koreans in their modernization efforts. In regard to the struggle of the Koreans with the Chinese, the Americans adopted a dual policy of taking a neutral position on the issue of Korean–Chinese relations, while trying to help the Koreans maintain their sovereignty. Unfortunately, the Koreans were not able to move vigorously and efficiently in the direction of modernization, and the nation became, at the end of this period, a target in the power struggle between two powerful neighbors—China and Japan.

The following twelve years from 1894 to 1904 were the most crucial years in the modern era of Korean history. They were also important years for the development of Korean–American relations. During these years, the East Asian international subsystem was transformed from a balance-of-power system to one-power domination. These changes endangered the very independence of the Kingdom of Korea. In these years of crises, Korean–American relations had to go through a period of severe testing to discover what a distant Western nation with minimal national interests in Korea would do at a time when the ancient East Asian kingdom was in the process of decline and demise.

By the spring of 1894, the Japanese Empire, which had been successfully modernizing during the previous two and a half decades, was ready to test its strength against the Chinese Empire, which had been less successful in responding to the coming of the West. When the armies of the two empires landed on Korean soil by using the Tonghak Rebellion as a pretext, the Korean king turned to the United States in an effort to prevent a war which would surely destroy the independence of the small kingdom. The American government, under the leadership of President Grover Cleveland and Secretary of State Walter Q. Gresham, responded to the Korean king's plea and offered good offices to the two belligerent powers to try to prevent the war. When this offer was not heeded, the American government fell back to the policy of strict neutrality throughout the war. The American republic, with small interest in the peninsula kingdom, could not do more. When the war ended with an overwhelming Japanese victory, the Chinese had to retreat from the Korean peninsula, leaving Japan as the dominant power.[4]

The Korean peninsula during the decade between 1895 and 1904 witnessed a repetition of the events of the previous decade with a partial change of players. Due partly to the circumstances created in the fall of 1895 by the crude Japanese act of assassinating the Korean queen and the king's flight to the Russian legation, and partly to the perennial Russian interest in the Korean peninsula, the Japanese Empire had to spend another decade dealing with one more antagonist in Korea. For the Koreans, the decade gave them another chance to meet the challenges facing them and save their independence from assault by predatory powers. In those years of turmoil, American interests grew through more trade and almost monopolistic concessions for building railways, mining, and other enterprises. Nonetheless, the American government's interest in Korea in those years under the leadership of President William McKinley and Theodore Roosevelt declined, and U.S. policy gradually switched from neutrality to indifference.[5]

The Japanese position in Korea was so strong by 1904 that the Russians tacitly acknowledged Japanese control before the outbreak of the Russo–Japanese War, and the war was fought mainly over control of Manchuria. President Theodore Roosevelt's interest in the maintenance of the balance of power in the Far East and his personal interest in the "Japanese race" led him to favor a Japanese victory. Going beyond indifference to the Korean cause, he cooperated with the Japanese as they took over the Korean peninsula. The Portsmouth Peace Treaty, to which Roosevelt made an important contribution, formally removed the last obstacle preventing the subjugation of Korea, and by the fall of 1905, Korea was practically in the hands of the Japanese. Roosevelt volunteered to withdraw the American legation in Seoul, and the United States became the first nation to remove its legation from Korea. There were no direct diplomatic relations between the two nations during the following five-year period; the United States maintained the consulate general in Seoul to 1910, when the Japanese formally annexed Korea.

Thus, the United States became the first Western nation to come and the first nation to leave Korea. Ironically, when the United States returned to the Korean peninsula forty years later, it replaced the Japanese Empire.[6]

The initial Korean–American relationship of two decades indeed reveals the nature and extent of each nation's interests with regard to the other. It should be pointed out that the two-nation relationship began with the Americans knocking on the Korean door. Aside from that, the American republic had little national interest in this small, distant Asian kingdom, and even the need for improvements in the treatment of shipwrecked seamen on the Korean coast was much exaggerated by the policy makers in Washington. As the Korean officials aptly pointed out, the traditional Korean policy had been to treat humanely the strange shipwrecked seamen on their coast, and there was no need to make a "special arrangement." Trade and other economic interests were secondary to the Americans, while American security and international relational interests relating to Korea were almost nonexistent in the 1880s. Nevertheless, American missionary activity was relatively large in Korea, although not very important for American diplomacy. Altogether, America took little interest in Korea, certainly not an important nation for the United States.

When we switch our attention to the Korean side, we find quite a different situation. In those years, the Koreans were desperately struggling to survive among their three powerful neighbors—China, Japan, and Russia—and they thought that quickly building a "wealthy and strong" nation through the process of modernization was the key that would solve the problem. In their efforts to meet this urgent national need, the Koreans could not have found a better nation to turn to than the United States—distant, wealthy, powerful, and without imperialistic ambitions in the Korean peninsula. The Koreans badly needed American help, but Korea had very little to offer the Americans. Asymmetry, the key problem for Korean–American relations, posed the question for the Koreans of what and how much this disinterested but friendly nation would do for them. Twenty-three years experience showed that the United States would not offer much beyond good offices, indifference, and eventual collaboration with an adversary.[7]

Between 1910 and 1948, Korea and the United States did not have a formal diplomatic relationship. During this long period, there was also little opportunity to develop a people-to-people relationship between Koreans and Americans. Only during the last seven years of this period, beginning in late 1941, did activities increase between the two nations. Of course, this kind of gap occurs frequently in international society, but it is by no means a normal phenomenon.

The Koreans suffered much during the first decade of Japanese rule, but they were not able to do much to resist the imposition of alien rule during this decade of worldwide crisis brought on by World War I. However, Korean grievances exploded like a volcano toward the end of the decade.

The year 1919 was a very special year, indeed a turning point, for the history of Korean nationalism. Although there was considerable planning and organizational leadership behind the March 1 Movement of 1919, the outburst of demands for independence from Japanese rule by Koreans on the whole peninsula was almost spontaneous. The Americans were involved in the March 1 Movement in two ways: First, the impetus behind the movement came directly from President Wilson's idea of national self-determination; second, many Americans, including a good number of congressional leaders, expressed sympathy for the Korean cause. For many American missionaries in Korea, the magnitude of the March 1 Movement, in which an estimated seven thousand Koreans were killed, was more than a surprise, and the cruelty of the Japanese authorities in crushing the nonviolent movement was a shock.[8] They did not hesitate to express their feelings about these bloody incidents. American presses in Korea were also active, and some nine thousand articles were published in the United States on the movement between March 1 of that year and the end of the following year.[9] The missionary reports were used later in a comprehensive report by the Commission on Relations with the Orient of the Federal Council of Churches of Christians in America, which made the important contribution of informing the American public about the incidents and of moving American congressmen.[10]

In addition to these sources, both the Korean Provisional Government and the League of the Friends of Korea provided the American public and the government with information about the situation in Korea. The Korean Provisional Government was established in Shanghai in the spring of 1919 by a group of prominent Koreans, and it became the single most important organization for Korean–American relations during the two and a half decades before the latter part of the 1940s. It was active in the United States through a committee headed by two illustrious leaders—Syngman Rhee and Philip Jasohn (Sŏh Jae-pil). Failing in their direct appeal to President Wilson for his help in improving the situation in Korea, committee leaders turned to the American public and the Congress through mass media and public lectures.[11] The League of the Friends of Korea was established in Philadelphia in 1919 by Senator Floyd W. Tompkins and seventeen other Americans with the purpose of helping the Koreans by appealing to the American public. Joined by many influential Americans in various sectors of the society, the organization, with nineteen branches in the country, became active for the Korean cause. One of the members—A. C. Whiting—delivered as many as 266 speeches on behalf of the Koreans.[12]

By early summer, enough information on the Korean situation since March had reached the United States to disturb many Americans, including a number of senators. On June 30, Senator Selden P. Spencer of Missouri submitted a resolution to the Senate, which was read and referred to the Foreign Relations Committee, requesting the Secretary of State to inform the Senate whether the situation in Korea at the time was such as to "indicate the necessity and wisdom of the United States exerting its offices on behalf of Korea."[13] Two weeks later, on July 15, Senator George W. Norris presented to the Senate the report of the Presbyterian Church of America on the condition of Korea, which had been printed in the *New York Times* on July 13.[14] Two days later, a full, detailed report on the atrocities in Korea prepared by the Federal Council of Churches of Christ in America was presented to the Senate.[15] The senators who had been bringing shocking Korean atrocity stories to the Senate floor did not stop there. They made public during the summer and fall the background to the incident in Korea by tracing what the Japanese had been doing to the Koreans since 1905, when the Japanese Empire had become the virtual ruler of the Korean peninsula. The "injustice" committed by the government of the United States under Theodore Roosevelt in collaborating with the ambitions of the Japanese government was also publicized. Senator Philander C. Knox, who headed the Department of State under the Taft administration, even labeled the hasty withdrawal of American legation in the fall of 1905 a "serious blunder in American diplomacy."[16]

The information which had been brought to the U.S. Congress in the summer and fall of 1919 apparently created much sympathy in the minds of American congressmen. Resolutions expressing sympathy with a recognition of the aspiration of the Korean people were introduced in both houses (S. Res. 200 and H. Res. 359) and referred to committees.[17] The introduction of the resolutions themselves is significant, but an important question is what effect did they have upon the executive branch of the U.S. government. No doubt a certain amount of sympathy was created in the minds of some officials in the American government, but there was no way to translate this feeling into actions against the Japanese government, given the power realities of the moment.[18]

Some Koreans, probably a good number of them, thought the United States was the "greatest friend" Korea had.[19] A story was circulated among the Koreans that President Wilson would come to Korea in an airplane and would set the suffering Koreans free from Japanese imperialism. Some of the Koreans might have wished to believe in the story, and those who believed in this story must have been disappointed in not seeing Wilson descending from the sky to save them from the Japanese yoke. However, a more realistic and exciting episode related to Korean–American relations happened in 1920. A party of nine American congressmen, one senator, along with their assistants and their families, visited Northeast Asia in the summer and managed to include Korea on their itinerary. The Koreans set up elaborate plans to demonstrate to the American dignitaries their predicament under Japanese rule, but all welcoming activities for these visitors were successfully blocked by the Japanese authority except a speech given by a congressman at the YMCA in Seoul. The American visitors left Seoul within twenty-four hours, one of many disappointments the Koreans experienced during this period.[20]

The next opportunity the Koreans had to make an appeal to the outside world concerning their plight under the Japanese rule was the Washington Conference held in late 1921 and early 1922. The Korean Provisional Government sent a group of delegates headed by Syngman Rhee to the international conference, but the demands of the group for participation in the conference were rebuffed, and the effort to include the issue of Korea in the discussion failed.[21] Again disappointed, the Koreans changed their strategy to cultivate their strength for later days. The following two decades before 1941 were the most quiet period in Korean–American relations. The "Korean problem" became a part of the Japanese domestic politics, nonexistent as an international issue in the eyes of the American government.

During this quiet period the work of missionaries helped the Koreans by providing needed services in medicine, education, and other practical fields. By 1930, there were at least fifty missionary hospitals and dispensaries in Korea, and missionaries operated the Severance Medical School in Seoul.[22] By far the most important sector of missionary activity in Korea was education. Since the mid-1880s, American missionaries had established a sizable number of schools in Korea, which continued to operate through the 1920s and the 1930s. They made a very valuable contribution by educating young Korean men and women who otherwise would not have had the opportunity of receiving a modern education, since there were a very limited number of modern schools in Korea under the Japanese rule. However, Japanese cultural imperialism did not leave the missionary educational activities undisturbed. Through the ordinances of 1911 and 1915, the Japanese government had begun to control both the preparatory schools and the specialized (technical) schools. In 1915, the missionary schools were prohibited from teaching the Bible and courses like geography and history, which might nourish a sense of national consciousness in the minds of young Koreans. The American missionaries reacted somewhat differently to the Japanese control measures: The Methodists decided to take a more conciliatory line and to go along with the Japanese authorities, while the Presbyterians decided to resist the Japanese measures and accept the consequences of closing many of their schools. The severest test for mission work came in the 1930s on the issue of Shinto shrine visiting. All schools, including the missionary schools, were instructed to participate in the shrine visits. The two American missions took a similar line in resisting this Japanese pressure, and the outcome was the same: The Presbyterians had to close more schools during the latter part of the 1930s. With the Japanese attack on Pearl Harbor, all American missionary work in Korea had to stop, and all missionaries had to leave the country.[23]

The scale and the nature of the activities of the Korean Provisional Government in China in the years between the two world wars had been inevitably conditioned to a large extent by the nature of political developments in China, where it was located. In the 1920s, when China itself was going through a difficult period of uncertainty, this organization of self-exiled

Korean patriots were not able to do much. But the following decade, an eventful period in Chinese history gave these Koreans an opportunity for action. After 1931, when the Japanese seized control of Manchuria, the Chinese started to sense a bond between the destiny of their country and that of Korea. They began to assist the Korean organization with money and by training Korean military officers at the Chinese military academies and special training centers. In 1934, the Korean Provisional Government established the Commission for Diplomatic Affairs and sent representatives to the United States and Europe. Syngman Rhee was appointed again to head the representative group in the United States. Another three years passed, and the 1937 Japanese invasion of China presented a even better opportunity to the Koreans in that country; the Koumintang government began to give more positive assistance to the Koreans. The Korean Liberation Army was formally organized in the fall of 1940 with the officers who had been trained in the past years at the Chinese military institutions.[24]

Geographically and culturally, Korea and the United States were far apart, and under normal circumstances, they were not expected to have even a normal internation relationship in the latter part of the nineteenth century. Because of unique circumstances—Korea being in need of some special assistance from an amiable nation to usher in the modern world, and the United States, a fast-rising industrial nation with a strong desire to play a role of a world power—the two nations entered a somewhat special relationship. But this relationship soon reached its limit; before the end of the century, the remote Western nation with little critical interest in the tiny Asian kingdom began to find difficulty except for providing a missionary service. This reluctance remained for the rest of the period, up until the outbreak of the Second World War.

NOTES

1. Chay Jongsuk, *Diplomacy of Asymmetry; Korean–American Relations to 1910* (Honolulu, Hawaii: University of Hawaii Press, 1990), pp. 17–27; Lee Yur-bok, *Diplomatic Relations between the United States and Korea, 1866–1887* (New York: Humanities Press, 1970), pp. 22–26.

2. Chay Jongsuk, *Diplomacy of Asymmetry*, pp. 27–33; Lee Yur-bok, *Diplomatic Relations*, pp. 26–30; Kim Wŏn-mo, *Kŭntae Han-Mi kyos ŏpsa* (The modern history of Korean–American relations) (Seoul: Hongsŏngsa, 1979), pp. 235–371.

3. Chay Jongsuk, *Diplomacy of Asymmetry*, pp. 36–59; Lee Yur-bok, *Diplomatic Relations*, pp. 36–51; Frederick Foo Chen, *The Opening of Korea: A Study of Chinese Diplomacy, 1876–1885* (New York: Shoe String Press, 1967); Kim Key-hiuk, *The Last Phase of East Asian World Order: Korea, Japan, and the Chinese Empire, 1860–1882* (Berkeley and Los Angeles: University of California Press, 1980); Martina Deuchler, *Confucian Gentleman and Barbarian Envoys: The Opening of Korea, 1875–1885* (Seattle: University of Washington Press, 1977).

4. Chay Jongsuk, *Diplomacy of Asymmetry*, pp. 92–107.

5. Chay Jongsuk, *Diplomacy of Asymmetry*, pp. 108–133; Raymond A. Esthus, *Theodore Roosevelt and Japan* (Seattle: University of Washington Press, 1967), pp. 3–23.

6. Chay Jongsuk, *Diplomacy of Asymmetry*, pp. 134–171; Esthus, *Theodore Roosevelt and Japan*, pp. 76–111.

7. Chay Jongsuk, *Diplomacy of Asymmetry*, pp. 1–16, 172–176; idem, ed., "The Dynamics of American–Korean Relations and Prospects for the Future," in *The Problems and Prospects of American–East Asian Relations*, ed. Chay John (Jongsuk) (Boulder, Colo.: Westview Press, 1977), pp. 189–204.

8. Sin Yŏng-il, "American Protestant Missions to Korea and to Awakening of Political and Social Consciousness in the Koreans between 1884 and 1941," in *U.S.–Korean Relations, 1882–1982*, ed. Kwak Tae-hwan, John Chay, Cho Soon Sung, and Shannon McCune (Seoul: Kyŏngnam University Press, 1982), p. 211.

9. Son Po-ki, " Samil Untongkwa Mikuk" (The March 1 independence movement and the United States), in *Han-mi sukyo 100-nyŏnsa* (The hundred year history of Korean–American relations), ed. Kukche Yŏksahakhoeŭi Hankuk Wiwŏnhoe (KYHW) (Seoul: KYHW, 1982), p. 243.

10. Son Po-ki, "Samil Untongkwa Mikuk," pp. 249–250.

11. Sin Chae-hong, "Taehanminkuk Imsichŏngpuwa tae-Mi oekyo" (Interim Government of the Republic of Korea and her diplomacy toward the United States), in *Han-Mi sukyo l00-nyŏnsa*, ed. KYHW, pp. 274–281.

12. See Sin Chae-hong, "Taehanminkuk Imsichŏngpuwa tae-Mi oekyo," pp. 277–281.

13. *Congressional Record*, 66th Cong., 1st sess., vol. 58, part 2, p. 2035.

14. *Congressional Record*, 66th Cong., 1st sess., vol. 58, part 3, pp. 2594–2600.

15. *Congressional Record*, 66th Cong., 1st sess., vol. 58, part 3, pp. 2697–2717.

16. *Congressional Record*, 66th Cong., 1st sess., vol. 58, part 4, pp. 3924–3926, vol. 58, part 6, pp. 5595–5597, vol 58, part 2, 6611, 6812–6826.

17. *Congressional Record*, 66th Cong., 1st sess., vol. 58, part 5, pp. 4476, 6172.

18. For a similar view, see Son Po-ki, "Samil Untongkwa Mikuk," pp. 258–259.

19. Pak Yong-sŏk, "Mikuk wiwŏntan nae-Han" (A visit to Korea by a United States Congressional delegation), in *Han-mi sukyo 100-nyŏnsa*, ed. KYHW, p. 261.

20. Pak Yong-sŏk, "Mikuk wiwŏntan nae-Han," pp. 260–271.

21. Sin Chae-hong, "Taehanminkuk Imsichŏngpuwa tae-Mi oekyo," pp. 273, 286.

22. Sin Yŏng-il, "American Protestant Missions to Korea," pp. 214–216.

23. Son In-su, "Kyoyuk" (Education), in *Han-Mi sukyo 100-nyŏnsa*, ed. KYHW, pp. 341–347, 354–355; Lee Man-yŏl, "Sŏnkyo" (Missionary work), ibid., pp. 338–340; Sin Yŏng-il, "American Protestant Missions to Korea," pp. 216–217.

24. Lee Yŏn-bok, "Kwangpokkunŭi ch'amchŏn" (Participation in the war by the Liberation Army), in *Han-mi sukyo 100-nyŏnsa*, ed. KYHW, pp. 367–371; Sin Chae-hong, "Taehanminkuk Imsichŏngpuwa tae-Mi oekyo," p. 287.

CHAPTER 2

The Two-Nation Relationship during the Second World War

The outbreak of the Second World War and the American intervention in the war after the Japanese attack on Pearl Harbor presented a new opportunity to the Korean people. After initial successes, the Japanese invasion of China began to have great difficulties, and difficulties for the Japanese could mean opportunities for the Koreans. The Korean Provisional Government had begun to approach the American government even before the attack on Pearl Harbor. On June 6, 1941, six months prior to Pearl Harbor, the executive head of the Korean organization in Chungking, Kim Ku, wrote a letter to President Roosevelt, which did not reach its destination until early following year. In this letter Kim expressed his wish for "the restoration of that friendly relationship for mutual benefit."[1] The receipt of Rhee's letter of February 7 to the secretary of state, in which Kim's letter was enclosed, was simply acknowledged about two weeks later by Assistant Secretary of State Adolf A. Berle.[2] Toward the end of March, Rhee wrote a letter to the secretary of state explaining the status of the Korean Provisional Government based on the treaty of 1882, the first treaty between Korea and the United States. This letter seems to have been left unanswered, for no copy has been found in the State Department file.[3] Thus, efforts to open communications between the Korean Provisional Government and the American government did not produce any result in the spring of 1942. However, during the same period, much effective communication took place between the American representative in China and the foreign policy makers in Washington. One important piece of the U.S. policy toward Korea during World War II was made at this time—a policy of nonrecognition toward the Korean Provisional Government.

On February 12, 1942, Ambassador C. E. Gauss in China wrote a communication which was received in Washington exactly a month later, to report to the secretary of state that Tjosowang (Cho So-hang), who had introduced himself as the foreign minister of the Korean Provisional Government, had sought an interview with the ambassador and had expressed the desire of his government for recognition and for military and financial aid from the American government. Gauss added in his report his impression that Cho tended to be "evasive and secretive."[4] While Gauss's dispatch was on the way to Washington, the State Department informed the British government of the American government's posture toward the Koreans, that it was not contemplating recognizing any Korean group as the "primary movement" against the Japanese, and that it was not making any commitment for future recognition of Korea. The British government had about the same view on the whole question. Thus, by early February 1942, the State Department had made an initial decision not to recognize the Korean Provisional Government or any other Korean group.[5]

The following two months (April and May 1942) were an important period for the "Korean question." The U.S. government handled the question in close coordination with the government of China. On April 8, President Roosevelt sent a copy of a memorandum from T. V. Soong, the Chinese foreign minister, to Acting Secretary of State Sumner Welles asking for his view on the Korean issue. Soong's memorandum gave a detailed description of the Korean Provisional Government and other Korean civilian and military groups in China and the Soviet Union and suggested that if the "United Nations," particularly the members of the Pacific War Council, wished to promote Korean independence, two measures might be taken: (1) promotion of a fusion of the Korean groups, which could be done without much difficulty, and undertaking the raising, arming, and supporting of an irregular Korean fighting force of possibly fifty thousand men; and (2) the announcement at an opportune time by the Pacific War Council of its determination that postwar Korea would be independent.[6] This was a very optimistic view for the Korean revolutionary groups. Five days later, on April 13, Welles responded to President Roosevelt, observing that the Korean irregular army should be assisted with regard to its organization and equipment and that, even though the Pacific War Council's announcement of its decision in favor of Korean independence was an agreeable idea in principle, it was not the right time to do so.[7] Five days later, the American ambassador in Chungking brought news on the Korean issue: The Chinese government had reexamined the issue of the recognition of the Korean Provisional Government and had concluded that it would be desirable to extend the recognition without delay. Gauss added in his telegram that the Chinese government wished to find out the American government's view on the matter and would not take any action until the American view was obtained.[8] Toward the end of April, Secretary of State Cordell Hull expressed his view that the issue of the recognition of the Korean Provisional Government had "complicated and delicate aspects" because of the sensitivities of both China and the Soviet Union.[9] On May 1, Secretary Hull informed Gauss about one of the most important decisions of the American government toward Korea during World War II: The U.S. government had no "immediate intention" of recognizing any Korean group. Hull gave as reasons for this decision: (1) the lack of unity among the Korean groups, and (2) the groups outside of Korea had little association with the Koreans on the peninsula. Within a week, Welles reported from Chungking that the matter of recognizing the Korean Provisional Government was being reconsidered by the Chinese government and that it was very likely that the recognition would be postponed until some more "favorable moment."[10] This favorable moment did not come soon; a year later, the Chinese government still held the position of "letting the matter rest."[11]

The year 1943 was one of the most important years for Korean–American relations during World War II. The United States came forward with a definite policy statement regarding Korean independence after the liberation of Korea from Japanese rule. The idea of a Korean trusteeship was brought out for the first time, and it was debated in international conferences. In addition, the famous "in due course" phrase was attached to the matter of Korean independence before the end of the year. It is not altogether clear when President Roosevelt conceived the trusteeship idea for Korea, but it apparently was one of the issues he and British Foreign Minister Anthony Eden discussed in March of that year. When Chinese Foreign Minister T. V. Soong inquired on March 29 about the "general impression" of the conversation, one day before the end of the Roosevelt–Eden talk, Welles revealed that the three nations (China, the United Kingdom, and the United States) were in agreement that after the war Korea would be independent under a "temporary international trusteeship." Within a week after the end of the conversation, a press report from London on the Korean trusteeship was published in the United States.[12] Thus, by spring, the American government had reached the point where it had sounded out the view of its major ally regarding the question of what to do with Korea after the war. However, on the question of the recognition of the Korean Provisional Government and the question of independence of Korea, related but separate issues, the governments of the United States and China maintained for the time being the same posture of "letting the matter rest."[13] Now the task left for the Roosevelt administration was to obtain an agreement from the three other powers (the United Kingdom, the Soviet Union, and China) in favor of Korean independence after the war under an international trusteeship, and Roosevelt took this task to Cairo and Teheran toward the end of the year.

Between March and November 1943, representatives of the Korean Provisional Government and the Chinese government in a responsible position presented their views on recognition of the Provisional Government and

Korean independence to the American government. On May 15, Syngman Rhee, in his capacity as chairman of the Korean Commission in the United States of the Provisional Government, addressed a letter to President Roosevelt, in which he pointed out that it was time "to rectify the wrong and injustice" done to the Korean people and their nation during the past thirty-five years and requested American recognition of the Provisional Government. Rhee also told the American government that he had reports indicating that the Soviet Union was aiming at the establishment of a Soviet republic in Korea and that independent Korea should be allowed to play the role of a "bulwark" of peace in the Orient against communism.[14] In mid-August, General Wang Peng-sheing, an adviser to Chiang Kai-shek on Japanese affairs and the liaison officer between Chiang and non-Chinese groups in China, wrote a letter to the American Embassy in Chungking expressing his view that the Korean problem should be solved before the end of the year and that the solution should be a "complete restoration of Korean independence." He also expressed the Chinese hope that the United States would play an important role in "underwriting" independence for the Koreans.[15] It is easy to surmise that Rhee's letter did not influence American thinking, but that Wang's words made an impression on State Department officials and perhaps even on President Roosevelt.

The Cairo–Teheran summit conference of 1943 was the most significant event for Korea and Korean–American relations during World War II.[16] The three major powers participating in the conference—the United States, the Soviet Union, and the United Kingdom—consolidated their policy lines on the postwar status of Korea and publicly declared their agreed-upon policy that "in due course Korea shall be independent." Along with Stalin, Chiang Kai-shek was the main target of Roosevelt's efforts at persuasion in Cairo. During the November 23 meeting with Chiang, one of a series of meetings at Cairo in late November and probably the most important occasion for Korea, Roosevelt advanced his view that China and the United States should reach "a mutual understanding" on the future status of Korea. Concurring with Roosevelt's views, Chiang stressed "the necessity" of granting independence to Korea.[17] During the following three days, the communiqué summarizing the outcome of the meetings was drafted and repeatedly revised. On the afternoon of November 24, Harry L. Hopkins, the special assistant to President Roosevelt, drafted the communiqué which read in part, "We are mindful of the treacherous enslavement of the people of Korea by Japan, and are determined that country, at the earliest possible moment after the downfall of Japan, shall become a free and independent country." Many of the words were charged with emotion, and some stylistic changes were inevitable. But it was unfortunate that the phrase, "earliest possible moment," was revised twice and became the words which made the Koreans most unhappy. President Roosevelt replaced the phrase with "proper moment"; the British came forward with the phrase "in due course," which was adopted for the final version of the communiqué. The author of the British draft is not known, but it is certain that the British draft received the approval of Winston Churchill.[18] Four days later, on November 30, at Teheran, Stalin "thoroughly" approved the content of the communiqué and specifically added that "it was right Korea should be independent."[19] On December 1, the communiqué was released by the White House, and Korean independence, or more appropriately the restoration of Korean independence, had received international assurances, but with the "in due course" phrase.[20] Thus, the intention of the American government to make a general public statement which had been contemplated since March of 1942 was realized in a multinational format.[21]

Along with the issue of independence, another important issue of Roosevelt's Korea policy at the time of the Cairo–Teheran conference was the matter of trusteeship. Both before and after the conferences, President Roosevelt made clear statements on the subject. On November 19, he told the Joint Chiefs of Staff that Chiang "desired" a trusteeship over Korea, one that would be administered by the Soviet Union, China, and the United States as trustees. On January 12, at the meeting of the Pacific War Council, he told the representatives of the Pacific allies that Stalin at Teheran had "specifically agreed" with the idea that the Koreans were not yet capable of exercising and maintaining independent government and that they should be placed under a 40-year tutelage."[22] However, no record of such an agreement made at Cairo and Teheran has been found.[23] Of course, this does not mean that such an agreement was not made verbally. It is clear that at least Roosevelt had at this point the idea of forty-year trusteeship for the Koreans.

The Koreans in China almost immediately showed their reaction to the "in due course" phrase. On December 3, a local paper reported a statement by the foreign minister of the Korean Provisional Government expressing "Korean pleasure" at the Cairo Declaration and suggesting that the United Nations now should recognize the Provisional Government and extend lend-lease aid to the Liberation Army. This statement was made before the release of the full text of the declaration in China. On the next day, representatives of the two major Korean groups at Chungking requested from the American embassy an interpretation of the phrase "in due course."[24]

Many authors have been very critical of the inclusion of the "in due course" phrase. Some thought it was an "unfortunate phrase," and some called it an act of a "stupidity."[25] Bruce Cumings thought that the provision reflected the "paternalistic" attitude of the great powers.[26] James Irving Matray, however, provides a different view: such criticisms are "unjustified," for the Koreans were unprepared for independence and they deserved a delay in the attainment of independence.[27] It is true that Korea was a part of the Japanese empire at this time, and as the winners of the war, the allied powers, especially the United States, had the power to decide what to do with Korea. However, because of the general principles of Cairo and Teheran and also the principles of the Atlantic Charter, including (1) liberation of the nations which had been subjugated by Japanese "violence and greed," (2) no territorial aggrandizement by the victorious powers, and (3) self-determination for the people concerned, the wishes and the expressed will of the liberated Koreans should have been given consideration. They were, however, completely ignored at Cairo and Teheran. It also cannot be denied that James Matray has a point, and his point seems to be based on the idea of so-called modern democracy. From this point of view, the Koreans who had been ruled by autocratic monarchs for a millennium and more recently by the Japanese imperial rulers were certainly "unprepared" for democracy. But another even more important point is that if this yardstick was used as the basis for judging every nation's qualifications for independence, only a few nations in the world would make it at this time. This is exactly the reason why the principle of self-determination emerged at the end of the World War I and continued to play its role throughout the years toward the end of the World War II. Matray and others who have the same opinions on the subject should be reminded that the Korean peninsula went through the process of evolving from tribes to tribal states to petty kingdoms and reached the stage of one kingdom on the peninsula about two centuries before Anglo-Saxon England went through the exactly same process. And, we are also reminded that direct democracy, in that sense the only genuine democracy, ended with emergence of a powerful kingdom, either on the British Isles or the Korean peninsula, or anywhere else.

All these arguments regarding independence and nonindependence come from confusion between a "denotation" or "description" of a "status" or "state" of a nation (e.g., independence) and a mode of governing of a nation (e.g., democracy). An independent nation can be democratic or nondemocratic; there have been a great number of nondemocratic independent nation-states in history. And, it is logical that once a human community reaches a status of nationhood, when a temporary, external imposition of dependency was removed from that nation, the nation automatically returns to the status of independence. All the controversies about independence and nonindependence for Korea at the end of World War II was a sheer luxury of the victorious great powers.

The year 1944 was a year of action. The Normandy landing operation and the subsequent military actions absorbed all the attention of the allied powers, and there was no international wartime conference that dealt with Korean question until the Yalta Conference of February 1945. And, both the Yalta and the Potsdam Conferences were far less important for the post–World War II situation in Korea than the previous ones at Cairo and Teheran. No new agreement was made concerning Korea at the two 1945 conferences; the major role of these two meetings was to confirm what the major allied powers had agreed to at the previous conferences.

The main objective of the United States at the Yalta Conference was to bring the Soviet Union into the Pacific theater of operations and to enhance the Chinese international position as one of the four major world powers. Korea accordingly occupied a small place among the subjects discussed at the conference. On the afternoon of February 8, Roosevelt and Stalin, meeting without Churchill and with only a few aides present, touched upon this subject. According to Charles E. Bohlen's minutes, Roosevelt told Stalin that he had in mind a Korean trusteeship composed of representatives of three powers (the Soviet Union, the United States, and China) and that the only experience his country had with trusteeships was in the Philippines, where it had taken about fifty years to prepare the people for self-government. Roosevelt thought that twenty to thirty years might be enough for the Koreans. Stalin commented that the shorter the period of trusteeship the better. Returning to the subject of the nations to be involved in the trusteeship, Roosevelt expressed his feeling that it would not be necessary to invite the British to participate. Stalin's replied that if the British were not invited they would certainly be offended and they should participate in the Korean trusteeship. This seems to have been all that was said about Korea at the conference.[28] However, for Korea, the Yalta Conference was not insignificant; the discussion of the possibility of a Korean trusteeship became more open and official and its likely duration and participants reached a stage of open discussion.

There was one other aspect of the Korean question that was probably conceived long before the spring of 1945.[29] This was the matter of the military occupation of Korea after the war, and it was articulated at the Yalta Conference. In a briefing paper dated January 18, 1945 and prepared by the State Department for the coming summit meeting, it was simply stated that there would be a military occupation and a military government in Korea after the completion of the military operation. The paper explained in detail why the military occupation and government should be international in character and that participants should come from the four powers (the United States, the United Kingdom, the Soviet Union, and China). Further, the paper pointed out that the military government in Korea should be organized on the principle of a centralized administration with all of Korea administered "as a single unit." In addition, the paper indicated that the four powers should participate in the trusteeship arrangement if such an arrangement could be decided upon. This paper also argued that the trusteeship in Korea would be necessary to shorten the duration of the military occupation and prepare the people for democracy.[30] It is clear that the American government was very keen about other major powers concerns, especially those of the Soviet Union, because it emphasized the international nature of both the military occupation and the trusteeship in Korea. And, even though the American government's original intention was to keep the Korean peninsula as a single administrative unit under one military government, regrettably this principle of centralized government was not brought up in the discussions at the conference.[31]

One more summit meeting was held before the end of the war, but the Korean issue did not see any further development at the Potsdam Conference, which was held in the summer of 1945. By the time the conference was convened, Harry S. Truman had succeeded to the commanding position in Washington.

While handling through a series of summit meetings the central issue of what to do with Korea after the war, the United States had to manage the lesser problem of responding to the desires and requests of the Korean Provisional Government. Through the 1920s and the 1930s, the Korean Provisional Government kept alive its desire of being recognized by the United States and other powers. Meanwhile, as the war expanded in the Pacific from the early 1940s through the attack on Pearl Harbor and the U.S. entry into the war, the Koreans switched their strategy from a diplomacy of the verbal petition to a wartime action policy. The Korean Liberation Army, which was formally established on September 17, 1940, grew to a three-hundred-man force within a year. A year later, in May 1942, a significant event for all the Korean groups in China took place. The *Chosŏn Ŭiyŏngtae* (The Korean Volunteer Army) decided to join the Korean Liberation Army. This troop was organized in 1938 under the leadership of Kim Wŏn-pong, a leftist leader and a 1925 graduate of the Whangpoa Military Academy, and its integration with the Korean Liberation Army was significant both militarily and politically for all the Korean groups in China that were working for national independence. Now, the Koreans had formed a unified front for both political and military activities. The size of the unified Korean military force did not grow as it was initially hoped (some hoped for a twenty-thousand-man force within two years) but the Army had at least the strength of five-hundred to six-hundred men, the core of which had been trained at the Chinese military academies.[32] The Korean Liberation Army was severely hampered by the lack of a financial base, and it had to rely on the support of the Chinese government. This support began in early November 1941, a month before Pearl Harbor. At the same time the Korean troops became a part of the Chinese fighting force under the nine-point regulations which were drawn up by the Chinese government. The Koreans tried to get out of this predicament but they did not have much chance without independent financial resources. This unsatisfactory condition lasted for three years, until early April 1945.[33] The Korean Liberation Army formulated a plan to undertake an action on the Korean peninsula against the Japanese army in September of that year, but because the war ended earlier than expected, this plan was not executed.[34]

After Pearl Harbor, the Korean military forces' desire for active participation in the war was expressed in Washington through formal Chinese diplomatic channels. T. V. Soong, the Chinese foreign minister in the United States at this time, sketched for President Roosevelt some of the possible actions the United States and other Allied powers might take in dealing with the Korean problem. Soong presented to Roosevelt the possibilities in terms favorable for the Koreans by pointing out that an irregular Korean Army of some fifty-thousand men might be raised and used for sabotage and intelligence activities in Korea, Japan, and North China. He also suggested that to encourage Korean aspirations, the Pacific War Council could announce at some "opportune moment" its determination to see Korea as an independent nation and that the Korean Provisional Government might be recognized at the same time or later by the powers.[35] Acting Secretary of State Sumner Welles, responding to the president's request for comments, suggested that the allied powers should assist the Korean Army with its organization and equipment and that the suggested activities could be carried out from Chinese bases. He also indicated that even though in principle he supported an announcement by the allied powers in favor of the independence of Korea, he did not think that it was the right time to do so because such an announcement would be unrealistic. He omitted a comment on the issue of the recognition of the Korean Provisional Government.[36] This dual line of thinking by Welles in the spring of 1942 became U.S. policy toward Korea for the rest of the war years. The Korean Army would be supported and used for the allies war activities, and Korean independence might be announced at a certain time in the future, but the Korean Provisional Government would not be recognized.

Some Korean Liberation Army troops were trained by OSS members in the spring of 1943, and a joint intelligence operation was carried out with the allied forces. Captain Clarence B. Weems, a son of a former American missionary in Korea, played a key role in coordinating the operation. It seems that a sizable number of Korean soldiers were dispatched to the India–Burma theater, according to an agreement with the British and Indian governments. There was a good possibility that the Korean Liberation Army would grow, and if the war had lasted a little longer in the Far East, it might have had an opportunity to join military operations on the Korean peninsula. Had such events taken place, the history of the nation and the history of American and other countries involvement on the peninsula in the post–World War II years might have been somewhat different.[37]

With the death of Roosevelt in mid-April 1945, the twelve-year-long Roosevelt era ended. Likewise, a phase in the relationship between Korea and the United States also reached an end. An overall examination of the relationship between the two nations during this period can be attempted from the viewpoints of each of the two nations. If we turn first to the Korean side, which took a more active posture mainly because of the circumstances, we can note that the Koreans perceived accurately the nature of events in the world in the 1930s and the early 1940s and tried to use them for realization of their goal of liberation from Japanese rule and restoration of their independence. A fundamental question for the Koreans was how this wish could be realized and what they had to do to achieve this seemingly impossible task. Not much could be expected from the Korean population under the Japanese control during this period; they were gripped by a sense of hopelessness and resignation, and there were few sources of energy for positive action. There was not enough will for resistance among the Korean people on the peninsula. T. V. Soong caught well the mood of the Koreans when he described it to Roosevelt in early 1942: "Held down by a large Japanese army of occupation, the mood of the Korean people is that of sullen submission, with memories of historic injustice rankling."[38] The only source of energy for the realization of the Korean wish was those Koreans living outside of the peninsula, especially the group in China, the Korean Provisional Government.

There is no question that the leaders of the Korean Provisional Government did their best under the given circumstances during the little over three year period from the spring of 1942 to the end of the war. Despite the formation of the unified military forces of the rightist and the leftist Korean groups in China by the spring of 1942, it is still questionable how much cooperation there was among the Koreans in China during this period. Other questions are why such a small force of not more than six hundred was raised and why it was so far from the fifty thousand T. V. Soong envisioned in the spring of 1942. With the base in Chungking, away from the center of the Korean population, the army must have had difficulty with recruitment. With this limitation, it is still regrettable that the strength of the army never reached a significant level.

Two major scholars on U.S. policy toward Korea have expressed opposite views on the Roosevelt administration's Korea policy. Bruce Cumings declared that Franklin Roosevelt was naively idealistic in adopting an internationalist approach for the Korean problem. In contrast, James Irving Matray thought Roosevelt was realistic in adopting the internationalist approach because the Korean problem had so much of an international character, especially with the Soviet involvement.[39] The difference between these two interpretations comes from the different meanings the authors gave to the same conceptual framework of idealism and realism. It also partly comes from the limitations of this kind of analytical framework for an understanding of foreign policy. On the issue of the recognition of the Korean Provisional Government, James Matray and Michael C. Sandusky seem to agree. Matray thinks that the U.S. government had valid reasons for a nonrecognition policy toward the Koreans because of the lack of unity among Korean revolutionary groups and because these groups lacked direct connection to the Korean population in their homeland. Sandusky also points out the lack of cohesion among the Korean groups and argues that the Koreans themselves were responsible for the American nonrecognition policy.[40]

Brief comments are in order regarding the key issues of Roosevelt's policies toward Korea: (1) the declaration for Korean independence, (2) support for the Korean Liberation Army, (3) recognition of the Korean Provisional Government, (4) the delay of independence for Korea, (5) the trusteeship, and (6) the military occupation. It was logical for the United States and the Allied powers to declare at Cairo that Korea would be independent after the war because the Atlantic Charter already had clearly adopted the principle of self-determination. One of the key principles at this summit meeting in dealing with the territories the Japanese had "stolen" or had taken by "violence and greed" was the restoration of property to the former owners. The Korean peninsula was one of those pieces of land which had been "stolen" or had been taken by "greed" and in an action close to "violence." Some may question the timing, but the delay is understandable because the Allied powers wanted to wait until their victory was assured before declaring their postwar policy. The United States was also logical to assist the Korean Liberation Army in their efforts to participate in the Allied fighting, because the United States was doing everything possible to win the war by utilizing all available resources. However, one may question the U.S. government's policy of denying recognition of the political wing of the Korean organization (the Korean Provisional Government) while trying to utilize the military wing of the same organization.

From the beginning of its existence, one of the major objectives of the Korean Provisional Government was to receive international recognition, especially that of the United States. However, until Pearl Harbor, U.S. recognition of the provisional government was simply unthinkable because the U.S. government would not wish to antagonize unnecessarily the Japanese government. After Pearl Harbor, recognition of the Korean Provisional Government became a possibility for the United States. Lack of cohesion and cooperation among the Korean revolutionary groups, lack of an association with the main body of the Korean population on the Korean peninsula, and a caution designed not to create a precedence for similar cases were stated to be the reasons for the nonrecognition policy.[41] There is no question that each of these reasons had a basis. But on the bases of both practicality and formality, it should be pointed out that there were also grounds for the U.S. recognition of the Korean Provisional Government. It is true that after two decades of its existence, the Provisional Government did not have much association with the Koreans at home, but it is also true that this organization had a more representative character than other Korean organizations abroad. Moreover, the Korean Provisional Government had a structure with branches corresponding to the actual branches of a government. It had an adequate structural basis for recognition if any government had seriously considered the action. And there was a pragmatic aspect of recognition: If recognized as a government in exile, the Korean Provisional Government would have much more effectively mobilized military forces for the Allies during the war years, and it would have provided an invaluable service to the United States and the Allied powers if they did not intend to carry out the military occupation of the Korean peninsula.

Among the remaining issues, the trusteeship issue was the most important, and Roosevelt was involved more personally in this issue than in any other issue. His conception of the idea may have gone back to the spring of 1942.[42] By the fall of 1943, it became the most important part of Roosevelt's Korea policy. The main stated reason for Roosevelt's decision in favor of a trusteeship of Korea was his belief that the Koreans were unprepared for self-government. Another reason was that the international trusteeship would protect the Koreans from new imperial desires of great powers.

As for the matter of Korean readiness for independence, it is true that the Koreans during the thirty-five year period of Japanese rule never had an opportunity to experience modern representative government. But, the Koreans had a two-thousand-year tradition of self-government, and if they had been thrown into water, they would have had an opportunity of demonstrating to the world their ability to swim through its treacherous currents. The multinational aspect of the trusteeship would have been helpful for the protection of Korea against new imperial desires, but this alone was certainly not a sufficient condition for Korean security; as has happened many times before, imperialistic powers often choose to split their victims if occupation by one power is not feasible. Both Matray and Cumings recognized that benevolent intents and strategic considerations lay behind Roosevelt's idea of a trusteeship for postwar Korea, but Cumings also pointed out that the mandate system in this new form was anachronistic.[43] After the loss of their independence for over three decades, the Koreans were impatient, and what they wanted was not sympathy or benevolent paternalism but immediate restoration of their independence, which they had for thousands of years, but lost when the Japanese had stolen it unjustly. It was difficult for Roosevelt and his aides to understand Korean feelings at this point, and even if they had understood them, it is questionable how much weight they could have had in the American policy-making process regarding Korea.

The decision to delay Korean independence, made manifest by the insertion of the "in due course" phrase, was closely related to the trusteeship issue. Since the trusteeship for Korea was Roosevelt's most important concern, it was inevitable that he would favor a delay. Comments on this issue have been made earlier in this chapter, and a more detailed discussion of the American occupation of Korea after World War II is made in Chapter 3. A brief discussion will accordingly suffice at this point. If the American decision in favor of a military occupation of Korea after World War II was made in the spring of 1944, then the American position was firm by the time preparations were made for Yalta Conference.[44] In its Briefing Book Paper of January 18, 1945, the State Department clearly stated that military occupation was necessary. And, interestingly enough, the paper indicated that a trusteeship was necessary to shorten the duration of the occupation. It also placed an emphasis on multinational involvement in the occupation, especially that of the Soviet Union.[45] An important question to be raised here is whether a military occupation was appropriate for Korea. After all, Korea was to be a liberated land, not a conquered territory. In this context, it also should be remembered that the most important principle articulated at Cairo and Teheran with regard to the former Japanese possessions was the restoration of the land to its former owner. Finally, if the decision in favor of military occupation was taken as a practical precaution against "potential Soviet duplicity," it would have been simpler and more beneficial in the long run for the United States had an alternative course—simple liberation—been taken.[46]

In the final analysis, it may be argued that at the bottom of these four key issues—the recognition of the Korean Provisional Government, the Korean trusteeship, the delayed independence of Korea, and the plan for a military occupation—lay a strong sense of confidence and pride on the part of the Americans in their power and culture. The United States was at its height of power in the mid-1940s and the people, especially the elite in Washington, had a tremendous amount of power and confidence in their cultural superiority. This attitude seems to have been the main force behind the decisions on these issues, as it was on many other issues regarding Korean–American relations over the following years.

In mid-April President Roosevelt died, and Truman took over the administration. For American–Korean relations, this change at the head of government in the United States did not have much immediate impact. American policies toward Korea would be continued, but with of course some changes of emphasis and style. Two of the major policy issues—the matter of trusteeship and military occupation—had already been decided upon by the former president, and the new president did not have any choice other than continuing the same policy unless and until the situation surrounding Korea changed drastically. However, an important point to be noted is that Truman did not have as much confidence as Roosevelt had in the future prospects of cooperation with Stalin in dealing with post–World War II problems. Together with differences in general outlook and diplomatic styles, this factor was destined to have an impact upon the course of the policies and actions employed to handle the Korean problems in the coming years.

The new president wished to ascertain whether Stalin intended to carry out agreements made with Roosevelt. Harry Hopkins was accordingly sent to Moscow in May, soon after Truman became president, and he obtained Stalin's assurance that the four-power trusteeship plan for Korea would be carried out.[47] In early June, Acting Secretary of State Joseph C. Grew reviewed American policy regarding Korea and pointed out that his country would not recognize the Korean Provisional Government or any other similar organization so as not "to compromise the right of the Korean people to choose the ultimate form and personnel of the government."[48]

One more summit meeting was necessary for the Allied powers' successful completion of the war. At the Potsdam Conference, which was held in late July and early August of 1945, there was a good possibility that the four powers would come to some concrete and definite understanding on the issues concerning Korea. Even though American foreign policy makers clearly saw this need,[49] the Korean issue failed to draw enough attention from the participating powers at the conference, and the only action taken at the conference regarding Korea was a reaffirmation of the Cairo declaration.[50] This lost opportunity was certainly a matter of regret for Koreans, but in fact the Korean issue was not significant enough for the major Allied powers at the conference to give it more attention.

The decision to divide the Korean peninsula at the 38th parallel was the single most significant action taken by the United States during the decade of the 1940s, or even during the whole period of American–Korean relations for that matter, even though the decision was rather hastily done. Without this division, there would not have been a tragic war, and most of the miseries experienced on the Korean peninsula could have been avoided. The roots of the decision to divide the nation at the 38th parallel are deep, and they need to be examined in detail, but the context in which the decision to divide was made is surprisingly simple and clear.

One of the most important concerns of the United States in the East Asian theater toward the end of World War II was how to finish the fighting with the Japanese without too much more American sacrifice. Of course, this concern was natural for the United States, or for any nation fighting a major war, and a major American objective during the last two summit meetings was to obtain Russian assistance for a speedy ending of the war. A price needed to be paid by someone for this deal, and at least part of it was paid by the Koreans. The only event which might have saved the Koreans from this unfortunate situation was the dropping of the two atomic bombs on Japan in early August 1945, but even then the Japanese surrender came a little too late for the Koreans.[51]

Even though there were some discussions that an agreement was made between the United States and the Soviet Union at Yalta and some detailed arrangement was made between the two powers at Potsdam regarding division of the Korean peninsula at the 38th parallel, a definite step toward the division of the Korean peninsula was not made by the United States until the Rusk–Bonesteel decision of August 10–11, 1945.[52] As Dean Rusk, one of the two colonels who made the fateful decision regarding the future of Korea, later recalled, the process was surprisingly simple and straightforward. Instructed by Secretary of State Byrnes, the Department of State asked the military to come up with a line for the division of the Korean peninsula as far north as possible in Korea for receiving the surrender of the Japanese troops. Within a half hour, the fateful decision, which had such a great impact upon millions of lives and many nations of the world, was made by two colonels—Dean Rusk and C. H. Bonesteel. As it was explained by one of the participants, the two tried to "harmonize the political desire" of the

United States with "the ability of the U.S. forces to reach the area."[53] Within five days the decision received the approval of the State-War-Navy Coordinating Committee (SWNCC), the Joint Chiefs of Staff, the State and War Departments, and the president. It was dispatched to General MacArthur as a part of the General Order No. One, the instrument for the Japanese surrender. Because the Korean peninsula had already been marked out as an area for Soviet military action and because the Soviet invasion of Korea was in progress, the Soviet acceptance of the American decision for the division of the peninsula at the 38th parallel relieved the anxiety of the Americans, who had worried about the Soviet reaction, and even Rusk was surprised at this turn of events.[54]

The consequences of the division of Korea at the 38th parallel were great. To the Koreans on both sides of the parallel, the division became the very source of all their future difficulties, pains, and sufferings. The 38th parallel, a geodetic line, which cuts Korea indiscriminately, created a critical situation on the peninsula economically, politically, and socioculturally. Economically, it cut the agricultural south from the industrial north, which had 92 percent of Korea's electricity, as well as 71 percent of the coal reserves and 83 percent of the mineral resources of the peninsula. By early November 1945, the line became a closed border and ideologically opposite political systems began to take root on both sides of the line. Socially and culturally, it was equally disastrous. Two entirely different styles of society and culture began to emerge on the peninsula. On September 24, only two weeks after his arrival in Korea, General John R. Hodge, the commanding general of the U.S. occupation forces in Korea, wrote, "In my opinion the Allied Powers, by this division, have created a situation impossible of peaceful correction."[55] Within five years, the Koreans had to suffer a war. Whatever the reasons for dividing nations at the end of a great war, the great powers inevitably made terrible mistakes. Two of the four divided nations—Korea and Vietnam—suffered wars, while the third barely escaped one. These great powers were, quite naturally, summoned to the battlefields of both wars.

Authors have been critical of the division of Korea at the end of World War II. They have pointed out that it was a "wholly American action," that the line was "arbitrarily chosen," and that the action was "undesirable" and "unfortunate." Some even thought it was a "tragic" act.[56] Syngman Rhee, in early December 1945, called it a "most serious blunder."[57]

Causal factors are always important to ascertain, but they are difficult to determine for any historical event, and the case of the decision to divide at the 38th parallel is no exception. Many authors have expressed their views on this question, and the subject has already been well explored. No one by this time believes that the real reason for the division of Korea was sheer military expediency; or, if expediency was a factor, it was not a significant one. Many authors think that the real reason was strategic and political. The decision to divide Korea was thus a part of the U.S. strategy for waging the

Cold War; it was, in other words, part of the containment policy, or a "de facto containment." The U.S. strategic interests dictated a division to prevent the Soviet occupation of the whole Korean peninsula. Because of the strategic value of the peninsula for the protection of Japan, the whole peninsula could not be allowed to be occupied by the Soviet Union. But since Soviet occupation of at least part of the peninsula was unavoidable due to the Soviet's military presence in the northern part of the peninsula, the decision to divide meant that at least part of Korea would not fall under communist control.[58]

If the decision for divided military occupation of the Korean peninsula was made solely on the basis of the strategic interests of the two great powers at the end of World War II, a question arises as to whether it was really the best choice for the two powers national interest, or whether a better way could not have been found. Division of the land of a defeated nation seems to be one of the most expedient ways to handle a dispute at the end of a war; however, an artificial division of a nation is always temporary, and the created unstable system demands a very high price from the nations involved. Often, short-term expediency proves very costly in the long run. There were at least two alternative routes which could have been considered for the Korean peninsula at the end of World War II: a short period ("shorter better," as Stalin expressed at one point) of joint trusteeship, to be followed by independence, or the simple returning of the "stolen" land to the former owner, as envisaged at Cairo two years earlier. If the latter route was too altruistic in an international transaction, even though it was the least costly and the best in the long run for all powers involved, the other alternative—an international trusteeship—deserved serious consideration by the two powers. The Soviet Union seems to have preferred "socialism in [at least] one zone" by the middle of August 1945 rather than the cumbersome and uncertain nature of a joint trusteeship arrangement. What was needed here, however, for the policy makers in both Moscow and Washington was a real understanding of the peculiar nature of the Korean peninsula as a buffer area. Not much imagination was necessary for this understanding; only some long-term consideration of the outcomes of the policy choices and plenty of courage would have been sufficient for the Americans to do the job of persuading the Soviet leaders to take the whole Korean peninsula as a buffer zone instead of "socialism in one zone" and democracy in the other zone. For the Koreans, not even persuasion was necessary in the middle of August 1945. It should also be pointed out that since the U.S. decision to divide the Korean peninsula at the 38th parallel on August 11, 1945 was two days after the second atomic bomb was dropped over Nagasaki, one day after the Japanese offered surrender, and one day before the Soviet troops stepped onto Korean soil, the division at the 38th parallel was too generous for the Soviet Union. The division could have been made along the 39th parallel, or at least the Chinnamp'o-Wŏnsan line, a little south of the 39th parallel, which then would have reduced the possibility of the later northern invasion of the south. The short-sighted and hasty decision for expediency came at very high cost, to be paid before long on a bloody battlefield.

NOTES

1. Kim Ku to Franklin D. Roosevelt, June 6, 1941 in Syngman Rhee to the Secretary of State, February 7, 1942, Department of State, *Foreign Relations of the United States (FRUS), 1942* (Washington, D.C.: U.S. Government Printing Office), 1: 859–860.

2. Adolf A. Berle to Syngman Rhee, February 19, 1942, *FRUS, 1942*, 1: 862.

3. Rhee to the Secretary of State, March 24, 1942, *FRUS, 1942*, 1: 865.

4. Gauss to the Secretary of State, February 12, 1942 (received March 12), *FRUS, 1942*, 1: 860–861.

5. Welles to Gauss, March 20, 1942, *FRUS, 1942*, 1: 862–864.

6. Memorandum by the Chinese Minister for Foreign Affairs (Soong), in Roosevelt to the Acting Secretary of State, April 8, 1942, *FRUS, 1942*, 1: 867–869.

7. Welles to Roosevelt, April 13, 1942, *FRUS, 1942*, 1: 870–872.

8. Tel., Gauss to the Secretary of State, April 18, 1942, *FRUS, 1942*, 1: 872–873.

9. Hull to Roosevelt, April 29, 1942, *FRUS, 1942*, 1: 873.

10. Tel., Hull to Gauss, May 1, 1942, *FRUS, 1942*, 1: 873–875; tel., Gauss to the Secretary of State, May 7, 1942, ibid., p. 875.

11. Memorandum of conversation, by Assistant Secretary of State Adolf A. Berle, Jr., May 12, 1953, *FRUS, 1943*, 3: 1092.

12. Memorandum by Maxwell M. Hamilton, the Chief of the Division of Far Eastern Affairs, to the Secretary of State, April 22, 1943, *FRUS, 1943*, 3: 1090–1091.

13. See the memorandum of conversation, by the Assistant Secretary of State (Berle), May 12, 1943, *FRUS, 1943*, 3: 1092.

14. The Chairman of the Korean Commission in the United States (Rhee) to Roosevelt, May 15, 1943, *FRUS, 1943*, 3: 1093. See also Gauss to the Secretary of State, December 6, 1943, ibid., pp. 1095–1096.

15. Atcheson, Chargé in Chungking, to the Secretary of State, August 20, 1943, *FRUS, 1943*, 3: 1094–1095.

16. Carl Berger, *The Korea Knot: A Military History–Political History* (Philadelphia: University of Pennsylvania Press, 1957), p. 37; Chŏng Yong-sŏk, *Mikukŭi tae-Han chŏngch'aek, 1945–1980* (U.S. policies toward Korea, 1945–1980) (Seoul: Ilchokak, 1976), p. 383.

17. Roosevelt–Chiang dinner meeting, November 23, 1943, 8 P.M., Roosevelt's villa, Chinese Summary Record, *FRUS, The Conferences at Cairo and Teheran, 1943*, p. 325.

18. American draft of the communiqué with amendments by President Roosevelt, *FRUS, The Conferences at Cairo and Teheran, 1943*, pp. 399–400; revised American draft of the communiqué, ibid., p. 402; British draft of the communiqué, ibid., p. 405; final text of the communiqué, ibid., pp. 448–449.

19. Roosevelt–Churchill–Stalin luncheon meeting, November 30, 1943, 1:30 P.M., Roosevelt's quarters, Soviet Embassy, *FRUS, The Conferences at Cairo and Teheran, 1943*, pp. 565–566.

20. "The War: Conference of President Roosevelt, Generalisimo Chiang Kaicheck, and Prime Minister Churchill in North Africa," *The Department of State Bulletin* 9 (December 4, 1943): 393.

21. Welles to Gauss, March 20, 1942, *FRUS, 1942,* 1: 863. See also Gauss to Welles, March 28, 1942, ibid., p. 867.

22. Minutes of the president's meeting with the Joint Chiefs of Staff, November 19, 1943, 2 P.M., Admiral's cabin, USS *Iowa, FRUS, The Conferences at Cairo and Teheran, 1943,* p. 257; minutes of a meeting of the Pacific War Council, January 12, 1944, ibid., p. 869.

23. Minutes of a meeting of the Pacific War Council, January 12, 1944, *FRUS, The Conferences at Cairo and Teheran, 1943,* p. 869, footnote 6.

24. Tel., Gauss to the Secretary of State, December 7, 1943, *FRUS, 1943,* 3: 1096.

25. Berger, *The Korea Knot,* p. 35; Cho Soon-sung, *Korea in World Politics, 1940–1950: An Evaluation of American Responsibility* (Berkeley and Los Angeles: University of California Press, 1967), p. 20; E. Grant Meade, *American Military Government in Korea* (New York: King's Crown Press, 1951), p. 44.

26. Bruce Cumings, *The Origins of the Korean War: Liberation and the Emergence of Separate Regimes, 1945–1947* (Princeton, N.J.: Princeton University Press, 1981), p. 106.

27. James Irving Matray, *The Reluctant Crusade: American Foreign Policy in Korea, 1941–1950* (Honolulu: University of Hawaii Press, 1985), p. 21.

28. Bohlen minutes, Roosevelt–Stalin meeting, February 8, 1945, 3:30 P.M., Livadia Palace, *FRUS, The Conferences at Malta and Yalta, 1945,* p. 770. See also the memorandum by the Assistant to the President's Naval Aide (Elsey), n.d., ibid., *FRUS, Conference of Berlin, 1945,* vol. 1, pp. 309–310.

29. Bruce Cumings puts the date back to the spring of 1944: Cumings, *The Origins of the Korean War,* pp. 113–114.

30. "Post-War Status of Korea," Briefing Book Paper (January 18, 1945), *FRUS, The Conferences at Malta and Yalta, 1945,* pp. 358–360.

31. See Cho Soon-sung, *Korea in World Politics,* p. 34.

32. Lee Hyŏn-hi, *Samil Tokrip Untongkwa Imsi Chŏngpuŭi pŏpt'ongsŏng* (The March 1 Movement and legitimacy of the Korean Provisional Government) (Seoul: Tongpang Tosŏ, 1987), pp. 190, 193, 251–252.

33. Lee Hyŏn-hi, *Samil Tokrip Untongkwa Imsi Chŏngpuŭi pŏpt'ongsŏng,* pp. 252, 256.

34. Lee Hyŏn-hi, *Samil Tokrip Untongkwa Imsi Chŏngpuŭi pŏpt'ongsŏng,* p. 257.

35. Roosevelt to Welles, April 8, 1942, *FRUS, 1942,* 1: 868–869.

36. Welles to Roosevelt, April 13, 1942, *FRUS, 1942,* 1: 870–871.

37. Lee Hyŏn-hi, *Samil Tokrip Untongkwa Imsi Chŏngpuŭi pŏpt'ongsŏng* pp. 374–379; Lee Wŏn-sŏl, "Kwangpokkwa Mikukŭi tae-Han chŏngch'aek" (The liberation and U.S. policy toward Korea), in *Han-mi sukyo 100-nyŏnsa* (Hundred-year history of Korean–American relations), ed. KYHW, p. 398.

38. Roosevelt to Welles, April 8, 1942, *FRUS, 1942,* 1: 808.

39. Bruce Cumings, "Introduction: The Course of Korean–American Relations, 1943–1953," in *Child of Conflict: The Korean–American Relations, 1943–1953,* ed. Bruce Cumings (Seattle: University of Washington Press, 1983), p. 4; Matray, *The Reluctant Crusade,* p. 18.

40. Matray, *The Reluctant Crusade,* p. 14; Michael C. Sandusky, *American Parallel* (Alexandria, Va.: Old Dominion Press, 1983), p. 315.

41. Welles to Roosevelt, March 20, 1942, *FRUS, 1942*, 1: 863; Acting Secretary Grew, "Review of Policy Regarding Korea," *Department of State Bulletin* 12 (June 10, 1945): 1058.

42. Matray, *The Reluctant Crusade*, p. 8.

43. Matray, *The Reluctant Crusade*, p. 15; Cumings, *The Origins of the Korean War*, pp. 15–16, 19, 103–105.

44. Cumings, *The Origins of the Korean War*, pp. 113–114.

45. "Post-War Status of Korea," Briefing Book Paper (January 18, 1945), *FRUS, The Conferences at Malta and Yalta, 1945*, pp. 358–361.

46. See Cumings, *The Origins of the Korean War*, p. 113.

47. Memorandum by the Assistant to the President's Naval Aide (Elsey), undated, *FRUS, Conference of Berlin, 1945*, vol. 1, p. 300. See also Matray, *The Reluctant Crusade*, pp. 35–36.

48. Acting Secretary Grew, "Review of Policy Regarding Korea," *Department of State Bulletin* 12 (June 10, 1945): 1058.

49. "Briefing Book Paper," undated, *FRUS, Conference of Berlin, 1945*, vol. 1, p. 927.

50. See Chŏng Yong-sŏk, "Cairo, Yalta, Potsdam hoei" (Conferences at Cairo, Yalta, and Potsdam), in *Han-mi sukyo 100-nyŏnsa*, ed. KYHW, p. 391; Cumings, *The Origins of the Korean War*, p. 112.

51. See Matray, *The Reluctant Crusade*, pp. 39–43.

52. Acting Secretary Grew, "Review of Policy Regarding Korea," *Department of State Bulletin* 311 (June 10, 1945), p. 1058; Lee Wŏn-sŏl, "Kwangpokkwa Mikukŭi tae-Han chŏngch'aek," pp. 409–410, 473–474; Cho Soon-sung, *Korea in World Politics*, p. 387.

53. Draft memorandum to the Joint Chief of Staff, undated, *FRUS, 1945*, 6: 1039.

54. See Cumings, *The Origins of the Korean War*, p. 121; Matray, *The Reluctant Crusade*, p. 46.

55. Memorandum of Hodge to MacArthur, September 24, 1945, *FRUS, 1945*, 6: 1055.

56. Bruce Cumings, "American Policy and Korean Liberation," in *Without Parallel: The American–Korean Relations since 1945*, ed. Franklin Baldwin (New York: Random House, 1973), p. 46; Matray, *The Reluctant Crusade*, p. 52; Meade, *American Military Government in Korea*, p. 92; Mark Paul, "Diplomacy Delayed: The Atomic Bomb and the Decision of Korea, 1945," in *Child of Conflict*, p. 91.

57. Resolution of the Korean Congress of Political Parties, by Chairman Syngman Rhee, United Central Council, *FRUS, 1945*, 6: 1110.

58. See Chin Dŏk-kyu, "Mi kunchŏng" (The U.S. military government), in *Han-mi sukyo 100-nyŏnsa*, ed. KYHW, pp. 424–425; Leon Gordenker, *The United Nations and the Peaceful Unification of Korea: The Politics of Field Operations, 1947–1950* (The Hague: Nijhoff, 1959), p. 241; Matray, *The Reluctant Crusade*, pp. 45, 47; Cumings, "Introduction," p. 13; Cumings, *The Origins of the Korean War*, pp. 117, 121; Sandusky, *American Parallel*, p. 333.

CHAPTER 3

U.S. Military Occupation of South Korea

The three years between 1945 and 1948 was a transitional period in Korean–American relations, as well as in the Korean history. In 1945 the Koreans were liberated from thirty-five years of Japanese rule. After three years of difficulties, the period of the two half Koreas began in 1948. For the Koreans, these three years were a time of great uncertainty. Also, this period was the beginning of eight years of difficulty, even tragedy, which ended only in 1953—the termination of the Korean War. Before long, we may look back upon these years as the linkage in the middle of the almost one hundred years of misfortune for the Korean nation, a period which stretches from the beginning of the twentieth century to the early part of the next.

The entry of twenty-one American naval vessels into Inch'ŏn harbor on September 8, 1945, with an occupation force was a conspicuous event in the history of Korean–American relations. The Americans had returned to the peninsula after an absence of forty years, and the leave taking and subsequent return occurred under quite different, almost opposite, circumstances. In 1905, the Americans left Korea, abandoning the peninsula kingdom in the hands of the Japanese; nearly a half century later, they returned to take over at least half of the peninsula from the same Japanese hands. One wonders if there was any cause–effect relationship between these events.

Even though it did not amount to very much, the Koreans at least took an active posture during the thirty-five year period between 1910 and 1945; naturally, the United States took a passive posture with regard to the Koreans during this period. However, beginning with the end of the war, those playing active and passive roles reversed their positions, and this condition continued until the end of the Korean War. In the harsh environment of the Cold War, Koreans were not given much freedom of action, and the peninsula became not much more than a geographic space for the struggle between the two major powers.

Among a number of dynamic factors within any international interaction, national interests are always in the foreground. This is especially the case for Korean–American relations. Traditionally, the United States had relatively minor interests in the Korean peninsula, mainly because of the physical and psychological distances separating the two and the difference in the size of the two nations.[1] However, American interest in the Korean peninsula changed and increased in the post–World War II years. An important question concerns the magnitude of these interests in Korea during those years.

Earlier, at the turn of the century, the United States had considerable economic interests in Korea—especially investments—and this economic factor became increasingly important again as the century approached its end.[2] However, the economic factor had little importance for the Americans in Korea during the post–World War II years. If there was any importance at all in this area, it was probably a negative factor, for there was a real possibility that Korea would become an economic burden for the United States. It is also doubtful if there was much sociocultural importance behind American interests immediately after World War II. The interests the United States had in Korea in this period were in two principal areas: the military and the political.

In the hierarchy of military strategic areas, Korea occupied a low priority in terms of its strategic importance for the United States. In the spring of 1947, Korea ranked fifteenth among the sixteen nations ranked by the Strategic Subcommittee of the Defense Department in terms of strategic priorities.[3] Whether the strategic importance of the Korean peninsula was adequately or fully appreciated by the American military strategists in this ranking is beside the point; the important point is that the American defense establishment considered Korea not important for American security. There were, however, some who appreciated the strategic importance of the Korean peninsula and, as will be discussed in the following pages, the American view also changed over the years.[4]

One of the most important facts for Korean–American relations during this period was the return, along with the United States, of Russia, then the Union of Soviet Socialist Republics, to the peninsula. This was the nation that had been forced out of Korea by Japan when it lost the war in 1905. The return of the two nations to the peninsula occurred under very special conditions, later called the Cold War, which had great implications for the relationship between Korea and the United States. The two other major powers in the region—Japan and China—were in no position to contest the position of two superpowers on the peninsula. Without any force to moderate their behavior, the two powers placed on the Korean stage played out their roles fiercely.

Beside the strategic and political considerations, another important factor for Korean–American relations was the geopolitical position of the Korean peninsula. The peninsula is a classic example of the buffer state, which was especially important in the post–World War II environment. It does not matter whether the powers on the stage were conscious of this factor; the geopolitical factor is always important for international relations on the Korean peninsula. It seems that both American and Korean policy makers during this three-year period were aware of the importance of Korea as a buffer state. Some of them considered this factor extremely important for the solution of the problems on the peninsula. For example, as will be discussed later, Kim Kyu-sik and his associates always recognized clearly its importance, as did General John Reed Hodge and others on the American side.[5]

Like most other bilateral relationships, the role of policy makers was important for Korean–American relations in the post–World War II period. On the American side, the president and the secretaries of state—Harry S. Truman, James F. Byrnes, George C. Marshall, and Dean G. Acheson—were men who possessed great leadership qualities and were directly involved in deciding the general direction of the nation's foreign policy and in making major policy decisions for the Korean case. However, because of the relative unimportance of Korea for the United States, most of the policy making toward the Korean peninsula was done by persons who ranked below these levels—the assistant secretaries, bureau chiefs, and the representatives in the field. Hugh Borton, John Carter Vincent, John M. Allison, Walton Butterworth, William R. Langdon, H. Merrell Benninghoff, and General John Reed Hodge played important roles in shaping American policy toward Korea during this three-year period. Along with the National Security Council, the role of the interdepartmental coordinating committees, the State-War-Navy Coordinating Committee, was also important for the formulation of Korea policy.[6] On the Korean side, there were a number of capable and dedicated persons like Syngman Rhee, Kim Kyu-sik, Kim Ku, Yŏ Un-hyŏng, and Cho Man-sik, but, unfortunately, partly because of their difficulties in cooperating with each other and partly because of the circumstances under which they had to work, they were not able to organize effectively their efforts to manage the critical period.

Since the containment policy was the major policy line guiding the United States in fighting the Cold War during the near half century after the end of World War II, a key question concerns the role it played in shaping U.S. policy toward Korea in the early post–World War II years. Many historians think that the United States definitely applied this policy to the Korean peninsula, not to mention other countries in the region.[7] The role of policy makers was important because the containment policy was a broad, general conceptual framework used by the United States during the Cold War years, and there is no controversy over its wide application to countries around the world, including Korea. The question to be asked is when it began to be applied to Korea and to what extent or how well it was applied. If definitive formulation of the containment policy goes back to early 1946, the time of George F. Kennan's telegram from Moscow, there is a question about how the actions the United States took to fight the communist threat in Korea before that time can be explained.[8] The Cold War on the Korean peninsula can be considered to have begun during the Roosevelt era and to have continued through the Truman years, at least from late 1944. Between Pearl Harbor and the establishment of the two Koreas, three major actions regarding Korea were taken to fight this Cold War: Roosevelt's suggestion of a trusteeship, Truman's decision to divide Korea at the 38th parallel, and the military occupation of Korea. Bruce Cumings calls the pre-1946 U.S. actions in Korea a "de facto containment policy."[9] The label probably does not matter; the fact is that the U.S. government began to take measures to prevent communist expansion in Korea, that is, to fight the Cold War there, much earlier than 1946.

Despite Korea's low ranking among the nations in which the United States had strategic interests in the post–World War II era, the United States still had some interest in the peninsula. Described in more concrete terms, U.S. objectives during the post–World War II years ranged between the establishment of a "friendly," democratic (and economically viable), single nation on the peninsula to denying control over the whole peninsula to the Soviet Union.[10] In the direction of accomplishing this objective, the Washington policy planners had already taken a big step in the summer of 1945 when they drew the line along the 38th parallel. However, the division and the military occupation of the peninsula by the two contending powers made achievement of the maximum objective of the nation—controlling the whole peninsula—difficult at the very least.

The U.S. decision to occupy Korea was one of the most important policy decisions concerning Korea in the 1940s. Why was the decision made to treat Korea as a "conquered" instead of a "liberated" land, despite the fact that the three great powers had already decided and declared that Korea would be liberated from Japanese rule? There was a definite relationship between the decision in favor of military occupation and the plan for a Korean trusteeship, and both were connected with the containment policy. The trusteeship idea had either always been present since Roosevelt's decision or it was revived at a certain point by the Truman administration. It does not appear that the decision on occupation replaced the trusteeship idea; rather, the two had a complementary relationship. The U.S. government seemed to have thought both were necessary to prevent Soviet domination of the whole peninsula. The idea of a military occupation of Korea may go back as far as 1943; by early January of that year, the planners in the State Department thought that a trusteeship, or an international arrangement similar to it, would be necessary to reduce the duration of the occupation period.[11] It is interesting to note that by this time occupation was considered more important than a trusteeship. Hardly anyone thought that the occupation of Korea was a correct decision, even though it was a "peaceful" one. Why then was Korea treated as a "conquered" (or a part of a conquered) nation instead of a "liberated" land? Writing in early June of 1945, the acting secretary of state said, "Responsible officials of the Department of State reiterated that Korea will be liberated from Japan and that intentions embodied in the Cairo Declaration will be carried out."[12] The same word "liberation" was used by Dean Acheson in 1947: "We feel however that there are substantial reasons for regarding Korea as a special case, due to its status as a liberated area."[13] Another State Department official in a responsible position voiced the same view in even clearer terms. Charles E. Saltzman, the assistant secretary of state for occupied areas, wrote in early 1948, "The view, namely, that U.S. armed forces stationed in Korea should pay their way therein as from the date of liberation of Korea, September 9, 1945, is consistent with the policy and commitments of this Government to treat Korea as a liberated and not a conquered country."[14] Thus, Korea was clearly perceived as a "liberated" area in the minds of the highest level officials in the State Department through the crucial years from 1945 to 1948. Nevertheless, the country was treated as a "conquered" land, and the consequences of this policy were grave. The reason for this unfortunate course may be found as already explained at a high policy level: to prevent Soviet domination of the whole peninsula. If not the whole of Korea, then at least half of it will be built as a "bulwark" for American security against the expansionist communist Russia. The idea that Korea would serve as a "bulwark" goes back to the spring of 1943, when Syngman Rhee picked up this concept in his futile effort to persuade the U.S. government to support the Korean Provisional Government's effort during World War II, a concept that gradually settled in the minds of the policy makers in Washington.[15]

Soon after the occupation began, the situation in Korea became very difficult for the occupation authorities to handle, and the mistake of the decision for the occupation became immediately apparent.[16] Immediate correction of the policy was necessary to eliminate or at least reduce the difficulties and decisive action was needed from Washington in the fall of 1945. When a correction was not easy, the difficult situation dragged on.

Some historians think that 1947 was the most important year between 1945 and 1950 for U.S. policy in Korea.[17] In a sense it was an important turning point for Korean–American relations because the United States took important action by bringing the Korean issue to the United Nations in the fall of the year. However, in terms of the degree of force behind the U.S. government's intention to fight communism on Korean peninsula, the year 1946 should be considered more significant. By late summer, the policy makers in Washington had come up with a firm, forceful anticommunist policy for Korea. Both William Langdon and W. Averell Harriman probably had some influence upon President Truman and his advisers.[18] The impact of Edwin W. Pauley, who had just returned from Korea as the special envoy of the president, on President Truman was clear. He began his June 22 report to the president with an opening statement that made clear he was greatly concerned about the U.S. position in Korea because it was not, in his view, receiving the attention it deserved. Then he presented clearly his view that Korea was "an ideological battleground" upon which the entire U.S. success in Asia might depend. After sketching the possible Soviet objectives in Korea, he made recommendations to strengthen the U.S. policy in Korea.[19] In his reply of July 16, President Truman expressed candidly his agreement with Pauley on the symbolic value of the Korean peninsula, and stated that the government was incorporating into the "revised policy for Korea" most of Pauley's recommendations for specific actions and that it would involve the Koreans in the governing process and also improve the economic and cultural programs.[20] Acting Secretary of State Dean Acheson, in his press conference of August 30, emphatically pointed out that the United States intended to remain in Korea and carry out its duty there until it had achieved its purpose of establishing an independent nation.[21] However, unfortunately, no active and positive actions emerged. The year 1946 was also a year of exploration: Following the foreign ministers' conference in Moscow, the Joint Commission in Seoul tried in the spring to see if the two superpowers could cooperate at the field commanders' level to solve the Korean problem. The U.S. military government also tried to involve Koreans in the administration and made an attempt to find an alternative to relying on rightist groups by turning to the neutral force. When all of these efforts proved futile, the U.S. government in 1947 decided that significant change was needed.

The year 1947 proved to be the year of change in American policy toward Korea. On February 25, the Special Interdepartmental Committee established with the specific purpose of preparing policy recommendations with regard to Korea came up with a draft report. The report shows clearly the alternative paths the United States could consider. After sketching five different possible courses under two headings—without agreement with the Soviet Union or in collaboration with the Soviet Union—the report lists four recommendations. Under the heading of "Without Agreement with U.S.S.R.," the report pointed out the difficulties with the continuation of existing policies and programs: insufficient funds and a lack of Korean cooperation. It also indicated that establishing an independent government in South Korea might lighten the burden on the United States but would not solve any problem in Korea. On the possibility of referring the Korean problem to either a group of (four) ministers or to the United Nations, the report was clear that such a course would not only admit American failure but would also give the Soviet Union an excuse to accuse the United States of not carrying out the international agreement (made at the Moscow Foreign Ministers Conference) and stated that bringing additional protagonists would not help solve the Korean problem. Then, the report turned to the last course under the heading of an "aggressive positive program for south Korea." It clearly stated that if the United States wanted to remain in Korea and wanted to achieve any success in solving the Korean problem, it should "initiate an aggressive, positive, long-term program." Under the heading of possible courses of action in collaboration with the Soviet Union, the report listed two courses: local negotiations in Korea, which had been tried and failed, and government negotiations, which were later proposed and rejected. The report ended with several recommendations. To implement the "aggressive and positive program," the committee recommended taking the steps necessary to secure an appropriation of $250,000,000 for fiscal year 1948, the gradual civilianization of the military government in Korea, and the dispatch of high-level business–industry and educational groups to Korea to make recommendations. The committee also recommended that doors be kept open for more negotiations with the Soviet Union.[22] The report was comprehensive, thorough, and clear; the group did a meritorious job by presenting clearly the policy choices the U.S. government had in Korea at this point. An important point to be noted is that in the early spring of 1946, Washington planners, at least the middle-level officials, still had a firm posture toward Korea. However, whether these recommendations would solve the Korean problem is a different question.

Intra and interdepartmental discussions took place in March. On March 28, Acting Secretary of State Acheson indicated to the Secretary of War Robert F. Patterson the need for a congressional authorization of $540 million for Korea over the following three years—$35 million less than the amount recommended by the interdepartmental committee.[23] Then came Secretary of War Patterson's "bomb shell." In his letter of April 4 to Acheson, Secretary Patterson declared that he was convinced that the United States should pursue forcefully a course of action whereby the nation would "get out of Korea" by an early date and that he believed that the early withdrawal of troops from Korea should be an "overriding objective." He also voiced doubts that the U.S. Congress would appropriate $540 million for the next three-year period and pointed out the possible adverse effects of this appropriation on the total War Department budget.[24] The bombshell effect of this statement did not come from its content because the idea had long been in the minds of many Americans; the effect came rather from the fact that a person in his position as secretary of war came forward and actually made the statement in a formal interdepartmental communication. The State Department seemed to have absorbed the effect of the Patterson statement, and Secretary of State Marshall in his letter of July 14 to the political adviser in Korea stressed that the only American policy in Korea was the establishment of "an independent united nation" and that the creation of a separate government in southern Korea could not be even considered by the government in Washington.[25]

However, before long, signs of a response from the State Department emerged. In his letter, which probably was written on July 23, John M. Allison, the assistant chief of the division of Northeast Asian affairs, brought up for a discussion purpose for an interdepartment group the long-term problems in Korea. One of the problems that concerned him was what to do with the Joint Commission of the two occupation authorities in Korea which had long been in a state of stalemate. The other problem was the matter of internal administration in South Korea. More important, he stated in the memorandum that consideration might be given to "the possibility of presenting the Korean problem to the United Nations."[26] Within a week, on July 29, Allison came up with future U.S. policy alternatives regarding Korea in more concrete and clear terms. The essence of his proposal stated that if the Soviet Union breaks off or drags down the work of the Joint Commission in Korea, a four-power conference would be requested. Then, if either the conference fails to agree on the establishment of a government in Korea or the Soviet Union refuses to meet, the United States would take the Korean case to the United Nations, and a working team would be organized immediately to prepare the case for this course of action. He also indicated that efforts to secure approval for a Korean grant-in-aid program should continue.[27]

Six days later, the Ad Hoc Committee on Korea presented a report that followed the lines Allison had presented, although some refinement and minor changes were added. In its conclusion, the report said, "The U.S. cannot at this time withdraw from Korea under circumstances which would inevitably lead to Communist domination of the entire country." It also stated that every effort should be made "to liquidate or reduce the U.S. commitment of men and money in Korea as soon as possible without abandoning Korea to Soviet domination." The committee suggested that the liquidation or reduction of the U.S. commitment in Korea without abandoning the peninsula to the Soviet Union could be accomplished by turning over the case to the United Nations. Further, the report indicated that in view of the possibility of failure by the United Nations to solve the Korean problem the U.S. government should be prepared for the possible necessity of granting independence to South Korea. This idea had not even been a possibility to Secretary of State Marshall a month ago. The recommendation also suggested continuing efforts to obtain the grant-in-aid legislation.[28] A compromise measure between the State and War Departments emerged. This was also a compromise between the maximum and minimum objectives of the United States in Korea. Now, one more step was left to be taken: military confirmation of measures which had been drafted from the point of view of political considerations.

On September 15, the SWNCC addressed a memorandum to the Joint Chiefs of Staff requesting its views on the value of the military occupation of South Korea from the point of view of the military security of the United

States.[29] Five months previously, Secretary of War Patterson had already stated the military view by saying that the United States should leave Korea. Leaving, of course, included the withdrawal of U.S. military forces from the Korean peninsula. Since the purpose of the SWNCC request was to confirm existing U.S. policy, the substance of the answer was anticipated. The opinion of the joint chiefs was that the United States had "little strategic interest" in maintaining the troops and bases in Korea, and it suggested the forty-five-thousand-man force in Korea could well be used elsewhere.[30] Of course, military opinions were important for foreign policy decisions, especially regarding U.S. policy toward Korea at this time. An interesting note to be added is that between September 15 and 29, George F. Kennan, the author of the containment framework and now the director of the policy planning staff of the State Department, said to Butterworth, director of the Far Eastern Affairs, that in light of the military's views on Korea, the United States should cut its losses and get out of the place "as gracefully and promptly as possible."[31]

Certainly, 1947 was an important year of change for the U.S. policy toward Korea. The following year was largely anticlimactic, and at the policy level nothing new happened. Both Cumings and Matray argue that the containment policy extended to the Korean peninsula in 1947. Charles Dobbs and others, however, point out that Korea was becoming a symbol for the U.S. anticommunist stance in the Far East.[32] Many interpreted the U.S. decision to take the Korean issue to the United Nations as an effort to find an alternative policy that would minimize the possible damage from a change of policy as a face-saving device or as an effort to find a midway compromise.[33] Each of these views seems to describe eloquently certain aspects of the whole picture. The problem with them is that the application of the containment framework to the Korean peninsula and simultaneous proposals for a U.S. retreat from Korea through the turning over of the issue to the United Nations do not seem to fit well together. After an examination of the occupation actions, an overall evaluation of the policies and actions will be attempted.

Since E. Grant Meade and others have already made detailed descriptive studies on the American military occupation of Korea, only a brief sketch of the organization and processes of the American military government in Korea will be made for the purpose of assessment.[34] The military occupation of Korea, which had begun on September 8, 1945 with the landing of American troops at Inchon harbor, was carried out by the three divisions—the 6th, the 7th, and the 40th—of the XXIV Corps commanded by Lieutenant General John Reed Hodge. Soon after the occupation began, the three divisions were replaced by special military government units in the provinces. In Seoul, the military governor acted as the governor general, assisted by the civil administrator, who had the important role of coordinating the functions of the military governor, the secretariat, and the bureaus. The central administration of the military government had bureaus for finance, mining and industry, agriculture and commerce, public safety, public health, education, justice, communication, and transportation. The secretariat included sections for foreign affairs, civil service, intelligence, information, property custody, planning and accounts, and other special functions of the military government. In the provinces, the provincial military governors commanded the civil affairs troops in their areas and were responsible directly to the military governor of South Korea.[35]

The most important official for the military occupation in Korea was General Hodge, commanding general of the XXIV Corps, who was in charge of the execution of occupation policies under the supervision of General Douglas MacArthur in Tokyo. Born in 1893 in Illinois, he was in his early fifties by the time he arrived in Korea, but he was characterized as "a premature cold warrior." "Pugnacious" and often independent to the extent of being insubordinate to his superiors, some thought he came to Korea as "a conqueror," not a "liberator." Beside these undesirable personal characteristics, he also lacked understanding of the Korean people and culture. To be fair, he demonstrated the capability to perceive accurately the essence of the situation in Korea and did not hesitate expressing candidly to his superiors what he saw.[36] Even if he was a "soldier's soldier," he was definitely not suitable for the job he was given in Korea. Had he had qualified assistants with him in Korea, his shortcomings would have been moderated to a certain extent, but such, unfortunately, was not the case. His staff were equally ignorant about Korea, and, even worse, most of them simply did not care much about Korea or its problems. H. Merrell Beninghoff and William Langdon, Hodge's political advisers, were judged to be lacking "an adequate caliber" to perform satisfactorily their duties in Korea.[37]

When the American occupation forces arrived at Inch'ŏn Harbor, they were greeted by the delegates of the Kŏnkuk Chunpi Wiwŏn Hoe (Committee for Preparation of Korean Independence). The committee was organized immediately after the end of World War II by Yŏ Un-hyŏng, one of the most capable and colorful Korean politicians of the time and a man with a liberal orientation. General Hodge had not expected the reception, and he did not know how to handle the situation. During his years in Korea, he had the opportunity to use Yŏ's organization for constructive purposes, but he was not able to meet the challenge presented by the organization. With an understanding from the Japanese Governor General Abe Nobuyuki, Yŏ organized the committee with the objective of preparing for Korean independence. Within a brief period of time, the committee organized people's committees throughout the peninsula, and these local organizations greatly contributed to the maintenance of security. Then, on September 2, Yŏ learned that the peninsula would be divided at the 38th parallel and would be occupied by the two powers. The committee began immediately to organize a meeting of a "National Assembly," which was held in Seoul with thousands of delegates representing various groups throughout the peninsula. The assembly declared the establishment of the People's Republic, elected Syngman Rhee as the chairman and Yŏ as the vice chairman, and appointed prominent Korean politicians as cabinet members, including Kim Ku, Kim Kyusik, and Cho Man-sik. This was done two days prior to the arrival of the American forces, and the announcement of the organization of the republic was made throughout the peninsula—both north and south.[38]

The People's Republic stood for land reform, elimination from the government of Korean officials formerly associated with the Japanese government, cooperatives, and immediate independence.[39] If not "nefarious and abnormal," the ideas may be labeled as at least too liberal or leftist-oriented for the Americans. Probably the most difficult part for the American military authority was the declaration of "immediate independence." President Truman, in his September 18 statement in Washington, clearly indicated that it would take some time for the Koreans to achieve independence: "The assumption by the Koreans themselves of the responsibilities and functions of a free and independent nation and the elimination of all vestiges of Japanese control over Korean economic and political life will of necessity require time and patience."[40] The U.S. military occupation of Korea had been decided on the basis of fairly firm objectives, and the U.S. government would not tolerate such an organization as the People's Republic. The organization was gradually weakened by mid-December of the year, and the stress produced by this process split its diverse political elements into leftist and rightist groups. The declaration of the People's Republic was one of the very few opportunities the United States could have used to establish a unified and independent nation on the peninsula, but the Americans had a different agenda in mind.

The first few months of the U.S. military occupation was the most critical time, because by the end of this period the outcome of the occupation had already become clear. After the entry into Inch'ŏn harbor, General Hodge's occupation force quickly moved to Seoul City, and on the next day, September 9, it received the surrender of some 180,000 Japanese troops. Had U.S. policy been liberation rather than military occupation, the responsibilities of the troops could have ended at this point, and their evacuation from the peninsula would have been possible. When the military occupation began, the Korean people, who had expected liberation, not military occupation, were surprised and greatly disappointed. Military occupation is rarely welcomed by a people under any circumstances. Especially in the Korean case, after the people had suffered for almost four decades under harsh Japanese rule and had been in a jubilant mood of liberation from colonial rule since August 15, the feeling of disappointment was understandable. This feeling on the part of the Koreans in the early stage of the occupation may be characterized as a mixture of disappointment and a certain amount of puzzlement and curiosity. Later, the feeling of disappointment shifted to resistance.[41]

The first mistake the American occupation authority in Korea made was the decision to retain the Japanese in their administrative positions. The Americans thought this temporary measure was necessary, but it was a serious matter in the eyes of the Koreans. When the mistake was realized, the American government immediately took corrective action by removing all Japanese from their positions and by making a clear explanatory statement in Washington. The importance of this seemingly minor mistake by the American occupation authority in Korea is that it revealed clearly how little the Americans understood the Korean situation and made American intentions even more suspicious in the eyes of the anxious Koreans.[42]

Another mistake made by the American authority in Korea during the early period of occupation was the removal of all the restrictions placed by the Japanese government on the production, collection, and marketing of rice. American intentions were good. They thought a free market system should be introduced into the Korean economy for this important commodity. However, the outcome was disastrous. Korean farmers would not release their valuable commodity, and city people soon began to cry out for rice. Early the following year, the military government returned to the control system, but much damage had been done to the reputation of the American military government. Meade called this "the height of stupidity." Typically, the original intention of the Americans had been good, but because of their lack of real understanding of the Korean situation, the actions had deplorable consequences.[43]

The participation of capable Koreans in the process of the military government was an important part of the American administrative policy in Korea. They wished to give a sense of participation to the Koreans, since the advice of a group of prominent Koreans might be useful for practical purposes. As before, the results were disappointing. On October 5, 1945, the military governor, Brigadier General Archibald V. Arnold, who had occupied the position for only about three weeks, appointed an eleven-member Advisory Council. With Kim Sŏng-su, Song Chin-u, Yŏ Un-hyŏng, and Cho Man-sik as members, the council was certainly an organization of prominent Korean politicians. When its composition is analyzed, however, it is clear that it was filled with rightist elites, with the exception of one leftist (Yŏ), that it had eight college graduates and six Christians, and that most of them were wealthy and spoke English. The characteristics of this group showed in this early period the orientation of the American military government in Korea and gave an unsatisfactory impression to the Korean public. The formation of provincial advisory councils, which soon followed, had the much more devastating effect of becoming an impetus for the organization of parties, associations, and groups in the provinces.[44]

Among the numerous problems Korea experienced in the post–World War II era, political problems were most important and most difficult to resolve, especially the problem of the relatively small amount of Korean experience with self-government under Japanese rule. If we confine our discussion only to the modern period, in the latter part of the 1890s, then a limited number of Koreans had the experience of participating in the open discussion of national problems and policies. But, even this experience had happened a half century ago, and most Koreans in the latter part of the 1940s had no personal experience of meaningful political participation, and only a very small number of them had an understanding of modern political processes. Another equally serious problem for Korean politics was the proliferation of political parties and social groups and their polarization into two groups—rightist and leftist. Soon after liberation, the conservative Korean Democratic Party was organized under the leadership of Song Chin-u and Kim Sŏng-su. More parties were born in the following weeks, and by the middle of October, there were over forty political groups in south Korea. Among these groups, the Korean People's Republic (KPR) and the Korean Democratic Party (KDP) remained the two major political groups, and as time passed, the political polarization became more conspicuous. The American military government, which at first remained aloof, began to side with the conservative groups, especially the KDP, an alignment that had important consequences for political developments in Korea.[45] In a brief period of time, the Korean peninsula had become a battlefield of two opposing ideologies, and this extreme polarization created a situation difficult for the American military government to handle.

The political situation in South Korea became extremely difficult in the early fall of 1945. Reporting in the middle of September, the political adviser Benninghoff said, "Southern Korea can best be described as a powder keg ready to explode at the application of a spark." He explained the reasons underlying this situation. The Koreans had understood the "due course" phrase in the Cairo declaration to mean independence as "very soon" or "in a few days" and when they found out that such was not the case, their disappointment was very great.[46] Late in September, Hodge reported to MacArthur a similar observation: "Continuation of separation of the country into two parts under opposed ideologies will be fatal."[47] By late November, the situation became so difficult that the acting political adviser Langdon recommended to the secretary of state that the idea of trusteeship in Korea be dropped and that Kim Ku should be permitted to organize a governing commission which would soon evolve into an interim government and take over the function of the military government.[48]

After a careful analysis of the situation in Korea in his mid-December memorandum to the Joint Chiefs of Staff, General MacArthur summed up his view: "The U.S. occupation of Korea under present conditions and policies is surely drifting to the edge of a political–economic abyss from which it can never be retrieved with any credit to United States prestige in the Far East." He concluded, "Positive action on the international level or the seizure of complete initiative in South Korea by the U.S. in the very near future is absolutely essential to stop this drift."[49] A month earlier, General Hodge had already reported to General MacArthur that there would be no prospects of working out differences at the level of field commanders until decisions were made between the two governments on a higher level.[50] Thus, by December of 1945, the need for some kind of high-level action by policy makers in Washington had become clear.

The American government decided to take up the Korean issue, along with others, at the Moscow Three Foreign Ministers Conference in late December. The Truman administration brought out the trusteeship measure, which had been put on the back burner as part of a scheme for achieving the dual objectives of establishing a unified nation on the peninsula and at the same time preventing Soviet domination of the whole peninsula. The communiqué, published on December 28, two days after the end of the conference, announced an "agreement" among the foreign ministers of the Soviet Union, the United Kingdom, and the United States of America. A joint commission of representatives from the two occupying powers would be established, which would meet within two weeks to prepare recommendations for the four powers, including China, for the establishment of a unified nation on the peninsula. The agreement also specified that a Korean provisional government would be established with the assistance of the Joint Commission, which would prepare a proposal for the consideration of the four powers for the establishment of a trusteeship of Korea of up to a five-year period.[51]

The Moscow Foreign Ministers Conference itself was significant because it seemed to signal a continuation, or restoration, of the wartime allied cooperation. The decision by the three foreign ministers to try to solve the Korean problem by establishing the Joint Commission seemed to be an important step forward for the two occupying powers. The Koreans, however, considered the trusteeship issue the most important matter discussed in Moscow and vehemently opposed it. News of the Moscow agreement reached Korea early on the morning of December 29, and the news immediately caused an uproar among the politicized Koreans. The South Korean press reported the agreement with emotional phrases like "[a] second Munich," "another mandatory rule," and "[an] insult to Korea." The Korean politicians seized the opportunity and called for strikes against the trusteeship idea. Not knowing exactly what took place in Moscow, General Hodge tried to calm the Koreans by persuading them that disorderly actions would hurt the Korean cause. Anger, at least against the Americans, was reduced, but strikes continued against the Soviet Union. The Russians were not pleased at being targets of Korean wrath. Tass and the head of the Soviet military mission in Seoul, Colonel General Terenti Shtykov, immediately revealed that the American, not the Russian, delegate in Moscow had proposed establishment of a trusteeship in Korea. The Soviet press release damaged the already low American prestige in Korea. The Soviet source disclosed that the American delegate had first proposed the trusteeship in the discussions, that the Americans suggested a possibility of extending the trusteeship for another five years, and that there would be no Korean provisional government during the trusteeship period.[52]

Belatedly the policy makers in Washington realized that damage control would be necessary as a response to the embarrassing developments in Korea, and something of a retreat was made. While reporting to the nation on the Moscow Foreign Ministers Conference on December 30, Secretary of State James F. Byrnes suggested that the Joint Commission might find it possible "to dispense with a trusteeship."[53] Byrnes's position to dispose with the trusteeship issue remained firm; early in the following year, Acting Secretary of State Dean Acheson and the Director of the Office of the Far Eastern Affairs John Carter Vincent talked on the subject in the same language.[54] Because of the definite negative feeling of the Korean people on the issue, the trusteeship idea did not have much possibility of realization in any form and duration; nevertheless, it remained as one of the issues for the Joint Commission to discuss.

Thus, the U.S. military occupation of South Korea that began in an atmosphere of uncertainty in early September remained unchanged at the end of the year. The situation on the Korean peninsula was becoming much more difficult for the satisfactory execution of U.S. military occupation policy. However, early in the following year, there was some hope and expectation that the Joint Commission, which was to convene soon in Seoul, might find some solution.

The commanding generals of the two occupying powers quickly agreed on a meeting of the Joint Commission, and the Soviet delegation, headed by Colonel General Terenti Shtikov, arrived in Seoul on January 15, 1946. The meeting began on the following day. The American delegation was headed by Major General Archibald V. Arnold, assisted by the political adviser Beninghoff and others. The Koreans, especially those familiar with the situation in North Korea, were very apprehensive about the prospects of the commission; others, however, had some hope that the commission might accomplish something.

By January 18, the commission had come up with a list of what to discuss and what to avoid during the meetings, and the list revealed the already limited scope of the commission's work.[55] It made some progress in the area of the coordination of transportation and communication. However, these were relatively minor areas of discussion. With regard to the major task of taking steps toward the establishment of a provisional government, it experienced great difficulties. How to choose which Korean political and social organizations would be consulted became the major issue for the conference. The American delegates stood firm in defense of freedom of speech, press, and travel for Korean organizations; the Russians insisted that any organization opposing the Moscow agreement should be excluded from the list for consultation. The problem for the Americans was that all the rightist groups in South Korea opposed the Moscow agreement on the trusteeship issue and would therefore be eliminated from the consultation list if the Russian proposal was adopted. For the Americans, the execution of the agreement reached in Moscow was important, but the exclusion of all rightist Korean groups from the political process in Korea was impossible to accept. The issue of freedom of speech and of the press was not a trivial issue for the Americans, who were quite serious about it. But, whatever the surface arguments and issues, the underlying question for both occupying powers was who would control the provisional government—either the rightist group, friendly to the United States, or the leftist group, friendly to the Soviet Union? Both sides would not yield, and after twenty-four futile sessions, the commission adjourned on May 8.[56]

As was the case with policy making, or probably because of what happened at the policy level in Washington, the year 1946 was an important year for events at the operational level. In addition to the Joint Commission meetings, a number of important actions and events in the political arena took place during that year. These included the American military government's efforts to create a coalition of the mild rightist and leftist Korean political groups, the various Korean political parties' efforts to unify in pursuit of the common goal of establishing a unified Korean government, the establishment of an interim legislative assembly as a step toward the establishment of an independent Korea, and the outbreak of rebellions in South Korea.

The American military authority in Korea tried in the early spring of 1946 to encourage moderate rightist and leftist Korean politicians to create a coalition. The effort was undertaken not from any philosophical conviction, but because of the need to work together with the Russians and to make a unified Korean government possible. The Koreans, to a certain extent in response to American encouragement and probably also because they recognized the need for a unified government, tried to find a way for the rightist and leftist groups to work together. But neither American nor Korean efforts succeeded. The general political atmosphere on the Korean peninsula was already permeated with the diametrically opposed ideologies of liberal democracy and totalitarian communism, and meaningful cooperation between the two groups representing these views was impossible. The failure of the effort to create a coalition actually brought about the opposite effect; the gap between the two groups widened even more, and the leftist group itself split into the moderate nationalistic leftist Yŏ Un-hyŏng group and the more doctrinaire communist Pak Hŏn-yong group.[57]

With the good intention of creating an advisory body of representative Korean politicians that would serve until the construction of the South Korean Interim Legislative Council, General Hodge established in early spring the Representative Democratic Advisory Council (RDC). The fate of this body was about the same as its predecessor, the advisory council of the previous year. A large majority of the body—twenty-four out of twenty-eight—were rightists headed by Syngman Rhee, and, as Leonard Bertsch quipped, the RDC was neither representative nor democratic. And, more important, it failed to give the intended counsel.[58] In the fall, the organization of the last and most important of the advisory institutions took place. On October 14, General Hodge announced the establishment of the ninety-member organization, the South Korean Interim Legislative Council (SKILC) (Nam Chosŏn Kwato Ippŏp Wiwŏnhoe), with half its membership to be elected and half to be appointed by him. When the election was held, a large majority of those elected—thirty-one of forty-five—represented the right. To balance the institution, Hodge appointed moderate rightists and leftists, including Kim Kyu-sik and Yŏ Un-hyŏng. Even though the title of the organization indicated that it was to be "legislative," and Hodge's original intention for the organization was probably more than advisory, its actual function did not go beyond an advisory role. It is doubtful how much of a meaningful role the organization played even within that limited scope. As Cumings has pointed out, the creation of the SKILC had the negative result of being one more step toward the establishment of a separate government in South Korea.[59]

Some advances were made in the administrative domain of the American military government in Korea in 1946. Overseas Koreans had been repatriated, all the Japanese in South Korea were deported, a police force was created, communication and educational systems were restored, and an operational framework for administrative and judicial systems were assembled. Late in August Langdon observed that some Koreans were grateful for the sundry achievements of the American military government.[60] However, it seems that those Koreans who praised the American achievements were limited to a small and special group, "the small articulate element of the population," in Langdon's words. Overall, the year 1946 was a time of suffering for ordinary Koreans, especially farmers and workers. Before the end of the year, their grievances exploded in the form of a "peasant rebellion." The disturbances began in late September when a railway workers' strike broke out in Pusan and then developed into peasants' and workers' rebellions, which spread to Kyŏngsang and Chŏlla provinces in October and November with casualties estimated at two hundred policemen and over one thousand civilians. Three causes of the rebellion were identified by the Joint American–Korean Conference, organized by General Hodge to come up with measures to deal with the problematic situation. Grievances included (1) enmity against the police, the role of the former Japanese collaborators and interpreters in the military government, the corruption of some Korean officials, and the activities of the agitators; (2) inequities on the rice collection and distribution program, inflation and high prices, refugee problems, and the slowness of economic recovery; and (3) delay in distribution of former Japanese property, and party influences. This list indicates that grievances were prevalent in virtually every area of life in South Korea—political, economic, and social.[61] The uprisings came as quite a shock to the Americans.[62] Since the uprisings were severe in the area where the leaders of the Peoples' Committee were active, their role in fomenting the rebellion seems to have been significant. It is also true that great numbers of peasants and workers in South Korea in 1946 had substantial grievances. The impact of the rebellion was great. It ended the Peoples' Committees and mass organizations like workers' unions; it marked a turning point for the rightist institutions, especially the police; and it highlighted the universal failure of the American military government.[63]

Thus, 1946, a decisive year, had begun with a reasonable amount of hope and even some expectation for cooperation between the two occupying powers through the Joint Commission and between the rightist and leftist Korean politicians, but ended in violence and great disappointment. After the failure of efforts to bring about cooperation between the two occupying powers and the two groups of opposing parties in Korea in the establishment of a unified government, there was not much hope left that it could be achieved peacefully in the years to come.

As the Cold War intensified and the policy of containment was adopted formally on the policy level by the U.S. government, the struggle between the rightists and the leftists intensified in Korea. In 1947 the level of violence spread from the provincial to the village level. As the situation worsened, both Hodge and MacArthur urged Washington to take action at a high level before it was too late.[64] Some planners in Washington also began to feel the same need. John Carter Vincent, the director of the Office of the Far Eastern Affairs, thought by late January that a long-range economic aid program for Korea, which was under consideration at that point, might influence the Russians to cooperate on the Korean problem.[65] Secretary of State Marshall took up the Korean problem with Soviet Foreign Minister Molotov during the fourth Council of Foreign Ministers meeting in April and managed to reach an agreement to reconvene the Joint Commission in Korea in late May. The five-month meeting of the Joint Commission meeting began, but the result of this second round of meetings was exactly the same as the first one. Soon after the meeting resumed, the two sides again deadlocked on the same issue of which Korean groups would be consulted, or which groups—the rightist or the leftist—would control the provisional government. The two delegates could not even agree to submit a joint report to the Council of Foreign Ministers, and the meeting adjourned on October 22 without any accomplishments.[66]

The failure of the Joint Commission in 1947 presented grave implications. When the work of the commission looked hopeless in the summer, the policy makers in Washington searched for alternatives. They soon decided to turn over Korea to the United Nations. The 1947 Joint Commission meeting was the last U.S. effort to solve the Korean problem through cooperation with the other occupying power in Korea. Obviously, most Koreans were disappointed at seeing another failure by the Joint Commission. But, it is also questionable how much the Koreans expected from the efforts for American–Soviet cooperation in 1947. The rightists clearly saw that if the Joint Commission succeeded the result would be the birth of a communist state on the Korean peninsula.[67]

Once the United States decided to take the Korean question to the United Nations, actions followed swiftly. Warren Austin, the U.S. representative at the United Nations, presented the case on September 17 to U.N. Secretary General Trygve Lie. The First Committee of the General Assembly resolved to take up the case in the following month and, on November 14, the General Assembly passed a resolution that elections would be held in Korea no later than March 31, 1948 to select the representatives of the Korean people for the organization of the National Assembly and the establishment of the National Government and that a U.N. temporary commission on Korea would be established for the purpose of facilitating and expediting the process of nation building in Korea.[68] The communist bloc simply did not have enough negative votes, and there was no way for it to block the U.S. move in the General Assembly. Thus, by late November, the United States had successfully turned the Korean problem over to the world organization; at least, so it seemed at that point. Even though it was a decisive step for the fate of Korea, the Koreans did not have a chance to say a word about this move. Even if some Koreans voiced their views on it, their views could not influence the process. It is doubtful how much effect General Hodge's placating words had on the Koreans.[69]

Authors have discussed U.S. objectives for taking the Korean case to the United Nations in 1947. Some argue that the United States was not really giving up or abandoning Korea, but was simply exploring an alternative method for pursuing the objective of founding a democratic and viable unified nation on the Korean peninsula, or that the U.S. government had found a tool of diplomacy in the world organization.[70] However, an important question is why did the policy makers in Washington think that the United Nations would be able to solve a problem that two superpowers had not been able to solve through bilateral efforts? It was very unlikely that the Soviet Union would cooperate with the United States to solve the Korean problem through the international organization when it refused to do so bilaterally. To fall back to the position that, despite the full knowledge that the United States would not be able to achieve the objective through the United Nations, it was simply dumping the "hot potato" into the lap of the young world organization. Of course, the U.S. government had good reasons for the action: It attached little military strategic value to the peninsula; it desired the withdrawal of the occupation troops for financial reasons; and it had exhausted the alternatives outside of the United Nations.[71]

The United Nations Temporary Commission on Korea (UNTCOK), which was soon established to solve the Korean problem, faced many problems from the outset. Canada, for example, was very hesitant to send its representative to the organization. Since the absence of Canada as part of the commission would hurt its status, President Truman managed to persuade the Canadian government to send its representative to Korea.[72] In early January 1948, the commission began its work in Korea, but when it encountered a refusal to cooperate by the North Koreans, a serious question arose as to what the commission should do, and it referred the problem to the Interim Committee of the General Assembly. Despite much hesitation and even objections from some of the powers allied with the United States, the U.S. proposal that an election should be held in South Korea, where its observation by the commission would be possible, was approved by the Interim Committee on February 24.[73] The issue of whether the election should be held only in South Korea then split Korean political groups: The rightists wholeheartedly supported the election in South Korea; the leftists raised strong objections; and the Kim Kyu-sik and Kim Ku group also opposed it. What the commission would have done if the Koreans had been united against holding the election only in South Korea poses a good question. The February 28 decision to implement the resolution of the Interim Committee was definitely not an easy task for the commission to carry out. Kim Kyu-sik and his colleagues argued that the commission should return its mandate to the General Assembly and get a new mandate. This position impressed some members of the commission, but they were not able to make much headway against the strength of the rightist groups.[74]

Before the election was held in South Korea, Kim Kyu-sik and Kim Ku made one more effort to see if it was possible to unite the will and strength of the Koreans, both in the north and the south, to prevent the establishment of two separate governments on the Korean peninsula. The effort materialized in the North–South Korean Leaders Conference, which was held in P'yŏngyang in late April. The two Kims and fourteen other rightist South Korean delegates attended the conference along with 695 delegates from the north. Typical of the communist style, at this conference delegates had no chance to express their opinions or discuss options, and the group returned to Seoul very disappointed. The American occupation authority could not do anything for or against this meeting, but at least some Korean leaders had made one more effort to prevent decisive action toward a permanent division of the peninsula.

The election in South Korea took place according to the schedule on May 10, the first election ever held in Korea based on universal suffrage. The response of the Korean electorate was good: 7,837,504, or 79.7 percent of the eligible voters registered, and 7,487,649 of them voted, or 75 percent of the potential voters cast their votes. Two days after the election, Secretary of State Marshall sent a congratulatory message to the Korean people.[75] The commission did its best under the circumstances to carry out its duties: With a relatively limited number of human resources, the commission could not do more than spot checking and concluded that the election was held in a "reasonably free atmosphere."[76] No one political party had a clear-cut victory, but, as had been expected, the rightist conservative parties managed to obtain enough seats to organize the new government. In the following two months, the representatives took the steps necessary for drawing up the constitution and elected Syngman Rhee as the first president of the republic. The independent nation of South Korea was born officially on August 15, 1948, three years after the liberation, and at midnight, the American military occupation officially ended.[77]

Although efforts in the political and administrative areas had certainly been an important and difficult part of the three-year American military government in Korea, the economic and sociocultural problems were also significant. The Korean peninsula was not rich in 1945, but with proper management, adequate agricultural resources existed for feeding the people and a small industrial base produced textile and other consumer goods. However, because of the division at the 38th parallel, both the agricultural south and the industrial north had suffered since the end of World War II. In addition, the political and administrative confusion and the Soviet refusal to cooperate with the Americans in the economic domain made the situation much worse.

Food and fuel shortages made life difficult for the common people. Food production during the occupation period in South Korea was insufficient because of the great population increase brought about by the postwar repatriation, the influx of refugees from North Korea, and by a fertilizer shortage. By 1947, the production of rice, the main food item for Koreans, reached preoccupation levels, but other grain items—barley, wheat, millet, and soybeans—had not reached the level of the prewar years. After the initial difficulty, the collection of rice and summer crops and their distribution in 1946 and 1947 was worked out satisfactorily. Management of land naturally was important in this predominantly agricultural society. In early 1946, only 14 percent of the Korean farmers were owner-operators; 33 percent of them were part owner–part tenant; and 51 percent of them were tenant farmers. The tenants' payment to landlords had been very high; in the spring of 1946, the military government reduced the rent to a maximum of one-third of the annual yield. The sale of a substantial amount of good agricultural land in Korea, which the Japanese had owned, helped reduce the number of tenant farmers. North Korea's cost-free land distribution in the spring of 1946 applied some pressure for a similar reform in the South, and the U.S. military government also had a genuine interest in its own land reform for the South Korean farmers. It reduced in the fall of 1946 the extremely high rate of rent for tenant farmers to a maximum of one-third of the annual yield; it made a serious effort for land reform through the Interim

Legislative Assembly; and it carried out in the spring of 1948 the sale of all formerly Japanese-owned land with fifteen-year spread-out payments.[78]

The industrial sector in the post-liberation era suffered much. The suffering came from the separation of the agricultural south from the industrial north, the sudden departure of Japanese technicians, who had occupied 80 percent of the total number of technical positions in Korean industry, and a relatively low priority the American government gave to industrial recovery and development. In 1948, after three years of military occupation, Korean industry employed only 30 percent of the 1941 Korean labor force, and industrial production had fallen to 17 percent of the 1941 figure.[79]

Three major problems developed in the South Korean industry during the occupation period. Because the Hŭngnam Chemical Fertilizer Company, which had produced 90 percent of the total output of chemical fertilizer in Korea prior to the liberation, was located in the north, the total capacity of chemical factories in the south was small. Moreover, these factories in the south produced only a meager portion of this limited capacity. In 1946, the three major chemical fertilizer factories in the south produced only 3,603 metric tons of fertilizer, less than 1 percent of their capacity and only 0.6 percent of the annual average of the ten-year period between 1935 and 1944. Construction of new chemical fertilizer companies in the south did not begin until the post–Korean War years. The huge gap between the need for fertilizer and its production in the south in those years was met by importations with the fund from Government Appropriation Relief in Occupied Areas (GARIOA). The production of cotton goods in those years was also low mainly because of the shortage of technicians and a lack of management skill. In 1946, the textile factories in the South, with twenty-five thousand spindles, produced only 40 percent of the prewar annual average. Even though South Korea's share of coal mining was small, it was important as a source of power, especially after May 1948, when electric power from the north was cut off completely. In 1948, 713,742 metric tons of coal were produced by the four major coal mines in the south, a substantial increase over the two previous years. Prior to May 1948, as much as 66 percent of the power supply had come from the north, and despite the increase from alternative sources in the south by 100 percent between January and December 1948, the total supply of electricity that year in the south declined from the previous year's 816.8 million kilowatt hours to 693.8 million kilowatt hours. Other industries like cement, common brick, and rubber shoes were either very small or not significant for the national economic life during the occupation period.[80]

Trade in South Korea during the three-year occupation period was conducted mainly by the military government for the purpose of economic stability, and it was occupied largely with the importation of food and other essential consumer goods from the United States with U.S. government appropriated funds. Government imports in 1946 and the following two years totaled $47,636,000, $172,723,000, and $176,501,000 respectively, while private imports, also controlled by the government, were a little over $1 million in 1947 and a little over $7 million in the following year. Foodstuffs, the most important import item, occupied between 38 percent and 45 percent of total imports, followed by fertilizer and coal. Export items, primarily seafoods, went mainly to Japan and the United States and a small amount to Hong Kong.[81]

One of the most difficult aspects of Korean economic life in the postliberation era, one from which people suffered considerably, was the extremely high rate of inflation. Records indicate that between August 1945 and July 1948 the average rate of inflation for all commodities was 900 percent. The price of grain rose only 386 percent, but inflation rates for some other items essential for ordinary life were extremely high. Fuel, textiles, and building materials rose in three years 21, 52, and 86 times, respectively. A large part of this inflation was caused by excessive government withdrawals from the Bank of Korea, the sum total of which reached over W1 billion by June 1948. For example, between April 1, 1947 and March 31, 1948, the government's actual spending was W22.7 billion against revenue of W15.3 billion, a deficit of W7.4 billion for the year.[82]

Economic and financial conditions in postliberation South Korea necessitated a fair amount of American aid. Writing to the secretary of state in the summer of 1947, nearly two years after the American occupation had begun, General MacArthur said, "Koreans are hungry but not starving, they are clothed but not well-dressed."[83] In the post–World War II years, when everything was in a state of confusion and uncertainty and with the population swelling with refugees and repatriates, just keeping the people above the level of starvation and nakedness, not an easy job, was part of the obligation of the occupation power. Fortunately, the United States was in a position to be able to provide the Koreans with the minimum necessities through economic aid. The United States spent a total of $137 million on civilian supplies from the U.S. Army during this transitional period to the end of 1948, when the Economic Cooperation Administration (ECA) took over aid operations in Korea. With this sum, which came from the GARIOA appropriations, the army obtained almost exclusively relief items like food, clothing, fertilizer, and petroleum. Military authorities purchased some raw materials for Korean industries, but no capital goods. Although the Korean share of U.S. aid during the transitional period was small, only 0.9 percent, this economic assistance in Korea, an absolute necessity in this period, made a great contribution in keeping the Korean economy from total bankruptcy. Because of the negative Soviet attitude, the assistance from the United Nations Korea Reconstruction Agency (UNKRA), was small.[84] In 1947, long-term economic aid for Korea with the specific purpose of recovery began to be contemplated in Washington, but it came at a time of dragged-out policy debates and produced no action for the Korean economy during the occupation period.

In the cultural sphere, education was considered important by both Koreans and Americans, and actions taken by the military government were easily recognizable. Captain Earl N. Lockard, an artillery officer, was in charge of the education division of the military government, and he proceeded energetically to carry out his assignment. On September 16, 1945, he established an advisory body, the Korean Committee on Education, and with the assistance of Dr. Oh Ch'ŏn-sŏk, an American education specialist, appointed seven prominent Korean educators including Paik Nak-chun and Kim Hwal-nan. American assistance for Korean education soon became visible, and a month and a half later on October 31 Lockard created another organization, the Korean Council on Educational Aid from America, with the particular mission of making a study for an aid program. This council, with nineteen prominent Koreans and key American advisers from the military government, produced by November 22 an elaborate educational aid program: It included inviting over a hundred American education specialists and teachers for an investigation of the Korean educational environment, education of some Korean teachers and students, and the sending of some four-hundred Korean educators and students to the United States for observation of the American educational system and study. A part of this ambitious plan was carried out in the following years. To help implement this plan, the Korean Education Commission, with six Korean educators including Chang Li-uk and Ko Hwang-kyŏg, was dispatched to the United States in the following April. During their four-month stay, they had a number of meetings with officials from the Office of Education and a number of prominent American educators on the possibility of developing Korean education with American assistance. In the spring of 1946, the American government approved an eight-member, two-month American survey mission, but it was blocked by MacArthur's headquarters in Tokyo. When it took place a year later, its size and length of stay was trimmed to six members and eighteen days. The members of the Arndt Mission, headed by C. O. Arndt of New York University, had conferences with the military government officials and visited provincial educational institutions and presented a report to General Hodge before their departure.

Outside of the military government's domain or, to a certain extent even against the wishes of the authorities, study organizations were established to make contributions to the development of Korean education during the occupation period. One of them was the Korean Committee on Educational Planning. If the function of the two organizations created by the military government—the Korean Committee on Education, and the Korean Council on Educational Aid from America—was mainly in the area of administrative management in education, the function of this organization centered on the area of educational philosophy and organization. Naturally, the structure of the organization was comprehensive, and the issues dealt with more long-term educational measures. Paik Nak-jun, Yu Ŏk-kyŏm, and Ko Hwang-kyŏng—who served for the American organization—were also members of this group, but the group also included other scholars like Chŏng In-po, Yu Chin-o, Cho Yun-che, Chough Pyŏng-ok, Chang Dŏk-su, and Chang Myŏn.

Because of the changing political environment in Korea and its impact upon some of the committee members, the life of the organization was short. Nevertheless, over sixty members, including eleven Americans, began their work in mid-November 1945, and the ten subcommittees made four-month intensive studies of practically every aspect of the Korean education system. The impact of the subcommittees studies was significant. For example, in the summer of 1946, another educational organization was born in Korea. An Ho-sang, who had been educated in Germany and had been excluded consistently from the military government's educational advisory groups, in cooperation with the more nationalistically oriented groups of Korean educators, organized the Democratic Education Studies Association. How much contribution was made by this group is not clear, but this group at least represented an alternative to the approach taken by the other groups.[85]

One of the concrete achievements of the American military government's three years of efforts to develop Korean education was the training of new teachers for the increasing student population in Korea and the retraining of old teachers. In three years, the primary school population in Korea doubled, and the number of students in secondary education tripled. To meet these needs, the military authority established eight new normal schools, while operating short-term teacher-training institutions. Over two thousand secondary school teachers were produced in 1946 and 1947 through the secondary school teacher-training institutes at fifteen colleges and universities. The retraining of existing Korean teachers received special attention from the military government for political reasons. Some 7,800 went through the retraining program beginning in the winter of 1945. The most conspicuous American effort in this category was the establishment of the Teacher Training Institute, which became the first effort of the education reconstruction program of the United States in Korea toward the end of the occupation. The institute, which opened its doors on August 1, 1948, with a $340,000 budget from the GARIOA fund and 20 teachers from the United States, gave eight-week training sessions to a total of 567 Korean teachers. The new American democratic educational ideology and methods were very popular among Korean teachers and had an impact upon Korean education for years after the end of the occupation.[86]

Thus, the American military government in Korea vigorously approached the restoration, development, and reorientation of Korean education during the occupation period. Some critics called the American education policy an action of "cultural penetration" or even "cultural imperialism." It has been noted that in the summer of 1946, the American government switched from the maintenance of the status quo to a more positive developmental policy to fight the Cold War in Korea. In mid-July, writing to Ambassador Edwin W. Pauley, who had recommended a more active educational policy in Korea, President Truman said, "You will be glad to learn that we are incorporating into our revised policy for Korea most of your recommendations for specific action there." "We intend to carry on," Truman continued candidly, "an international and educational campaign to sell to the Koreans our form of democracy and for this purpose to send American teachers to Korea and Korean students and teachers to this country."[87] It is not possible to say that all of the educational system changes the Americans made in Korea during those three years were good for the Koreans, as was the case in Japan in the post–World War II period. But it is true that Korean schools in those years needed restoration, development, and reorientation and required outside assistance. It is also true that too many unfamiliar educational institutions and procedures were brought in during a short time span, and necessary modifications were made later. As far as the Americans were concerned, they had firm confidence in their own educational system, and the anticommunist element they brought into Korea in those early Cold War years was unavoidable.

Maintaining order and security in restless and turbulent Korea in the postliberation period was an important and difficult task. At the time of liberation only 30 percent of the police force in Korea was Korean. The American military government immediately reopened (October 15, 1945) the police academy for short-term training to reduce the shortage of security personnel. Military authorities also appointed high-level officials for the Korean police force, and they were criticized for relying too heavily on personnel of the conservative Korean Democratic Party like Chough Pyŏng-ok.[88]

The story of the birth of the Republic of Korea Army (ROKA) is much more complicated. From the beginning of the occupation, the military authorities realized that a police force would not be adequate to handle internal disorder and defend the border and began to contemplate establishment of a "national defense force." On November 10, 1945, two months after the occupation had begun, General Hodge appointed a board of officers to study this issue and make recommendations. Before even seeing a report from this group, he created on November 13 the Bureau of Armed Forces. The study that came from the board recommended the establishment of a forty-five-thousand-man army with two fighter squadrons and a five-thousand-man navy and coast guard. Hodge approved the plan, but MacArthur in Tokyo thought it an issue beyond his authority and referred it to Washington. Hodge apparently did not have much confidence that his grand plan would receive approval from the authorities in Washington and, while a debate on the plan was going on in Washington, he proceeded to implement a "small" plan. With the assistance of Lee Hyŏng-kun, a former officer in the Japanese Army, he opened the English Language School for Korean Military Officers in Seoul with some sixty candidates, including Lee Ŭng-chun, Wŏn Yong-tŏk, Yu Chae-hŭng, and others who had served in the Japanese Army. For political reasons, the SWNCC in Washington recommended in late December the postponement of the grand plan for establishment of the defense force in South Korea. Hodge took immediate action to carry out an alternate plan called BAMBOO, a project for creating a twenty-five-thousand-man constabulary-type police reserve force for national emergency cases. The plan proceeded quickly: Recruitment began on January 14 of the following year, and by the end of April there were some two-thousand men in eight regiments, one in each of eight provinces, and they were equipped with captured Japanese rifles. American officers and men provided infantry-type training for the program, and the constabulary grew steadily and reached the twenty-thousand-man level by late 1947.

The year 1947 was a year of change in U.S. policy toward Korea, and in October the Department of the Army asked both Hodge and MacArthur for recommendations regarding the Korean defense force. Hodge proposed to create an eight-division defense force within a year; MacArthur, however, recommended expanding the constabulary to fifty-thousand men. The Joint Chiefs of Staff authorized on March 10, 1948 the equipping of the Korean constabulary force with small arms, armored cars, and cannons; in the same month, the strength of the constabulary reached the target figure, and standardized training began in July of that year. Thus, by the spring of 1948 the foundation of the Republic of Korean Army was firmly laid by the American military government.[89]

With a few exceptions, most of those who have examined the American military occupation of Korea have been critical. One writer described it as "the most unfortunate legacies of World War II," pointing out the inconsistencies, uncertainties, and confusions. Another thought it was simply "a miserable failure."[90] To be more specific, one of the problems the Americans faced was unpreparedness. The XXIV Corps was picked as the occupation force because it happened to be at Okinawa, the nearest location to the Korean peninsula, at the end of the war, and John Reed Hodge's assignment as the commanding general of the troops was also not by careful choice. Thus the job fell to particular units by chance, and there was no special reason to expect more or less preparedness for the task; the XXIV Corps was just an average American unit, and the average American soldier knew little about Korea. General Hodge has been criticized by some, but to others, especially his superiors on the Joint Chiefs of Staff and W. Averell Harriman, the president's special envoy in the Far East, thought that he was a competent soldier ably carrying out his assigned duties. It is unlikely that the Washington military authorities could have found a better-prepared occupation force under a betterqualified commander for the task of occupation in Korea than the XXIV Corps. However, had the U.S. government planned earlier, perhaps as soon as it decided upon the occupation, it could have provided some personnel with a working knowledge of Korea and the Korean language by the time the occupation force was dispatched. Behind the negligence, one may detect the lack of significance the Americans had assigned to Korea.[91]

Many also have pointed out that the American authorities in Korea relied on the wrong groups of Koreans when assistance was needed. The Korean interpreters had considerable influence with the military government, and the Americans used the administrative and advisory services of only conservative, wealthy, and English-speaking Koreans.[92] This criticism is well founded. At the same time, it may be pointed out that these decisions were reached mainly because of expediency. Some have suggested that if the military government had involved the Korean Provisional Government from China in the civil government of Korea, then American prestige would have increased. The Americans never had any confidence in this organization, but if they had modified their views about it and cooperated with it, the job could have been much easier.[93]

Beside the organizational difficulties, there were also behavioral problems. Some critics have pointed out that the American military government was oppressive, more oppressive than even the Japanese colonial rule. Critics also characterize the Americans in Korea as arrogant and patronizing toward the Koreans. In the post–World War II years, the United States was enjoying the peak of its power and wealth, and the Americans were proud people. A danger inherent in the arrogance of power and the pride of wealth seems to be insensitivity and blindness to other peoples' legitimate needs and desires, soon cocooned in a cozy closed system. E. Grant Meade has aptly pointed out that the worst effect of the American cultural superiority complex was that it prevented them from seeing the real national needs and listening to the wishes of the Korean peoples.[94]

Despite all the mistakes and problems, it must be recognized that the Americans made important and positive accomplishments in Korea during the occupation period. After three and a half decades of Japanese rule, including eight years of war, which were especially hard for the Korean people, the Korean peninsula was in a very difficult situation. There were shortages of food, fuel, housing, and other necessary items for the people's daily lives; inflation was extremely high; the administrative system had broken down; political expectations were inflated, and extreme confusion and uncertainty reigned; two contending ideologies were beginning to do battle; and, above all, there was a sudden disappearance of order and stability. In this extremely difficult situation, the task of restoration of an orderly, normal life in Korea would have been a tremendously difficult task for any nation. Restoration of the local administration, educational facilities, transportation and communication; the reclamation of arable land and an effort for land reform; the initiation of a reforestation program; improvements in flood control; the rehabilitation of the fishing industry; and, most important, the prevention of widespread starvation were some of the major contributions of the American military government in Korea.[95] Undoubtedly, the Americans could have done a better job, but it is doubtful whether any other nation could have done a better job than the Americans did in Korea during those difficult years.

An important question to ask is whether there were any meaningful alternatives to the military occupation of the divided Korea. We can consider at least three possibilities: a U.S.–Soviet joint occupation of the whole peninsula; a three- or four-power joint occupation of the whole of Korea; or returning Korea to the Koreans, dismissing altogether a military occupation. The first two approaches would have entailed much cooperation and coordination among the occupation powers and would have been difficult to execute. But one big advantage of this approach would have been the fact that the inconvenience of the occupation would have shortened its length. The third alternative, the simple execution of the Cairo Declaration, would have been best not only for the Koreans but also for the powers involved. Of course, the most difficult part for the United States and the Soviet Union would have been that they might have lost the chance for getting the whole peninsula or at least a part of it. As a classical case of the buffer state, the contending powers would wish to obtain the whole buffer area. A question is whether possession of part of the buffer area by the contending powers was necessarily better than having the whole in the hands of the buffer state, perhaps with certain conditions such as a possibly temporary international guarantee of neutrality and security of the peninsula. It seems reasonable that the contending powers should have chosen to preserve Korea as a unified and neutral buffer state over the more troublesome alternative of possessing either part or the whole of the contended area. There is a good reason why the idea of a united and neutral Korea returned again and again to the minds of some Americans in the 1940s and 1950s, but much wisdom, vision, and courage would have been required for the adoption of this approach, and unfortunately, these conditions were lacking at this time.[96]

Some social scientists have been optimistic in believing that if the American authorities had recognized de facto the control of the People's Republic in the south in the fall of 1945, the independence and unification of Korea would have been possible.[97] How much the leftist elements dominated the People's Republic and the People's Committee is an important question that still needs to be answered. At the early stage of the occupation, these organizations were composed of people of many ideological shades, but later they gradually became leftist oriented and even radicalized. If the People's Republic ever had some chance of success, it was in the early fall of 1945, soon after the beginning of the occupation in both north and south. By the end of the year, the republic had no chance for success. It would have been at least a hypothetically interesting test to send the Koreans back to the pre-Three Kingdom era to see if they could redevelop a real democratic society, as their ancestors had done two thousand years ago. If they could have done it, could the two superpowers, under the particular circumstances, or under any circumstances, have done such an unselfish act as to allow a tiny nation to develop a democratic system? The People's Republic and the People's Committee indeed had very little chance of success.

In the north, a parallel phenomenon developed in the same three-year period. When the news of the Japanese surrender arrived, the Japanese police force evaporated overnight, and the local people immediately organized a security or self-protection force. Soon there followed the organization of people's committees on different levels. These actions took place within two or three weeks, and on September 6, the six provincial committees sent delegates to Seoul to explore the possibility of establishing one provisional government for Korea. Soon, however, the control of the Soviet occupation authority was established. In early spring of the following year, a provisional people's committee was established with Kim Il-sung as the chairman, the first big step toward the establishment of a separate government in the north. In early November of that year, W. Averell Harriman in Moscow already foresaw a strong possibility that the Soviet Union would establish an "independent friendly" regime in Korea with a strong military force and withdraw its military forces.[98] The establishment of the North Korean Workers Party in the summer of 1946, the all-level elections in the fall and the establishment of the Supreme Peoples Assembly in the following spring, the preparation of a constitution in the fall of 1947 and the following spring and its final ratification, and the appointment of Kim Il-sung as the premier on September 3, 1948 were systematic steps taken to establish a separate state in north. Building the armed forces proceeded in a like manner: First came the birth of the Security Corps (*Poantae*) in early October 1945, and then the establishment of the de facto armed forces with a navy in the summer of 1946 which obtained formal status by February of the following year.[99]

Because of its geographical location, the Russians have traditionally had much interest in the Korean peninsula (not so much as the Japanese and the Chinese, but definitely more than the Americans) and in 1945, they returned to the peninsula after four decades of absence. Probably domination of the whole peninsula was the maximum objective, while the minimum was preventing control of the whole of Korea by their adversaries, the Americans. In a sense, their objective was not dissimilar from that of the Americans. The difference was a matter of degree. Because of a higher level of interest, the level of their commitment was naturally more intense. In addition to a conventional national interest and objective, a revolutionary zeal was also there as an additional factor.[100] Authors seem to agree that the Soviet Union did better in carrying out their occupation policy in Korea. They were better prepared for the occupation than their counterparts, and they were more systematic and efficient in the execution of their policy; indeed, they were often ruthless. And, probably they were also strategically cost effective in taking the backseat after establishing a tightly organized state and a powerful armed force.[101]

In late summer and early fall of 1948, two separate states were born on the Korean peninsula. The three years of military rule in Korea may not have been as harsh as the thirty-five years of Japanese rule. Nevertheless, it was still foreign rule, and the Koreans in the north experienced unprecedented crudity at the hands of the Russians. In a real sense, however, the Koreans had to share some of the blame for what went wrong during the three-year period. The ideological cleavage was not of their making and to a large extent they cannot be blamed for it. Likewise, a lack of experience with modern democratic practices after some four decades of Japanese rule was also not their fault. But, they were not wise and courageous enough to bury their individual and group differences and unite their efforts in eliminating foreign rule and building their own independent and sovereign nation during those three years. Of course, the two occupation powers have to bear much of the responsibility for what occurred on the Korean peninsula in those years. First, they erred in deciding upon a divided occupation. National interest helps to explain the reason behind the occupation of Korea. All nations must protect their national interests, but when they become too selfish and short-sighted, especially when these two failings are combined and multiplied, the effects become fatal. Perhaps because of the fierce ideological and power struggle, it was very difficult for the two superpowers to avoid the mistakes made on the Korean peninsula. Nevertheless, they also could not escape from their responsibilities for what they had done; two years later, they were dragged to the battlefield by these mistakes.

In the final analysis, the United States and the allied powers, as the victors, had the power to decide the fate of Korea at the end of World War II, and the Koreans, as part of the defeated nation, had no voice in this decision. If the Koreans had a choice for their future, they would have chosen immediate independence. If they had to choose among various formats of delayed independence, the next choice would have been a short period of joint military occupation and even a very short-term trusteeship before independence. Though temporary military occupation and trusteeship would have been emotionally annoying, in a practical sense they would not have affected the real life of the people. The last and worst choice for the Koreans was long-delayed independence with divided military occupation. For the Americans and their allies, however, the most expedient way to handle the Korean situation was divided occupation. For the Truman administration, which, unlike the previous one, did not have much confidence in working with the Soviet leaders, this was the easiest to choose. Immediate independence of Korea would have been a difficult choice for the United States and the allies, because it would have meant a wasted opportunity—the opportunity of reserving the land which had belonged to a defeated power for a possible future use—quite similar to the situation the victorious powers had in the Middle East after World War I, with some risk of the whole Korean peninsula falling under communist control. However, in the long run, execution of the Cairo Declaration was the best choice for the United States and the allied powers. The problem was that this choice looked too altruistic for the victorious powers. If Korea had been allowed to handle its own affairs soon after the liberation and allowed to play out fully its role as a buffer state between the two fast-developing ideological camps of communism and liberal democracy, it would have been the best solution for both the Koreans and the Americans and their allies. Regrettably for all nations involved, the American leaders and their allies at this critical point did not adequately perceive the peculiar geopolitical characteristics of the Korean peninsula as a buffer state.

One final question to raise is whether the process of hardening the division of the Korean peninsula during the three-year occupation period could have been stopped and possibly even reversed. Academics often read too much between and behind the lines. If we take the American policy makers' reason for the decision for the division along the 38th parallel at the end of World War II as it was stated—a division of the peninsula for receiving the Japanese surrender—what went wrong in Korea seems to have been not the division itself but an extensive mismanagement of Korean affairs after the Japanese surrender. For the Americans to give a chance to the reestablishment of Korea as a buffer state required much patience and initiative. When they turned to Kim Kyu-sik and Yŏ Un-hyŏng for the formation of a mild rightist-and-leftist coalition in Korea in the spring of 1946, they were on the right track. Since both extreme rightists and leftists lacked broad support of the Korean public—Kim Kyu-sik providing leadership for Korean intellectuals and Yŏ Un-hyŏng, with his brilliance and charisma, popular with the Korean public—if the Americans had pushed with much more vigor and patience this approach of forming a strong center group through the rest of 1946 and 1947, they could have had a better chance of success at the second joint commission meeting. President Truman and Secretary of State James F. Byrnes should have come up in the summer and fall of 1946 with a more positive and imaginative response to the recommendation of Edwin W. Pauley who had returned from his fact-finding trip to Korea. Even the spring of 1947 was not too late for an American initiative. Secretary of State George C. Marshall, while in Moscow for a foreign ministers conference, should have had frank and serious talks with Molotov and Stalin to solve the vexatious Korean problem in a more fundamenatal way. If the leaders of the two superpowers had taken up the idea of building a wide, long buffer belt around the globe between the two camps, democracy and communism, including the Korean peninsula, they could have had much less difficulties managing the Cold War in the following decades. Characteristic American impatience became quite costly in dealing with the Russians. The communists almost succeeded in eliminating American influence from the Korean peninsula when the Americans became frustrated and impatient with the Korean situation and decided in the spring of 1947 to get out of Korea. Fortunately, it was not a perfect exit for the Americans because they turned over Korea to the United Nations, and an easy success of the Soviet attempt was denied. The consequence of lacking a long-term vision, wisdom, and courage was grave; soon, the two contending powers were summoned to the battlefield for a settlement.[102]

NOTES

1. Chay Jongsuk, "The Dynamics of American–Korean Relations and Prospects for the Future" in *The Problems and Prospects of American–East Asian Relations*, ed. idem (Boulder, Colo.: Westview Press, 1977), pp. 189–204; idem, *Diplomacy of Asymmetry*, pp. 1–16.

2. Chay Jongsuk, *Diplomacy of Asymmetry*, pp. 1–4.

3. Thomas H. Etzold and John L. Gaddis, eds., *Containment: Documents on American Policy and Strategy, 1945–1950* (New York: Columbia University Press, 1978), p. 79. See also Cumings, "Introduction," p. 19; Matray, *The Reluctant Crusade*, p. 128.

4. See E. Grant Meade, *American Military Government in Korea* (New York: King's Crown Press, 1951), p. vii; Cumings, "Introduction," p. 79.

5. For the subject, see Jongsuk Chay and Thomas E. Ross, eds., *Buffer States in World Politics* (Boulder, Colo.: Westview Press, 1987), especially pp. 191–212.

6. For the subject, see the discussions in Cumings, *The Origins of the Korean War: Liberation and the Emergence of Separate Regimes, 1945–1947* (Princeton, N.J.: Princeton University Press, 1981), p. 113; idem, *The Origins of the Korean War*, vol. 2, *The Roaring of the Cataract, 1947–1950* (Princeton, N.J.: Princeton University Press, 1990), pp. 59–60; Matray, *The Reluctant Crusade*, p. 30.

7. Cumings, "Introduction," pp. 7, 17; idem, *The Origins of the Korean War*, pp. 186, 226; Matray, *The Reluctant Crusade*, p. 74; Stephen Pelz, "U.S. Decisions on Korean Policy, 1943–1950," in *Child of Conflict: The Korean–American Relations, 1943–1953*, ed. Bruce Cumings (Seattle: University of Washington Press, 1983), p. 109.

8. Joseph M. Siracusa, "Will the Real Author of Containment Please Stand Up: The Strange Case of George Kennan and Frank Roberts," *The Society for Historians of American Foreign Relations Newsletter* 2, no. 3 (September 1991): 1–27.

9. Cumings, "Introduction," p. 15. See also his *The Origins of the Korean War*, vol. 2, p. 48.

10. Basic initial directive to the Commander in Chief, U.S. Army Forces, Pacific, for the administration of civil affairs in those areas of Korea occupied by U.S. forces, undated (between October 12 and 17, 1945), *Foreign Relations of the United States (FRUS), 1945*, 6: 1074. See also Cumings, "Introduction," pp. 18, 22; Kim Yong-myŏng, "Hankuk chŏngch'i pyŏntongkwa Mikuk" (Political changes in Korea and the United States), *Hankuk Chŏngch'ihak Hoepo* 22 (1988): 97.

11. "Post-War Status of Korea," Briefing Book Paper (January 18, 1945), *FRUS, The Conferences at Malta and Yalta, 1945*, p. 360. For a discussion on the topic, see Cumings, *The Origins of the Korean War*, p. 438.

12. The Acting Secretary of State to the Chairman of the Korean Commission in the United States (Rhee), June 5, 1945, *FRUS, 1945*, 6: 1029.

13. The Acting Secretary of State to the Secretary of State, in Moscow, April 11, 1947, *FRUS, 1947*, 6: 630–631.

14. The Assistant Secretary of State for Occupied Areas (Saltzman) to the Comptroller General of the United States (Warren), April 6, 1948, *FRUS, 1948*, 6: 1174. For the discussion on the subject see also Cumings, *The Origins of the Korean War*, pp. 126–128.

15. The Chairman of the Korean Commission in the United States (Rhee) to President Roosevelt, May 15, 1943, *FRUS, 1943*, 3: 1093. See also Cumings, *The Origins of the Korean War*, p. 136; Meade, *American Military Government in Korea*, p. 82; Joyce Kolko and Gabriel Kolko, *The Limits of Power: The World and the United States Foreign Policy, 1945–1954* (New York: Harper and Row, 1972), p. 283.

16. The Secretary of State to Harriman, November 3, 1945, *FRUS, 1945*, 6: 1109. See also the Political Adviser in Korea (Benninghoff) to the Secretary of State, September 15, 1945, ibid., p. 1049; memorandum of General R. Hodge to General Douglas MacArthur, September 24, 1945, ibid., p. 1055; the Assistant Secretary of War (McCloy) to the Undersecretary of State (Acheson), November 13, 1945, ibid., p. 1124.

17. William Stueck, *The Road to Confrontation: American Policy toward China and Korea, 1947–1950* (Chapel Hill: University of North Carolina Press, 1981), p. 6; Charles M. Dobbs, *The Unwanted Symbol: American Foreign Policy, the Cold War, and Korea, 1945–1950* (Kent, Ohio: Kent State University Press, 1981), p. 103.

18. The Political Adviser in Korea (Langdon) to the Secretary of State, May 24, 1946, *FRUS, 1946*, 8: 685; Matray, *The Reluctant Crusade*, p. 80.

19. Edwin W. Pauley to Truman, June 22, 1946, *FRUS, 1946*, 8: 706–709.

20. Truman to Edwin W. Pauley, July 16, 1946, *FRUS, 1946*, 8: 713–714. See also the draft of a letter from Truman to the Secretary of War (Patterson), July 3, 1946, ibid., p. 721.

21. The Acting Secretary of State to the Political Adviser in Korea, August 30, 1946, *FRUS, 1946*, 8: 734.

22. Memorandum by the Special Inter-Departmental Committee on Korea, February 25, 1947, *FRUS, 1947*, 6: 608–618.

23. The Acting Secretary of State to the Secretary of War (Patterson), March 28, 1947, *FRUS, 1947*, 6: 621–623.

24. The Secretary of War (Patterson) to the Acting Secretary of State, April 4, 1947, *FRUS, 1947*, 6: 625–628.

25. The Secretary of State to the Political Adviser in Korea (Jacobs), July 14, 1947, *FRUS, 1947*, 6: 701–703.

26. Memorandum by the Assistant Chief of the Division of Northeast Asian Affairs (Allison), n.d. *FRUS, 1947*, 6: 713–714.

27. Memorandum by the Assistant Chief of the Division of Northeast Asian Affairs (Allison), July 29, 1947, *FRUS, 1947*, 6: 734–736.

28. Report by the Ad Hoc Committee on Korea, August 4, 1947, *FRUS, 1947*, 6: 738–741.

29. Memorandum by the State-War-Navy Coordinating Committee to the Secretary, Joint Chiefs of Staff, September 15, 1947, *FRUS, 1947*, 6: 789–790.

30. Memorandum by the Secretary of Defense (Forrestal) to the Secretary of State, September 26 [29] 1947, *FRUS, 1947*, 6: 817–818.

31. Memorandum by the Director of the Policy Planning Staff (Kennan) to the Director of the Office of Far Eastern Affairs (Butterworth), September 24, 1947, *FRUS, 1947*, 6: 814–815.

32. Cumings, "Introduction," p. 18; idem, *The Origins of the Korean War*, vol. 2, pp. 46, 48; Matray, *The Reluctant Crusade*, p. 2.; Dobbs, *The Unwanted Symbol*, pp. 92, 97, 108, 110, 128, 160; Callum A. MacDonald, *Korea: The War before Vietnam* (New York: Free Press, 1986), pp. 13, 16.

33. Stueck, *The Road to Confrontation*, pp. 85, 86; Matray, *The Reluctant Crusade*, pp. 99, 133–134; John Lewis Gaddis, *The Long Peace: Inquiries into the History of the Cold War* (New York: Oxford University Press, 1987), p. 95; Cumings, *The Origins of the Korean War*, pp. 438–439.

34. Meade, *American Military Government in Korea*; Cho Soon-sung, *Korea in World Politics, 1940–1950: An Evaluation of American Responsibility* (Berkeley and Los Angeles: University of California Press, 1967), pp. 61–160; Cumings, *The Origins of the Korean War*, pp. 135–381; Matray, *The Reluctant Crusade*, pp. 52–150.

35. Meade, *American Military Government in Korea*, pp. 76–78.

36. See Cumings, "Introduction," p. 15; idem, *The Origins of the Korean War*, pp. 123, 128, 229–230, 440; Sandusky, *American Parallel*, pp. 289, 291; Kolko and Kolko, *The Limits of Power*, p. 282.

37. Meade, *American Military Government in Korea*, pp. 225, 228, 235; Cumings, *The Origins of the Korean War*, p. 229; Matray, *The Reluctant Crusade*, p. 53.

38. Cho Soon-sung, *Korea in World Politics*, pp. 65–73; Meade, *American Military Government in Korea*, pp. 54, 71; Gregory Henderson, *Korea: The Politics of Vortex* (Cambridge, Mass.: Harvard University Press, 1968), p. 118.

39. Meade, *American Military Government in Korea*, p. 228.

40. Annex in a memorandum by the Acting Secretary of State to President Truman, September 14, 1945, *FRUS, 1945*, 6: 1048.

41. See the memorandum by the Acting Secretary of State to President Truman, September 14, 1945, *FRUS, 1945*, 6: 1047; the Political Adviser in Korea (Benninghoff) to the Secretary of State, September 15, 1945, ibid., p. 1049; the Acting Political Adviser in Korea (Langdon) to the Secretary of State, November 20, 1945, ibid., p. 1131; resolution of the Korean Congress of Political Parties, Seoul, November 4, 1945 (a copy was transmitted to the State Department on December 1, 1945), ibid., p. 1110. See also Cumings, *The Origins of the Korean War*, p. 137; Matray, *The Reluctant Crusade*, p. 50.

42. Memorandum by the Acting Chairman of the State-War-Navy Coordinating Committee, September 10, 1945, *FRUS, 1945*, 6: 1044; memorandum of the Acting Secretary of State to President Truman, September 14, 1945, ibid., pp. 1047–1048.

43. See Meade, *American Military Government in Korea*, p. 66; Cumings, *The Origins of the Korean War*, p. 204.

44. Meade, *American Military Government in Korea*, p. 158; Chin Dŏk-kyu, "Mi kunchŏng" (The U.S. military government), in *Han-mi sukyo 100-nyŏnsa*, ed. KYHW, p. 430; Cumings, *The Origins of the Korean War*, p. 147; Matray, *The Reluctant Crusade*, p. 55.

45. Cho Soon-sung, *Korea in World Politics*, pp. 73–75; Chin Dŏk-kyu, "Mi kunchŏng," pp. 434–440; Cumings, *The Origins of the Korean War*, pp. 135, 141–142, 145.

46. The Political Adviser in Korea (Benninghoff) to the Secretary of State, September 15, 1945, *FRUS, 1945*, 6: 1049.

47. Memorandum of Lieutenant General George R. Hodge to General of the Army Douglas MacArthur, September 24, 1945, *FRUS, 1945*, 6: 1055.

48. The Acting Political Adviser in Korea (Langdon) to the Secretary of State, November 24, 1945, *FRUS, 1945*, 6: 1130–1133.

49. MacArthur to the Joint Chiefs of Staff, December 16, 1945, *FRUS, 1945*, 6: 1147.

50. MacArthur to the Joint Chiefs of Staff, October 11, 1945, *FRUS, 1945*, 6: 1071–1072.

51. "Korea," *Department of State Bulletin* 13 (December 30, 1945): pp. 1027–1030.

52. Cho Soon-sung, *Korea in World Politics*, pp. 100–110; Matray, *The Reluctant Crusade*, pp. 64–66; Cumings, *The Origins of the Korean War*, pp. 215–217.

53. "Korea," *Department of State Bulletin* 13 (December 30, 1945): 1036.

54. "Korea," *Department of State Bulletin* 13 (December 30, 1945): 1027; ibid., 14 (January 27, 1946): 108.

55. Hodge to the War Department, January 18, 1946, *FRUS, 1946*, 8: 611–612. See also the Joint Chiefs of Staff to MacArthur, January 5, 1946, ibid., pp. 607–608.

56. For the discussions on the subject see Matray, *The Reluctant Crusade*, pp. 70–85; Cumings, *The Origins of the Korean War*, pp. 39–46; Cho Soon-sung, *Korea in World Politics*, pp. 114–118.

57. The Political Adviser in Korea (Benninghoff) to the Secretary of State, January 28, February 9, 1946, *FRUS, 1946*, 8: 627, 631; MacArthur to the Secretary of State, February 24, 1946, ibid., p. 641; Langdon to the Secretary of State, March 19, April 10, May 14, August 23, 1946, ibid., pp. 648, 658, 677–678, 726. See also Cumings, *The Origins of the Korean War*, p. 264.

58. See Cumings, *The Origins of the Korean War*, pp. 235, 237; Cho Soon-sung, *Korea in World Politics*, p. 80; Matray, *The Reluctant Crusade*, p. 78.

59. The Political Adviser in Korea (Langdon) to the Secretary of State, November 14, December 27, 1946, *FRUS, 1946*, 8: 767, 780. See also Chin Dŏk-kyu, "Mi kunchŏng," pp. 421–422, 431–432; Cho Soon-sung, *Korea in World Politics*, p. 131; Cumings, *The Origins of the Korean War*, pp. 260–261; Matray, *The Reluctant Crusade*, pp. 95–96; Kolko and Kolko, *The Limits of Power*, pp. 291–292.

60. The Political Adviser to Korea (Langdon) to the Secretary of State, August 28, 1946, *FRUS, 1946*, 8: 726.

61. The Political Adviser in Korea (Langdon) to the Secretary of State, November 14, 1946, *FRUS, 1946*, 8: 767.

62. See Cumings, *The Origins of the Korean War*, p. 351.

63. Cumings, *The Origins of the Korean War*, pp. 351–352, 379–381, 432–433; Kolko and Kolko, *The Limits of Power*, pp. 291–292.

64. Memorandum of the Director of the Office of Far Eastern Affairs (Vincent) to the Secretary of State, January 27, 1947, *FRUS, 1947*, 6: 601–602. See also Cumings, *The Origins of the Korean War*, vol. 2, p. 237.

65. Vincent to the Secretary of State, January 27, 1947, *FRUS, 1947*, 6: 602–603.

66. The Secretary of State to the Acting Secretary of State, April 2, 1947, *FRUS, 1947*, 6: 623–625; the Soviet Minister for Foreign Affairs (Molotov) to the Secretary of State, April 19, 1947, ibid., pp. 632–635; the Political Adviser to Korea (Langdon) to the Secretary of State, May 30, 1947, ibid., pp. 656–657; Hodge to the Secretary of State, June 26, July 3, 10, 1947, ibid., pp. 679–680, 685–687, 697–700; the Political Adviser in Korea (Jacobs) to the Secretary of State, July 3, 14, 1947, ibid., 687–688, 701–703. See also Matray, *The Reluctant Crusade*, pp. 108–124; Cumings, *The Origins of the Korean War*, vol. 2, pp. 68–70; Cho Soon-sung, *Korea in World Politics*, pp. 139–155, 161; Russell D. Buhite, *Soviet–American Relations in Asia, 1945–1954* (Norman: University of Oklahoma Press, 1981), p. 154.

67. The Political Adviser in Korea (Jacobs) to the Secretary of State, July 7, 1947, *FRUS, 1947*, 6: 691.

68. Acting Secretary of State to the Embassy in the Soviet Union, September 16, 1947, *FRUS, 1947*, 6: 792; United Nations Official Records of the Second Session of the General Assembly, Resolutions, September 16–November 29, 1947, pp. 16–18; "Request for the Inclusion of the Added Items in the Agenda of the Second Regular Session," U.N. Document A/BUR/185, September 17, 1947, United Nations, Official Records of the Second Session of the General Assembly; Plenary Session of the General Assembly Verbatim Record, September 16–September 29, 1947, vol. 2, 110th–128th meetings, November 13–November 29, 1947, p. 858.

69. The Political Adviser in Korea (Jacobs) to the Secretary of State, October 8, 1947, *FRUS, 1947*, 6: 825.

70. Matray, *The Reluctant Crusade*, pp. 123–125; Cumings, *The Origins of the Korean War*, vol. 2, pp. 65–67; Cho Soon-sung, *Korea in World Politics*, p. 183; McDonald, *Korea: The War before Vietnam*, p. 14.

71. See Matray, *The Reluctant Crusade*, pp. 123, 125; Cumings, *The Origins of the Korean War*, vol. 2, p. 67; Pelz, "U.S. Decisions on Korean Policy," p. 111; Cho Soon-sung, *Korea in World Politics*, pp. 165, 184–185.

72. Memorandum of conversation by the Acting Secretary of State, January 3, 1948, *FRUS, 1948*, 6: 1079; Secretary of State to the Acting Political Adviser in Korea (Langdon), January 6, 1948, ibid., p. 1083; Truman to the Canadian Prime Minister (Mackenzie King), January 24, 1948, ibid., 1087–1088.

73. The Political Adviser in Korea (Jacobs) to the Secretary of State, February 2, 5, 8, 1948, *FRUS, 1948*, 6: 1090, 1093, 1096; the Secretary of State to the Acting Political Adviser in Korea (Langdon), February 27, 1948, ibid., p. 1134; U.N. Document, A/583.

74. The Political Adviser in Korea (Jacobs) to the Secretary of State, February 12, 1948, *FRUS, 1948*, 6: 1103.

75. The Secretary of State to the Political Adviser in Korea (Jacobs), May 12, 1948, *FRUS, 1948*, 6: 1195.

76. The Political Adviser in Korea (Jacobs) to the Secretary of State, April 27, 28, 1948, *FRUS, 1948*, 6: 1182, 1184.

77. The Political Adviser in Korea (Jacobs) to the Secretary of State, August 9, 1948, *FRUS, 1948*, 6: 1268–1269; Cho Soon-sung, *Korea in World Politics*, pp. 205–211; Matray, *The Reluctant Crusade*, pp. 148–150.

78. The Political Adviser in Korea (Langdon) to the Secretary of State, March 19, 1946, *FRUS, 1946*, 8: 650; "Economic Review of the Republic of Korea, 1948," International Reference Service (Office of International Trade, U.S. Department of Commerce), 6, no. 42 (June 1949): 1–2; Yu In-ho, "Haepanghu nongchi kaehyŏkŭi chŏnkae kwachŏngkwa sŏngkyŏk" (The process and characteristics of land reform in the postliberation era) in *Haepang chŏnhusaŭi insik* (Understanding of the history of the pre- and postliberation era), vol. 1, ed. Song Kŏn-ho (Seoul: Hankilsa, 1989), pp. 422–423, 431, 434–435; Lee Chŏng-hun, "Mi kunchŏng kyŏngchaeŭi yŏksachŏk sŏngkyŏk" (The historical characteristics of the economic policies of the American military government), in ibid., pp. 488, 491; Chang Sang-hwan, "Nongchi kaehyŏkkwachŏnge kwanhan silchŭngchŏk yŏnku" (A study on the process of the land reform), in ibid., pp. 305, 309. See also Hwang Han-sik, "Mi kunchŏngha nongŏpkwa t'ochi kaehyŏk chŏngch'aek" (Agriculture and land reform policy under the U.S. military government) in *Haepang chŏnhusaŭi insik* (Understanding of the history of the pre- and postliberation era), vol. 2, ed. Kang Man-kil et al. (Seoul: Hankilsa, 1985), pp. 266, 270–280; Yu In-ho, "Haepanghu nongchi kaehyŏkŭi chŏnkae kwachŏngkwa sŏngkyŏk" (The developmental process and characteristics of land reform after the liberation), in *Haepang chŏnhusaŭi insik*, vol.1, ed. Song Kŏn-ho, pp. 406, 414, 430–435.

79. See Lee Chŏng-hun, "Mi kunchŏng kyŏngchaeŭi yŏksachŏk sŏngkyŏk," p. 509.

80. "Economic Review of the Republic of Korea, 1948," pp. 3–4; Lee Chŏng-hun, "Mi kunchŏng kyŏngchaeŭi yŏksachŏk sŏngkyŏk," pp. 509–513.

81. "Economic Review of the Republic of Korea, 1948," pp. 5–7; Lee Chŏng-hun, "Mi kunchŏng kyŏngchaeŭi yŏksachŏk sŏngkyŏk," pp. 514–522.

82. National Economy Board, United States Army Military Government in Korea, "South Korean Interim Government Activities," no. 33 (June 1948), pp. 32, 126; "Economic Review of the Republic of Korea, 1948," p. 5.

83. MacArthur to the Secretary of State, July 2, 1947, *FRUS, 1947*, 6: 684.

84. William Adams Brown, Jr., *American Foreign Assistance* (Washington, D.C.: Brookings Institution, 1953), pp. 115–116, 373–374. The State Department came up with a much larger figure, a total of $250 million of U.S. economic aid for Korea between September 1945 and July 1948, which probably came from a different method of counting: Department of State, Publications 3305, Far Eastern Series 28, "Korea 1945 to 1948; A Report on Political Development and Economic Resources with Selected Documents," Washington, D.C., 1948, p. 39.

85. For this and the preceding paragraph, see Lee Kwang-ho, "Mi kunchŏngŭi kyoyuk chŏngch'aek," (The American military government's policy for education) in *Haepang chŏnhusaŭi insik*, vol. 2, ed. Kang Man-kil et al., pp. 493–528, especially pp. 501–510; Han Chun-sang, "Mikuŭi munhwa chimt'uwa Hankuk kyoyuk," (American cultural penetration and Korean education), in *Haepang chŏnhusaŭi insik* (Understanding of the history of the pre- and postliberation era), vol. 3, ed. Pak Hyŏn-chae (Seoul: Hankilsa, 1989), pp. 541–607, especially pp. 558, 573–594.

86. Lee Kwang-ho, "Mi kunchŏngŭi kyoyuk chŏngch'aek," pp. 509–511.

87. Han Chun-sang, "Mikukŭi munhwa ch'imt'uwa Hanguk kyoyuk," pp. 541, 542, 596; Lee Kwang-ho, "Mi kunchŏngŭi kyoyuk chŏngch'aek," pp. 494–495, 500; memorandum of the Assistant Secretary of State for Occupied Areas (Hilding) to the Operational Division, War Department, June 6, 1946, *FRUS, 1946*, 8: 693–694; Truman to Edwin W. Pauley, July 16, 1946, ibid., p. 713.

88. Robert K. Sawyer, *Military Advisers in Korea: KMAG in Peace and War* (Washington, D.C.: Office of the Chief of Military History, Department of the Army, 1962), pp. 8–10; Cumings, *The Origins of the Korean War*, p. 162.

89. The Acting Political Adviser in Korea (Langdon) to the Secretary of State, November 20, 1945, *FRUS, 1945*, 6: 1133; the Joint Chiefs of Staff to MacArthur, January 9, 1946, ibid., p. 1157; Sawyer, *Military Advisers in Korea*, pp. 9–31; Kim Chŏm-kon, *The Korean War: The First Comprehensive Account of the Historical Background and Development of the Korean War, 1950–1953* (Seoul: Kwangmyŏng, 1973), pp. 246–248; Cho Soon-sung, *Korea in World Politics*, pp. 248–249; Cumings, *The Origins of the Korean War*, pp. 172–177.

90. Matray, *The Reluctant Crusade*, pp. 52, 95–96; Kim Chŏm-kon, *The Korean War*, p. 181. See also Cumings, "Introduction," pp. 14, 16; Kolko and Kolko, *The Limits of Power*, pp. 284, 287.

91. Meade, *American Military Government in Korea*, pp. 228, 225, 235; Cumings, *The Origins of the Korean War*, pp. 123, 128, 229–230, 440; Sandusky, *American Parallel*, pp. 289, 291.

92. Meade, *American Military Government in Korea*, pp. 61, 228–299; Cumings, *The Origins of the Korean War*, pp. 138, 141; Matray, *The Reluctant Crusade*, pp. 53–54.

93. Cho Soon-sung, *Korea in World Politics*, p. 90.

94. Kolko and Kolko, *The Limits of Power*, pp. 291–292, 299; Meade, *American Military Government in Korea*, p. 235; Kim Chŏm-kon, *The Korean War*, p. 161. See also MacArthur to the Joint Chiefs of Staff, December 16, 1945, *FRUS, 1945*, 6: 1145; memorandum of conversation by the Deputy Director of the Office of Far Eastern Affairs (Penfield), October 31, 1946, *FRUS, 1946*, 8: 753.

95. See Meade, *American Military Government in Korea*, pp. 225, 233; Dobbs, *The Unwanted Symbol*, p. 150.

96. See James Burnham, *The Struggle for the World* (New York: John Day, 1947), p. 233.

97. Cho Soon-sung, *Korea in World Politics*, pp. 69–73. See also Henderson, *Korea: The Politics of Vortex*, pp. 117–118; Meade, *American Military Government in Korea*, pp. 8, 54, 71, 158.

98. The Ambassador in the Soviet Union (Harriman) to the Secretary of State, November 12, 1945, *FRUS, 1945*, 6: 1122.

99. The Acting Political Adviser (Langdon) to the Secretary of State, February 20, 1948, *FRUS, 1948*, 6: 1122; Hodge to the Secretary of State, February 24, 1948, ibid., pp. 1129–1131; Cho Soon-sung, *Korea in World Politics*, pp. 82, 128, 211; Cumings, *The Origins of the Korean War*, pp. 187, 382, 384; Kim Chŏm-kon, *The Korean War*, pp. 242–257; Erik Van Ree, *Socialism in One Zone: Stalin's Policy in Korea, 1945–1947* (Oxford: Berg, 1989), pp. 85–186.

100. For the Russian objectives see Buhite, *Soviet–American Relations in Asia, 1945–1954*, p. 139; Cumings, *The Origins of the Korean War*, vol. 2, pp. 331, 326, 330; Matray, *The Reluctant Crusade*, p. 55; Van Ree, *Socialism in One Zone*, pp. 1–12, 268–277.

101. Meade, *American Military Government in Korea*, p. 58; Cumings, *The Origins of the Korean War*, p. 426; Matray, *The Reluctant Crusade*, p. 55.

102. Proposed message to the General of the Army Douglas MacArthut drafted in the Department of State, *FRUS, 1946*, 8: 645–646; memorandum of the Far

Eastern Affairs (Vincent) to the Secretary of State, January 27, 1947, ibid., p. 601; the Secretary of War (Patterson) to the Acting Secretary of State, April 4, 1947, ibid., pp. 625–628; report by the Ad Hoc Committee on Korea, August 4, 1947, ibid., pp. 738–741. See also Yang Tong-chu, "Haepanghu chaik untongkwa minchuchui minchok chŏnsŏn" (The leftist movement and democratic nationlist front after the liberation), in *Haepang chŏnhusaŭ insik*, vol. 3, ed. Pak Hyŏn-chae, pp. 107–119; Lee Tong-hwa, "8.15 rŭl chŏnhuhan Yŏ Un-hyŏngŭi hwaltong" (Yŏ Un-hyŏng's activities during the pre- and the postliberation era), in *Haepang chŏnhusaŭ insik*, vol. 1, ed. Song Kŏn-ho pp. 381–385.

PART II

THE CRITICAL TWO YEARS

CHAPTER 4

Establishment of
the Republic of Korea

The two-year period between the summer of 1948 and the summer of 1950 was critical for Korea. A series of events and actions had already taken place by this time: the Cairo Declaration of 1943, the division of the peninsula at the 38th parallel in 1945, the military occupation of the peninsula by the two major Cold War adversaries between 1945 and 1948, the failure of these two occupying powers to unite the two halves of the nation peacefully during the three-year period, the U.S. decision to take the Korean question to the United Nations in 1947, and the birth of the two half states in 1948. These events and actions naturally conditioned to a large extent the events and actions that would take place in the following two years. With a number of buttons already in the wrong holes, it was not easy to straighten out the whole process. Still, it was not impossible, and this was the difficult task faced by those responsible for the policies and actions taken during those two years in Seoul, P'yŏngyang, Washington, Moscow, and Beijing. Both what they had done and what they had failed to do largely determined what happened at the end of the period.

A number of salient issues dominated Korean–American relations during these two years: U.S. troop withdrawal and its policy implications, U.S. economic aid for Korea and the Korean economy, U.S. military aid and the status of Korean defense forces, the nature and development of the Korean political system and its impact upon Korean–U.S. relations, and the role and function of the U.N. Commission in Korea.

Our story will begin with the establishment of the two governments in the summer of 1948. The Koreans greeted August 15, 1948, the day on which the government of the Republic of Korea was established, with mixed feelings. By this time, they recognized with a keen sense of disappointment that even though their wish for a reunited nation was great, the forces blocking this goal were too powerful. The establishment of a government in the south would soon follow in the north, and the division along the 38th parallel would become firmly fixed. There was also a sense of resignation in the minds of many Koreans; they felt that there was no other way than to face political reality and save at least a half of the peninsula from communism. In the midst of these mixed feelings, the ceremony of inauguration for the birth of the republic in South Korea was held on the day of the third anniversary of liberation of the nation from Japanese rule.

Newspapers reported the inauguration ceremony with their usual eloquence and considerable exaggeration. "The Korean people, in every village and hamlet," one of the leading Korean newspapers reported, "enjoyed fully the glorious celebration of the fifteenth of August in the atmosphere filled with the auspicious signs permanently promising the future of the nation."[1] The *New York Times* was equally eloquent: "A nation sold down the river forty-three years ago into slavery to Japan was reborn yesterday in the centuries old city of Seoul when the newly formed Korean government formally took office." The paper added, "May Korea in the years ahead justify its history as the Flowery Kingdom, the Land of Morning Calm. It has an opportunity as a reborn nation to set an example for the rest of Asia and help lead the billions of the people of the Far East down the road to democracy and to peace."[2] General Douglas MacArthur was the most honored guest, and he spoke first when the ceremony began. His oratory began, "I am profoundly moved to stand on the soil of Korea in this historic hour, to see liberty born, the cause of right and justice prevail." After praising the heroic works of the Korean patriots in their endeavor for regaining freedom, he continued, "Yet in this hour, as the forces of righteousness advance, the triumph is dulled by one of the great tragedies of contemporary history—an artificial barrier has divided your land. This barrier must and will be torn down." Words of encouragement followed: "Nothing shall prevent the ultimate unity of your people as freemen of a free nation. Koreans come from too proud a stock to sacrifice their sacred cause by yielding to any alien philosophies of disruption."[3] Then, General Hodge, the U.S. official delegate for the occasion, spoke in more sober tones.[4] In his carefully prepared inaugural speech, President Syngman Rhee thanked the nations—especially the United States—the United Nations, and individuals for their contributions to the founding of the new republic and explained the six "fundamental principles" of the nation: a firm faith in democracy; freedom of speech, freedom of assembly, freedom of religion, and freedom of thought; "respect and guard" for freedom; tolerance and cooperation; improving living conditions of the people; and the need for economic assistance.[5]

Soon after the inauguration, formal diplomatic relations with the United States were reopened, after a forty-three year interval that began in 1905 when the American government closed its legation in Seoul. John J. Muccio was appointed by President Truman as the head of the American diplomatic mission in Seoul, a good choice in view of the service he rendered later for the two governments. President Rhee wished to have a man of the caliber of W. Averell Harriman in the post, but it was not only impossible but also even unwise to have such a person in Korea during the war years. An Italian-born bachelor and career diplomat, Muccio had years of service in the Far East and Latin America; he also had an assignment in Europe working on the German problem, which was useful for his Korean assignment.[6]

Even though Muccio arrived in Korea a week after the inauguration (August 22), because of the delay of full recognition of the Korean government, which came in the beginning of the following year, he served for four months as the special representative of the president with a personal rank of ambassador.[7] The Korean government and the people did everything possible to welcome this important emissary from the United States. When he arrived at Kimpo Airport near Seoul, he was greeted by the key cabinet members of the Korean government—the prime minister and foreign and home ministers—and a nineteen-gun salute. When he presented his credentials to President Rhee, the Korean police and troops lined up between the Bando Hotel, where his office was located, and the Kyŏngmutae, the presidential office building, and many American and Korean officials, thousands of the Korean citizens, and the police on horseback followed his car.[8] The Korean government offered Muccio the Bando Hotel, one of the two best hotel buildings in Seoul and the most suitable building for a foreigner's establishment of an office and residence in the city.

After forty years of absence, the reestablishment of diplomatic relations was not an easy task for the new republic. With the exception of a few, who had some experience of dealing with a limited number of governments during the intervening years, practically no Korean had any experience in diplomacy. Chang T'aek-sang, who was chosen by President Rhee as the minister of foreign affairs, was a graduate of Edinburgh University in Scotland and had limited experience with international conferences, but he was not happy with his assignment and stayed in the office for only five months. The position was taken over by Im Pyŏng-chik, President Rhee's long-time associate in the United States who had done diplomatic work for the Korean independence movement. President Rhee chose Chang Myŏn as the first representative of the republic to the United States and Han Pyo wook as his assistant. Both of them were good choices: Chang, educated in the United States, was a capable and amiable person. Han, a graduate student at the University of Michigan, was a capable young man who also gave valuable service to the young republic in those early years of Korean diplomacy. Unlike Muccio in Korea, who, despite numerous inconveniences in Seoul in the late 1940s, had at least sufficient human and material resources for the position, these two men in Washington had to manage their official diplomatic functions with meager resources—an assistant, two secretaries, and four rooms which were rented in an office building in the northwestern section of the city. Later, the Korean government purchased a building and spent $200,000 for purchase, repair, and expansion.[9]

The American military occupation officially ended at midnight August 15. The immediate task facing the new republic and the American representative in Seoul was the transfer of the governing authority and its property. For this important and not small task, President Rhee appointed Prime Minister Lee Pŏm-sŏk, Foreign Minister Chang T'aek-sang, and Home Minister Yun Ch'i-yŏng; on the American side, General Hodge gave the work to Major General Charles G. Helmick, chief of the civil affairs section of the XXIV Corps, and Minister Everett F. Drumright.[10] Even though the Koreans were impatient about the slowness of the transfer, these people worked hard, and most of the work was completed by the end of September. The transfer of the businesses of the South Korean interim government to the new government moved expeditiously. By September 25 most of the transfer was completed, except for two categories—security and the settlement of finance and property—which were scheduled to be finished by the middle of December.[11]

The transfer was not smooth in these two areas, however. There was a considerable amount of discussion on one, and an intensive debate on the other. The State Department complained later about inadequate documentation of the process of debate concerning the transfer of Korean security matters, and communications from Seoul do not explain the details of the nature of the dispute on security matters. Fortunately, the first two articles of the August 25, 1948 agreement seem to give a fair indication of the nature of the dispute between two sides. The first article stated that the commanding general of the U.S. armed forces in Korea "will continue to organize, train and equip" the security forces of the Republic of Korea until the completion of the withdrawal of U.S. troops. There is no reason why the Koreans should have been unhappy with this stipulation. However, they probably were concerned about the statement in the second article, which directed that the U.S. forces would transfer the "direction" of the Korean security forces "progressively" and "as rapidly as they would deem compatible with common security." The Korean concern must have been about the manner of the transfer and the discretionary power of the American commander to judge the speed of the transfer. Very possibly in the minds of both Americans and Koreans there was a connection between the two articles; in view of the American contribution, which was specified in the first article, the Koreans would not be in a position to complain about the speed of the transfer of the control of the Korean security force by the American commander.[12]

Intensive debates took place concerning the settlement of finance and property. Whereas in other areas, the transfer was a matter of organization and management, substance was involved in terms of numbers of won and dollars, an area important to both sides. After eight meetings, an agreement was reached and was signed by both sides on September 11. The outstanding items in the financial and property agreement included turning over all government property and accounts of the South Korean interim government to the new government; transfer of cash and sales contracts from the sales of formerly Japanese-owned property and the unsold property which had been held in trust and administered by the American military government; the gift to Korea of the relief and rehabilitation supplies distributed in South Korea since Liberation Day, worth about $250 million; turning over of the foreign assets created by the military government; settlement of the $25 million Korean Liquidation Commission loan by the United States to Korea; U.S. payment for the services rendered to the occupation troops by the Korean people; and transfer of miscellaneous assets including $7 million worth of locomotives and $32 million of capital improvements. The total property and accounts involved in the settlement were valued at over $100 million and W600 billion, and a total of over $25 million and W7 billion cash was also turned over to the new government. It should also be noted here that because Korea was considered a "liberated" area, the occupation cost was borneby the U.S. government. The U.S. government was generous in many respects, especially regarding relief and rehabilitation and payment for the service provided by the Korean people during the occupation period, and Koreans were grateful. But, two seemingly minor clauses in the agreement, at least from the American view point, caused "violent discussions" in the Korean National Assembly. One dealt with the acquisition of Korean property by the American government, and the other was an unpaid debt on the part of Korea. Some members of the assembly were apprehensive about the implications of Article IX, c. 2, which stated that the American government would be able to purchase any piece of property in Korea in which it had an interest. Some of the Korean representatives in the assembly even reminded their colleagues of the treaties Korea made with Japan in the 1900s. Clearly, in this debate the assembly was very sensitive on the issue of national sovereignty, which they saw as just being restored after a half century of loss. General Helmick's explanatory letter, taken as an assurance of U.S. motives, was effective in calming these Korean concerns, and the agreement was approved by the assembly by a 78 to 28 vote with 3 abstentions. The debate on the loan resulted from a misunderstanding and lack of information on the nature and background of the settlement, as was pointed out by Muccio. A succeeding government was obligated to take over the debt as well as the assets of the former government.[13]

Thus, the first important piece of work for Korean–American relations after establishment of the South Korean government was successfully completed. Although the transfer of the governing authority from one nation to another within one month was not an easy task, it was accomplished without much difficulty. In the transfer some give and take between the two governments was required. This rather difficult operation in two different cultural contexts, where such giving and taking was handled differently, occurred without noticeable complication, despite some apprehension on the Korean side about the issue of acquisition of their property by the American government. Ambassador Muccio saw in the debate in the Korean National Assembly an assertion of independence of the legislative branch vis-a-vis the powerful executive branch of the government under President Rhee.[14]

Whenever a new state or a new government is born, its recognition by the international community becomes its first important business. The Republic of Korea in 1948 was no exception. It was even more important for this new nation to achieve recognition given the state of complication and uncertainty on the peninsula and as an issue of special importance for Korean–American relations. This was the first question that the two nations would take up in the international arena, and how much cooperation the two governments would show in dealing with it on the world stage would establish a precedent. The United Nations was inevitably involved in the question, and how the question would fare in this world organization in this early stage was important in view of the role the world organization would play two years later.

For the Korean government, receiving international recognition, especially that of the United States, was the most important task in the fall of 1948, and it occupied first place among a number of objectives for the new republic's diplomacy as listed by the first Foreign Minister Chang T'aek-sang.[15] The president himself, who had specialized in international law in his graduate studies in the United States, must have clearly seen its significance. The American government took seriously this question, and the State Department began to examine soon after the May 10 election in Korea the various aspects involved in the question. In his May 25 memorandum to Ernest A. Gross, the legal adviser for the department, W. Walton Butterworth sketched out the policy alternatives for the U.S. government regarding the recognition question. After listing the reasons for the special relationship the United States had with Korea, the director of the Office of Far Eastern Affairs laid out the positive and negative factors involved in the immediate recognition of the new government, concluding that the possible risks involved in immediate recognition of the Korean government by the United States would be outweighed by the adverse effects in terms of the U.S. prestige and stability of the government. He also pointed out that the recognition should not necessarily be complete and without reservation, hinting that it could be limited to a provisional recognition pending the review of the question by the U.N. General Assembly in the coming annual meeting in Paris. He then asked the legal adviser whether limited recognition would be a legally tenable proposition and, if so, what form the recognition should take.[16]

In response, the State Department's legal adviser first pointed out that the recognition question should be divided into two parts, recognition of the state and recognition of the government, and that in the Korean case, both actions would be necessary. He then pointed out that recognition of the state should not be limited and should be a full recognition. With regard to the recognition of the government, Gross explained that it could take any form, depending upon the political expediencies of the recognizing government, and that the U.S. government would be free to choose either a de jure or a de facto recognition of the Korean government without any restrictions coming from the U.N. General Assembly. The former was to be preferred, he said, because from a legal standpoint de facto recognition is "somewhat nebulous." He further suggested that if limited recognition was adopted by the U.S. government, the form might involve full recognition of Korean sovereignty or de facto recognition of the government. He also suggested sending a "special mission," rather than a regular diplomatic mission, to Korea, noting that treaty making would be possible after a de facto recognition.[17] For whatever reason, the State Department dismissed completely the part about recognition of the state and followed the portion of the suggestions of the legal adviser for recognition of the government of Korea.

By early July of the year, the State Department firmed up its view that a provisional de facto recognition would be accorded the government in South Korea soon after its formation and that a declaration would be made to the effect that the U.S. government would regard the new government as "the National Government of Korea" envisaged by the U.N. General Assembly resolution of November 14, 1947. In addition, it asked its representatives in the capitals of the nations represented on the UNTCOK (United Nations Temporary Commission on Korea) and a couple of other major nations to sound out the views of the governments in those capitals regarding the statement on the "final decision" of the government.[18] Secretary Marshall explained in this circular that as the occupation power the United States would have to decide its attitude before entering into negotiations with the new government for the transfer of the governmental functions and the withdrawal of troops and that not to recognize the new government in Korea, whose organization was based on an expression of the will of the Korean people through the recent election as the "national government," would amount to admitting the "impotence" of the United Nations. The powers consulted were split in their views on the U.S. government's intended action: The British Commonwealth countries—the United Kingdom, Australia, Canada, and India—were unanimously critical of the U.S. position on both the "national government" issue and immediate recognition; the rest—China, Syria, the Philippines, and El Salvador—expressed favorable views regarding the U.S. position.[19] British officials were quite candid in expressing their view that to recognize the South Korean government as the national government of Korea would be "very dubious" because the new government controlled only half of the country and the phrase was not accurate; furthermore, the U.S. action would cause resentment and dissension among the members of the United Nations, and the Soviet Union might exploit the opportunity for propaganda purposes and also might find in this step some justification for proclaiming the puppet government in the north as the "national government" of Korea. Philip Jessup, the acting U.S. representative at the United Nations, also suggested to Secretary Marshall not to take the contemplated action because of concerns about the U.S. position in the United Nations.[20] After considering the opposing views on the question of recognition, the policy makers in Washington decided to proceed with the proclamation of recognition, and the proclamation was made on August 12, not long after the formation of the new government and three days before its inauguration. The U.S. government did, however, compromise by taking out the word "national" and by calling the new government simply the "Government of Korea envisaged by the General Assembly resolution of November 14, 1947."[21]

Under normal circumstances, collective action for the recognition of a state or a government is not necessary, but because of the U.N.'s involvement in the Korean problem since 1947, the recognition of the government in Seoul by the world organization was a necessity rather than merely a matter of desirability for the South Koreans. The government in P'yŏngyang would not miss the opportunity, at least for demonstration purposes. The U.S. government clearly recognized the importance of the Paris General Assembly meeting for the world recognition of the new government in South Korea, which was established under its auspices. It was a small-scale test case for the United States to see how the issue would fare in the organization in which it had a strong leadership against the opposing camp. The management of the Korean case in the fall 1948 U.N. General Assembly meeting had another and equally important meaning. The South Korean government had an opportunity to work with the U.S. government for the first time on the world stage on an issue in which they had a common interest.

President Rhee fully recognized the importance of the 1948 U.N. General Assembly meeting for his government, and he sent to Paris a team of nine capable Koreans and Robert T. Oliver, his special assistant. The team was headed by Ambassador Chang Myŏn, and Chough Pyŏng-ok played his special role of assisting the chief of the mission. The two men's personalities and work styles were almost like those of John Quincy Adams and Henry Clay at Ghent in 1814, and the system of complementary roles worked out well. Chung Il-hyŏng and the rest of the group also provided able assistance, and the presence of two women delegates—Kim Hwal lan and Mo Yun-suk—was also helpful for the fulfillment of the mission.[22] Some American delegates were not happy with some of the personal activities of the Korean delegates in Paris, especially the role of Oliver, but the selection of the Korean delegates was done well. The American delegation, with over seven-hundred members, was huge and impressive, and Secretary Marshall participated for a considerable length of time in the conference. Joseph Jacobs, who had been in Seoul as a political adviser and was familiar with the Korean problems, joined the American delegation in Paris.

The American government naturally took a leading role in the joint effort for the collective recognition of the South Korean government in Paris, and the American position on the Korean issue was sketched out by Dean Rusk, the director of the Office of the United Nations Affairs in the State Department, in his memorandum of early September to Undersecretary Robert Lovett, and it went through the whole process in Paris without much modification. The American position on the Korean issue was (1) to advocate that the government of the Republic of Korea was entitled to be regarded as the government of Korea envisaged in the General Assembly resolution of November 14, 1947; (2) to support the South Korean government's wish to be heard at the meeting without participation in the debate; (3) not to oppose the North Korean delegates' request to be heard at the meeting if the assembly would be favorably disposed toward it; (4) to support the early withdrawal of all occupation forces from the Korean peninsula; (5) to advocate taking steps toward the unification of Korea; (6) to recommend reconstruction of the present commission on Korea or appointment of a new commission; and (7) to support approval of the reports of the United Nations Temporary Commission on Korea.[23]

A month later in early October, the American delegate in Paris drafted the U.S. delegate's position paper with exactly the same content as in Rusk's position paper.[24] The American government, through its active diplomacy, tried to get support of the members of the General Assembly. After two weeks of diplomacy, however, the American government decided to modify its stand on at least one point: "the government of Korea," the phrase adopted originally to characterize the South Korean government, was replaced by "a lawful government," a simple and unloaded phrase. Since this was an important part of the original U.S. position on Korea, the concession was not a minor one, even though it is doubtful whether the American policy makers thought they could succeed in retaining the phrase.[25] On October 29, the draft resolution of the United States on Korea for the General Assembly was completed in Washington and was sent to Paris on November 8. The proposal was basically the same as the U.S. delegation's position paper of October 22, but the principles received some modifications, and specifications regarding the works of the commission on Korea were added. One of the modifications was that, after the early version of characterization of the South Korean government as "a lawful government" and "the only such government in Korea," the South Korean government was further characterized as "the Government envisaged in the Resolution of November 14, 1947." This modification was actually a restoration of Rusk's phrase of early September. The troop withdrawal issue was then clearly and emphatically stated: "The occupying Powers [would] withdraw their armed forces from Korea as early as practicable, if possible, within ninety days."[26]

The U.S. proposal on Korea of early November received two modifications by the end of the month in the process of diplomatic maneuvering at

Paris. One came from the Australian delegate, who was uncomfortable with the American version of the characterization of the South Korean government, and the American–Australian joint proposal of mid-November deleted the phrase referring to the General Assembly resolution of November 14, 1947. The joint proposal also modified the approval of the commission report from the whole report to only the conclusion. As Secretary of State Marshall pointed out in his comparison of the two proposals, the two were essentially the same except for these modifications. For the final American–Australian–Chinese proposal, the Chinese delegate, who had been unhappy with the troop withdrawal clause in the two-nation proposal and whose opinion reflected (nationalist) Chinese feelings, persuaded the other two delegates to drop the ninety-day restriction.[27] By late November, the three-nation joint proposal was completed, and it was not much different from the original American version, even after the alternately weakening and strengthening process of negotiation. However, the Australian and Chinese modifications were not insignificant, since they played the role of moderators by reflecting their sensitivity to the communist side's feelings on the Korean issue and by expressing their concern about hasty withdrawal of the American military forces from Korea.[28]

The three months of preparatory work on the Korean issue since the early fall were brought to the final stage in early December. On December 7, the First (Political) Committee of the General Assembly took up the Korean issue, dealing first with the question of seating the delegates of the two governments in Korea. The committee, with a vote of 6 for to 34 against and 8 abstentions, rejected the Czech motion to hear the North Korean delegate; the committee then voted for the Chinese motion of hearing the delegate of the South Korean government, with 39 votes for to 6 against and 1 abstention. Next, the committee approved the joint Australian–Chinese–United States proposal by a vote of 41 to 6, with 2 abstentions. The voting was very much along the political line up; the delegates from the six communist countries voted together. For the South Korean government, the delegates from the United States, China, Philippines, Australia, New Zealand, Canada, United Kingdom, and a number of other countries (a total of twelve) gave strong supporting speeches.[29] The 1948 U.N. General Assembly meeting in Paris was crowded with many important issues, and even though the Americans and the Koreans worried that the meeting might adjourn before reaching the Korean question, the issue was taken up on the very last day, December 12. Again, eloquent speeches were made. When the assembly came to vote, the outcome was as expected along the lines of the political divisions, and approval of the three-power joint resolution was by a vote of 48 for, 6 against, and 1 abstention (Sweden).[30]

Since the two Koreas, or half Koreas, were a reflection of the Cold War and one Korea's winning meant a loss by the other Korea, North Korea lost and lost badly. The desire of the other Korean government to be heard at the conference was as strong as that of the South Korean government, and even though the support of the six communist delegates was firm and consistent the number was simply too small against the opposite side of forty or more. On December 6, the Czechoslovakian delegate's motion in the First Committee to hear the North Korean representative was rejected by a vote of 6 against 34, with 8 abstentions. The North Korean government was, naturally, unhappy or indignant with the outcome of the consideration of the Korean question at the Paris U.N. General Assembly meeting.[31]

The handling of the report of the U.N. Temporary Commission on Korea and a decision concerning continuation of U.N. commission work in Korea was important for both the American and Korean governments. It was especially for the latter, since it occupied an important part of the whole Korean question. Approval of the commission report by the General Assembly was considered necessary, and it was understood that the commission work would go on in Korea either through a continuation of the existing commission or the creation of a new one. From early September, as it was clearly expressed in the Rusk memorandum, the American government was firm in support of the approval of the commission report; only when it met with the resistance from the Australian delegate did it compromise reluctantly. On the last day of the meeting, a Canadian proposal for the establishment of a new commission, the U.N. Commission on Korea, with representatives from Australia, China, El Salvador, France, India, Philippines, and Syria was approved by the assembly by a vote of 42 to 0 with 1 abstention. Canada and France had been reluctant to serve on the new commission, and only Canada succeeded in the effort for being deleted from the list of the new commission members. The Soviet proposal to abolish the U.N. Temporary Commission on Korea was defeated by a vote of 46 to 6 with no abstention. The final resolution contained detailed specifications regarding the operation of the new commission.[32]

The American newspapers accurately grasped the meaning of the U.N. actions on the Korean question and made positive comments. The *New York Times* called the final U.N. action for Korea "logical and just" and considered it an "event of world history." The paper also pointed out that retreating from the recognition of the South Korean government as "the national government of Korea" to the "legal government" constituted a weakness. The statement on troop withdrawal also caught the eyes of the journalists: the *New York Herald Tribune* noted that the U.S. government left the statement "intentionally vague," and the *Kansas City Star* even "welcomed the considerable leeway."[33]

The Koreans in the southern half of the peninsula were naturally happy with the General Assembly action. President Rhee, in one of his public statements, exclaimed, "All loyal Koreans—men, women, and children—are profoundly grateful to the United Nations in general and the United States in particular and their gratitude will remain in the hearts of the Korean people for generations to come." The Korean National Assembly sent its message to President Truman thanking him for the cooperation and support of the American government for the U.N. recognition.[34] For the South Korean government, still young and without personnel with the kind of experience required at the Paris U.N. conference, participation in the conference was a real challenge. The Korean representatives in Paris mobilized all the wisdom and energy they had and tried to meet the challenge, and they did well. They tried to work closely with the delegates of the friendly powers, especially the United States. The American delegates, at least some of them, were not quite happy with some of the Korean delegates' activities in Paris, but it seems that the Koreans received a good amount of cooperation from the Americans. Many other delegates, especially those of China, the Philippines, and India, also exhibited ample sympathy for the Korean cause.[35] Both the legal effect of the collective recognition of the United Nations and its moral support for the South Korean government resulting from the action of the General Assembly at Paris in late 1948 was important for the young republic, especially in view of what came a year and a half later.

The achievement of the American government at the 1948 Paris conference regarding the Korean question was also considerable. The South Korean government, for whose birth the American government had a large share of responsibility and hence a large stake, was recognized by the United Nations as the "lawful government" of Korea. As was widely recognized, it was a watered-down version of the "government of Korea." In a sense, the compromise was not a small one, but it was wise for the U.S. government not to insist too much on its original position, not only against an ally like Australia but also against an antagonist like the Soviet Union. Often too much victory is costly. Approval of the UNTCOK report and a continuation of the commission's work in Korea was also important for the United States, and these were accomplished without much difficulty. Inclusion of a statement regarding the troop withdrawal from Korea was also important for the U.S. government. The ninety-day restriction had to be dropped because of the sensitivities of both Koreas and the Chinese. Here also, the concession was not a bad idea, because the U.S. government might have been trapped by its own restrictions and, as many newspapermen saw, the vague and flexible words would better serve the interests of the nation. The manner in which the American delegates cooperated with the Korean delegates was also commendable. Probably the amount of American support was not as much as the Koreans would have wished to have, but the Americans gave enough guidance and encouragement to the Korean delegates at the Paris conference.

NOTES

1. *Seoul Sinmun*, August 16, 1948, no. 1: 1–5.
2. *New York Times*, August 15, 1948, sec. IV, 8: 2.

3. CINCFE to USAFIK, August 14, 1948, Douglas MacArthur Memorial Archives and Library (MacArthur Library), Record Group (RG) 9, box 148, blue binders.

4. CG USAFIK to Secretary of the State, August 15, 1948, MacArthur Library, RG 9, box 148, blue binders.

5. CG USAFIK to JCOS, August 16, 1948, MacArthur Library, RG 9, box 148, blue binders. See also, Charles M. Dobbs, *The Unwanted Symbol: American Foreign Policy, the Cold War, and Korea, 1945-1950* (Kent, Ohio: Kent State University Press, 1981), p. 150.

6. Jacobs to the Secretary of State, July 18, 1948, in Niles W. Bond to Bromley K. Smith, August 2, 1948, National Archives (NA), Decimal File 1945-49, box 2108; Marshall to Truman, April 27, 1948, Truman Library, White House Central File, State Department Correspondence 1948-1949, folder 12; John J. Muccio, U.S. Ambassador to Korea, NA, RG 469, Records of U.S. Foreign Affairs Agencies, 1948-61, Division of Korea Program, Office of Director, Outgoing Letters, box 1; John J. Muccio, Truman Library, oral history interview transcript, p. 5.

7. The Secretary of State to Jacobs, July 27, 1948, *FRUS, 1948*, 6: 1263; Jacobs to the Secretary of State, August 23, 1948, ibid., pp. 1286-1287; *Department of State Bulletin* 19 (August 23, 1948): 242.

8. "Pisa oekyo 30-nyŏn" (Confidential history of a thirty-year diplomacy), *Seoul Sinmun*, April 15, 1982, no. 19; ibid., August 24, 1948, 1: 1-5; Im P'yŏng-chik, *Im P'yŏng-chik hoekorok: Kŭmtae oekyo imyŏnsa* (Im P'yŏng-chik memoirs: The inside history of modern diplomacy) (Seoul: Yŏwŏnsa, 1956), p. 334.

9. CG USAFIK to the Secretary of State, December 29, 1948, MacArthur Library, RG 9, blue binders; Han P'yo-wook, *Han-Mi oekyo yoramki* (The early years of the Korean–American diplomatic relationship) (Seoul: Chungang Ilbosa, 1984), pp. 47-55; *Sichŏng Wŏlpo* (Administrative monthly report) 4 (July 23, 1949): 43; "Pisa oekyo 30-nyŏn," *Seoul Sinmun* no. 6 (October 1949), March 23, 1982: p. 5; idem, no 9 (February 1950), March 28, 1982, p. 5; idem, no. 10 (April 1950), March 31, 1982, p. 5; Cumings, *The Origins of the Korean War*, vol. 2, *The Roaring of the Cataract, 1947-1950* (Princeton, N.J.: Princeton University Press, 1990), p. 223.

10. Jacobs to the Secretary of State, August 17, 1948, *FRUS, 1948*, 6: 1279; *New York Times*, August 15, 1948, 1: 3; *Seoul Sinmun*, August 18, 1948, 1: 1-3.

11. Muccio to the Secretary of State, October 1, 1948, NA, RG 59, Decimal File, 1945-49, box 3828; minutes of the first meeting, August 16, 1948, NA, RG 84, Seoul Mission, Records of American Economic Aid to Korea, 1948-1949, box 1; *Seoul Sinmun*, August 22, 1948, no. 1: 1-5.

12. Jacobs to the Secretary of State, August 18, 24, 1948, *FRUS, 1948*, 6: 1282-1283, 1287-1288; Jacobs to the Secretary of Sate, August 24, 1948, NA, RG 59, 740.00119 control (Korea)/8-2448; Acting Secretary of State (Lovett) to Seoul Embassy, January 13, 1949, NA, RG 59, Decimal File 1945-49, box 3828.

13. Muccio to the Secretary of State, September 3, 11, 16, 25, 1948, NA, RG 59, Decimal File 1945-49, box 3238; *Sichŏng Wŏlpo* 2 (March 10, 1949): 51-56; *Seoul Sinmun*, September 19, 1948, 1: 1-7.

14. Muccio to the Secretary of State, September 25, 1948, NA, RG 59, Decimal File 1945-49, box 3828.

15. *Sichŏng Wŏlpo* 1 (January 5, 1949): 13.

16. Memorandum of the Director of the Office of Far Eastern Affairs (Butterworth) to the Legal Adviser (Gross), May 25, 1948, *FRUS, 1948*, 6: 1204-1206.

17. Memorandum of the Legal Adviser (Gross) to the Director of the Office of Far Eastern Affairs (Butterworth), June 1, 1948, *FRUS, 1948*, 6: 1211–1213.

18. The Secretary of State to certain diplomatic and consular officers abroad, July 10, 1948, *FRUS, 1948*, 6: 1235–1237.

19. The Ambassador in the United Kingdom (Douglas) to the Secretary of State, July 13, 19, 1948, *FRUS, 1948*, 6: 1239–1240, 1247–1248; the Chargé in Australia (Nielsen) to the Secretary of State, July 14, 1948, ibid., pp. 1241–1242; the Chargé in India (Donovan) to the Secretary of State, ibid., pp. 1246–1247; the Secretary of State to the Embassy in Soviet Union, July 21, 1948, ibid., p. 1252; the Ambassador in China (Stuart) to the Secretary of State, July 15, 1948, ibid., p. 1243; the Chargé in the Philippines to the Secretary of State, July 16, 1948, ibid., 1245; the Ambassador in El Salvador (Nufer) to the Secretary of State, July 30, 1948, ibid., p. 1266.

20. The Acting U.S. Representative at the United Nations (Jessup) to the Secretary of State, July 20, 1948, *FRUS, 1948*, 6: 1249–1251.

21. *Department of State Bulletin* 19 (August 22, 1948): 242.

22. "Pisa oekyo 30-nyŏn, *Seoul Sinmun* no. 24, April 24, 1982; Release no. 1, October 13, 1948, Paris, NA, RG 59, Decimal File 1945–49, box 2111.

23. Memorandum of the Director of the Office of the United Nations Affairs (Rusk) to the Undersecretary to the Secretary of State and the Undersecretary of State (Lovett), September 10, 1948, *FRUS, 1948*, 6: 1299–1300.

24. Joseph E. Jacobs to Niles Bond, October 9, 1948, NA, RG 59, 501.BB Korea/10–948.

25. U.S. Delegation Position Paper, October 22, 1948, *FRUS, 1948*, 6: 1315–1317.

26. The Acting Secretary (Lovett) to the American Embassy in Paris, November 8, 1948, NA, RG 59, 501.BB Korea/11–848; Draft Resolution on Korea for the United Nations General Assembly, *FRUS, 1948*, 6: 1321–1323.

27. Marshall to the State Department, November 16, 1948, NA, RG 59, 501.BB Korea/11–1648; the Secretary of State to the Acting Secretary of State, November 16, 1948, *FRUS, 1948*, 6: 1327–1329. See also the editorial note regarding the Chinese position, ibid., p. 1317.

28. Marshall to the State Department, November 8, 1948, NA, RG 59, 501.BB Korea/11–1848; the Secretary of State to the American Embassy in Seoul, November 27, 1948, ibid., 11–2748.

29. Dulles to the State Department (for Chang to Rhee), December 6, 7, 8, 1948, NA, RG 59, 501.BB Korea/12–648, 12–748, 12–848; the Acting Representative at the United Nations (Dulles) to the Secretary of State, December 6, 1948, *FRUS, 1948*, 6: 1335.

30. Lovette to Dulles, December 10, 1948, NA, RG 9, 501.BB Korea/12–1048; the Acting U.S. Representative at the United Nations (Dulles) to the Secretary of State, December 12, 1948, *FRUS, 1948*, 6: 1336–1337; *Department of State Bulletin* 19 (December 19, 1948): 760.

31. The Acting U.S. Representative at the United Nations (Dulles) to the Secretary of State, December 6, 1948, *FRUS, 1948*, 6: 1335; the U.S. Embassy in Moscow (Smith) to the State Department, December 13, 1948, NA, RG 59, 501.BB Korea/12–1348.

32. The Acting U.S. Representative to the United Nations (Dulles) to the Secretary of State, December 9, 12, 1948, *FRUS, 1948*, 6: 1336, 1337; *Department of State Bulletin* 19 (December 19, 1948): 760.

33. *New York Times*, December 13, 1948, 22: 1–2; the State Department to the U.S. Embassy in Seoul, December 14, 1948, NA, RG 59, 501.BB Korea/12–1448.

34. Shinnnicky to the U.S. President, December 15, 1948, NA, 501.BB Korea/11–1548; *New York Times*, December 14, 1948, 25: 1.

35. Jacobs to Bond, October 14, 1948, NA, RG 59, 501.BB Korea/10–1448; Jacobs to the State Department, October 30, 1948, ibid., 10–3048; Muccio to the State Department, November 4, 1948, ibid., 11–448; "Pisa oekyo 30-nyŏn," *Seoul Sinmun* no. 30 (April 24, 1982).

CHAPTER 5

The Policies of the Two Republics

Because of its importance, American policy toward Korea from the establishment of the new republic in the summer of 1948 to the outbreak of the war in June 1950 has received much attention from a number of historians. These scholars may be divided into three major groups according to their interpretation of the general trends, or the continuity or change, of the U.S. policy during the period. The first group considers that U.S. policy toward Korea was consistent throughout the latter half of the 1940s, arguing that the U.S. had no intent of "shirking" its responsibility toward the new republic.[1] The second group takes the opposite view that the United States changed its policy and "abandoned" the new republic.[2] These extremists are a small minority, the large third group chooses the middle line between the two extremes. They take the position that the United States did not completely abandon its responsibility in Korea in those years, but that certain changes were made in the two-year period. They recognize that the troop withdrawal, which took place in mid-1949, was a significant step for Korea, even though there were good reasons for it. Despite the retreat, according to this third group, the United States came forward, with the turning point occurring in late 1948 and the following year, somewhat vigorously to offer a containment policy in Korea by means of economic and military aid for the Koreans. They also admit that the execution of this policy presented difficulties.[3] A brief examination of the declarations and actions of the United States government in those years will be made first before an evaluation of the policy.

Throughout the entire two-year period, the long-term, basic objective of the United States in Korea remained the same: the establishment of a unified and democratic nation in Korea. The National Security Council (NSC), which played an important role in U.S. policy making toward Korea during this period, was firm and consistent in stating the long-term objectives for Korea in the NSC 8 series. This series, which was approved by President Truman on April 8, 1948, defined the broad objectives of the United States with respect to Korea as the "establishment of a united and independent nation with sound economy and educational system." In the same document, the council also sketched three principal courses of actions the nation might pursue in the future: (1) to abandon the South Korean government, (2) to provide military and economic aid to Korea to facilitate the derivative objective of the termination of military commitment "with the minimum of bad effects," and (3) to guarantee the political independence and territorial integrity of South Korea—and choose the middle road.[4] A year later, in NSC 8/2, which fixed the final date of the troop withdrawal, the council kept the same broad national objective in Korea and reaffirmed the middle course of action and specified the amount of military and economic aid for the South Korean government.[5]

A close examination of the National Security Council's Document 8 series shows that, while the broad U.S. objective and the main course of action to be pursued in Korea remained the same in 1948 and in the following year, the derivative objective, the orientation, and the policy line went through changes and a hardening. The single most important derivative objective of the U.S. government in Korea in 1948 and in the early part of the following year was the withdrawal of troops from South Korea. The rendering of military and economic aid to the republic would be the means to achieve this objective with "the minimum of bad effects." In the spring of 1949, however, through NSC 8/2, the U.S. government not only elaborated the aid programs, but also clearly stated that the aid program would be used to build the ROK security force "as a deterrent to the external aggression and as a guarantor of internal order in South Korea."

Beside the National Security Council documents, there were other statements coming from responsible government officials in Washington that revealed the nature of U.S. policy toward Korea during the two-year period. Secretaries of State Marshall and Acheson reiterated the long-term U.S. policy objectives of the realization of a unified and democratic nation on the Korean peninsula.[6] Two cogent and important documents emerged in Washington late in 1948 and early in the following year, one in the Division of Northeast Asian Affairs and the other from the Central Intelligence Agency. In a December 17 memorandum, which was directed to W. Walton Butterworth, director of the Office of Far Eastern Affairs, Niles Bond and Max Bishop presented their view that the Korean issue dealt with in NSC 8 should be reviewed as "part of an overall Pacific policy." The central point of their argument was that if a "premature" withdrawal of U.S. troops from the Korean peninsula took place, it would be followed by the Soviet domination of the whole peninsula and that holding Japan within the sphere of the United States would become very difficult. Their view first persuaded their superiors in the department and later Defense Department officials, and the proposed review resulted in NSC 8/2. Their geostrategic argument—that if the Korean peninsula fell into the hands of Soviet bloc, then the Japanese position would become extremely untenable—convinced a good number of officials in both departments.[7] In its February 28 analysis, the Central Intelligence Agency pointed out the military and political importance of Korea. Even though the agency conceded to the military view that the Korean peninsula would have little value for the United States in the case of an outbreak of a general war, it rather convincingly argued that the Korean peninsula as a military base in the hands of the Soviet Union would become a great menace to Japan—a classical argument for the role of a buffer state. The analysis further pointed out that Korea would represent to Japan and other countries a "symbol" of U.S. determination to resist the further encroachment of the communist forces in East Asia.[8] Exactly what effect this document had on policy modifications by the United States in the following months is not known, but the document must have had some effect in view of the position of the agency and the weight of the argument. The American military perhaps still did not want to change its view on the strategic value of the Korean peninsula, but the geopolitical importance of Korea, and the symbolic value of the republic, was widely recognized by the circle of foreign policy makers in Washington, and it seems to have become a significant factor for the U.S. policy-making process toward Korea during this period.[9]

Regarding U.S. economic and military aid policy for Korea, Secretary Acheson made a statement in mid-March of 1949 that in addition to the U.N. General Assembly resolution of December 12, 1948, and apart from the troop withdrawal issue, it was the intention of the United States to provide economic, technical, military, and other assistance for the achievement of economic and political stability of the new republic.[10] Among the statements denoting U.S. policy changes during the period, Niles Bond's recollection is most straightforward. Because it is a later recollection, there is room for doubting its accuracy. However, because of his intensive involvement, first as the assistant chief of the Division of Northeast Asian affairs and later as the officer in charge of Korean affairs in the State Department, the reliability of his recollections is enhanced. He recalled in late 1973 that up to the beginning of 1949 the State Department pretty much went along with the view of the military that Korea lacked strategic value for the United States, but said that from that point on the department began to change its view and attached a political interest to the new republic.[11] NSC 8/2 was completed in the spring of 1949 and Bond's recollection was accurate. But, since the first suggestion of a policy modification came up in Bishop's December 17 (1948) memorandum, initiation of the change goes back at least to mid-December of the previous year. The reason for the change cited by Bond in his recollection is interesting—the State Department officials' sense of responsibility for the Koreans.

An examination of the available historical documents makes it clear that the broad, long-range U.S. objectives of the establishment of a unified and democratic Korea remained the same throughout the two-year period. After the decision was taken to achieve a derivative objective, or the short-term objective of terminating "as soon as possible," by the end of June 1949, the military commitment of the United States in Korea, the U.S. government modified its policy. Between late 1948 and early 1949, the U.S. government came forward with a policy of preventing a communist takeover of South Korea through economic and military aid, or a containment policy by the means of the aid for the Republic of Korea. We will see how this policy was executed to achieve the objective of deterring a war and how the policy and its execution is connected with the Korean War. Before turning to an examination of U.S. policy for and actions in Korea during the year and a half period preceding the war, we will briefly consider the Korean side of the story.

Korean–American relations during the two years preceding the Korean War—or even throughout the whole period for the two-nation relationship until very recent years—were very uneven, or asymmetrical, and there is no way to talk about Korean policy and diplomacy toward the United States as one does about the U.S. policy toward Korea. Not only is this the case because the Korean side was too small and its role in the two-nation relationship was too insignificant, but also because of the inadequacy of the presently available Korean material. In short, there is no way to tell the full story of Korean policy and diplomacy on an equal basis. Of course, this does not mean that there is no story on the Korean side; rather, it is partial and tentative, like so many other stories in history.

Many authors are critical of the South Korean government and the conditions in Korea in those years. The government under Syngman Rhee was helplessly corrupt and authoritarian, conditions in Korea were bleak, and the scope of political and economic decay was serious.[12] Of course, this judgment has much truth in it, but one needs to examine more closely the conditions and look at the situation in a broader perspective for a real understanding of Korea and the Koreans in those years. South Korea, during the two-year period between the establishment of the new government and the outbreak of the war, was beset with serious problems: threats coming from rebellions, guerrilla groups, and the North Korean invasion; an inordinately high deficit budget, an incredibly high inflation rate, and other economic difficulties; and the inefficient and overcentralized government system. Even though an explanation of the Korean situation in the early months of the new republic by the Koreans themselves is desirable, the observations of others are also useful. There is a good amount of information about the situation in

Korea at this time available from the American representatives in Seoul. This information may not be perfectly accurate for a real picture of Korea, representing only the views of these individuals, or more accurately, reflecting America's image of the Korean situation in these months. Nevertheless, these images are important and valuable, because, whatever the accuracy of the images, policy decisions about Korea were made in Washington based on them, not on the true, but little-known, picture.

The late October 1948 U.S. intelligence report and the mid-November Muccio report presented detailed information to Washington about the Korean situation. The former provides a picture of the political, economic, and military situation in Korea. It observed that the new republic gave evidence of a successful start in the direction of responsible government. The government had a strong executive branch under the leadership of President Rhee with "certain superficial features" of a parliamentary system. Its concern was the lack of a healthy minority opposition and the danger of the National Assembly being reduced to a rubber-stamp institution. It reported that the most serious economic problem in Korea in the fall of 1948 was a shortage of food supplies, which depended upon the collection and distribution of grain. It also pointed out that shortages of electric power, coal, petroleum, raw cotton, fertilizer and a lack of skilled administrators and managers in the economic life of the nation were problems. The report indicated that one of the most serious problems confronting the new government was the military and observed that the Soviet Union and the North Korean government had enough capability to use force to implement the downfall of the republic in the south, but that a formal invasion by the North Korean Army would "remain a possibility," but not a "probability."[13]

Muccio's report during this period was not as full as the intelligence report, but it was fair and perceptive. Writing on November 12, he observed that the Rhee government was not a strong government according to the American standard. It was young and inexperienced; the Korean officials lacked confidence in themselves, in each other, in the security forces, and in the possibility of defeating a communist invasion from the north of the 38th parallel; and the future of the republic was uncertain. In his later dispatch, Muccio reported that the people in South Korea were shaken by the Yŏsu-Sunch'ŏn revolt, which took place in late October of the year.[14] Korean sources also divulged the inexperience and difficulties during the early months of the new government. Even though the Korean government had drawn up a balanced budget for the first six months of the operation of the new administration, from October 1948 through March of the following year, the circulation of the currency, the major source of the revenue and the key factor behind the inflation, increased drastically—45 percent from W29.9 billion to W43.3 billion.[15]

Two major civil disturbances occurred during the two-year period. Both came in the early months of the new republic: one, a large-scale uprising in

Cheju Island, which had begun in the spring of 1948 and flared up again in the fall, and the other, a brief rebellion in Yŏsu and Sunch'ŏn cities, which broke out in the fall of 1948 and was carried out mainly by the ROK military personnel. The Cheju people, who had a long tradition of autonomy and had been troubled by harsh treatment by the national police and the government-supported youth groups (Sŏpuk Ch'ŏngnyŏntan), rose after the establishment of the separate government in Seoul. The rebellion was crushed by early May of the following year with casualties of over five-thousand island people in the seven-month period. The Yŏsu-Sunch'ŏn incident of October 1948, a relatively small-scale rebellion, broke out on October 19, when some of the Fourteenth Regiment, established in the spring of the year and infiltrated heavily by leftists, resisted the order to go to Cheju Island for the mopping-up operation. Some civilians joined in attacking police stations, and the rebellious group swiftly occupied Yŏsu and nearby Sunch'ŏn in less than twenty-four hours. The government response was swift: It took only a week to recapture the two cities from the rebel forces. Both incidents seemed to show that the leftist force was quite strong in the southern provinces, and the dissatisfied citizens in those provinces were a real challenge to the new government in Seoul.[16]

Regular diplomatic mission work did not begin on both sides until early 1949. But Muccio's work began in Seoul soon after the inauguration of the new government in Korea, and Chough Pyŏng-ok, President Rhee's special envoy in Washington, who was considered Muccio's counterpart, made an effort to carry out his diplomatic mission in the United States. Chough as the special envoy of President Rhee was a good choice. He belonged to the opposite party but was the best qualified person for the important mission because of his caliber and capability. Chough was on the way to Paris for the U.N. General Assembly meeting and stayed only two weeks in the United States. But he had enough time to talk with key officials in the State Department and Pentagon, and he briefly saw President Truman. His main objective was to thank the American officials for past assistance in the establishment of the new republic and to ask for continuation of the assistance. He did not stay long enough to irritate State Department officials this time, and he seems to have impressed President Truman as being "quite a man."[17]

For the government in Seoul, the United States was not just the most important country, but it was also very "special" in a real sense. The special relationship was recognized even by the British government. For the new republic, U.S. aid, both economic and military, was essential for its existence in those early months and was the very heart of the "active" relationship. Recognition of the South Korean government by other powers, the improvement of international trade, and the collection of intelligence about North Korea were additional tasks for the new republic's diplomats.[18] In late October, President Rhee traveled to Japan with the purpose of discussing with General MacArthur the issues of U.S. troop withdrawal and regional organization. The Koreans thought that MacArthur's response was positive (for the Koreans) about the troop withdrawal but was "lukewarm" on the issue of the Pacific pact. It seems to be that MacArthur's purpose behind the invitation was to soften up the old Korean patriot's age-old hard feeling toward the Japanese, but how successful the general was in achieving this objective is questionable.[19]

The year 1949 was another important year for the Korean peninsula. It took several months for the two governments to establish themselves, and the months in the fall and winter of 1948 were spent for that purpose. A crisis was fast approaching in the early months of 1950, and there was not much time left for the Koreans to find a peaceful resolution to the situation. If there was any possibility for the Koreans to resolve peacefully among themselves a situation which had been created by outside forces, this was the year in which they had to work it out. But the task was too great and the time was too short, and the two half Koreas moved to opposite directions during this period.

The most important and vexing internal problems for South Korea in 1949 were the civil disturbances, guerrilla warfare, and poor financial and administrative management. Despite some fluctuations in the Korean situations, these problems continued to exist throughout the year. In late January, Muccio was afraid that the following few months would be the most critical time in Korea.[20] January and February were certainly difficult months, but the situation looked a little better in the following two months. In the late January report to the State Department, Muccio deplored several conditions: that the administration was generally poor, that rivalries existed within the cabinet, and that the quarrel between the executive and legislative branches of the government continued. He also pointed out the difficulty with rice collection for the urban population, the continuing budget deficit, and the inability of the Koreans to handle the problem of economic administration effectively. At the same time, Muccio did not neglect the positive side of the picture in Korea. The "infant government," he said, was still basically weak but stronger than two months ago. The relationship between the executive and legislative branches had improved, and the latter was exercising its checking influence over the executive branch. In the economic sector, he also saw a positive side: The shortage of electric power had gradually been overcome, the large variety of domestic goods available in small towns and villages seemed to suggest that home craft industries were meeting well the needs of the people, and the farm population, representing two-thirds of the total population, was still "relatively well-off." In his mid-March reevaluation, Muccio reported that the rebellion on Cheju Island was getting worse and that guerrilla activities were still continuing in the Chŏlla Provinces and elsewhere in South Korea. He also indicated in this report that the South Korean government finally admitted that the grain collection was a failure.[21]

After the somewhat gloomy picture of South Korea in January and February, the situation was perceived to be a little better in the following months and remained about the same for the rest of 1949, except during the months of May and June. After a two-week survey trip through the South Korean provinces, two officials from the American Embassy reported to the State Department in their March 17 dispatch that most Koreans were still "well-fed" and simple crafts and furniture shops were in operation. Toward the end of March, Chargé Everett F. Drumright's report to Washington about conditions in Korea contained a similar mixed evaluation but with a more optimistic tone: While corruption and inefficiency still remained, food stocks were believed to be adequate and the inflationary spiral had slowed down. In his May 1 report, Muccio considered the restoration of public peace as the most noteworthy achievement of the month of April. The all-out guerrilla extermination campaign ended successfully on Cheju Island, and the six-week antiguerrilla campaign in the Chŏlla Province and the vicinity also ended during the month.[22]

May and June in Korea were plagued with difficulties connected with the American troop withdrawal, and other events and problems—notably the death of Kim Ku, one of the most illustrious political leaders of the nation—heightened executive–legislative discord, serious outbreaks on the 38th parallel, and two considerable guerrilla raids in North Kyŏngsang Province.[23] July was characterized as the period of "holding the line" for the Republic of Korea, and the following five-month period may be summarized with the same description.[24] Minor clashes along the 38th parallel and the guerrilla raids continued throughout the months, but not at an intolerable level.

Beneath the relative quiet, there were increasingly disturbing concerns by the two countries, which did not begin during this period but were becoming more salient at this time: the American concern about the tendency of increasing centralization of power in the Korean political system and the Korean concern about the uncertainty of American policy in Korea and elsewhere in the Far East.[25] These two concerns were independent in their origins and development, but at times they had a countering relationship. This relationship showed up in 1949, especially through the conversations between Chough Pyŏng-ok, the special emissary of President Rhee who had met a number of times with the American officials in the early period of the new republic. In an early January conversation between Chough and State Department officials, the countering tendency already appeared and continued through the similar conversations of the year. Chough indicated serious concerns about developments in China, referring to U.S. policies toward Chiang Kai-shek's government; Butterworth responded by pointing out that the new Korean government should avoid the mistake of becoming "static and anti-progressive (the mistake of the Chinese)." Chough countered by saying that he entirely agreed with the theory, but that it was a "luxury" in the real world where the new government was fighting for its existence. Later in the same year, when Chough tried to tie the troop withdrawal to military and economic aid, the American side countered with the point that

Korean needs had to be examined in "the light of the requirements of all." Irritated by Chough's arguments, the Americans indicated that Chough's efforts in Washington were "detrimental" to the two-nation relationship.[26] Chang Myŏn, however, began in late March of the year to represent the South Korean government in Washington, and he mitigated the negative effect of the Chough mission.

One of the continuing problems in South Korea since its liberation was inflation, which was especially high in 1949. According to Korean and American government sources, the currency circulation increased from W43.4 billion to W74 billion in 1949, an increase of 70 percent. This was considerably lower when compared with the months of the previous year and the three-year occupation period, which was 45 percent between August and December 1948—an annual rate of 135 percent—and 510 percent between August 1945 and August 1948—an annual rate of 170 percent, a lower rate but still certainly high. The U.S. Foreign Assistance Agencies in charge of the Korean program thought the inflation stemmed from (1) a succession of supplementary budgets and borrowings, (2) heavy expenditures for the maintenance of the security forces, (3) large subsidies for the operation of the government enterprises, (4) inadequate tax collections, and (5) excessive voluntary contributions and "squeeze." In the following spring, the inflation rate became one of the most serious issues between Korea and the United States.[27]

Understanding how conditions developed in South Korea during the first half of 1950, up to the outbreak of the war, and the communication and actions—or lack of certain communication and actions—between the Republic of Korea and the United States during the same period is important for understanding the outbreak of the war and the nature of the relationship between a big power and a small power. During the first six-month period (January to June), the internal Korean condition deteriorated markedly. Power was concentrated more and more in the hands of the chief executive, and the relationship between the executive and legislative branches of the government reached a level of crisis. The inflation rate also reached an alarmingly high level. These domestic conditions were the basis for controversies between the two nations, while different views, attitudes, actions, and reactions developed through the spring and early summer of the year. For Washington, the key policy issue was intervention in another nation's domestic problems, while for Seoul, it was a question of how to respond to a friendly nation's well-intended intervention.

President Rhee experienced many difficulties in dealing with the National Assembly. At age seventy-five, his extreme pride, confidence, and high sense of self-righteousness combined with an unfortunate rigidity and stubbornness. Another problem was his dim view of the role of political parties in Korea in the early years of the new republic. He used nationwide youth and other organizations for his own political purposes and took political issues directly to the Korean people. Although Korean parties at this point were not much more than parliamentary groups, they controlled the National Assembly. Unless he worked with them as the head of the executive branch, he could not accomplish anything in the legislative branch. Predictably, he lost the support of the assembly. The Democratic National Party (Minkuk Tang), the successor to the Korean Democratic Party (Hanmin Tang), which President Rhee had abandoned after using its support for his assumption of presidency in 1948, decided to challenge President Rhee's power in the spring of 1950. By this time Rhee had also lost the confidence and trust of the Korean people as a whole, a fact which was revealed when he lost the election held at the end of March. Because of these serious problems, President Rhee turned to crude measures of using national police and youth groups to deal with the opposition force in the National Assembly.

The executive–legislative struggle in Seoul resulted in early March in a proposal in the National Assembly for a constitutional amendment to change the National Assembly from a unicameral to a bicameral body and to make the cabinet responsible to the assembly, not to the president. When the voting took place on March 14, many members of the assembly abstained from voting, and only 79 voted for amendment, far short of the 123 needed. The March attempt to amend the constitution seems to indicate that the political turmoil in Korea at that time came not only from personality factors, but also from a gradual strengthening of the legislative branch—not an unhealthy phenomenon, even though Korea was not quite ready yet for a modified cabinet system with more responsibilities in the cabinet.[28]

The problem in South Korea in the spring of 1950 considered most serious by the Americans was inflation. In his early January visit, Philip C. Jessup, the American ambassador at large, pointed out to the Korean prime minister that inflation was one of the two most important problems confronting the new republic; the other was the guerrilla threat. On January 14, Muccio conveyed to President Rhee Washington's serious concern about inflation with a mild threat by saying that unless the Korean government could bring about internal conditions necessary for the success of the recovery program, the entire Korean aid program of the American government would have to be reviewed in terms of feasibility. Three days later, on January 17, and again on January 21, he complained that Rhee was not responding satisfactorily to his request. On January 20, Chang Myŏn in Washington told a State Department official that his government was taking measures to combat inflation in response to Butterworth's expressed concern about the problem. The next day President Rhee in Seoul told the press that inflation was under control.[29] Communication on the two sides seem to indicate that the Americans fully expressed their view on the problem and the Korean side responded, or at least attempted to respond, promptly to the American concern.

American pressure on Koreans to control inflation escalated in the following months, culminating in Acheson's *aide memoire* of April 3. In his

February 14 dispatch, Acheson instructed Muccio to inform President Rhee cordially that very serious questions were raised in the House of Representatives, when it passed its $60 million authorization bill for Korea, as to the ability of the Republic of Korea (ROK) to control inflation. President Rhee received the message "in extraordinarily good heart" and assured Muccio that he would make efforts to seek measures to curb inflation.[30] In mid-March, a State–ECA joint meeting was held in Washington, and extensive discussion took place regarding the economic and political problems in Korea, and the idea of recalling Ambassador Muccio for consultation emerged. On March 23, the recall message was sent by Acheson, and on the same day ECA Director Paul G. Hoffman wrote a strong letter responding to Korean Prime Minister Lee Pŏm-sŏk's letter of March 4. Hoffman bluntly voiced his candid opinion that the prime minister's appraisal of the current Korean economic situation (deflation instead of inflation) was invalid and warned that unless the Korean government took the necessary measures to satisfy the ECA mission in Korea and himself that the inflationary problem in Korea would be dealt with effectively, the advisability of requesting an amount of appropriation less than $60 million would be considered, and a further review of the request of $100 million for the fiscal year 1951 would be undertaken. On the same day—actually, thirteen hours earlier—President Rhee sent to the National Assembly a revised budget for FY 1950, balanced at W180 billion, with a 300-percent increase in tax revenues, a 100-percent increase in railroad rates, and a 50-percent increase in government tobacco production. On March 29, Muccio reported to Washington that cooperation with the Korean government was working out and that progress had been made in the effort to control inflation.[31]

A series of intercommunications and interactions between Seoul and Washington after January reached a climax in early April through Acheson's *aide memoire*, which was handed to the Korean Ambassador who was scheduled to return to Seoul soon. In the *memoire*, Acheson solemnly declared his government's deep concern over the mounting inflation in Korea. After pointing out the factors thought to be causing the problem, Acheson informed Chang that unless the Korean government were able to take satisfactory and effective measures to counter the inflationary forces, it would be necessary for his government to reexamine, and perhaps to make adjustment in, the ECA assistance program in Korea.[32] When Ambassador Muccio delivered Acheson's *aide memoire* in Seoul, President Rhee was much concerned, and he asked the ambassador what would be necessary to satisfy the secretary of state and the director of the ECA. The Korean government took seriously the communication from the two responsible American officials and came up with fifteen economic projects to cope with the situation. The *New York Times* praised the Korean government's efforts to comply with the "friendly suggestions" of the American government.[33]

The Koreans received, in general, the American warnings in good heart. Muccio reported to Washington that Prime Minister Lee, whose letter had provoked Hoffman's response, termed the *aide memoire* "friendly advice" and admitted Korea's responsibility. The members of the Korean National Assembly took the American message more seriously and took it as a "stern warning." Some of them showed immediate resentment. Yun Ch'i-yŏng, the vice chairman of the institution, charged that the *aide memoire* was an "interference." The Korean press reaction to the American government was in general thoughtful. Some thought the tone of message was a little too stern, but most of the Korean papers took the message more constructively. The *Seoul Sinmun*, the *Kyŏghyang Sinmun*, the *Chosŏn Ilbo*, and the *Donga Ilbo*—the major newspapers in Seoul—all agreed that the Koreans better seize the opportunity and take bravely the necessary steps. The *Yŏnhap Shinmun*, a paper close to the government, one of few exceptions, thought the message was rather severe.[34]

The American pressure on the Koreans in the spring of 1950 to take drastic measures to combat the high inflation rate, which culminated in the messages of the director of the ECA and the Secretary of State in March and April, was characterized as "friendly advice," a "warning," a "stern warning," or "interference." Thus, the perceptions differ between "advice" and "interference" depending upon one's standpoint, but the message was issued. Accordingly, a few questions may be raised regarding the decision. First, was the message necessary at all? Second, were the style and tone of the message appropriate, if the message was necessary? Third, was the message effective in producing the desired results? Clearly, American officials thought the inflation rate of Korean economy in the spring of 1950 was too high to be tolerated, but the statements were made without any numerical references, and it is difficult to determine exactly the level of the inflation at this point. One later analytical study indicates that retail prices during the first half of 1950 to the outbreak of the war rose 19 percent, which was certainly not high if compared with the preceding period or if compared with the occupation period.[35] The particular style and tone of the message, the essence of which was a threat, seemed to have been chosen purposely for its effectiveness. Both messages of Acheson and Hoffman were formal and solemn, even stern, and this seemed to have come partly from the personal style of the two men who signed the messages, but also from a decision—again to make it effective. Last, the message seems to have achieved its objective: The message was received correctly by the Koreans as a stern message as it was intended to be; and the Koreans responded seriously and took immediate actions. Even the outspoken Yun Ch'i-yŏng, the vice chairman of the Korean National Assembly, who called the *aide memoire* an "interference," saw the need for compliance, and the 19 percent inflation rate of the first six months seems to indicate the effectiveness of the Korean response. Since inflation is difficult to control in any country under any circumstance, it is rather surprising that the Koreans were able to control it at this time.

Very much like the financial problem, the political problem of the centralization of power in the Republic of Korea had long been one of the main concerns of the American government. In the spring of 1950, it crystallized in an election issue. During his April 3 conversation with Ambassador Chang, Dean Rusk, at that time the Assistant Secretary of State for Far Eastern Affairs, showed great concern about information that President Rhee wished to postpone arbitrarily the early May National Assembly elections. He explained that the action would weaken the support of the nations in the world whose continuing support through the United Nations would be needed for the new republic and that the action would also affect the American public and congressional opinion. On the following day, Acheson, in his *aide memoire*, forcefully pointed out that both the military and economic aid of the United States was predicated upon the existence and growth of democratic institutions in the republic and said that holding the election according to the schedule was "urgent." Ten days later, Acheson requested that Muccio provide him with the fullest possible reports and analyses of activities connected with the election. This instruction resulted in at least eighteen dispatches from Seoul. The American pressure was not only over the date of the election, but also over Rhee's attempt to change all police chiefs who were under the control of the interior minister, an opposition party man. Rhee had no choice but to give in to the American pressure, and the election was held on May 30. It was a fair election and was praised by many. Muccio was pleased with both the fair manner in which the election was held and the outcome; only 48 Rhee supporters were elected out of 210 total seats in the assembly, and the opposition National Democratic Party did not do any better, winning only 19 seats. With the election of 120 independents, the real victor was the Korean people and the democratic process, and the Americans deserved some credit for this election.[36] Rhee's struggle with the National Assembly continued in May, and, when he threatened the representative body with dissolution, another letter of advice from the American government, this time from the president, was written to restrain him.[37]

In the spring of 1950, the Koreans had difficult problems in the areas of security, politics, and economics. In all three areas, the Koreans needed assistance and the cooperation of the United States. To be sure, the Koreans wished to get the necessary assistance without any restrictions. But this was not possible, and the price paid by the Koreans was intervention. Even the hawkish Yun Ch'i-yŏng conceded that the price was necessary. The Americans had themselves a long history of struggle for independence and avoidance of outside interference, and they probably wished not to interfere with the domestic life of the Koreans. As mentioned already, in early April, Rusk tried to explain to the Koreans the rationale for American intervention in Korean financial affairs by citing future U.N. support and U.S. domestic opinion. Two months later, Louis A. Johnson, in his memorandum to Secretary Acheson, raised the question of whether the interests of the United

States required "the drastic action of intervening directly in the Korean political affairs" and answered himself by concluding that if the intervention was not made, then U.S. and U.N. interests would receive severe damage.[38] This situation in which something was given and received reluctantly had to take place because of sheer necessity.

NOTES

1. James Irving Matray, *The Reluctant Crusade: American Foreign Policy in Korea, 1941–1950* (Honolulu: University of Hawaii Press, 1985), p. 151.

2. Cho Soon-sung, *Korea in World Politics, 1940–1950: An Evaluation of American Responsibility* (Berkeley and Los Angeles: University of California Press, 1967), p. 246; Ohn Chang-il, "The Joint Chiefs of Staff and U.S. Policy and Strategy Regarding Korea, 1945–1953," Ph.D. dissertation, University of Kansas, 1983, p. 72.

3. William W. Stueck, *The Road to Confrontation: American Policy toward China and Korea, 1947–1950* (Chapel Hill: University of North Carolina Press, 1981), pp. 100, 105, 110, 162; Bruce Cumings, ed., *Child of Conflict: The Korean-American Relations, 1943–1953* (Seattle: University of Washington Press, 1983), pp. 26, 29, 31–32, 49–50; idem, *The Origins of the Korean War*, vol. 2, *The Roaring of the Cataract, 1947–1950* (Princeton, N.J.: Princeton University Press, 1990), p. 325; John Lewis Gaddis, *The Long Peace: Inquiries into the History of the Cold War* (New York: Oxford University Press, 1987), p. 95; idem, "Korea in American Politics, Strategy and Diplomacy, 1945–50," in *The Origins of the Cold War in Asia*, ed. Y. Nagai and A. Iriye (New York: Columbia University Press, 1977), p. 202; Charles M. Dobbs, *The Unwanted Symbol: American Foreign Policy, the Cold War, and Korea, 1945–1950* (Kent, Ohio: Kent University Press, 1981), pp. 139, 157, 159, 161–162; Calum A. MacDonald, *Korea: The War before Vietnam* (New York: Free Press, 1986), pp. 18–19, 22–23.

4. NSC 8, in a note by the Executive Secretary of the National Security Council (Sources) to President Truman, April 2, 1948, *Foreign Relations of the United States (FRUS), 1948*, 6: 1164–1169.

5. NSC 8, *FRUS, 1948*, 6: 1164–1168; NSC 8/2, *FRUS, 1949*, 7: 969–978.

6. The Secretary of State to the Embassy in India, February 24, 1948, *FRUS, 1948*, 6: 1128; the Acting Secretary of State to the Special Representative in Korea, September 24, 1948, ibid., p. 1312; *Department of State Bulletin* 19 (October 3, 1948): 433–434; the Secretary of State to the Embassy in Korea, June 6, 1949, National Archives (NA), RG 59, 740.00119 control (Korea)/6–649.

7. Memorandum by the Chief of the Division of Northeast Asian Affairs (Bishop) to the Director of the Office of Far Eastern Affairs (Butterworth), December 17, 1948, *FRUS, 1948*, 6: 1337–1340. See also Stueck, *The Road to Confrontation*, p. 105; Cumings, ed., *Child of Conflict*, p. 26.

8. "Consequences of Troop Withdrawal from Korea in Spring 1949, "ORE 3-49, published February 28, 1949, Central Intelligence Agency, NA, RG 319, Assistant Chief of Staff, G-3, Decimal File 1949–50, P. O. 350.05 T. S. F/W.11.

9. See appearance of the word "symbol" in President Truman's message to the Congress, June 7, 1949, *Congressional Record*, 81st Cong., 1st Sess., vol. 95, pt. 6, p. 8359; Merchant to Bruce, February 16, 1950, NA, RG 84, Seoul Embassy Top

Secret Records, box 1; "Interdepartmental Meeting on the Far East," April 27, 1949, NA, RG 59, 795.00/4-2750.

10. The Secretary of State to certain diplomatic offices, March 18, 1949, *FRUS, 1949*, 7: 968.

11. Niles W. Bond, oral history interview transcript, December 28, 1973, Truman Library, p. 34.

12. Gaddis, *The Long Peace*, p. 94; Joyce Kolko and Gabriel Kolko, *The Limits of Power: The World and United States Foreign Policy, 1945-1954* (New York: Harper and Row, 1972), pp. 567-569; Cumings, *The Origins of the Korean War*, vol. 2, p. 216; Stueck, *The Road to Confrontation*, pp. 162-163; Dobbs, *The Unwanted Symbol*, p. 188; Park Hong-kyu, "American-Korean Relations, 1945-1953; A Study in United States Diplomacy," Ph.D. dissertation, North Texas State University, 1981, p. 174.

13. "Prospects of Survival of the Republic of Korea," October 28, 1948, Truman Library, President's Secretary's File, box 255, ORE 44-48, CIA. See also Muccio to the Secretary of State, July 28, 1949, NA, RG 59, Decimal File 1945-49, NA, RG 9, 501.BB Korea/7-2489.

14. Muccio to the Secretary of State, November 12, 1948, NA, RG 59, 740.00119 control (Korea)/11-1248; Muccio to the Secretary of State, NA, RG 59, Decimal File, NA, RG 59, 501.BB Korea/7-2489.

15. "Pisa oekyo 30-nyŏn" (Confidential history of a thirty-year diplomacy), *Seoul Sinmun,* no. 19, April 15, 1982; *Sichŏng Wŏlpo*, 8 (January 20, 1950): 8; Im P'yŏng-chik, *Im P'yŏng-chik hoekorok: Kŭntae oekyo imyŏnsa* (Im P'yŏng-chik memoirs: The inside history of modern diplomacy) (Seoul: Yŏwŏnsa, 1956), p. 334.

16. Lee Chang-hun, "4.3 minchu hangchaengŭi chŏnkaewa sŏngkyŏk" (The development and characteristics of the April 3 democratic struggle), in *Haepang chŏnhusaŭi insik* (Understanding of the history of the pre- and the postliberation era), vol. 4, ed. Choe Chang-chip (Seoul: Hankilsa, 1989) pp. 260-304; Hwang Nam-chun, "Chŏnnam chipang chŏngch'iwa Yŏ-Sun Sakŏn" (Chŏnnam local politics and the Yŏ-Sun incident), in ibid., vol. 3, ed. Pak Hyŏn-chae (Seoul: Hankilsa, 1987), pp. 413-455.

17. Joseph E. Jacobs to the Secretary of State, August 14, 1948, NA, Decimal File 1945-49, box 2110; Memorandum of conversation by the Acting Secretary of State, September 23, 1948, *FRUS, 1948*, 6: 1309-1311; Truman to J. D. Harvey, October 5, 1948, Truman Library, OF471 (1945-48).

18. U.S. Ambassador in London (Douglas) to the Secretary of State, August 13, 1948, NA, RG 59, Decimal File 1945-49, box 2110; *Sichŏng Wŏlpo* 1 (January 1949): 12-14; "Pisa oekyo 30-nyŏn," *Seoul Sinmun*, March 3, 1982, no. 9. p. 5; ibid., March 28, 1982, no. 10; Im Pyŏng-chik, *Im Pyŏng-chik hoekorok*, pp. 325, 331.

19. Commanding General, U.S. Armed Forces in Korea to the Secretary of State, October 9, 1948, Douglas MacArthur Memorial Archives (MacArthur Library), RG 9, box 148; "Pisa oekyo 30-nyŏn," 28, *Seoul Sinmun*, October 20, 1982, p. 8.

20. Muccio to the Secretary of State, January 27, 1949, *FRUS, 1949*, 7: 951.

21. Muccio to the Secretary of State, March 14, 1949, NA, RG 59, Decimal File 1945-49, 895.00/1-1449.

22. American Embassy in Korea to the Secretary of State, March 17, 1949, NA, RG 59, Numerical File 1945-49, 895.00/3-1749; Chargé of the American Mission in Korea to the Secretary of State, March 28, 1949, *FRUS, 1949*, 7: 979; Muccio to

the Secretary of State, April 18, May 1, 1949, NA, RG 59, Numerical File 1945–49, 895.00/4–1849, 895.00/5–1749; Muccio to the Secretary of State, April 2, 1949, NA, RG 59, 501.BB Korea/4–2649.

23. Muccio to the Secretary of State, June 13, July 11, 1949, NA, RG 59, Numerical File 1945–49, 895.00/6–1349, 895.00/7–1149.

24. Muccio to the Secretary of State, August 10, September 13, October 7, November 7, NA, RG 59, Numerical Files, 1945–49, 895.00/8–1049, 895.00/9–1349, 895.00/9–10749, 895.00/11–749.

25. Muccio to Niles W. Bond, September 12, 1949, NA, RG 59, Numerical File 1945–49, 895.00/8–3149; Memorandum of conversation by the Secretary of the Army (Royall) with Rhee and Muccio, February 8, 1949, *FRUS, 1949*, 7: 958; *Jayu Sinmun*, May 12, 1949, 1: 1–7; ibid., July 7, 1949, 1: 1–5; *Donga Ilbo*, August 21, 1949, 1: 1–7; *Kyŏnghyang Sinmun*, August 22, 1949, 1: 1–8.

26. Memorandum of conversation by the Director of the Office of the Far Eastern Affairs (Butterworth) with Cho and Bond, January 5, 1949, *FRUS, 1949*, 7: 940; memorandum of conversation by Butterworth with Cho, Chang Myŏn, and Bond, April 11, 1949, ibid., pp. 984–985; Muccio to the Secretary of State, June 3, 1949, NA, RG 59, Numerical File 1945–49, 740.00119 control (Korea)/6–349; Muccio to Bond, July 11, 1949, *FRUS, 1949*, 7: 1061.

27. "The Financial Situation," by J. E. Collbert, January 13, 1950, NA, RG 469, Records of U.S. Foreign Assistance Agencies, 1948–61, Division of Korea Program, Office of Director, Outgoing Letters, 1949–50, box 1; *Sichŏng Wŏlpo* 8(January 20, 1950): 7–9.

28. Drumright to the Secretary of State, April 17, 1950, NA, RG 59, Numerical File 1950–54, 795B.00/4–1750; *New York Times*, March 14, 1950, 10: 2.

29. Memorandum by Ambassador at Large Philip C. Jessup, January 14, 1950, *FRUS, 1950*, 7: 4; Muccio to Rhee, January 14, 1950, enclosure in Muccio to the Secretary of State, January 17, 18, 1950, NA, RG 59, Numerical File 1950–54, 895.00/1–1850, 895.00/1–2150, 895.00T/1–2150, 895.00R/1–2150; memorandum of conversation by John Z. Williams of the Office of the Northeastern Asian Affairs, January 20, 1920, *FRUS, 1950*, 7: 13.

30. The Secretary of State to Muccio, February 14, 1950, *FRUS, 1950*, 7: 28; Drumright to the Secretary of State, February 21, 1950, ibid., p. 29.

31. Memorandum of conversation by the Officer in Charge of Korean Affairs (Bond), March 15, 1950, *FRUS, 1950*, 7: 30–33; Acheson to Muccio, March 23, 1950, ibid., p. 35; the Deputy Administrator of the Economic Cooperation Administration (Foster) to the Embassy in Korea, March 27, 1950, ibid., p. 36; Edgar A. J. Johnson to Paul G. Hoffman, March 23, 1950, NA, RG 469, Records of U.S. Foreign Assistance Agencies, 1948–61, Division of Korea Program , Office of Director, Outgoing Letters, 1949–50, box 1; Chief KMAG to CINCFE, March 24, 1950, MacArthur Library, RG 9, box 43, KMAG; Muccio to the Secretary of State, March 29, 1950, *FRUS, 1950*, 7: 37–38.

32. The Secretary of State to the Korean Ambassador (Chang Myŏn), *Aide Memoire*, April 3, 1950, *FRUS, 1950*, 7: 43–44.

33. Muccio to the Secretary of State, April 4, 1950, *FRUS, 1950*, 7: 44; Lee Yulmo, "The Merits and Demerits of American Assistance to Korea," *Koreana Quarterly* 6 (1964): 42; *New York Times*, April 27, 1950, 28: 1.

34. Drumright to the Secretary of State, April 28, 1950, *FRUS, 1950*, 7: 52–58. See also *Kyŏnghyang Sinmun*, April 9, 1950, 1: 1–7.

35. Lee Yul-mo, "The Merits and Demerits," p. 42. See also the *New York Times*, April 22, 1950, 5: 2, for passage by the National Assembly of the 1950 balanced budget bill and Senator Knowland's April 10 remarks in the Senate regarding the American pressure for the inflation in Korea which had been difficult to control in the United States, *Congressional Record*, 81st Cong., 2d Sess., vol. 96, part 4, p. 4985.

36. The Secretary of State to the Korean Ambassador (Chang), *Aide Memoire*, April 4, 1950, *FRUS, 1950*, 7: 44; Muccio to the Secretary of State, April 1, 1950, ibid., pp. 39–40; Muccio to the Secretary of State, April 20, 1950, NA, RG 59, Numerical File 1950–54, 795.00/4–2050; Chargé Drumright to the Secretary of State, May 2, 3, *FRUS, 1950*, 7: 62–63, 66; Muccio to the Secretary of State, May 27, 1950, ibid., p. 91; Muccio to Rusk, June 1, 1950, ibid., p. 98; *New York Times*, June 1, 1950, 10: 5; ibid., June 2, 1950, 22: 3; Acheson to Muccio, April 14, 1950, NA, RG 59, Numerical File 1950–54, 795.00/4–1450; Cho Soon-sung, *Korea in World Politics*, p. 262.

37. American Embassy in Korea to the Secretary of State, June 3, 1950, Truman Library, State Department File, box 13, selected records relating to the Korean War. See also Allison to the Secretary of State, June 5, 1950, ibid.

38. Memorandum of conversation by Dean G. Rusk with Chang Myŏn and Niles Bond, April 3, 1950, NA, RG 59, Numerical File 1950–54, 795.00/4–350; Johnson to Acheson, June 2, 1950, Truman Library, Department of State File, box 13, selected records relating to the Korean War. For a general discussion on the subject of intervention, see Richard A. Falk, *A Global Approach to National Policy* (Cambridge, Mass.: Harvard University Press, 1975), pp. 122–125.

CHAPTER 6

The U.S. Troop Withdrawal Issue

For Korean–American relations during the year and ten-month period between the establishment of the Republic of Korea and the outbreak of the
Korean War, the issues of the withdrawal of American troops from Korea
and U.S. economic and military aid for the new republic became most important. These two, though related in certain ways, were also separate issues, and the former, much more important than the latter with regard to the
outbreak of the war, is taken up first. Three decades after the event, William Stueck wrote, "In the year and a half prior to the outbreak of war, the most
important United States action in Korea was the removal of its troops from that
country."[1] Indeed, not just for that period, but for the whole five-year period
between the decision to divide the peninsula in mid-August 1945 and the outbreak of the war, the withdrawal of the troops was the most important event in
South Korean history. Three events in 1945, 1947, and 1949 (the occupation, the transfer of Korea to U.N. control, and the troop withdrawal) were
definitely causally linked, and there is no doubt that these three—especially
the third one—were linked to a fourth major event—the Korean War. For a
better understanding of the problems surrounding the withdrawal of the
troops, a few questions may be asked: What was its nature and meaning?
What were the bases for and the process of the decision making? What was
the process of its execution? And, what were its consequences?

The exclusion of foreign troops from a nation's territory is one of the
most important practices of the modern nation-state system, and nations
abhor to see the presence of any foreign troops on their soil, except in
special circumstances. The Koreans during the period under consideration

were very sensitive about their recently recovered sovereign rights, and they should have been happy to see foreign troops departing from both the northern and southern parts of the peninsula. Unfortunately, however, during this period Korea was caught within a set of a very special circumstances, and most Koreans in the south, with the exception of a small number of ultraidealistic nationalists and the leftists, wished the American troops to stay until their defense forces were strong enough to defend the nation. For the Americans, withdrawal of their troops from Korea after the birth of the new republic in the southern part of the peninsula was not only logical, but also very desirable because the troops could be used elsewhere in the world. The Americans, however, were also trapped by the Cold War in Korea, and the matter of the troop withdrawal became problematic.

The decision to withdraw the American troops from Korea had already been made before the summer of 1948, and the point under discussion during this period was not whether to withdraw, but when to do it and how to do it. With the transfer of the Korean question to the United Nations, which was soon followed by the establishment of the two half-Korean states on the peninsula, the decision to withdraw troops was also made because the withdrawal of the occupation troops would automatically follow the birth of a new nation.[2] Further, for the origin of the decision to withdraw the troops, we have to go back to mid-August 1945, when the military occupation of Korea was decided upon, because without a military occupation, there would be no withdrawal problem. And behind the occupation and troop withdrawal sat the ever-present Cold War. Without the U.S. desire to prevent communist expansion, there would have been neither the occupation nor the troop withdrawal question.

Even though the two departments—State and Defense—which were involved most intensively in discussions of the troop withdrawal issue had in mind quite different views and strategies, the two agreed that American troops would have to leave Korea sooner or later. The only disagreement the two departments had was on the matter of the schedule of the withdrawal, which was important because it mattered very much whether the American troops would leave Korea in 1948, immediately after the establishment of the new republic, or a year or two later. Had the final departure of American troops taken place a few years later, then the history of Korea during the past four decades would have been much different. The Koreans agreed with the Americans that American troops would have to leave Korea sooner or later; what they wished for was a delay in the troop withdrawal until their own army was strong enough to defend their country from communist threats.

Throughout the spring of 1949, when the date for the final withdrawal of American troops in Korea was finally fixed at a National Security Council meeting, the interdepartmental struggle continued between the State and Defense Departments. The military was in a stronger position in this struggle because the matter of troop withdrawal was more a military operation than political. Furthermore, the military decision that the Korean peninsula did not have any strategic value, which had already been made the previous fall, and the general post–World War II national mood for smaller government spending and a small defense expenditure added strength to the military position. However, withdrawal of the troops was certainly not an exclusively military matter. It also had an international political dimension, and the final decision would have to be made politically, hence the State Department would have a large voice. Overall, however, the Defense Department was in a stronger position, and the State Department had to make an extra effort in the struggle.

Throughout the whole period of the interdepartmental squabble, the U.S. military establishment clearly showed its eagerness to withdraw its troops as soon as possible from Korea. In fact, the withdrawal had been going on since the previous fall, for it began as soon as the government decided to transfer the Korea problem to the United Nations. U.S. forces in Korea had declined from 45,000 to 26,072 in the three months between the end of September 1947 and January 1 of the following year (a drop of 42 percent), and the decline was to continue until the level of 18,000 was reached by March 1. In brief, in five months, between the fall of 1947 and the spring of 1948, more than half of the American troops (60 percent) had left Korea.[3] Hence, the so-called "troop withdrawal" meant the completion of the process of the withdrawal, not a debate over the whole process.

On January 16, 1948, the Department of the Army formally requested from the State Department a "termination" of the military occupation of Korea. Four days later, MacArthur optimistically estimated the strength of the Republic of Korea Army and indicated that the "optimum short-range conditions for withdrawal" would be created by April. A month later, a reaction came from the State Department. Niles Bond, the assistant chief of the division of the Northeast Asian affairs, suggested postponement of the troop withdrawal until the upcoming session of the U.N. General Assembly, which was scheduled to begin in Paris in September. Interdepartmental communication and discussions in the early spring of 1948 regarding the troop withdrawal process resulted in the NSC 8, the most basic document for the issue, which was published on April 2 and was approved, with instructions for its implementation, by President Truman on April 8. After an analysis of the U.S. objectives in Korea and conditions in that country, the paper concluded that the United States should be prepared to proceed with the implementation of the withdrawal and that every effort should be made "to create conditions for the withdrawal of occupation forces by 31 December 1948." Later, the date was reconsidered and changed, but the basic guidelines for the evacuation of troops established in this document remained.[4] NSC 8 was a consensus which was reached at that point between the two departments; the Defense Department made one forward step in fixing a target date and the State Department also won a first battle in putting the final withdrawal date off until the end of the U.N. General Assembly meeting.

Now it was the turn of the military to take steps to implement the policy decision. MacArthur proposed beginning preparations for the withdrawal on May 15, commencing the "tactical withdrawal" on August 15, and to complete the whole process by December 15. The proposal was approved by Washington, and preparations for the withdrawal began officially on May 19. In fact, the planning had already been ordered by the Department of Army in late March, and "logistical preparations" were also ordered by the department in late April.[5] In June, the military took steps to organize the Korean Military Advisory Group (KMAG) as part of the preparations. Thus in May and June preparations for the troop withdrawal were proceeding expeditiously. At this moment, however, the situation in China was quickly deteriorating for the nationalist side, and the State Department became quite uneasy about the possible impact of the withdrawal of troops from Korea upon the Chinese situation. On June 23, Secretary Marshall accordingly asked Secretary of the Army Kenneth C. Royall to maintain "sufficient flexibility" in the preparation and execution of the withdrawal plans. On the same day, crossing with Marshall's letter, Royall wrote Marshall asking for the State Department's concurrence on the initiation of the "tactical withdrawal" on August 15. Toward the end of June, the State-Army Ad Hoc Committee on Korea in its report accommodated the wishes of both departments—fixing the beginning and the ending dates of the withdrawal and maintaining flexibility in the execution of the plan. Early the following month, on July 8, Undersecretary of State Robert A. Lovett responded positively to Royall's request by saying that the State Department had no objection to the proposed dates for the initiation and the completion of the withdrawal on August 15 and December 15. He also reiterated Marshall's request for flexibility in case "suspension, delay or other adjustment" was necessary.[6] Thus, by early July, it seemed that the hurdle had been removed for the preparation and the initiation of the withdrawal, leaving only the completion of the withdrawal to be undertaken.

But an adjustment had to be made soon. On July 20, at the request of the State Department, a decision was made to delay the withdrawal for one month; the revised date for the commencement of the withdrawal was set for September 15, 1948 while completion was scheduled for January 15 of the following year. Even after the arrangement for a one-month delay, State Department officials felt considerable unease about the time table for the troop withdrawal and expressed their feelings on the matter throughout the month of August. On August 8, John M. Allison and Niles Bond suggested a high-level interdepartmental consideration of the subject; on August 14, Muccio recommended to the department that the withdrawal plan not be implemented until the situation in Korea reached the point at which the withdrawal would not jeopardize the American "operation"; and on August

17, Butterworth argued that even though the date for the initiation of the withdrawal had been set for September 15, the U.N. General Assembly meeting would begin on September 21, and the withdrawal of the troops should not begin until after the United Nations had considered the subject, except for an "appropriate reduction and regrouping" of the American troops in Korea. While words were exchanged and ideas were shared within the State Department, the Defense Department did not delay in taking action to implement the U.S. withdrawal policy. On September 27, the Department of the Army ordered the commanding general in Korea to undertake "continued implementation" of the plan. Actually, so much of a "reduction" had been made by the spring of 1948 that by the end of March only a small "residual force" was left, and it had almost no combat strength. The army's estimate in the summer of the year was that November 15 was the date beyond which the continued withdrawal would make occupation "untenable."[7]

In the fall of 1948, the news of the Soviet troop withdrawal from North Korea complicated the troop withdrawal question. With this new element, withdrawal emerged for the first time as an open policy issue. Up until this time, the discussion of the troop withdrawal was kept strictly within American government circles, and the Koreans were not consulted or even informed about the subject. The American public also was kept in the dark. On September 10, the Supreme National Assembly of (North) Korea addressed the governments of the Soviet Union and the United States requesting the simultaneous and immediate withdrawal of their troops from the Korean peninsula. The presidium of the Supreme Soviet of the Soviet Union responded by instructing the Council of Ministers to complete the withdrawal of the Soviet troops in North Korea by the end of the year. The presidium also expressed its hope that the American government would do likewise within the same time period. On September 18, the Soviet government informed the North Korean government of its decision. The immediate reaction by the U.S. government was cautious. The Secretary of State instructed the ambassador in Moscow to convey the message that the U.S. government had taken note of the decision of the Soviet government, that the U.S. government considered the question of a troop withdrawal as "part of the larger question of Korean unity and independence," and that its views would be presented at the appropriate time to the General Assembly of the United Nations.

The Korean reaction to the communist move was somewhat mixed. President Rhee's immediate reaction was that withdrawal of Soviet troops from the North was "the right thing" to be done; at the same time he expressed his wish that the United States would not "play into the Soviet game" by making any agreement without consulting the Koreans. His view was that U.S. troops should stay in Korea until the ROK defense forces were strong enough to handle the nation's defense. The immediate reaction in the National Assembly was also mixed, and it divided into pro and con groups on the issue of troop withdrawal.[8]

Members of the American press took great interest in the news, and its overall reaction was cautious, similar to the government posture. They warned the government not to be deceived by Soviet propaganda tactics. News commentators were convinced that the Soviet proposal for the withdrawal of military forces from both Koreas was a propaganda move designed to put the United States on the spot before the U.N. General Assembly and that the Soviet Union was prepared to evacuate from North Korea because the military force in the north was strong enough to take over the rest of the Korean peninsula eventually. *Time* magazine equated the Soviet Union with a cat smiling at a canary, and the *New Orleans State* said that for the Americans to withdraw from South Korea would be tantamount to "handing it over to Moscow on a silver platter." Other papers expressed their views on the issue. The *Washington Star* anticipated a "crisis of far-reaching significance over Korea" after the American troop withdrawal; an attack on the new republic by the North Korean army would constitute defiance of the United States and the United Nations alike; and such "barefooted aggression" would clearly require positive action on the part of both. Two other papers expressed a different view: the *Christian Science Monitor* asserted that Korea was no longer considered a strategic necessity, and the *Chicago News* also discounted the strategic and diplomatic value of Korea, indicating that it was secondary to other areas like Western Europe. *The Washington Post* suggested using the opportunity more positively by taking up the Soviet proposal and coupling it with a demand for elections under U.N. auspices for the whole Korean peninsula that would result in the formulation of a united government.[9] It was useful for the American government to see the American people's response to the Soviet move. An even more valuable byproduct was information about where the American people stood on the whole issue of troop withdrawal from Korea.

Since the fall of 1947, when the U.S. government had taken the Korean question to the United Nations, the world organization played an important role in Korean–American relations. Its role in the fall 1948 meeting was significant, both for the questions of troop withdrawal and the recognition of the new republic. It provided a convenient place for the U.S. government to deal with the Soviet challenge with the proposal of simultaneous troop withdrawals; it also provided the Koreans with a forum for expressing their view on an important issue concerning their very existence. On September 10, before the Soviet proposal had been made, the issue of the troop withdrawal was already on the American agenda for the Paris conference. Dean Rusk, in his memorandum to Undersecretary of State Lovett, indicated that one of the U.S. delegate's jobs would be supporting "early withdrawal of all occupation forces" from Korea—a modest term, but the word "all" denoted both the United States and the Soviet Union. On October 22, a month after the Soviet proposal had reached Washington, the U.S. delegate's position paper included the troop withdrawal matter with a little more elaboration. It referred in a general way to the November 14, 1947 U.N. resolution, which partly read "complete withdrawal from Korea of their armed forces as early as practicable and if possible within ninety days," but without any more clear time reference. A week later, on October 29, the U.S. draft resolution on Korea for the U.N. General Assembly was cleared with the State Department and telegrammed to Paris on November 8. The U.S. draft contained a reference to a time schedule by adding a phrase, "if possible, within ninety days." At this point, when a proposal on Korea was shaping up between Paris and Washington, the situation in China was deteriorating quickly, and the Chinese delegates and the South Korean representatives in Paris were "alarmed." Their worries began to influence their activities in Paris.[10]

Chang Myŏn, the chief Korean delegate, must have become familiar by late October (between October 22 and 27) with the content of the American proposal, if not on the matter of the troop withdrawal, at least on the issue of Korean recognition. On October 27, he telegrammed through the American government communication channel a request to President Rhee for inclusion of a statement against the "wholesale withdrawal" of U.S. troops before the Korean military forces were adequately trained and equipped. This was the beginning of an official Korean reaction to the American plan for the withdrawal of troops. While the Korean reaction continued, State Department officials were also perturbed by the situation in China and the progress of the troop withdrawals. Charles B. Saltzman wrote to Lieutenant General Albert C. Wedemeyer, the director of Plans and Operations in the Department of the Army, in November expressing the State Department's view that the department regarded entering into "the final and irrevocable stages" of the troop withdrawal as "premature and prejudicial" to the interests of the nation and, pending the General Assembly action, the reduction of forces in Korea should not be permitted to progress beyond the critical point. Muccio on November 12 also reported on the critical condition in China and Korea and stressed that the continued presence of American troops would give the South Korean government a "period of grace."[11]

The ninety-day time restriction, which was added in the winter of 1947 to the troop withdrawal document by the American government and brought back a year later, was dropped by the time the U.N. General Assembly finally took action on the issue. The phrase was still there on November 16, when the draft of the U.S.-Australian joint resolution proposal was drawn up. Then, the Chinese and the other delegates' suggestions—the Chinese delegate definitely suggested this portion of the change—were incorporated into the November 27 draft of the three-power joint resolution, and the time restriction was dropped in the last proposal. The U.S.-Australian–Chinese proposal concerning Korea was approved on December 12 by the General Assembly without further changes, and the troop withdrawal clause contained no time restriction.[12]

By dealing with the troop withdrawal issue in the winter of 1948 through the United Nations, the State Department came out well. It responded successfully to the Soviet proposal through the world organization; it stopped, at least temporarily, the then accelerating withdrawal process; and it managed to satisfy the Korean desire to prevent the early evacuation of American troops from their country. Responding to Saltzman's appeal to Wedemeyer of November 9 to halt the process of reducing American forces in Korea, the Department of the Army ordered MacArthur a week later, pending reception of the authority to complete the final phase of the withdrawal, to retain in Korea for an "indefinite period" one regimental combat team of about 7,500 men. Even though the military had known that there would be a high level reexamination of the situation before the final phase of the troop withdrawal was completed, this was a definite accomplishment by the State Department.[13]

The State Department's dealings with the Koreans were much more complicated. Because the Koreans feared that withdrawal of the American troops would create a vacuum that would be filled by communist forces, they wished to retain American troops until their own defense forces were prepared to rebuff an invasion. Further, if necessary, President Rhee wished to appeal formally to the General Assembly for a resolution requesting the United States to retain "a token force" in Korea. Seeing that the task of persuasion was not easy, the Koreans decided to undertake a concerted effort for a month beginning in late October. President Rhee made a formal appeal to President Truman to retain the troops for the time being; the cabinet and the National Assembly passed resolutions asking for the same thing; and the public was mobilized for large-scale demonstrations designed to impress the delegates in Paris.[14] It is questionable how effective the Korean actions were. The Koreans had to do their best at the General Assembly meeting on the troop withdrawal issue, but the task was too difficult to achieve. Because of the U.S. determination to respond to the Soviet proposal, no nation could have persuaded the Americans to drop the general statement. Dropping the ninety-day time restriction was the most the United States could concede. Even though this accomplishment resulted largely from the contribution of the Chinese delegate, it was good for the Koreans, and they should have been happy with the accomplishment. Taking out the ninety-day phrase, which was already in the November 1947 U.N. resolution, not an easy task in December 1948, was no small accomplishment. It also may be said that the State Department's victory at the 1948 U.N. General Assembly meeting did not automatically mean a loss to the Department of the Army. The army did not give up anything essential; the process of the withdrawal—or reduction—had to stop at a certain point to wait for an authorization for the final step of the withdrawal.

The U.N. General Assembly meeting gave the parties involved in the struggle over the troop withdrawal issue a breathing space, and as soon as the meeting was over, they returned to the fierce last battle. Since the previous October, the Korean government had become a party to the struggle, and the issue became a three-party struggle on both the domestic and international fronts, with the Korean government the weakest and the army the strongest contestants. The army had no choice but to hold up the withdrawal process in Korea for a short period from mid-November pending the outcome of the U.N. General Assembly meeting. Once the meeting concluded with a resolution that was in accord with the same basic line of withdrawal, the army stepped up its efforts to complete the process without more delay. One source of its strength was the fact that the withdrawal was a military operation, and the army could act while others were talking. The real withdrawal had been going on for a long time under the names of "regrouping" or "reduction" of forces. By late 1948, the remaining American troops in Korea lacked the capacity to fight, and in a real sense the withdrawal had progressed beyond the "critical point." Soon the military came forward with a powerful argument that as long as the occupation forces remained in Korea they had an obligation to defend the republic, but they did not have the strength to do so; therefore they should be withdrawn. An additional, even more powerful, argument was that if South Korea were attacked under existing conditions, the United States would be trapped there unintentionally because of the small and useless military force remaining.[15]

On December 22, ten days after the end of the U.N. General Assembly meeting, the Department of the Army asked the Department of State to agree to the initiation of the final withdrawal on February 1, 1949, and to its completion by the end of March. On the same day, it simply announced the continuation of "withdrawal" operations in Korea, and before the end of the year, the 7th Division moved to Japan. A month later, on January 25, the army told the State Department that it wished to complete the withdrawal on May 10, as General MacArthur had recommended. Actually, the army was anxious to get out of Korea as soon as possible, if possible even before the May 10 deadline.[16] Officials in the State Department, however, were much more concerned about the situation in the Far East—especially developments in China and their impact on the region—and they would not easily give up the battle with the military. Even before the end of the General Assembly meeting on November 9, Saltzman told Wedemeyer that prior to the implementation of the final phase of the withdrawal a review by an appropriate agency was "assumed." Two weeks later, Butterworth pointed out to Saltzman that since April, when the early troop withdrawal from Korea was approved, the situation in the Far East had changed and that a "fundamental reassessment" of U.S. policy with respect to Korea must be undertaken in light of developments in China and elsewhere. What the outcome of the fundamental reassessment Butterworth contemplated might have been is not clear, but it definitely might have produced a delay in the troop withdrawals of more than one or two months. On November 12, Muccio wrote from Seoul and presented a grave picture of the situation in Korea. He said that only the continued presence of American troops would give the Korean government a "grace period." On December 17, a few days after the end of the General Assembly meeting, Max Bishop, chief of the Division of Northeast Asian Affairs, wrote a memorandum to Butterworth pointing out that "a careful review" of the conclusion regarding troop withdrawal from Korea set forth in NSC 8 was necessary and that U.S. policy in Korea should be examined as part of an overall U.S. Pacific policy. On January 10 of the following year, Butterworth officially proposed a National Security Council meeting to "reappraise, and if necessary redefine" U.S. policy with respect to Korea. The Department of the Army had to respond, and, as a part of it, Secretary Royall made a trip to Korea in early February to appraise firsthand the situation. He and Muccio met with President Rhee in Seoul, and he returned from Korea with the impression that if the United States would agree to provide "a reasonable amount of additional arms," Rhee would not object to an immediate U.S. withdrawal. Later, there was some controversy on the difference between his perception of Rhee's view and that of Muccio. Finally, the two departments agreed to iron out their differences on the troop withdrawal issue and to review the whole Korean problem. A National Security Council meeting was held on March 22, from which the NSC 8/2 emerged.[17]

One piece of analysis, which was produced about a month before the March National Security Council meeting and was available to the policymaking community in Washington, was the CIA report of February 28, "Consequences of the Troop Withdrawal from Korea in Spring, 1949" (ORE-49). In a carefully done analysis, the Central Intelligence Agency examined every angle involved in the troop withdrawal. The agency stated in its summary that the U.S. troop withdrawal would probably result in the collapse of the U.S.–supported Republic of Korea, an event which would seriously diminish U.S. prestige and adversely affect U.S. security interests in the Far East. It also stated that the troop withdrawal in the spring of 1949 would probably in time be followed by an invasion. Although it could be presumed that South Korean security forces would eventually develop sufficient strength to resist such an invasion, it would not have achieved that capability by the spring of 1949. As it turned out later, the agency was wrong about one prediction and right about the other one. Army intelligence filed a dissent to the CIA analysis, arguing that the North Korean invasion was a possibility but not a probability.[18] A question is what impact the CIA analysis had on the minds of the Washington foreign policy makers between February 28 and March 22. The army must have trusted its own intelligence division more than anyone else's, as was evident in the NSC 8/2.

NSC 8/2 followed exactly the same format and line of thought as NSC 8 had. It retained the original objectives of U.S. policy in Korea and chose the middle course, like the first document, for future U.S. policy toward Korea. An important part of the new document was a review of developments since April 1948. The review, however, treated the data much more teleologically and left out certain important aspects of the developments in the Far East during the period. For example, the April 1948 analysis estimated the size of the North Korean military forces at 125,000 and the South Korean military force at 57,000; a year later, the March 1949 analysis estimated 75,000 to 95,000 North Korean military forces and 114,000 troops in the South Korean security force. The changes underway in China and the impact of the American troop withdrawal on the region, especially Japan, were ignored completely in the analysis, and the review simply stated that for the survival of the South Korean government a limited amount of economic and military aid was needed, but the presence of an American military force was not necessary, an optimistic assumption which was later questioned in Congress. On the basis of this analysis, the National Security Council recommended completion of the troop withdrawal by June 30 of the year.[19] The revised U.S. policy guidelines for the troop withdrawal provided three more months than the original Army Department request and forty more days than the MacArthur recommendation; that much the army conceded and the state gained. Certainly even a few more months were helpful for the South Korean defense forces, but it was not enough to change the course of events. In view of what happened later, we know now that if the Republic of Korea Army had at least one more year and preferably two to develop, along with a small token force of troops present in Korea as a symbol of U.S. policy, Korean history in the 1950s and thereafter would have been much different. Bishop, Butterworth, and some others in the State Department, who had wished to see a much more substantial review of the past and a reorientation of future U.S. policy, must have been disappointed by the outcome of the meeting. However, this was the kind of consensus possible at this point, and in any case, the struggle over the troop withdrawal issue between the state and the army ended with NSC 8/2. Thus, by late March, the final adjustments to the U.S. policy regarding the withdrawal of troops were made. For execution of the policy, the main stage was moved to Seoul.

Even though NSC 8/2 stipulated that the Korean government, along with the U.N. Temporary Commission on Korea, would be "consulted" on the final phase of the withdrawal, practically no room was left by this time for the Koreans. The Americans knew what the Koreans would say and do if they had known earlier about the American plan to withdraw the troops, and they were kept in the dark about the policy-making process. To be sure, many Koreans must have felt that the American strategy was not fair for the Koreans because the land the troops occupied was theirs, and they would suffer most of the consequences of the withdrawal. But the Koreans lacked resources and leverage to back up their sense of justice, and even though they suggested some alternatives and made a last minute appeal, their voice did not prevail. After the final policy decision of the United States through NSC 8/2, Muccio's effort began in late March to explain to President Rhee the logic, or the inevitability, of the troop withdrawal. He was very successful in this task, or Rhee was reasonable in seeing why the eventual withdrawal of American troops would be not only unavoidable but also desirable. Muccio based his efforts at persuasion on the information in some of the conclusions of the NSC 8/2. The document was useful for the job: Only two of the ten items in the conclusion had nothing to do with the troop withdrawal; and only one of them would be harmful for the task of the persuasion. The other items related to what economic and military aid the U.S. government would give the Korean government after the withdrawal. President Rhee took "calmly" Muccio's explanation and, by April 11, he even agreed to make a public statement to explain the forthcoming event to the Korean people, which was carried out a week later. He parenthetically made the "suggestion" that the American authorities might review the "timing of withdrawal" in light of the December 12 resolution.[20]

Thus Muccio did well in selling the problematic proposal; so it seemed, at least at this point. But soon a difficulty rose. At least part of the reason for Muccio's easy persuasion of President Rhee was that he withheld from the president any reference to the withdrawal schedule. When the president received the press dispatch from the United States stating that the withdrawal would be carried out by about July 1 of the year, he was disturbed and began to protest. In his letter of April 14, he stated that such a withdrawal should not take place without "prior consultation" with his government and the U.N. commission in Korea, and suggested that, even though he trusted the content of the document signed by the president of the United States, the promise of economic and military aid for Korea should be made public so as to gain Korean understanding and support. He suggested also that the American government should publicly reaffirm the pledge contained in the Korean–American treaty of 1882. His suggestion for a reaffirmation of the first article of the 1882 treaty sounded at this point more like a condition for the troop withdrawal than one of the alternatives that he proposed when the early withdrawal seemed to be inevitable. Rhee's protest was the beginning of the Korean reaction to the U.S. troop withdrawal, which continued for a month, to the middle of May. Immediately, Muccio asked the Secretary of State whether a reaffirmation of the pledge in the old treaty would be possible and received a quick response from Acheson that the old treaty was no longer in effect but that negotiation of a new treaty of friendship and commerce might be considered. President Rhee promptly proposed to open negotiations for a new treaty. Before receiving a response from Washington, on April 18, he made a public explanation to the Korean people as he had promised. The reaction of the Korean press to the announcement of the troop withdrawal was reported to be in general favorable. Some papers appealed to the Korean people for a special dedication and determination for the defense of the nation.[21]

For a month beginning in late April, President Rhee made an effort, through words and actions, to appeal to the U.S. government. Realizing that direct communication with Washington would not be effective, he decided to use an indirect channel. The Philippines was one of the nations which sympathized with Korea's problem concerning the withdrawal issue, and it also had representation on the U.N. commission in Seoul. President Rhee decided to use the assistance of the Philippines, and the message was delivered to Washington through the Filipino representatives in Seoul and the United Nations. When Acheson received the message, he was angry. Frustrated, President Rhee turned to another route, and a much more risky one—the press. On May 7, the Office of Public Information released the president's statement: "In the case of an attack by an outside power, would the Republic of Korea be able to count upon all-out American military aid?" "This question is," his statement continued, "of far greater importance than the mere question of whether or not the remaining American troops are to stay in Korea." When a report reached Acheson, he became furious and instructed Muccio to tell Rhee that "this unfortunate utterance can only redound to disadvantage of the ROK and may well have serious adverse consequences in terms of pending requests for economic and military aid for Korea." Muccio delivered the secretary's words together with his own even stronger ones. Somewhat surprised and worried, President Rhee became defensive and retreated to the pretension that the statement was released without his authorization. A few days later, he also admitted that it was perhaps a mistake for him to try to force the hand of the U.S. government. Nevertheless, he still held his firm view that the U.S. government should make a public statement about its plan for economic and military aid for Korea and about the Pacific Pact, which was similar to the Atlantic Pact. It should be added that even though Secretary Acheson expressed in unmistakable terms the firm policy of the U.S. government regarding the troop withdrawal and Korean anxiety, some members of the State Department were genuinely concerned about the Korean situation. During a conversation with the Korean representatives (Chough Pyŏng-ok and Chang Myŏn), Butterworth expressed his view that the U.S. government had no intention of abandoning Korea and that there should be no objection to stating it at an appropriate time.[22] By the middle of May, the Koreans had exhausted the negligible means at their disposal to make an appeal, and were left with resignation and the last-moment emotional expression of their feelings on the issue.

May 17 was an important date for Muccio's mission in Seoul concerning the troop withdrawal issue. The Koreans began to show their sense of resignation and acceptance of the inevitable, even though they still did not know the date of final departure for the American troops. Once more President Rhee reiterated what he wished to see as alternatives if the American troops had to leave soon. He favored a Pacific pact, or the conclusion of a mutual defense agreement between the United States and Korea alone or with other nations, or the reaffirmation by the U.S. government of the amity clause of the 1882 treaty. Muccio clearly perceived signs of resignation among the president and his cabinet members to the fact of the early troop withdrawal. On May 20, during a conversation with the president, the American ambassador and the defense minister, Foreign Minister Im Pyŏng-chik, who had spent many years in the United States and had just returned to take up the job, "flew into a rage" and "declared the United States sold China down the river and were pursuing the same course for Korea." One more event in May was a mass demonstration in Seoul against the early troop withdrawal, for which some fifty thousand people were mobilized, but it was orderly and did not cause much concern to anyone. Even after resignation set in, probably because of it, the Koreans' worry for the future of their nation's security did not diminish. All along, Muccio made efforts to calm the Koreans by telling them how strong the Republic of Korea Army was and that the North Korean Army would not take such a rash act as invading South Korea. The South Koreans knew full well the comparative strength of the two armies, and these words rang hollow to them. On the last day of May, Muccio reported to the State Department, "Clamor and fear aroused by troop withdrawal have far exceeded my expectation. It now appears a sense of crisis bordering on panic has enveloped higher circles of the Korean Government which has in turn spread to people at large." Perhaps the expression was somewhat exaggerated, but the Korean people's sense of disappointment, helplessness, and fear was real and widespread in the spring of 1949.[23]

It has been said that April is the cruelest month. But, for ordinary Koreans, June was a crueler month. The Korean War started in June 1950. June 1949 was another cruel month for the Koreans. Some fifty thousand gathered in Seoul stadium to appeal to the Americans to keep their troops a littler longer in their country. This should have been a gathering to celebrate the departure of occupation troops and a gesture of thanks for their work in securing the future of Korea. But it was not, and the crowd must have sensed that something had gone wrong for the South Korean cause.

The first few days of June were used by the American government to inform the American public about the evacuation of American troops from Korea. A week later, in another press release, the American government added the explanation that the troop withdrawal from Korea in no way indicated a "lessening of United States interest in the Republic of Korea." It is possible that some in the government officials actually believed the statement. During the first week of the month, Chough Pyŏng-ok, one of the representatives of the Republic of Korea at the annual U. N. General Assembly meeting at Lake Success, New York, made a useless last-minute effort to keep the American troops in Korea for one more year. While the public announcements were made in Washington and anxious people marched through the streets in Seoul, the final phase of the withdrawal operation was carried out quietly, and the long, troubled operation was finally completed on June 29, 1949. On the same day, the *New York Times* reported, "The last United States combat troops today left Korea—Asiatic hot spot in the cold war." The paper also reported on the same day heavy fighting between the North and South Korean troops on the Ongjin peninsula, south of the 38th parallel. One Korean newspaper expressed regret at not being able to give a farewell ceremony for the departing American troops.[24] Two days after the completion of the U.S. troop withdrawal, the Korean Military Advisory Group began its formal operation with an augmented five-hundred-person authorized force for the purpose of training and other military assistance for the ROK defense forces. Providing five-hundred military advisers and leaving behind equipment with a $56 million estimated value by the departing U.S. troops for the ROK military forces, however, did not substitute for the troop withdrawal.[25]

On February 20, 1948, Ambassador Douglas in London had reported, "Foreign Office has strong impression US will soon withdraw forces South Korea." It was a perceptive statement, because it was made a month and a half before the NSC 8 was drawn up in Washington. An even more perceptive statement followed: "Having drawn foregoing conclusion, it clear UK has 'written off' Korea as lost to Soviets." The British observer had equated the troop withdrawal with giving up—or "abandoning"—the Republic of Korea. Giving up on Korea meant losing it to the Soviet Union, or a Soviet takeover. It is doubtful whether the British were the only perceptive ones who could see clearly the implications and consequences of the troop withdrawal in 1948 and 1949. Later, a number of those who were involved in the policy-making process spoke about the meaning of the troop withdrawal. William H. Draper, the undersecretary of the army between 1947 and 1949, later told an interviewer, "That, I suppose, acted as an invitation, or at least it didn't prevent the possibility, of an invasion from the North." In the fall of 1952, presidential candidate Dwight D. Eisenhower said, "It was certainly no secret to the Soviets that we had withdrawn our troops and had left behind a South Korean army which any competent military man on the scene knew could not stop the force the Soviets had built in North Korea." It may be added that General Dwight D. Eisenhower was a member of the Joint Chiefs of Staff in the fall of 1947. In the following spring, he also expressed his view that if the United States had kept a "reasonable military stature" and had not had to withdraw its troops from Korea, the war would not have occurred. These statements are hindsights, which we wish had been expressed at the time, but they still are valuable reflections by eyewitnesses and hence judgments of an important historical event. Of course, the troop withdrawal was not the only cause of the war, but it was certainly one of the most important causes.[26]

At the policy level, the most important question is whether the early withdrawal was appropriate in view of the circumstances. To answer this question, two related factors need to be examined—money and the strategic orientation of the United States. The Truman administration experienced a post–World War II money crunch, and the defense budget, which affected the size of the army, had to be kept small. Political leadership was the crux of the problem. As Eisenhower later pointed out, the postwar reduction of the military went too far; the political leadership needed to persuade the American people of the necessity for a larger defense force and more taxes. In principle, it is true that national policy should be made within the range of available resources. However, it is also true that when there are certain critical national needs, the means need to be found rather than sacrificing the ends. A further question is whether the money saved by the troop withdrawal from Korea was significant. The answer seems to be in the negative; a small force of only 7,500 men was involved. Another important factor was the strategic orientation of the U.S. government for the execution of the containment policy. The expansionist communist forces were constantly looking for weak spots in the containment dike, and the block-and-gap approach of the United States naturally ran the risk of endangering the whole system. Because of the common cultural background, the American decision to put Europe first is understandable. However, when this tendency was pushed too far, neglecting certain critical spots in Asia and elsewhere in the world, the risk was great.[27]

Further, the military view of the strategic value of Korea had some problems. Essentially, Korea is a typical buffer state, and as General Wedemeyer's August 30, 1948 analysis of the advantages and disadvantages related to the troop withdrawal seem to indicate, a buffer state is always difficult to defend but rarely initiates an attack. As a result, the neighboring larger powers are not often tempted to absorb either the whole or even part of a buffer state. Nevertheless, such a power always wishes to deny the buffer state to its adversaries. In another words, it was logical for the United States to consider Korea hard to defend, but it did not want to see the Soviet occupation of the whole peninsula either. However, the United States did not seem to care much whether the Soviets took over the peninsula. Wedemeyer and other military strategists overlooked Korea as a buffer state and assigned too little strategic value to the peninsula. In contrast, the CIA had greater appreciation for the position of Korea as a buffer state than the military did, but its view does not seem to have played much of a role in the policy-making process. It seems that the military had too great an influence on the process of policy making in the troop withdrawal issue and that it viewed the issue from a narrowly technical perspective; civilians like Butterworth, Bishop, and Bond and the CIA leaders should have been allowed to speak up more loudly. More important, President Truman and Secretary Acheson needed greater vision and courage to eliminate early one big factor that helped cause the war.[28]

A few comments may be made with regard to the execution of the troop withdrawal policy within the context of diplomacy between the South Korean and U.S. governments. The diplomacy of the troop withdrawal seems to illustrate well the pattern of diplomacy between two friendly powers, one large and powerful and the other small and weak. The role of personality was another factor in the diplomatic exchanges. The American policy makers not only did not allow any "consultation" with any Korean leader, but they also completely withheld all information regarding the policy discussions until the very last moment. In a sense, there was no diplomacy in this case, if diplomacy is to be understood as a transaction between two equal sovereign nations. One side was simply declaring—sometimes explaining without any room for any compromise—its decisions and actions to the other side, which was simply accepting the declaration. Of course, there is a limit to this kind of one-sided diplomacy, and if the other power's cooperation is needed, it would not work. Fortunately, for the United States, the cooperation of the Koreans was almost unnecessary in this case. Another restraining factor is that even a powerful nation cannot escape the consequences of its actions, a fact not often realized until it is too late. The Korean government tried its best under the circumstances, even though there was not much to be done. President Rhee discovered quickly that the U.S. withdrawal policy was firm and that no ordinary talk would bring any result. He therefore tried a few extraordinary methods by going through other friendly powers and by using public opinion; he even protested through mass demonstrations. None of these methods worked; even worse, he angered Secretary Acheson. He had no choice but to confess resignation and accept the inevitable, even though he knew full well the meaning and consequences of the troop withdrawal. His tactic of pushing matters to the limit did not work with Acheson, even though it later worked to a certain extent with Eisenhower and Dulles.

NOTES

1. William Stueck, *The Road to Confrontation: American Policy toward China and Korea, 1947-1950* (Chapel Hill: University of North Carolina Press, 1981), pp. 152-153.

2. See Memorandum by the Director of the Office of Far Eastern Affairs (Butterworth) to the Undersecretary of State (Lovette), October 1, 1947, *Foreign Relations of the United States (FRUS), 1947*, 6: 820.

3. Memorandum by the Secretary of Defense (Forrestal) to the Secretary of State, September 26 [29], 1947, *FRUS, 1947*, 6: 818; XXIV Corps to CINCFE, January 6, 1948, Douglas MacArthur Memorial Archives (MacArthur Library), RG 9, box 154, blue binder.

4. CSGPO to CINCFE, January 16, 1948, MacArthur Library, WARX 82838, RG 9, box 149, blue binders; memorandum by the Assistant Chief of the Division of Northeast Asian Affairs (Bond), February 17, 1948, *FRUS, 1948*, 6: 1113; "Report by the National Security Council on the Position of the United States with respect to Korea," NSC 8, enclosure in a note by the Executive Secretary of the National Security Council (Souers) to President Truman, April 2, 1948, *FRUS, 1948*, 6: 1163-1169.

5. Lt. General A. C. Wedemeyer, Director of Plans and Operations, to the Secretary of Defense, August 30, 1948, National Archives (NA), RG 330, Defense Department, Office of the Administrative Secretary, Numerical File 1947–50, CD 6-2-41; CSGPO to CINCFE, March 21, 1948, MacArthur Library, WARX 98020, RG 9, box 148; Department of Army to CINCFE, April 25, 1948, ibid., WARX 80362.

6. The Secretary of State (Marshall) to the Secretary of the Army (Royall), June 23, 1948, *FRUS, 1948*, 6: 1225; the Secretary of the Army (Royall) to the Secretary of State (Marshall), June 23, 1948, ibid., p. 1226; the Undersecretary of State (Lovett) to the Secretary of the Army (Royall), July 8, 1948, ibid., p. 1235; report by the State Army Ad Hoc Committee on Korea, June 29, 1948, NA, RG 59, Decimal File 1945–49, box 3828.

7. Memorandum from Allison and Bond to Butterworth, August 8, 1948, NA, RG 9, Numerical File 740.00119 control (Korea)/8–648; Muccio to the Secretary of State, August 14, 1948, ibid., 8–1448; memorandum by the Director of the Office of Far Eastern Affairs (Butterworth), August 17, 1948, *FRUS, 1948*, 6: 1276–1279; Lt. General A. C. Wedemeyer to the Secretary of Defense, August 30, 1948, NA, RG 330, Defense Department, Office of the Administrative Secretary, Numerical File 1947–50, CD 6-2-41; CINCFE to the Department of the Army, January 13, 1948, MacArthur Library, CX 67025, RG 9, box 64; Draper to Royall, March 30, 1948, ibid., box 146, blue binders; the Assistant Secretary for Occupied Areas (Saltzman) to the Secretary of State, September 8, 1948, *FRUS, 1948*, 6: 1299.

8. The Chargé in the Soviet Union (Kohler) to the Secretary of State, Sept 19, 1948, *FRUS, 1948*, 6: 1306; The Secretary of State to the U.S. Embassy in Moscow, September 27, 1948, NA, RG 59, Decimal File 1945–49, 740.00119 control (Korea)/9–2748; *Department of State Bulletin* 19 (October 10, 1948): 456; the Acting Secretary of State to Muccio, September 20, 1948, *FRUS, 1948*, 6: 1307; Muccio to the Secretary of State, September 20, 1948, ibid., p. 1307; *Seoul Sinmun*, September 21, 1: 4–7; ibid., October 9, 1: 4–5; *Chosŏn Ilbo*, October 14, 1948, 1: 1–5.

9. The Secretary of State to the Embassy in Seoul, September 22, 1948, NA, RG 59, Decimal File 1945–49, box 3828. See also the Secretary of State to the Embassy in Seoul, September 24, 1948, NA, RG 59, Numerical File 740.00119 control (Korea)/9–2448; *New York Times*, September 24, 1948, 24: 1–2.

10. Memorandum by the Director of the Office of United Nations Affairs (Rusk) to the Secretary of State and Undersecretary of State, September 10, 1948, *FRUS, 1948*, 6: 1299; United States Delegation position paper, October 22, 1948, ibid., p. 1315; Marshall to the Department of State, October 27, 1948, NA, RG 59, 501.BB Korea/10–2748; draft resolution on Korea for the U.N. General Assembly, the Secretary of State to the Acting Secretary of State, November 16, 1948, *FRUS, 1948*, 6: 1321–1323.

11. Marshall to the Department of State, October 27, 1948, NA, RG 59, 501.BB Korea/10–2748; CG EUSAK to Department of the Army, October 30, 1948, MacArthur Library, RG 9, box 149, blue binders; Muccio to the Secretary of State, November 9, 1948, *FRUS, 1948*, 6: 1323; the Assistant Secretary for Occupied Areas (Saltzman) to the Director of Plans and Operations, Department of the Army (Wedemeyer), November 9, 1948, ibid., p. 1324; Muccio to the Secretary of State, November 12, 1948, ibid., p. 1326; Muccio to the Secretary of State, November 19, 1948, NA, RG 59, Decimal File 1945–49, box 3829.

12. The Secretary of State to the Acting Secretary of State, November 16, 1948, *FRUS, 1948*, 6: 1327; the Secretary of State to the Acting Secretary of State, No-

vember 18, 1948, NA, RG 59, 501.BB Korea/11-1848; the Secretary of State to Muccio, November 27, 1948, NA, RG 59, Decimal File 1945-49, box 2111; the Acting U.S. Representative at the United Nations (Dulles) to the Secretary of State, December 12, 1948, *FRUS, 1948*, 6: 1336; *Department of State Bulletin* 19 (December 19, 1948): 760.

13. CSGPO to CINCFE, November 16, 1948, MacArthur Library, RG 9, box 149, blue binders.

14. Muccio to the Secretary of State, November 19, 1948, *FRUS, 1948*, 6: 1331-1332; *New York Times*, November 20, 1948, 4: 8; ibid., November 21, 1948, 30: 1-2; ibid., November 24, 1948, 3: 5; Muccio to the Secretary of State, November 23, 1948, NA, RG 59, Decimal File 1945-49, box 3829; *Seoul Sinmun*, November 21, 1948, no. 1: 1-5; ibid., November 22, 1948, no. 1: 1-2; Ibid., November 25, 1948, no. 1: 1-2; Muccio to the Secretary of State, November 27, 1948, NA, RG 59, Decimal File 1945-49, box 3829/740.00119 control (Korea)/11-2748.

15. CINCFE to DA, December 20, 1948, MacArthur Library, RG 9, box 64, blue binders.

16. The Undersecretary of State of the Army (Draper) to the Assistant Secretary of State for Occupied Areas (Saltzman), December 2 , 1948, *FRUS, 1948*, 6; 1343; DA to CINCFE, December 22, 1948, MacArthur Library, RG 9, box 154, blue binders; *New York Times*, December 29, 1948, 1: 7; *Seoul Sinmun*, December 30, 1948, no. 1: 1-3; The Secretary of the Army to the Secretary of State, January 25, 1949, *FRUS, 1949*, 7: 945; memorandum of conversation by the Secretary of the Army (Royall), February 8, 1949, *FRUS, 1949*, 7: 958.

17. The Assistant Secretary of State for Occupied Areas (Saltzman) to the Director of the Plans and Operations (Wedemeyer), November 9, 1948, *FRUS, 1948*, 6: 1324; the Special Representative in Korea (Muccio) to the Secretary of State, November 12, 1948, ibid., 1325-1327; memorandum by the Chief of the Division of Northeast Asian Affairs (Bishop) to the Director of the Office of Far Eastern Affairs (Butterworth), December 17, 1948, *FRUS, 1948*, 6: 1337-1340; memorandum by the Director of the Office of the Far Eastern Affairs (Butterworth) to the Secretary of State, January 10, 1949, *FRUS, 1949*, 7: 942-943; memorandum of conversation by the Secretary of the Army (Royall) with Rhee, Royall, and Muccio, February 8, 1949, *FRUS, 1949*, 7: 956-958; memorandum of conversation by the Special Representative in Korea (Muccio), February 25, 1949, ibid., pp. 958-959.

18. "Consequences of U.S. Troop Withdrawal from Korea in Spring, 1949," ORE 3-49, Truman Library, Intelligence File, box 256; "Dissent by the Intelligence Division, Department of the Army," Enclosure A in "Consequences of Troop Withdrawal from Korea in Spring, 1949," NA, RG 319, Assistant Chief of Staff, G-3, Decimal File 1949-50, P & O 350.05 T. S. F/W.11.

19. NSC 8, enclosure in a note by the Executive Secretary of the National Security Council (Souers) to President Truman, April 2, 1948, *FRUS, 1948*, 6: 1163-1169; NSC 8/2, report by the National Security Council to the President, March 2, 1949, *FRUS, 1949*, 7: 969-978.

20. Memorandum of conversation by Muccio with Rhee and Drumright, April 4, 1949, National Archives, RG 59, Decimal File 1945-49, box 3829; Muccio to the Secretary of State, April 9, 1949, *FRUS, 1949*, 7: 981; memorandum of conversation by Muccio with Rhee, April 11, 1949, NA, RG 59, Decimal File 1945-49, box 3829; Muccio to the Secretary of State, April 12, 1949, *FRUS, 1949*, 7: 986.

21. Draft letter from the President of the Republic of Korea (Rhee) to the Special Representative in Korea (Muccio), April 14, 1949, enclosure in Muccio to Rhee,

April 14, 1949, *FRUS, 1949*, 7: 990–991; Muccio to the Secretary of State, April 14, 1949, ibid., 988; the Secretary of State to the American Mission in Korea, April 15, 1949, ibid., 992; Muccio to the Secretary of State, April 16, 1949, NA, RG 59, Decimal File 1945–49, 711.952/4–1649; Muccio to the Secretary of State, April 17, 1949, NA, RG 59, 501.BB Korea/4–1849; *Sichŏng Wŏlpo* 5 (September 15, 1949): 55; memorandum by Butterworth to the Secretary of State, April 18, 1949, *FRUS, 1949*, 7: 992; Muccio to the Secretary of State, April 22, 1949, ibid., p. 994; *Jayu Sinmun*, April 20, 1949, 1: 1–5; *Donga Ilbo*, April 21, 1949, 1: 1–6.

22. The U.S. Representative at the United Nations (Austin) to the Secretary of State, May 4, 1949, *FRUS, 1949*, 7: 1006; the Secretary of State to Austin, May 5, 1949, ibid., p. 1008; Muccio to the Secretary of State, May 7, 1949, ibid., 1011–1102; *New York Times*, May 7, 1949, 4: 6; *Jayu Sinmun*, May 8, 1949, 1: 2–5; Muccio to the Secretary of State, May 9, 12, 1949, *FRUS, 1949*, 7: 1013–1014, 1021; Muccio to the Secretary of State, May 17, 1949, RG 59, Decimal File 1945–49, 740.00119 control (Korea); memorandum of conversation by Butterworth with Chough Pyŏng-ok and Chang Myŏn, May 11, 1949, ibid., p. 1020.

23. Muccio to the Secretary of State, May 17, 20, 26, 31, 1949, *FRUS, 1949*, 7: 1029, 1034–1035.

24. The Acting Secretary of State (Webb) to Muccio, June 1, 1949, NA, RG 59, Decimal File 1945–49, box 3829; *Department of State Bulletin* 20 (June 19, 1949): 781; Muccio to the Secretary of State, June 11, July 1, 1949, NA, RG 59, 740.00119 control (Korea)/6–1449, 7–149; the Acting U.S. Representative at the United Nations (Ross) to the Secretary of State, June 1, 1949, *FRUS, 1949*, 7: 1036; Muccio to the Secretary of State, June 6, 1949, ibid., p. 1039; *New York Times*, June 29, 1949, 1: 2–3; ibid., 11: 3; *Chosŏn Sinmun*, July 1, 1949, 1: 1–6.

25. See Muccio to the Secretary of State, June 11, 1949, *FRUS, 1949*, part 2, p. 1041, note 1. See also NSC 8/2, ibid., p. 977; the Secretary of State to the American Mission in Korea, April 5, 1949, ibid., p. 980; Muccio to the Secretary of State, June 24, 1949, ibid., pp. 1044–1045; Truman to Rhee, September 26, 1949, ibid., pp. 1084–1085.

26. Ambassador in the United Kingdom (Douglas) to the Secretary of State, *FRUS, 1948*, 6: 1121; William H. Draper, Truman Library, oral history interview transcript, p. 76; Shipley to C. D. Jackson, Eisenhower Library, Ann Whitman File, Campaign Series, box 7. See also Walter H. Judd, Truman Library, oral history interview transcript, pp. 41–42; Stueck, *The Road to Confrontation*, p. 105.

27. Minutes of the fourth meeting of the U.S. Delegation to the U.N. Assembly, September 21, 1950, *FRUS, 1950*, 7: 743–747.

28. Wedemeyer to the Secretary of Defense, August 30, 1948, NA, RG 330, Office of Administrative Secretary, Defense Department, Numerical File 1947–50, CD 6-2-41; John L. Gaddis, "The Strategic Perimeter: The Rise and Fall of the Defense Perimeter Concept," in *Uncertain Years: Chinese–American Relations, 1947–50*, ed. Dorothy Borg and Waldo Heinrich (New York: Columbia University Press, 1960), p. 105; Stueck, *The Road to Confrontation*, p. 154. For a discussion on Korea as a buffer state see Jongsuk Chay and Thomas E. Ross, eds., *Buffer States in World Politics* (Boulder, Colo.: Westview Press, 1987), pp. 191–212.

CHAPTER 7

Economic and Military Aid

Fortunately, despite the fact that the troop withdrawal was by far the most important event for Korean–American relations prior to the outbreak of the Korean War, it was not the only nor was it an isolated event. The U.S. government took a more positive and somewhat compensatory action by providing economic and military aid for the Republic of Korea. Some on the American and the Korean sides hoped that these remedial actions would work out and reduce the "bad effect" of the American military retreat. But they did not, and the consequences were grave. A number of questions may thus be raised concerning the subsquent economic and military aid: Was the aid really necessary? What were the reasons and goals of the aid program and how were aid policies formulated ? How were they carried out? What were the Korean reactions to the aid? Finally, what was its impact upon the coming major event—the war?

The condition of the Korean economy and finances can be approached from both the actual situation and American perceptions of the situation. After nearly a half century of Japanese colonial economic policy, eight years of wartime, and the three-year American occupation, the Korean economy in the late 1940s was anything but normal. Under Japanese domination, it was structured to serve the Japanese colonial economic policy by supplying food and raw material and by absorbing Japanese industrial products. The eight-year war distorted the Korean economic structure even more. When the liberation came, the departure of Japanese technicians and managers, who had occupied most of the key positions of Korean industry and other economic institutions, pushed the distorted economy into a state of chaos. Even more disastrous for the post–World War II Korean economy was the division of the peninsula at the 38th parallel, which caused the separation of the agricultural south from the industrial north. The south lost its sources of industrial products including fertilizer and hydroelectric power and a market for its agricultural goods. The suffering of the south from electric power shortages after 1948 was severe. The American military government spent a sizable amount of money and resources during the occupation period (a little over $200 million by the end of 1948), but its efforts concentrated on preventing hunger and disease, and the concern did not go beyond providing relief. At the end of the summer of 1948, only 30 percent of the factories in the south were in operation, and rehabilitation of the rest of the industry was necessary. Even though the food situation was improving, increasing the supply of fertilizer, practically all of which had been produced by the factories now in the north, was also necessary. In May 1948, when the north cut off all electrical power for political reasons, the south lost an important source of power, and the construction of electric power generating facilities was also now needed.[1]

Foreign trade and the state of the national finances were sectors needing even greater concern and assistance. South Korea urgently needed certain key items and they had to be brought in from the outside; these, which included food products, fertilizer, coal, and petroleum, occupied about 45 percent of total imports during 1948. Fortunately, the need for the importation of food products decreased drastically after 1948, but other items remained on a critical-need list. On the other hand, Korea at this point did not have much to export, with marine products being the main export item. Not surprisingly, the result was a major trade deficit; the ratio between imports and exports in 1948 was 11 to 1. In the following year, the gap decreased to 10 to 1, but it was still too large and most of it (87 percent for 1948) was filled by American aid. The fiscal and financial condition was likewise very serious. National security and other needs demanded a large budget from the new government, but mainly because of the relatively small tax collection, the revenue was extremely small, leaving a large gap to be filled either by overdrawing money from the Bank of Korea, which in turn created a serious inflationary spiral, or by outside help.[2]

The American perception of the Korean economic situation in the late 1940s was even more bleak. In early 1948, Major General Charles G. Helmick, the deputy military governor in South Korea, made a forecast about conditions in Korea to the State Department. Upon withdrawal of the U.S. occupation forces and the cessation of present supplies of coal from Japan, as well as food, oil, and gasoline from the United States, he argued, the South Korean transportation system would cease to function within a week or ten days; within two months, South Korea would be reduced to a "bull cart" economy; and some nine million nonfood producers would face starvation. Early in November of the same year, Glenn G. Wolfe, who had just completed a special survey mission in South Korea reported, "In terms of our Western technological civilization Korea is an impoverished nation. Sanitary conditions are less than rudimentary. Prevalence of disease is high, and transportation facilities within Seoul are non-existent for purposes of American personnel use."[3] There was some exaggeration here, but this was the condition of the Korea in 1948 as perceived by two serious American observers. Conditions were indeed serious. The problem the Republic of Korea faced in this early period was how to restore quickly what it had at the time of the liberation and then to move on to build an economic basis to fight the Cold War. Essentially, it was a problem of rehabilitation and reconstruction, and because of the ongoing fierce engagements of the Cold War, the problem had to be solved fast. For this large and urgent task, however, Korea did not have the necessary resources, and assistance was imperative.[4]

An accurate assessment of economic conditions in Korea at this time requires caution. It had the strength of a backward economy. The Korean economy in the late 1940s was probably close to what the United States had in its federalist or early republican period, an economy suitable for 150 years ago, and it was predominantly agricultural with some small-scale consumer industries. Like any similar economy, the Korean agrarian economy in the late 1940s had a basic toughness and a will to survive. As some American Embassy staff members who had traveled in the countryside observed, the people on the farms were surprisingly well fed and clothed and supplied with other items they produced on their land. These people were self-sufficient, and they were able to survive under very adverse conditions. Unfortunately, the land reform, which had just begun before the outbreak of the Korean War, was not carried out until after the war, but the tenant farmers in South Korea had a much better situation during this period with lowered rate of land rent. Furthermore, a good number of farmers became the owners of the land formerly held by the Japanese.[5] The problem concerned the urban population, and the collection of rice and rationing was needed mainly for them. The point is that, while there were severe industrial, commercial, and financial problems, the Korean economy was not about to collapse in two or three months without outside aid, as was repeatedly stated. Indeed, some authors argue that it would have been better if the Koreans had moved slowly and gradually to build their economy without reliance upon outside assistance, but an important factor that cannot be neglected here was the pressure coming from the Cold War. Unless South Korea moved quickly to rehabilitate and reconstruct its economy and then to build the stable and sound economy necessary to support a large security force, it would be taken over by the communist north. This pressure from the Cold War was a powerful factor favoring the reception and almost certainly favoring the giving of economic aid. Thus, for the Republic of Korea a speedy recovery and the rapid construction of a stable economy was a necessity. To meet the time pressure imposed by the Cold War, outside assistance was a necessity, not the luxury of choice.[6]

On the policy-making level, the task on the Korean side was simple, because it was not a matter of choice but necessity. From the very beginning of the new government, one of its most important national policies was to continue to receive American economic aid. As with the case of the withdrawal of the troops, some liked to use the word "withdrawal" in discussing economic aid, and this word accurately describes Korean thinking. Economic aid was a matter of necessity; consequently, its discontinuation amounted to a withdrawal. If receiving the economic aid in this case was a necessity, the giving was not, and in this sense, the matter was asymmetrical and a source of the problem. For the American government, economic aid was a matter of choice, and to give or not to give it to the Koreans at this point was a matter that caused much debate within and between the executive and legislative branches between 1948 and 1950.[7]

Because the NSC 8 series contains the most fundamental and comprehensive U.S. policy statement with regard to Korea, we have to return to it to ascertain the U.S. policy for economic aid for South Korea. NSC 8, which received presidential approval on April 8, 1948, is significant because it reveals American ideals, perceptions of the realities in Korea, choices for the U.S. government, and future plans for U.S. economic aid. The analysis started with the "broad objectives" of U.S. policy in Korea, and one of the three objectives was to "assist the Korean people in establishing a sound economy." The current situation in Korea was perceived to be so much dependent upon the importation of necessary commodities like coal and food items that the Korean economy would collapse within a matter of weeks after the termination of U.S. aid. It also revealed that if the requested appropriation was approved, then a total of $185 million would be available for Korea for the fiscal year 1949. The analysis also prescribed, as part of the middle course which was recommended, the extension of economic aid to Korea to forestall an economic breakdown, with a possibility of continuing the aid after the troop withdrawal. Even though U.S. policy at this point was still not quite clear about aid in the posttroop withdrawal years, continuation of the relief and rehabilitation aid program until June 1949 was certain. Also to be noted is the connection between economic aid and the troop withdrawal and an American ideal in U.S. foreign policy. The very first item of the conclusion read, "It should be the effort of the US Government through all proper means to effect a settlement of the Korean problem which would enable the U.S. to withdraw from Korea as soon as possible with the minimum of bad effects." The continuation of economic aid was part of the "means" for the "derivative objective" of the troop withdrawal. Along with all of the practical aspects of the national policy set out in this document, a remarkable part of this policy statement is that it has an ideal aspect, which was one of three "broad objectives" "to assist the Korean people in establishing a sound economy and educational system as essential bases of an independent and democratic state."[8]

Since the economic aid was needed by Korea, it was logical for the Korean government to initiate formal action for the continuation of aid after the republic was born. On September 1, 1948, two weeks after the establishment of the new republic, President Rhee wrote to President Truman asking for the continuation of the program for "economic rehabilitation and security." Rhee's letter was received in Washington on September 14, and President Truman responded promptly to the request by writing on September 21 that his government had given favorable consideration "to the continuance of U.S. aid and assistance" to Korea. Beside these formal actions at the level of the heads of state, there is no doubt that much contemplation had taken place on both sides of the Pacific Ocean. Even before the September 1 letter, a presidential instruction·for the ECA to take over the army's economic aid program on the first day of the following year had been issued, and Assistant Secretary of State Saltzman sketched on September 7 the choices facing the U.S. government regarding economic aid for the Republic of Korea. After explaining in detail the four choices, which ranged between termination of the relief program at the end of FY 1949 and a three and one-half year relief and economic development program, Saltzman concluded that American interests would be served best by planning a grant program of relief and economic development of several years duration, which included immediate expenditures for the most essential capital equipment and which was calculated to place the Republic of Korea on a self-supporting basis as rapidly as possible. The total price tag was set at $410 million, with an initial expenditure of $180 million. Saltzman emphatically pointed out that the long-term program was laid out only for planning purposes and that each annual program would stand on its own, with a periodical evaluation for its continuation. He also clearly pointed out in his memorandum that in the long run, a long-term plan would be most economical for the United States, because at the end of the three-year period Korea would be close to self-supporting. The State Department plan in the fall of 1948 was not only rational but also idealistic, and if it had been carried out, the Korean situation in the following years would have been considerably different. But unfortunately for both Korea and the United States, the plan had to go through a long struggle, and the result was probably realistic but not rational.[9]

After ten days of deliberation within the department, Secretary of State Marshall communicated to ECA Director Hoffman on September 17 the department's preferred three and one-half year plan, a plan that combined rehabilitation with economic development, and requested him to prepare a proposal for presentation to Congress. Two weeks later, Hoffman thanked Marshall for his policy guidance and submitted a budget proposal for an aid program to begin in FY 1950. The loss of half a year resulted from the time needed to implement the proposal. Soon, in early October, negotiations began between the representatives of the ROK and U.S. governments to draft guidelines for economic aid. After two-months work an agreement was signed in Seoul on December 10. The nine-point so-called "Dodge line" in the second article, which listed the measures the Korean government would undertake to strengthen and stabilize the economy in Korea, included maintenance of a balanced budget, controls over the issuance of currency, regulation of all foreign exchange transactions, establishment of foreign exchange, control of food prices, facilitation of private foreign investment, and the development of export industries.[10] Thus, by the end of 1949, the State Department had come forward with the best-possible economic aid program for Korea and a formal framework for execution of the program in Korea was established.

The first five months of 1949 were spent preparing the ECA's proposal for Korean economic aid, the proposed FY 1950, for presentation to the Congress. Otherwise, nothing was done during this period, and precious time was wasted. During this period, the reports that came from Korea on the economic condition continued to be bad. Late in January of the year, Muccio stated that even though the short-term view was not hopeless, the long-term view for rehabilitation and economic development was "as bleak as ever." Two months later, Counselor Drumright warned Washington that Korea's current progress and future health were dependent in large part on continuing U.S. aid, without which the Korean government would almost certainly collapse. Through its representative in Washington, the Korean government appealed to the U.S. government for urgent economic aid. And, during the first half of the year, the ECA continued in Korea the army-type economic aid program, mainly relief with some rehabilitation with the funds from the army.[11]

The executive branch's challenge began in early June when President Truman's message to the Congress called for an appropriation of $150 million for the fiscal year ending June 30, 1950. He persuasively argued that the current bare-bones relief effort would be more costly for the United States in the long run, but that the proposed recovery program would make Korea self-sufficient and less costly for the United States. He also pointed out that Korea had become a testing ground, and that the survival and progress of the republic toward having a self-supporting and stable economy would have an intense and far-reaching effect on the people of Asia. The next day, Acting Secretary of State James E. Webb and ECA Director Hoffman also persuasively argued the case for Korean assistance before the House Foreign Affairs Committee. The key points of their argument were that the program would be the most economical, that the republic was an outpost against communism, and that Korea was also a symbol for the Asian people. Hoffman's presentation contained some technical details, pointing out that the proposed FY 1950 aid program would have a capital development portion designed to increase production of coal, thermal power, fertilizer, which would cost about $32 million or about 20 percent of the program, and that the three-year program would cost somewhere between $350 million and $385 million. Acheson made a short but forceful statement before the same committee: The United States could not possibly guarantee South Korean protection with American military power, but the United States could and should provide economic aid along with military aid so that the republic would be able to defend itself against North Korea. He also pointed out that there was no assurance the program would be successful, but there was complete assurance that Korea would survive for the next two or three months with the aid. George Kennan also argued that the long-term aid program would be a good idea.[12]

Even though the House Committee for Foreign Affairs approved the Korean aid bill, some committee members expressed the view that the program would be "too little and too late," and it might be wiser for the United States to wait a while and let "the dust settle on Korea" before spending more of the taxpayers' money. Some members of the House thought it was utterly preposterous to combine the troop withdrawal with award of $150 million and tossing in a few more million dollars after abandoning Korea, an action which would make Korea only a richer prize for the communists. These words were an ominous sign, and the House of Representatives did nothing further for or against Korea until the following year. However, the Senate approved on October 12 Senate Bill 2319 with an appropriation of $150 million for FY 1950 after hearing mostly positive views like Senator Tom Connally's reference to Korea as an anticommunist "bastion," Senator William Knowland's concern about the effect of this aid for the Koreans in Japan and the Philippines, and Senator Henry Cabot Lodge's reference to the matter of faith. Because of the lack of legislative action to appropriate aid money for Korea for FY 1950, the ECA managed to continue until February 15 of the following year the army-type relief and rehabilitation program for Korea with two temporary appropriations which totaled $60 million. The handling of the economic aid issue for Korea by the U.S. government drew a good amount of attention from the press, both in Korea and the United States.[13]

January 19, 1950 was a momentous date for the Korean aid legislation in the U.S. Congress. When the House finally took up the delayed Korean aid bill, groups for and against the bill eloquently poured out their views on the issue. Representatives Maurice G. Burnside (D, W.V.), Harley Orrin Staggers (D, W.V.), Walter Henry Judd (R, Minn.), and Abraham A. Ribicoff (D, Conn.) stood on high moral ground with words like "moral obligation," "commitment," "responsibilities," "American honor," and "good name"; representatives William P. Bolton (D, Md.), John W. McCormick (D, Mass.), and Fred L. Crawford (R, Mich.) demonstrated recognition of the value of the Korean peninsula by using words like "the last foothold," "toe hold," and "the second triangle" of Aleutian–Philippines–Korea. The opposite group—Representatives Christian A. Herter (R, Mass.), John M. Vorys (R, Ohio), Donald L. Jackson (R, Calif.), and William Lemke (R, N.D.)—argued, employing words like "piecemeal palliative," "no strategic value," "indefensible," "no commitment," and "rat hole," and saying that spending money for Korea was pouring money into a "rat hole" without any strategic value. When the House counted hands after a long and heated debate, the $150 million Korean aid bill HR 5330 was defeated by 193 votes to 191. It is true that many political factors were involved in this foreign policy issue, and the Republicans, who were angry about the State Department's China policy, barely defeated the bill with the help of conservative Southern Democrats. But, other factors, like the ambiguous strategic value of Korea, the need to save money, and the military and economic relationship between the troop withdrawal and economic aid, contributed to the defeat.[14] It was a contest between the "toe hold" and the "rat hole" schools and a struggle between notions of "moral responsibility" and "no commitment."

Apparently the State Department had expected the economic aid for Korea to be passed by Congress. With "concern and dismay," it received the news of the defeat, according to Secretary Acheson. President Truman also received the news with "regret" and agreed with Acheson about the seriousness of the situation. Even for some congressmen, it was an "unexpected defeat" and a "shock." And even though the decision to give or not to give aid belonged to the Americans, the defeat certainly affected the Koreans most. Although greatly disappointed, they reacted calmly. President Rhee expressed his confidence that upon reflection the U.S. Congress and government would not fail to extend aid to Korea. Butterworth expressed pleasure at the soundness of President Rhee's reaction, and Acheson even thanked him for his temperate statement. These reactions and reactions to the reactions are rather interesting. It seems that the leaders of the executive branch in Washington were a little too optimistic about the aid bill's prospects, and that President Rhee and his assistants grasped more realistically the situation in Washington. Some expressed the curious view that the defeat in the House would have a "salutary effect" on President Rhee. The press was loud and critical in reporting and commenting on the event. The *New York Times* called the action in the House "a blunder" and "something of a legislative fluke" to be rectified. It said that the Republican critics of the administration's policy in China were decisive in bringing about the defeat and the so-called "rat hole" view was also a contributing factor. The Korean papers also loudly expressed their disappointment.[15]

The democratic leadership in the administration and Congress took seriously the setback and the republican challenge and acted promptly and effectively to mobilize their supporters in the Congress. This time they were successful, but the appropriation was reduced by $30 million from the original request of $150 million to $120 million for FY 1950. The $60 million in aid for Korea for the remainder of FY 1950, for the period between February 15 and June 30, 1950, was "sugar coated" by combining it with similar aid for the Nationalist Chinese government in Taiwan, and it went hurriedly through the House and Senate on February 9 and 10. The difference between the original and the revised economic aid program for Korea was not just the amount of money, as was pointed out by the House Committee on Foreign Affairs in its February 1, 1950 report, but there were also differences in the nature of the aid as well. A recovery program pared down too drastically would become a relief program. Moreover, as the Korean aid program was delayed in time, the effects of the delay also fell upon the recovery portion of the program. The key to the aid program was the three-year recovery plan that called for building fertilizer plants in 1950, power-generating facilities in 1951, and coal-mining facilities in the following and the last year. The attempt to save a relatively small amount of money—about 25 percent during the first year—defeated the whole purpose of building an anticommunist nation in Asia that would be economically sound and politically stable. The House apparently did not mind seeing a continuation of the limited economic aid program in Korea, and it approved during the following month $100 million for FY 1951. The Senate, after some debate, also approved two months later on May 27 the same amount for the program in Korea. The bill was signed by the president on June 5, three weeks before the outbreak of the war.[16]

For the Koreans in the spring of 1950, there was not much they could do to ensure continuation of American economic aid except making an appeal for the aid and thanking the Americans when the positive decision was made. President Rhee appealed through Ambassador Chang Myŏn in Washington for continuation of the aid, and he repeatedly showed his concern through the spring of the year. The National Assembly made an appeal to the American government right after the defeat of the House bill for reconsideration of the aid program. In late March, the chairman of the National Assembly made a special trip to Washington to thank the Americans for the approval of the revised aid bill in Congress. From the very beginning, the Koreans were clear about the reason for the economic aid and its character: Division of the peninsula had crippled the already distorted Korean economy in 1945, and recovery was a necessity. Some Americans agreed with the Koreans and saw the same necessity in Korea, but unfortunately that view did not prevail in Congress. The press continued to report diligently the process of the legislative actions for Korean economic aid. On May 7, 1950, the *New York Times* commented editorially that the assistance approved in Congress was a "moral must." "We have made a commitment in respect to the young republic that we cannot in honor evade or ignore," the comment continued. Late in March, *Seoul Sinmun*, one of the major papers in Korea, stated that the United States was one of the two powers that had created the division at the 38th parallel and that it therefore was responsible for active economic aid for Korea.[17]

Charles Dobbs reflected some three decades later on the U.S. decision in the spring of 1950 to continue economic aid to the Republic of Korea, saying that the origins of the American involvement in the Korean War were made in January and February 1950. The origins of the Korean War cannot be attributed to a single cause, and some go back well before 1950, but the point that the economic aid issue was significant is well made. An even more important point to be made regarding the subject is that it was a halfway measure. It should have been either all or nothing. Some republican congressmen—perhaps not a small number—thought that Korea had already been abandoned, and they did not want to see an additional waste of money. If the original program with the recovery part had been carried out, as Acheson and others wished, South Korea would have at least had some chance of avoiding the coming calamity. Moreover, the problem was not just the scale and nature of the aid; the time factor was important. By the spring of 1950, too much time had been lost, and as some congressmen thought, it was already too late. One more important point to be added concerns the psychological impact of the process and the defeat of the legislative action for Korean aid. The South Koreans might be ignored as helpless people on the receiving end of American largesse, but others who were watching the process, especially the North Koreans, certainly could not be so easily ignored.[18]

If the economic aid issue was important but not handled correctly, why did it happen? At least six points need to be clarified: (1) the scale and schedule of the aid, (2) the choice of a middle road, (3) the connection between aid and strategic considerations, (4) the issue of moral obligation, (5) the relationship between economic and military considerations, and (6) the cultural factor. Some Republicans sincerely thought they did not have a right to waste taxpayer's money for a hopeless project. We know now hindsight is one of the strengths of history and that when one of the congressmen said that his opponents were "penny-wise and dollar foolish," he was right. The loss of time was also serious, and it seems to have come about because of procedural negligence. The administration lost nine months between September 1948 and June 1949, while the House caused the loss of the other half in the fall and winter of 1949–1950. There is always a great inclination to take the middle road in the policy-making process—the road some call "a bureaucratic middle"—especially when the choice is a difficult one. But it is always possible that the middle-of-the-road approach is inadequate for the job or that it will result in much waste. Often this approach is chosen for sheer convenience and lack of decisiveness. One of the most controversial points in the discussion of Korean aid was the value of Korea for the United States. One group of representatives stood firm on the same ground as the military and claimed that the peninsula had no strategic value whatsoever; the other group thought that the peninsula was one of the last "toe holds" and that it should not be given up to the enemy. This debate might have been between the military value and the political—or symbolic—value of the peninsula. If such was the case, the consideration of ends and means comes in. An adjustment was needed between the two, instead of sacrificing the ends for the sake of the means. If it was a pure military and strategic issue, then the military view probably had some room for a reexamination. Many congressmen—the so-called "rat hole" school—showed their concern about the separation of military and economic factors in Korea and pointed out that there was no point in pouring money into the "rat hole" if the United States intended to withdraw its troops and leave the nation defenseless. If not all of them, at least some of them were serious about their assertion, and the argument had a firm logical basis and should not have been neglected, at least for purposes of clarification. The debate over Korean aid seems to have been a classic struggle between idealism and realism. Some thought the Americans had made a moral commitment and had a moral obligation to Korea because of the division of the peninsula and because the United States sponsored the birth of the half-Korean state in the south; others insisted there was no promise, no commitment, and no obligation to the Koreans. The real world has room for both idealism and realism and much more besides. Neglect of the moral aspects of the issue by many congressmen was one of the serious problems in this case. As Truman made clear in his June 1949 letter to the congressmen and some others, economic aid for Korea had some common characteristics with the Marshall Plan in Europe. There was no doubt that Europe was much closer to the hearts of most Americans, an emotional factor difficult to confront, but if a nation neglects some other areas of the world for cultural reasons, it still cannot escape the consequences. In addition, it should be pointed out that the administration mismanaged the process by misjudging the magnitude of the feeling of the Republicans in the House regarding the U.S. policy in China. If the Truman administration had acted much more carefully and actively mobilized the force of the Democratic Party in the House, which alone was adequate to pass the original aid bill, the January 19 defeat could have been avoided.

Economic aid was certainly important; however, even more important was the issue of military aid, for it was directly connected with the security of a nation. It was also aid that was given by one nation to another, and that gave it common characteristics with economic aid. The relationship between two nations, one as a giver and the other as a receiver, was very similar. The giver could decide to give or not to give, and the only thing the receiver could do was to explain why the aid was needed and make an appeal to the giver, or beg. As usual, even though the very existence of their nation was involved in the matter, the Koreans could not play much of a role in the decision process. At the center of the policy-making process were the U.S. Army and State Departments, and the State had a handicap as it had in the troop withdrawal case, because the aid was of a military nature, and the experts were supposed to have more weight. An important question concerns, as was the case of economic aid, the nature and magnitude of the U.S. military aid that was needed to deter war in South Korea. Further, what did the two governments do, or fail to do, to meet the challenge?

The North Korean challenge increased steadily through 1948 and 1949 and increased abruptly in the spring of 1950, and information about it was collected by both the Korean and American intelligence agencies. The South Korean government naturally felt keenly the threat from the north, and it made every possible attempt to respond by increasing its military capabilities to meet this challenge. Because of its technological and economic weakness, the South Korean government had no other choice than to turn to the American government for assistance. The role of the Soviet Union in the North Korean military build-up was a well-known fact, and this was more than enough of an excuse for the South Korean government to expect the same role from the American government in their endeavor to meet the challenge. The American government, however, did not feel so keenly as the South Korean government about the threat from North Korea, and it responded slowly and reluctantly. The different postures of the two governments in responding to the challenge presented by the North Korean and Soviet governments naturally created some friction and much unpleasantness between the two governments through these years, leading finally to the disaster of war.

The year 1948 was the year of initiation for diplomacy concerning military aid, and by the end of the year, the diplomatic process had already revealed its characteristics and problems. We have to start our survey of developments with an examination of NSC 8, a document that received presidential approval on April 8. As a part of its analysis of the current situation on the Korean peninsula, the document listed the military forces in the north and the south—125,000 northern troops and a Soviet occupation force of 45,000 compared with 57,000 southern troops and a U.S. occupation force of 20,000. The ratio of the force levels between the two sides was more than two to one, but there was no expression of any concern about this imbalance. However, as one of the steps to be taken by the American government in connection with the troop withdrawal, the policy statement prescribed "expeditious completion" of existing plans for the expansion of the South Korean constabulary to provide for the security of South Korea against "any but an overt act of aggression by North Korean or other forces." By mid-September, General John R. Hodge indicated during a conversation with Niles Bond that, when all of the already earmarked equipment would be transferred to the South Korean forces, South Korea would have an "adequately equipped" defense force. A couple days later, Secretary of State Marshall stated that he understood the role of the constabulary in South Korea to be maintenance of internal order and the offering of "token resistance" in case of an invasion from the north. This was the first time the concept of "token resistance" was officially expressed, and it remained in place until the time of invasion. Through NSC 8 and Marshall's statement, the U.S. government made it clear that the purpose of the South Korean military force was to maintain internal order and to handle patrols of the border, but the nation was not to have much, if any, security against an invasion from the north. Naturally, the South Koreans felt very insecure, and soon after the new republic was established, President Rhee expressed the need for strengthening the security forces of his country and requested American assistance. He appealed on September 29 to General MacArthur for arms and ammunition and in early November requested through Muccio a special mission to train an additional fifty thousand men for the South Korean defense force.[19]

The year 1949 was the most important time for the military aid issue in Korea, as it was for the matters of the troop withdrawal and economic aid. The North Korean challenge had escalated; the South Korean government became anxious about its ability to meet the challenge; and the American government was reluctant to respond to these challenges. Moreover, an interesting strategic concept emerged for Korean security during this period, making it even more important. Before NSC 8/2 established firm objectives and guidelines for military aid for the Republic of Korea in late March, Muccio and MacArthur reported to Washington on the military situation on the Korean peninsula. On January 27, Muccio made a detailed report on various aspects of the situation in South Korea and pointed out that South Korea had a 114,000-man defense force, including 45,000 policemen and 4,000 coast guardsmen (and 50,000 of 65,000 troops of the Republic of Korea Army had "generally sufficient" equipment) against North Korean military forces of about twice that number, including 64,000 soldiers in the Peoples Army, a 9,000-man border constabulary, and at least 100,000 Koreans fighting with the Chinese communist armies. He added the optimistic observation that the South Korean forces were adequate to maintain internal stability, and before long they would be adequate to handle even a northern invasion. A month later, MacArthur made somewhat different observations for the Department of the Army: He said that 50,000 was about the maximum feasible force for South Korea. Its capability was to control the border and offer "token resistance" in case of a northern invasion. A very important strategic concept was brought into the picture during this period: On March 3, Niles Bond wrote in his memorandum to John M. Allison that the purpose of the aid to Korea was to provide the Korean government with security forces capable of "serving effectively as a deterrent to external aggression" and as a "guarantor of internal order." What role the strategic concept of "deterrence" would play against the idea of "token resistance" is an important question.[20]

The factual side of the NSC 8/2 did not go much beyond what Muccio and MacArthur provided: The size of the South Korean security forces was listed as a total of 114,000, including a 65,000-man army, against a North

Korean Army of between 75,000 and 95,000 men and about an equal or a larger number of Korean military forces in Manchuria. The document added that the North Korean defense force also reportedly possessed a small number of fighter and reconnaissance aircraft transferred by the Soviet Army. In conclusion, the National Security Council stated that a well-trained and equipped army of 65,000 men, including air detachments, for the maintenance of internal order and border security and a coast guard of 4,000 men for suppression of smuggling, piracy, illegal entry, and hostile infiltration by sea into South Korea would be provided through continuing military aid from the United States. When compared with similar statements from the previous year, this was a much firmer and clearer statement of the American military aid policy, for it actually said that the small force would be well trained and well equipped and that it would include air detachments and a coast guard suitable to perform the designated function. However, it still left South Korea defenseless against a possible North Korean invasion; and it failed to adopt the concept of deterrence, remaining with the concept of "token resistance" for the South Korean defense. Even though it recognized the existence of some fighter planes in the north, it did not provide any countermeasures for the South Korean defense. The weight and firmness of the document naturally created rigidity which, combined with a general tendency toward slowness and reluctance, played a much greater role during the following months.[21]

The next three-month period, between late March and the end of June, or between the adoption of NSC 8/2 and the completion of the troop withdrawal, was the period in which the diplomacy of American military aid for the Republic of Korea was most active. Muccio came forward to speak up actively and rather courageously for strengthening South Korea's defense forces to counter the increasing threat from the north. The South Korean government wished to increase its army to 100,000 men and to obtain some air planes and ships to reduce the possibility of northern invasion, if it could not match with equal numbers the armed forces of the north. Earlier, Muccio told Washington that South Korea did not have any vessels or equipment of value for its coastal defenses; in late April, he recommended that the Korean coast guard be provided with thirty ships, including four patrol craft, sixteen sub chasers, and ten picket boats. In early May, he also requested forty planes for the Korean air defenses, consisting of twenty liaison craft, fifteen single engine trainers (AT-6s), and five transports (C-47s). In his repeated requests, he clearly pointed out that the additional and necessary assistance would be helpful in persuading President Rhee to accept the early troop withdrawal. On May 9, he received Secretary Acheson's negative response to his requests. Acheson firmly told Muccio that, even though he shared Muccio's concern about Korean defenses, neither equipment nor funds would be available in the near future and that granting the request for planes and ships was absolutely out of the question. Further, he added that he was under the impression that Rhee was progressively raising the price to extract every possible concession over the troop withdrawal issue. Muccio could not argue with Secretary Acheson, but he could not completely drop his worries and cautiously continued his efforts, often through the American military representative in Korea. However, the stern response of Acheson was enough to discourage President Rhee, and ten days after Acheson's message, he decided to purchase with Korean funds ten T-6 trainers from Canada and asked the American government for a detachment of nine trainees.[22]

Even though at times President Rhee and other Korean officials made extravagant statements and cited excessive figures that irritated their American friends, what they realistically wished to achieve was an increase of the Republic of Korea Army to the 100,000-man level. Such an increase would have improved the ratio between the northern and southern defense forces to a little less than two to one, if not one to one. They also wished to improve the nation's air and naval defenses by obtaining a limited number of planes and ships. Certainly, the transfer of arms and equipment, which occurred when the U.S. troop withdrawal took place and was worth $56 million, helped arm the 65,000-man ROKA forces and some police with light arms, but this was far from adequate to meet the threat from the north. On August 20, almost two months after the last American combat soldier left Inch'ŏn, President Rhee wrote to President Truman a somewhat vague letter asking in general terms for help: "I wish at this time to bring to your attention some of the serious problems which are troubling me and the Korean people." He continued, "As I sit in my home not much more than thirty miles from positions where soldiers of the Republic are defending with their lives the soil and the people of Korea against savage assaults of Communist armies, my thoughts most naturally turn to our grievous problems of defense. Unless I, and my government, with the aid of our friends, do find solutions, the immediate future for our nation is bleak and bloody." And, in a modest and humble tone he asked, "I trust, therefore, that you will pardon my request that you again consider the question of military aid after you yourself and the great nation which you lead have already shown such sympathy and generosity to my country." President Truman's response was equally general: After reminding President Rhee of the transfer of some $56 million worth of arms and pointing out to him that an efficient, compact army would be best for the Republic of Korea, President Truman told President Rhee that the subject of military aid was receiving the sympathetic consideration it merited. Behind these general words, a real struggle went on.[23]

During the six months following the withdrawal of American troops, Muccio persistently pursued his effort to strengthen the South Korean air and naval defense, and Washington showed some response by asking questions about the real needs in Korea. A couple of new elements came into the picture, making the diplomatic exchanges on the military aid issue between Seoul and Washington more lively and complicated. A good number of tanks were added to the North Korean arsenal and information about the existence of fighter planes in the North Korean Air Force became firmer. Further, the $10 million allocation for Korea from the Mutual Defense Assistance fund was announced. Despite the firm response he gave Muccio in early May on the air and naval needs of South Korea, after repeated prodding, Acheson asked Muccio on July 15 to make a reassessment of the minimum needs for the Korean Coast Guard and to estimate the annual costs for the maintenance, repair, and training involved. Muccio promptly responded to the secretary's instruction by reporting that the Korean Coast Guard's absolute minimum need was fifteen U.S. Navy-type, wood-hulled, 110-foot submarine chasers and fifteen ex-U.S.-type 45-foot, wood-hulled picket boats, and the total annual operating cost would be a little over $7 million. The figures were later revised to specify four ex-U.S.–PC type vessels, five picket boats, and five ex-U.S. Navy OS 2U or SOC-type engine seaplanes. Encouraged by the secretary's attention, Muccio, either directly or through the Korean Military Advisory Group, sent to Washington more requests for South Korean air and naval equipment. In his September 14 dispatch, Muccio recommended that the State Department set aside $500,000 for a number of surplus or secondhand vessels and $26,956 for seven L-4 aircraft and spare parts for South Korean defense forces. On October 10, the Chief KMAG informed the Department of the Army that minimum requirements needed by the South Korean air defenses to counter the confirmed strength of the North Korean Air Force which was believed to be forty F-51 or similar type aircraft and ten AT-6 type aircraft. Muccio made another important contribution by bringing into the picture the concept of a "small but compact and efficient army." President Truman adopted this idea in his effort to persuade President Rhee to favor a small army, and it seemed that this general principle gave some consolation to the helpless Koreans.[24]

The information that only $10 million of a total of an over $800 million Mutual Defense Assistance Bill was allocated for the Republic of Korea was greatly disappointing news in Seoul for both Koreans and Americans concerned about the respective state of military forces in the north and the south, and Muccio began early protests to Washington. On September 16, he pointed out to Washington that the amount would "obviously be inadequate" and repeated the same opinion on many occasions. On December 19, he recommended a minimum of $20 million for Korea. Of the $814 million in the 1949 Mutual Defense Assistance Bill, $500 million was allocated to Europe, more than $211 million to Greece and Turkey, and $27,640,000 to Korea, the Philippines, and Iran. In terms of the urgency and magnitude of the communist challenge, Korea, the hottest spot of the Cold War in the whole world, deserved a much higher position than the one assigned. Some officials in the State Department thought so, and Bond proposed in mid-September to move Korea up to another group to fit the prescription in the NSC 8/2. Apparently, his was a minority view, and it was ignored, just as his concept of "deterrence" had been. However, as was the case in May, the State Department could not ignore the Korean problem completely, and it asked Muccio in late November a series of questions so he could elaborate on the inadequacy of the $10.23 million.[25]

The spring of 1950, the last six months of the struggle for more military aid for South Korean defense, was the period, as it was in the case of economic aid, in which the limits of the American willingness to meet the increasing communist challenge on the Korean peninsula became evident. While Muccio continued his last-minute efforts, General William G. Roberts, head of the Korean Military Advisers Group (KMAG) and the U.S. military representative in Korea, played a somewhat questionable role. In addition, Bond brought up more ideas, which did not draw much attention, and the Koreans tried a last minute effort to draw a little more attention to their plight. After failing in the attempt, they fell back to a stance of resignation and bitterness.

In early January, President Rhee presented a formal request for U.S. assistance to strengthen the South Korean Coast Guard and tried to impress President Truman by pointing out the possibility of training some 250,000 Korean youths for security purposes. He received a perfunctory response. In the meantime, he acquired the assistance of experts in his effort to establish a small air force to counter the Northern air threat. Two retired U.S. Air Force generals studied South Korean air defense needs and presented elaborate plans to the U.S. government. Plan A called for a fleet of ninety-nine planes, including twenty-five fighters (F-51s) and six bombers (B-25s) with U.S. financial support; and Plan B was a scaled-down version of Plan A with Korean funds. When General MacArthur was asked for an opinion on the plans, his answer was firmly negative. In his judgment, South Korea did not need an air force, given her security needs, namely the maintenance of internal order, the patrol of her border, and the capacity to offer "token resistance" as specified in NSC 8/2. The Koreans were naturally disappointed, but they could not do much other than retreat to resignation and do whatever was feasible. The Korean government tried late in January to obtain a group of advisers and technicians from the U.S. government for the ten planes purchased from Canada—they wanted three flight instructors, three airplane mechanics, two radio mechanics, and one electrical technician. In February, the Koreans heard that there would soon be a number of planes replaced in Japan, and President Rhee tried to obtain these obsolete planes. Even had he been successful in this effort, not much could have been accomplished with few trainers and obsolete air planes against the already existing force of at least thirty and possibly up to one hundred fighter planes in the north. Greatly discouraged, President Rhee became bitter by early May.[26]

By the spring of 1950, there was nothing new that Muccio could try to deal with the South Korean insecurity problem, but he remained the person whom both governments in Washington and Seoul could rely upon in dealing with the difficult situation in Korea. On January 25, he repeated the point that the $10 million in military aid for South Korean security was far from adequate and recommended an additional $9.8 million. To Muccio's repeated appeal, Acheson on April 13 responded by stating the Defense Department's view on the matter of the Korean's need for air defenses: According to the authority and intent of NSC 8/2, the proposed South Korean Air Force was not necessary. But Washington gave Muccio a chance in early May to present his case to the State–Defense joint group, and partly because of his efforts and partly because of the contributions by Bond, the idea of reexamining NSC 8/2 with regard to military aid for Korea was entertained. In early May, the military went so far as to concede the transfer of U.S. fighter planes pending revision of NSC 8/2. Secretary Acheson also gave Muccio a chance to explain in what sense the South Korean defense forces were superior to the North Korean forces and how the maintenance and ground support of the desired planes could be handled by the Koreans. Thus, some ideas came up for a solution to the problem in Korea, some questions were asked and explanations were made, and even some explorations were tried. But the U.S. government in general, especially the military establishment in Tokyo and Washington, was so reluctant to make any more commitments for Korea that nothing came of these ideas, explanations, and explorations.[27]

Brigadier General William G. Roberts occupied a critical position in Korea as head of the Korean Military Advisers Group. It is no doubt that his job was not an easy one because of the great difficulties inherent in the Korean security situation, especially with regard to the matter of the military assistance program, and he did his best, given his capacities and the circumstances. But his role for or against U.S. military assistance was somewhat problematic. Assisting Ambassador Muccio, he made some genuine efforts to obtain air and naval equipment for the South Korean defense force, but he also helped both MacArthur's headquarters and the Washington military authorities to develop the impression that the Korean defense strength was adequate to handle the North Korean military threat and not just give a token resistance. At the same time, when he communicated orally with a person like Philip Jessup, the U.S. ambassador at large, and others in responsible positions in Washington, he did not hide the unpreparedness of the Korean defense forces and almost boasted that when five or ten North Korean bombers came over South Korea, there would be "great disaster." It was unfortunate for both the United States and the Republic of Korea to have this man, who gave mixed information to Washington on such an important matter at such a critical time. There was a natural tendency for the South Koreans to exaggerate the strength of the North Koreans, while the Americans had a tendency to be overly optimistic about the strength of the south when compared to the military capacity of the north. General Roberts added more confusion to this already difficult situation.[28]

The issue of U.S. military aid for South Korea did not attract as much press attention as the two other issues—troop withdrawal and economic aid. And most of the articles, with the exception of some news releases and editorials, were short news items based largely upon the small number of announcements issued by the government. In early April 1949, the *New York Times* published a long editorial on the issue, which opened with the sentence, "There is no reason why the case of Korea should require any special pleading." It continued, "The United States has clearly defined obligations and that obligation must be met." It also stated that, in the light of the U.S. obligation, a request is reasonable if it calls for adequate force to defend the Korean Republic. The view was clear and simple, and it succinctly stated what was probably the view of most attentive Americans on the issue. In late June the same newspaper published a missionary wife's story who had just returned from Korea, in which she said that "unless American aid [is] given to the Republic of Korea better armed communist forces in North Korea will overrun the republic and eventually take over the entire country." She added that she thought the American policy was short-sighted and that it would let Asia fall to communism by default. This was not just one person's view; she was expressing a prevailing opinion, not only in Korea but throughout all of Asia. In the spring of 1950, the *New York Times* printed a story about the Koreans purchasing a training ship with money donated by Korean sailors and naval officers. This probably was to most just a heart-warming story, but to some of the so-called attentive public, it must have been a pathetic and unpleasant story. The Korean newspapers did not publish much other than short news items on the subject.[29]

To evaluate Korean and American policies and diplomacy with regard to the issue of military aid, a reality–ideality test will be attempted. By the late 1940s, the key American strategic concept for fighting the Cold War was definitely deterrence. On February 23, 1950, Niles Bond, the officer in charge of the Korean affairs, suggested to Livingston Merchant, the deputy assistant secretary for Far Eastern affairs, the possibility of moving Korea from the fourth and lowest category of the Mutual Defense Assistance Program (MDAP), which was designed for "supporting the political orientation of the recipient," to the third. His objective was to ensure that the ROKA would be "capable of serving effectively as a deterrent to external aggression and a guarantor of internal order in South Korea." There were only four months left until the outbreak of the war, and it was getting too late to do something substantial to avert the coming crisis, but it still was not too late to at least signal the enemy camp, which was extremely important, only if the U.S. government had the intention to do so. We can consider the deterrent posture, or the building-up of the Korean defense force to discourage the North Koreans from attempting an invasion, as the ideal route. Then, the question becomes, What was needed to pursue this course? First, we would need an accurate picture of the reality on the Korean peninsula.

Chargé Drumright's mid-May 1950 comparative figures for the military strengths of the north and the south provides a good base. Together with some other studies and recent analyses, it gives a fair picture of the situation in Korea in the spring of 1950. Korean sources indicated that the north had a total of 300,000 fighting men, 173 tanks, 609 76-mm and 122-mm guns and howitzers, 1,162 82-mm and 122–120-mm motors, and 609 antitank guns. The same sources also estimated a total of 195 airplanes in the north. U.S. sources gave much smaller numbers, about one-half of what the Korean sources cited in general and sometimes even one-third less: The U.S. estimates were a 103,000-man military force, 65 tanks, 296 76.2-mm and 122-mm guns and howitzers, 780 82-mm and 120-mm mortars, 356 antitank guns, and 75–100 yaks, including some fighters. The big differences in the total number of the military forces seems to have come from not only the tendency of each side to either exaggerate or minimize, but also from differences over what units to include or not to include in the counting. Accordingly, a fair estimate of the total military forces of the north was somewhere between the two figures, or roughly 200,000 men. Since it seems to be the case that the north decided to launch the invasion with a roughly two to one superiority, the minimum superiority ratio for an offensive operation, the addition of some 35,000 forces to the ROKA would have had the effect of improving the deterrent factor. The northern offensive air power and the heavy artillery pieces and tanks they possessed must have also been an important factor in the decision to invade. If part of the additional $9.8 million MDAP fund had been spent for some more and heavier artillery pieces and 50 to 100 "obsolete" fighter planes which some thought were needed to block about the same number fighter planes in the north, it would have become an important additional deterrent factor.[30]

What, then, were the factors preventing the United States from adopting this policy, which seemed to be necessary to discourage North Korean aggression? Washington had all necessary, if not absolutely clear, information, and a useful conceptual framework was also available, but these ingredients failed to effect the necessary policy revisions in the spring of 1950. The first and most important question is whether the U.S. government had real intentions of preventing Korea from falling into the communist camp at this time. Even though the long-range U.S. policy in Korea foresaw the establishment of a unified, democratic, and economically viable nation, the immediate concern of the U.S. government in Korea, as stated in the NSC 8 series, was to withdraw the troops and provide a limited amount of military aid for the "maintenance of internal order and border patrol" and "token resistance" in case of a northern invasion. In a practical sense South Korea became defenseless after June 30, 1949. Bond called the South Korean defense force "a pitiful thing"; General Matthew Ridgway called it a "sorry force"; and on June 28, 1950, Acheson himself called the Republic of Korea an "undefended country." If the situation in Korea was created by default, then an explanation is necessary.

If the intention was to prevent a communist takeover of South Korea, the reason for the failure to translate this intention into action probably lies in the policy-making mechanism. The idea of "deterrence" does not seem to have gone beyond the level of the middle echelon of foreign policy makers, and if it did, it stopped in Secretary Acheson's office. With a fine educational background and rich experience, Acheson certainly was a capable policy maker and an effective administrator. But how much flexibility and imagination his fine legal mind included is a good question. At the last moment, even the military showed some flexibility in expressing their willingness to allot some "obsolete planes" for Korea pending a revision of NSC 8/2. But Acheson would not take the steps necessary to salvage the situation. Beyond questions about American objectives and the nature of the policy-making process, there were two other even more fundamental factors that helped produce inaction by default in Korea: first, the low position of Korea in the U.S. military aid priority list, and second, the middle-of-the-road approach preferred. In the Mutual Defense Assistance Program list, Korea was placed in the lowest group along with the Philippines and Iran and below the group of Greece and Turkey, which was below Europe. Who can argue that Europe had the highest offensive and defensive value or military strategic value? The priority list was based on something other than military or strategic concerns; its basis was political or even cultural. And if the list of priorities could be defended from a cultural viewpoint, it was indefensible from a Cold War viewpoint. Korea was a hot spot, certainly one that was hotter than Europe, Greece, or Turkey.

Another fundamental problem behind the lukewarm attitude of the U.S. government in dealing with the issue of military aid for Korea came from its middle-of-the-road approach, which allowed neither complete retreat nor a courageous stand that dealt with the reality of the situation. Some congressmen and others saw the danger in this policy orientation, but the Truman administration did not seem to see it. Of course, it is easy to take the middle road when one is not very sure which way the nation should go, and it is a trap that one easily falls into. Military and economic factors were closely tied, as it was pointed out by some congressmen, and could not be separated, but this point too was ignored by the administration. It does not make much sense to try to save $9.8 million in military aid while spending $100 million for economic aid on a country without adequate defenses, a policy that amounted to pouring that money into a "rat hole," to borrow an expression from an American congressman. Thus, the U.S. military aid for the Republic of Korea failed to pass a reality–ideality test. American policy makers failed to grasp accurately the reality of the security situation on the Korean peninsula and stopped far short of the ideal approach that was necessary to deal with reality.[31]

The Koreans also made many mistakes. One serious error was the exaggeration in estimating the size of the North Korean Army. They also often exaggerated their own capabilities. Some who were in responsible positions in the defense and diplomatic establishments talked sometimes as if the South Korean forces could march north on the following day and conquer the north in three days. Overconfidence is often more valuable than underconfidence in human life, and to a certain extent the boasting had a practical value in making them appear confident to their ever uncertain American friends and, even more important, to boost their own morale. But at the same time, the risk was also great. Korea's American friends received illusions about the strength of the South Korean defense force, and the Koreans themselves accepted a false sense of reality. On the other hand, some Koreans, especially President Rhee, tried to be realistic, and after pleading, knew how to retreat and to find their own way by purchasing some necessary equipment with their own money. A mendicant mentality not only does not work in international relations but is also self-destructive. Altogether, the military aid diplomacy did not work out well, and its failure became a direct cause of the coming disaster.

NOTES

1. See W. D. Reeve, *The Republic of Korea: A Political and Economic Study* (London: Oxford University Press, 1963), pp. 101–108.

2. "Economic Review of the Republic of Korea, 1949," Bureau of Foreign and Domestic Commerce, U.S. Department of Commerce, International Reference Service, 7 (July 1950): 3.

3. Memorandum of conversation by John G. Williams with Major General Charles G. Helmick, February 4, 1948, *Foreign Relations of the United States (FRUS), 1948*, 6: 1092; Glen G. Wolfe, Chairman, Special Survey Mission to Korea, to the Secretary of State and ECA Administrator, November 8, 1948, National Archives (NA), RG 165, Defense Department, Civil Affairs Division, 1948, Old Korea, box 410.

4. See Reeve, *The Republic of Korea*, pp. 101–108.

5. See Yu In-ho, "Haepanghu nongchi kaehyŏkŭi chŏnkae kwachŏngkwa sŏngkyŏk," (The development process and characteristics of land reform after the liberation), in *Haepang Chŏnhusaŭi insik* (Understanding of the history of the pre- and postliberation era), vol. 2, ed. Kang Man-kil (Seoul: Hankilsa, 1985), pp. 437–438, 443–444.

6. See the memorandum of conversation by the Acting Secretary of State (Lovette) with Chough Pyŏng-ok, Butterworth, and Bond, September 23, 1948, *FRUS, 1948*, 6: 1310; *Sichŏng Wŏlpo* 11 (May 11, 1959): 11–12; "Economic Review of the Republic of Korea," Bureau of Foreign and Domestic Commerce, U.S. Department of Commerce, International Reference Service, 7 (July 1950): 1–8; Chu Sŏk-keun, "Why American Aid Failed," *Koreana Quarterly* 4 (1962): 81–93; Wŏn Tong-sŏk, "U.S. Foreign Aid Program in Korea," ibid., 5 (1963): 95–99.

7. See *Sichŏng Wŏlpo* 11 (May 10, 1950): 11; ibid. 12 (June 1950): 184–185; Im Pyŏng-chik, *Im pyŏng-chik hoekorok*, p. 331.

8. NSC 8, report by the National Security Council on the position of the United States with respect to Korea, an enclosure in a note by the Executive Secretary of the National Security Council (Sowers) to President Truman, April 2, 1948, *FRUS, 1948*, 6: 1163–1169.

9. President Rhee to President Truman, September 1, 1948, an enclosure in Muccio to the Secretary of State, September 3, 1948, *FRUS, 1948*, 6: 1290–1292; Muccio to the Secretary of State, September 22, 1948, Douglas MacArthur Memorial Archives (MacArthur Library), RG 9, box 149, blue binders; memorandum by Truman to the Secretary of State, August 25, 1948, *FRUS, 1948*, 6: 1288–1289; memorandum by the Assistant Secretary of State for Occupied Areas (Saltzman), September 7, 1948, ibid., 1292–1298.

10. The Secretary of State to the Administrator of the Economic Cooperation Administration (Hoffman), September 17, 1948, *FRUS, 1948*, 6: 1303–1305; Hoffman to the Secretary of State, October 1, 1948, ibid., p. 1309; Muccio to the Secretary of State, October 6, 1948, NA, RG 9, Decimal File 1945–49, box 3828; "Agreement on Aid between the United States of America and Republic of Korea," Department of State Publication 3522 (Washington, D.C.: U.S. Government Printing Office, 1949).

11. Muccio to the Secretary of State, January 27, 1949, *FRUS, 1949*, 7: 950; Drumright to the Secretary of State, March 23, 1949, ibid., p. 980; *Sichŏng Wŏlpo* 4 (July 23, 1949): 42; House of Representatives, Committee of Foreign Affairs, 81st Cong., 2d sess., "Background Information on Korea, Report Pursuant to H. Res. 206," 1950, Report 2495; *Sichŏng Wŏlpo* 12 (June 30, 1950): 181.

12. *Congressional Record*, 81st Cong., 1st Sess., vol. 95, pt. 6, pp. 7358–7359; "Korean Aid," Hearings on HR 5330 before the Committee on Foreign Affairs, 81st Cong., 1st sess., pp. 8–9, 15–20, 27, 138, 192.

13. *Congressional Record*, 81st Cong., 1st Sess., vol. 95, pt. 11, pp. 14337–14339, 15090, vol. 95, pt. 15a, A4533; editorial note, *FRUS, 1949*, 7: 1039–1040; *New York Times*, June 9, 1949, 18: 3; ibid., June 10, 1949, 26: 3; ibid., June 11, 1949, 4: 4; ibid., June 21, 1949, 13: 1; ibid., June 25, 1949, 1: 2–3; ibid., June 28, 1949, 4: 2; ibid., July 1, 1949, 6: 7; ibid., July 2, 1949, 1: 2–3; ibid., July 3, 1949, IV, 6: 3; ibid., August 26, 1949, 3: 8; ibid., September 12, 1949, 15: 7; ibid., October 1, 1949, 12: 2; ibid., October 11, 1949, 11: 5; ibid., October 13, 1949, 7: 5; ibid., October 14, 1949, 26: 2; *Kyŏnghyang Sinmun*, September 25, 1949, 1: 1–7; *Seoul Sinmun*, October 21, 1949, no. 1: 2–7; *Donga Ilbo*, June 12, 1949, 1: 1–5; ibid., November 24, 1949, 1: 1–7; ibid., November 29, 1949, 1: 1–7; *Jayu Sinmun*, May 18, 1949, 1: 2–8; ibid., June 9, 1949, 1: 9–11; ibid., June 26, 1949, 1: 2–7.

14. *Congressional Record*, 81st Cong., 2d sess., vol. 96, pt. 7, pp. 632–656.

15. Acheson to Truman, January 20, 1950, NA, RG 59, Decimal File, box 5689.; *Department of State Bulletin* 22 (February 6, 1950): 212; *Congressional Record*, 81st Cong., 2d sess., vol. 96, pt. 13, p. A508; Acheson to Muccio, January 20, 1950, NA, RG 59, Decimal File, box 5690; memorandum of conversation by John Z. Williams of the Office of Northeast Asian Affairs with Chang Myŏn and Butterworth, *FRUS, 1950*, 7: 13; *Sichŏng Wŏlpo* 10 (April 1, 1950): 22–23; memorandum of conversation by the Officer in Charge of Korean Affairs (Bond) with Bunce, Johnson, Butterworth, Allison, and others, March 15, 1950, *FRUS, 1950*, 7: 31; *New York Times*, January 20, 1950, 1: 4; ibid., January 21, 1950, 1: 2; ibid., January 16, 1950, 1; February 2, 1950, 26: 2; ibid., February 11, 1950, 14: 2; *Seoul Sinmun*, January 21, 1950, no. 1: 1–5; ibid., February 21, 1950, 1: 2–5.

16. Memorandum of conversation for the Secretary of State, January 20, 1950, Truman Library, Acheson Papers, box 65; Memorandum of L. D. Battle to McFall, January 30, 1950, NA, RG 59, Decimal File, box 5689; Memorandum of conversa-

tion with the President, January 23, 1950 Truman Library, Acheson Papers, box 65; "Korean Aid," hearings before the Committee on Foreign Affairs House of Representatives, 81st Cong. 1st sess., on HR 5330, pp. 11, 15–16; *New York Times*, February 1, 1950, 13: 2–3; ibid., February 2, 1950, 3: 6, 26: 2; ibid., February 10, 1950, 1: 4; ibid., February 11, 1950, 6: 8; Acheson to Muccio, February 14, 1950, NA, RG 59, Decimal File, box 5698; *Department of State Bulletin* 22 (March 13, 1950): 405; House Committee on Foreign Affairs, "Economic Assistance to Certain Areas in the Far East," 81st Cong., 2d sess., Report 1572, 1950, p. 14; *New York Times*, April 1, 1950, 1: 8; ibid., May 26, 1950, 1: 8; ibid., June 6, 1950, 1: 23.

17. Memorandum of conversation by John Z. Williams of the Office of Northeast Asian Affairs with Chang Myŏn and Butterworth, January 20, 1950, *FRUS, 1950*, 7: 11–14; Chang Myŏn to President Truman, January 20, 1950, Truman Library, box 1304; memorandum of conversation March 22, 1950, ibid., box 65; *New York Times*, February 1, 1950, 13: 2–3; ibid., February 2, 1950, 3: 6; ibid., February 2, 1950, 26: 2; ibid., February 10, 1950, 1: 4; ibid., March 8, 1950, 6: 3; ibid., March 31, 1950, 18: 4; ibid., April 1, 1950, 1: 8; ibid., May 6, 1950, 1: 8; ibid., May 7, 1950, IV, 12: 2; *Seoul Sinmun*, January 21, 1950, 1: 1–2; ibid., January 23, 1950, 1: 1–6; ibid., January 31, 1950, 1: 1–6; ibid., February 9, 1950, 1: 1–6; ibid., February 11, 1950, 1: 1–5; ibid., February 12, 1950, 1: 1–4; ibid., March 22, 1950, 1: 5–7; ibid., March 29, 1950, 1: 7–13; ibid., March 31, 1950, 1: 1–2.

18. Charles M. Dobbs, *The Unwanted Symbol: American Foreign Policy, the Cold War, and Korea, 1945–1950* (Kent: Ohio: Kent University Press, 1981), p. 537. See also Robert M. Blum, *Drawing the Line: The Origins of the American Containment Policy in East Asia* (New York: Norton, 1982), p. 72; Cho Soon-sung, *Korea in World Politics, 1940–1950: An Evaluation of American Responsibility* (Berkeley and Los Angeles: University of California Press, 1967), pp. 243, 246, 283.

19. NSC 8, April 2, 1948, *FRUS, 1948*, 6: 1164–1169; memorandum of conversation between General Hodge and Bond, September 16, 1948, NA, RG 84, Seoul Embassy, Top Secret Records, 1950–56, box 1; the Secretary of State to the Secretary of the Army (Royall) September 17, 1948, *FRUS, 1948*, 6: 1303; Rhee to MacArthur, September 29, 1948, MacArthur Library; Muccio to the Secretary of State, November 5, 1948, *FRUS, 1948*, 6: 1320; Muccio to the Secretary of State, November 12, 1948, NA, Decimal File, 740.00119 control (Korea)/11–1248.

20. Muccio to the Secretary of State, January 27, 1949, *FRUS, 1949*, 7: 948–950; CINCFE to the Department of the Army, February 23, 1949, MacArthur Library, RG 9, box 148; Bond to Allison, March 14, 1949, NA, RG 84, Seoul Embassy, Top Secret Records, 1950–56.

21. NSC 8/2, March 22, 1949, *FRUS, 1949*, 7: 969–978.

22. Muccio to the Secretary of State, April 12, 26, 29, May 3, 6, 1949, *FRUS, 1949*, 7: 986, 996, 998, 1006; the Secretary of State to Muccio, May 9, 1949, ibid., 1014; Muccio to General MacArthur, May 19, 1949, in Muccio to Bonds, May 19, 1949, NA, RG 84, Seoul Embassy, Top Secret Records, 1950–55. See also Senator Knowland's concern about the uneven force level between the north and south, *Congressional Record*, 81st Cong., 1st sess., vol. 95, pt. 4, p. 4602.

23. The President of the Republic of Korea (Rhee) to President Truman, August 20, 1949, *FRUS, 1949*, 7: 1075–1076; President Truman to the President of the Republic of Korea, September 26, 1949, ibid., pp. 1084–1085.

24. Muccio to Bond, July 13, 1949, *FRUS, 1949*, 7: 1060; Acheson to Muccio,

July 15, 1949, ibid., pp. 1061–1062; Muccio to Acheson, July 25, 1949, ibid., pp. 1066–1067; Muccio to the Secretary of State, September 14, October 19, November 8, 10, 1949, ibid., pp. 1080, 1088, 1094, 1095; Chief of KMAG to the Department of the Army, October 10, 1949, NA, RG 84, Seoul Embassy, Top Secret Records, 1950–55, box 1.

25. *Department of State Bulletin* 21 (August 2, October 24, 1949): 267, 603–605; Bond to Wergle, September 16, 1949, NA, RG 84, Seoul Embassy, Top Secret Records, 1950–55, box 1; Muccio to the Secretary of State, September 16, November 19, December 19, 1949, *FRUS, 1949*, 7: 1079, 1099, 1102, 1112; Muccio to the Secretary of State, December 12, 1949, NA, RG 84, Seoul Embassy, Top Secret Records, 1950–55, box 1; the Acting Secretary of State (Webb) to Muccio, November 28, 1949, *FRUS, 1949*, 7: 1101–1102; the Secretary of State to Muccio, December 9, 1949, ibid., p. 1107.

26. Muccio to the Secretary of State, January 21, March 16, 1950, *FRUS, 1950*, 7: 14, 35; Chang Myŏn to Acheson, January 9, 1950, and draft letter, Truman to Rhee, January 10, 1950, in Acheson to Truman, January 10, 1950, Truman Library, box 1305; CINCFE to the Department of the Army, January 16, 1950, MacArthur Library, RG 9, box 64; Allison to the Director of the Office of Foreign Military Affairs, Office of the Secretary of State, January 31, 1950, *FRUS, 1950*, 7: 24.

27. Muccio to the Secretary of State, January 25, March 16, 1950, *FRUS, 1950*, 7: 15, 34; Acheson to Muccio, April 13, June 13, 1950, ibid., pp. 46, 104; Acting Secretary of State (Webb) to Muccio, May 19, 1950, ibid., p. 85; memorandum of conversation by Bond with Muccio, Major General Lemnitzer, and others, May 10, 1950, ibid., pp. 78–81; Bond to Merchant, February 23, 1950, NA, RG 84, Seoul Embassy, Top Secret Records, 1950–55, box 1.

28. The Chief of the U.S. Military Advisory Group to the Republic of Korea (Roberts) to the Ambassador in Korea, January 7, 1950, in Muccio to the Secretary of State, January 25, 1950, *FRUS, 1950*, 7: 17; memorandum by Ambassador at Large Philip C. Jessup, January 14, 1950, ibid., p. 5; Muccio to the Secretary of State, January 28, 1950, ibid., p. 19; the Chief of the U.S. Military Advisory Group (Roberts) to the Republic of Korea and all KMAG Advisers, May 5, 1950, in Muccio to the Secretary of State, May 29, 1950, ibid., p. 93.

29. *New York Times*, December 19, 1948, 12: 3; ibid., April 3, 1949, IV, 8: 2; ibid., June 30, 1949, 9: 5–6; ibid., September 1, 1949, 12: 3; ibid., January 27, 1950, 7: 2; ibid., February 1, 1950, 13: 5; ibid., June 2, 1950, 1: 8 and 2: 2–5; *Seoul Sinmun*, August 26, 1948, no. 1: 1–3; ibid., April 15, 1949, no. 1: 1–4; ibid., July 27, 1949, no. 1: 1–5; ibid., October 30, 1949, no. 1: 2–5; ibid., June 4, 1950, no. 1: 1–8; ibid., June 9, 1950, no. 1: 7–12; *Jayu Sinmun*, May 28, 1949, 1: 2–5; ibid., June 17, 1949, 1: 1–8; ibid., September 24, 1949, 1: 1–4.

30. Chargé Drumright to the Secretary of State, May 11, 1950, *FRUS, 1950*, 7: 84. See also Butterworth to Allison, October 9, 1949, NA, RG 84, Seoul Embassy, Top Secret Records, 1950–54, box 1; Muccio to the Secretary of State, November 10, 1949, *FRUS, 1949*, 7: 1095; Wright to Drumright, April 11, 1950, NA, Seoul Embassy, Top Secret Records, 1950–54, box 1; Drumright to Muccio, April 20, 1950, *FRUS, 1950*, 7: 46; Chief of KMAG to all KMAG Advisers, May 5, 1950, in Muccio to the Secretary of State, May 29, 1950, ibid., p. 93; Lee Ki-ong, "Pukhan taengknŭn chŏchihalsu isŏtta" (The northern tanks could be dealt with), *Donga Ilbo*, June 23, 1993, 1: 4–6.

31. Niles W. Bond, Truman Library, oral interview history transcript, p. 36; Mathew B. Ridgway, *The Korean War: How We Met the Challenge* (Garden City, N.Y.: Doubleday, 1967), p. 10; *Department of State Bulletin* 23 (July 3, 1950): 6; Frank K. Pace, Jr., Truman Library, oral interview history transcript, p. 95. See also William W. Stueck, Jr., *The Road to Confrontation: American Policy toward China and Korea, 1947–1950* (Chapel Hill: University of North Carolina Press, 1981), pp. 152–153, 159–162, 166, 170; Gaddis, "Korea in American Politics," pp. 247–248, 286–287; Cho Soon-sung, *Korea in World Politics*, p. 256; Pelz, "U.S. Decisions on Korean Policy, 1943–1950," in *Child of Conflict: The Korean-American Relations, 1943–1953*, ed. Bruce Cumings (Seattle: University of Washington Press, 1983), p. 75; Ohn Chang-il, "The Joint Chiefs of Staff and U.S. Policy and Strategy Regarding Korea, 1945–1953" (Ph.D. diss., University of Kansas, 1983), p. 271.

CHAPTER 8

The Four Episodes

Before closing this discussion of an important two-year period, we must turn briefly to four episodes which took place in the winter and spring of 1950 and played a role in the coming crisis in Korean–American relations. They were Secretary Acheson's Press Club speech in January, Senator Connally's May interview with a news magazine, and brief visits by two men to Korea, Philip Jessup in January and John Foster Dulles, right before the outbreak of the war.

Secretary Acheson's National Press Club speech on January 12 may be counted not merely as an episode but as one of the major events leading to the war. The speech contained an unfortunate and untimely statement about the "defense perimeter" in Asia. The speech itself, written by George Kennan and approved by President Truman beforehand, was an overall good speech. It offered a candid and comprehensive discussion of U.S. policy toward Asia. However, Korea received only a paragraph which dealt with the issue of economic aid. Some Koreans caught this independent section before reading the perimeter statement, and they immediately thanked Acheson. When the speech reached the question of security matters in the Pacific, Acheson specified that the U.S. defense perimeter ran along the Aleutians to Japan and then to Rykus and ended with the Philippines. He explained the special relationships the United States had with these places. Then, he made the most damaging statement: "So far as the military security of other areas in the Pacific is concerned, it must be clear that no person can guarantee these areas against military attack. But it must also be clear that such a guarantee is hardly sensible or necessary within the realm of practical relationship."

He gave a prescription for what would be needed if these other areas were attacked. First, the people would have to rely on themselves for initial resistance and then on the "entire civilized world under the Charter of the United Nations." It must have been very clear to anyone—the Americans, the South Koreans, the North Koreans, the Russians, or anyone else—that South Korea was left outside of the U.S. defense line. If Korea was attacked by outside force, she could not rely on the United States for her defense but would have to rely first on her own strength and then on the "entire civilized world" or the United Nations. Of course, this was remarkably close to what happened when the attack came, and Acheson was telling exactly what the United States would do in case of war in Korea. Also, his audience knew that Acheson's suggestion did not mean very much in a real sense, because the Republic of Korea did not have much to fall back on for self-reliance. It was an "unprotected" nation in Acheson's own words, and the United Nations in 1950 was certainly not even the organization of the 1990s, which has had difficulty handling a crisis the size of those in Somalia and Yugoslavia. The United Nations in 1950 was a weak and untested collective security system, and its capacity in a time of a fair-sized crisis was an absolutely unknown factor. Acheson's speech was treated as an important statement and stimulated a large number of comments, pro and con, both from contemporaries and later analysts. Acheson himself, probably naturally, did not think the speech had anything to do with the war. But, many others, including those who served on the military side, thought it influenced the communist decision to attack. Some even thought that it was the main cause of the North Korean invasion. In the fall of 1952, presidential candidate Dwight Eisenhower, in a campaign speech, said, "As I have pointed out before Secretary Acheson served notice officially to the Soviet Union that Korea was outside the U.S. defense perimeter in case of general war." On the other side, interestingly enough, John Muccio and Niles Bond, the two who tried to do the most for the Republic of Korea for the sake of American interests, later defended Acheson's speech.[1]

The reaction of the Koreans was intense, as might have been expected, even though some of them were confused, at least for a short while, about the meaning of the key passage in the speech. After a hasty reading, President Rhee and the legislative leaders were impressed by the secretary's statement on economic aid in the speech and immediately sent words of thanks to the secretary through Ambassador Chang. Before long, however, they grasped fully the meaning of the message for the more important security matter. Ambassador Chang attended the club meeting and said later that he was very much surprised and discouraged when the secretary excluded Korea from the defense perimeter and immediately called the State Department. The explanation he heard did not convince him at all. He said he thought the speech was one of the contributing factors for the North Korean decision to invade. Rusk and others in the State Department tried their best to explain the situation to the Koreans by pointing out that the United States had a very special relationship with the places included in the perimeter as an occupying power, and the exclusion of Korea did not mean at all the abandonment of that country, given the substantial material aid and political support the Koreans had received. However, these words did not have the strength to convince the disturbed Koreans, and they were much troubled by the implications of the speech.[2]

No direct evidence comes to light in the presently available communist sources to show the impact of Acheson's speech upon the communist leaders. However, the Russian archival materials indicate that Kim Il Sung on January 19—three days after the speech—made his first step to obtain Stalin's promise for assisting him specifically with preparation for the war. Stalin granted Kim the promise by the end of the month. This seems to indicate that the speech influenced the minds of the communist leaders. This subject has drawn a relatively large amount of scholarly attention. Many scholars think the speech must have had an impact upon the communist camp's decision to invade. John Gaddis has made some very thoughtful comments on the subject of the defense perimeter idea, which deserve special attention. One of the key points he makes is that the idea of a defensive perimeter idea with Korea outside of it was not anything new in Washington by this time and that Acheson was simply voicing well-established U.S. policy. Further, he points out that the defense perimeter idea made sense in view of the U.S. manpower shortage and its heavy reliance on military technology. He also points out that the speech eliminated the element of ambiguity with regard to U.S. responsibility for the South Korean defense and that the exclusion of Taiwan from the perimeter pushed more Republicans to vote against the Korea economic aid bill.[3]

Acheson's inclusion of the statement about the U.S. defense perimeter in Asia in the January 1950 speech was unnecessary and unfortunate. It is true that Acheson was simply summarizing well-established U.S. military policy and that he was not blundering into describing something nonexistent. Since 1947, the U.S. posture toward Korea had been clearly one of graceful withdrawal with a minimum of damage and adequate face-saving measures. Probably because of the element of grace and face saving, for the roots of which one must dig until he hits the rock of morality, the nation had been hanging somewhere between a wish to get out completely and to stay completely. Thus was created a sense of ambiguity for those who did not know the real U.S. intent and policy as articulated in the NSC 8 series and other documents. Of course, ambiguity in diplomacy entails its own hazards, but sometimes, to keep the enemy guessing about what one really intends to do, it has a definite advantage. As Gaddis astutely points out, this was the case in Korea at this time, and Acheson probably unintentionally destroyed this ambiguity by giving a fairly clear signal to the enemy. The military always have drawn strategic perimeters, both defensive and offensive, for the purpose of the effective use of available resources, but they usually do not announce them. In essence, drawing the defense line in this case came from the block-and-gap approach, which was a very questionable approach for the containment policy, as has already been pointed out, and it was corrected later. We are again in the midst of an argument over the primacy of ends and means. The manpower shortage and the other examples of military unpreparedness—the means—needed to be corrected; the other kind of adjustment—the adjustment of the ends to the existing means—is often much harder within international society. This is particularly true in this case because the communist intentions in Korea were clear. Rather than using a purely technical military strategic concept, Acheson could have adopted some sort of idea to explain the logic of the U.S. posture in Asia. He could have used, for example, the concept of a triangle made up of Korea, Japan, and the Philippines, as a congressman pointed out. It would have been even better if he had created a triangle made of Korea, Japan, and China, which was of course a political or a geopolitical perimeter. Even though MacArthur and other military leaders had been insistent about the Asian military defense perimeter, even the military in the spring of 1950 was willing to concede the political value of the Korean peninsula or its political strategic value. Another important aspect of the inclusion of the perimeter statement in the speech was its timing, as both General Ridgway and John Gaddis have pointed out. The debate and vote on the Korean economic aid bill was scheduled to be held only a week later, and the speech may have pushed more Republicans to vote against the bill. Since the bill was defeated by a margin of only two votes, the impact of the speech may have been very critical. The two events—the speech and the defeat of the aid bill—came too close together, and the two must have given a strong impression to the North Koreans and their friends. Discussion of the defense perimeter was a good subject for a military staff meeting, but it certainly was the wrong one for a U.S. Secretary of State's public speech that was also delivered at an inopportune time. Altogether, it was a very unfortunate episode.

About four months after the Acheson's speech, a somewhat similar incident occurred, which aggravated further the already very difficult situation in Korea. On May 2, while Senator Tom Connally was giving an interview to the editor of *U.S. News and World Report*, he divulged his views on the subject of the abandonment of Korea. He was asked a question about whether the suggestion that the United States would abandon South Korea was going to be seriously considered. His answer was clear and straightforward: "I am afraid it is going to be seriously considered because I'm afraid it's going to happen whether we want it or not." Like Acheson's case, what the senator was saying was not news to the people in Washington and was a simple confirmation in a slightly different way of what Acheson already had said in his speech. The Associated Press immediately reported the content of the interview, and the May 5 issue of the magazine printed its full text. Even before seeing the reaction of the Koreans, Chargé Drumright in Seoul began to worry about its damaging effect in Korea. He said that Korean reaction was unknown as yet but President Rhee and other Korean officials seemed almost certain to be "angered, and bewildered and dismayed," adding that it was highly desirable that the department issue a statement reaffirming the continuation of a U.S. interest in supporting Korea. Acheson responded to Drumright's suggestion and issued on May 3 an explanation by saying that the department "continuously stressed the importance which it attached to South Korea" by enumerating the efforts the United States had made to help the Koreans, and by concluding that he doubted very much whether Senator Connally took a different view from his. The Seoul newspapers first printed rather indignant comments on the interview and then printed a translation of Acheson's statement without comments. Drumright later reported to Washington that the damaging implications of the Connally statement had been largely offset by Secretary Acheson's subsequent statement. But how well the damage control measure worked out is doubtful, because under normal circumstances, Acheson's statement would not have impressed anyone very much. But because the Koreans were not living in normal circumstances in the spring of 1950 and were of a mind to believe anything that sounded helpful for their future, it is probable that Drumright's impression was not totally incorrect. In any case, President Rhee was so discouraged by the implications of the Connally statement that Drumright found his faith in the United States had been shaken and that he had become "bitter."[4] The Connally statement was, like the Acheson statement, unnecessary and unfortunate.

Squeezed between two large powers in Northeast Asia, the Korean people often felt neglected and ignored by the rest of the world. During the spring of 1950, this feeling was more acute for the South Koreans because of the multiplying difficulties the nation was going through and a pervasive sense of helplessness. Under these circumstances, any visitor would have been welcomed, especially ones from the United States. Muccio fully realized this problem and tried to impress upon Washington the desirability of sending some delegations to Korea. A number of U.S. senators and congressmen had come during the previous fall to see what was happening there and occasionally U.S. naval ships stopped by the Korean harbors, visits helpful for the Koreans, but more and more important visitors were needed. Two very important men came to visit Korea during the spring, and both Philip Jessup's visit in January and John Foster Dulles's in June boosted Korean morale, although not much else resulted from them.[5]

Philip Jessup was a very special visitor for the Koreans because of his background and position in Washington. As a prominent scholar in international law, he naturally commanded the respect of the Koreans. This scholar–diplomat came in his official capacity as an ambassador at large, and because of his important role in the U.S. foreign policy process, the Koreans rightly believed that whatever view he would take back to Washington would have an impact upon the future of U.S. policy toward Korea. The Koreans also wished to hear from him words of encouragement and assurance, if possible, of U.S. support for their country in the case of a future crisis. Koreans, government officials as well as the public, enthusiastically welcomed this very special guest with high expectations.

As soon as Jessup arrived at Kimp'o Airport on the afternoon of January 11, his busy two and a half day schedule began. During his short stay, he talked four times with President Rhee, had conversations with other government officials and educators, gave speeches at the National Assembly and the Chamber of Commerce, and received an honorary degree from Seoul National University. He also was briefed by American officials, saw the U.N. representative in Seoul, and took a trip to the 38th parallel. He easily impressed the people he met with his knowledge and intellectual power. When the Koreans tried to argue with him that American policy in the Far East was too mild, or even wrong headed, Jessup quickly reminded his hosts that they could not just sit back and expect the United States to solve their problems. When President Rhee and other Koreans tried to impress upon him their urgent need for planes, ships, and tanks, Jessup took it as a "familiar plea" and told them that the more fundamental way to fight communism would be the development of a sound democratic system and economic prosperity. At the National Assembly, he heard from Chairman Sin Ik-hi that, with U.S. economic and military aid, Korea could become a "bulwark" in Asia against communist aggression, an outcome that would be good for both Korea and the free world.[6]

The Korean people were happy to have the special visitor and were much impressed by his charm and poise as well as by his knowledge and integrity. The Korean newspapers enthusiastically welcomed him with reports and favorable comments. Drumright was very happy with the Jessup visit, and began his detailed report to Washington with the remark that the visit was one of the most successful visits to Korea by an American official. One of the most important aspects of the visit was an open exchange of views by both sides. Jessup expressed frankly American feelings regarding Korean domestic politics and economic conditions; in return, the Koreans were equally open in telling their visitor what seemed to be wrong with American policy in the Far East and what their urgent needs were to fight the Cold War in Korea. This kind of exchange, much needed by both sides, was done well. It is also true that whatever information and impressions Jessup picked up to take back from the frontiers of the Cold War to the conference rooms of Washington would certainly be useful. But beyond these exchanges of views and the acquisition of impressions and pieces of information, what was accomplished by his visit is not known. It was probably useful in that it provided him with background information, but his talks often sounded like idealistic lectures for people whose needs were urgent and whose very survival was at stake. For Koreans, who needed planes, ships, and tanks, the talks on freedom and democracy sounded too remote. The Koreans had expected a fresh message from Jessup, and to the extent they did so, they were disappointed. Jessup, of course, did not bring any new message; his trip was a fact-finding mission. While in Korea, he told the Koreans that their army was good and that Korean defenses were in good shape. Jessup was repeating to the Koreans what he had just heard during a briefing from General Roberts. A trip of two and a half days was just too short for anyone, however perceptive, to grasp fully the real situation, and it should be said that despite the shortcomings and disappointments involved in the visit, Jessup's January visit to Korea was good for both the Koreans and the Americans.

About six months later another important visitor came to Korea from the United States. John Foster Dulles's trip, which was made right before the outbreak of the war, aroused considerable emotion in Korea—on both sides of the parallel—and it remains something of a puzzle. Republican Dulles was giving bipartisan assistance to the Democratic administration and was closely associated with the State Department at the time when he made the short but important trip to Korea while undertaking explorations for a peace treaty with Japan. He probably lacked the intellectual charm and depth of knowledge possessed by Jessup, but he had magnanimity and breadth of thinking, and he was the right person to come to Korea at this point, a moment when the people needed real encouragement.

The purpose of the Dulles trip to Korea in late June was largely fact finding, much as Jessup's had been. But he also later indicated that during the trip he wished to counteract the feeling widespread among the Koreans—both in the south and the north—that the United States had abandoned South Korea as expendable. Probably, his intention was to accomplish both. He also had a busy schedule, crowded with talks with President Rhee and other leaders and filled with other activities like speeches, honorary degrees, and briefings. He also made a trip to the 38th parallel, and his purpose was to learn firsthand the nature of the situation along the dangerous line. Without question, his most important act during his visit with the Koreans was the speech he made at the National Assembly. He spoke using high-sounding words: "You are conducting what may go down in history as the Great Korean Experiment, an experiment which, in its way, can exert a moral influence in the twentieth century as profound as that which, in the nineteenth century, was exerted by what was then called the Great American Experiment." The words were purposely grand, chosen to encourage the Koreans. Then came the most important statement: "You are not alone. You will never be alone so long as you continue to play worthily in the great design of human freedom." It was a statement of a broad principle, and simply because of the context—the place and time—it became the subject for many different interpretations and even the target for accusations. Ambassador Chang Myŏn later recalled that he was the one who made the suggestion to Dulles that he give a speech at the National Assembly and utter strong words of encouragement. He also suggested that Secretary Acheson be contacted for approval. Beyond the great but general words of encouragement, Dulles could not offer concrete assurances, and he stopped with general advice to the Koreans to respect the principles of representative government, to make a real effort for self-control, and to do hard work to create a stable economy and government—words very much like those of Jessup.[7]

President Rhee and other Koreans were very happy with the morale boosting they received from Dulles. Of course, they read much into the general words they heard. The Korean newspapers gave him a generous welcome and printed words of thanks as well as news of his visit. Dulles's "You are not alone" statement was immediately subjected to different interpretations and conjectures as to its meaning. Some contemporaries thought that he was giving "the most explicit assurance of American protection." The North Koreans accused him after the outbreak of the war of "complicity" in "the South Korean invasion" of the north. Even the North Koreans found a way to extract propaganda value from the statement. Later writers thought that Dulles was promising positive action by the United States on behalf of the Koreans. Vague, general statements like Dulles's invite different interpretations. In this regard, Dulles's statement was the opposite of the one made by Acheson in January, when he drew a line clear to any observer. Both extremes involve particular risks and should therefore have been avoided. However, when either type is deemed necessary, its practical utility should have been calculated carefully according to the general principle of maximizing the benefits and minimizing the damage. Interpretations of John Foster Dulles's statements in Seoul brought considerable benefit to the Koreans and did little damage, so they fare well in this utilitarian test.[8]

The near two-year period between the establishment of the government of the Republic of Korea and the outbreak of the Korean War was somewhat like two periods the nation had gone through a half century earlier, first between 1882 and 1894, and then between 1895 and 1905. During each of these two periods, the Koreans had enjoyed a favorable environment when their three powerful neighbors (China, Japan, and Russia) were in balance with each other and when there was a good chance for transformation, but which the Koreans failed to take advantage of. A half century later, the Koreans seemed to have another chance for nation building and for moving in the direction of modernization, but once again they missed the opportunity. Of course, the situation on the Korean peninsula in the mid-twentieth century was quite different from that at the turn of the century. At midcentury, the period of a year and ten months was too brief. The United States and the Soviet Union were quite different from the three older powers in terms of their interests. The priority the two Cold War giants gave the maintenance of equilibrium on the Korean peninsula was questionable, and the Koreans faced the tremendous difficulty of a division into two parts and two competing ideologies. In terms of challenge and response, the Koreans were facing too many challenges for an optimum response. The choices and alternatives open to the Koreans during this period were almost nonexistent. Taking a middle road to neutrality was a very idealistic route. Earlier, during the occupation period, General Hodge had tried this route, and given their historical position as a classical buffer state, the idea has always been attractive in Korea. Kim Kyu-sik and Kim Ku toyed with the idea during this period, and their protest at the Paris U.N. General Assembly meeting in the fall of 1948 looked almost quixotic. Another approach open to the Koreans at this time was the opening of a dialogue between the north and the south. But even setting aside the factor of personality, the late 1940s were definitely too early for a north–south dialogue in Korea.

During this two-year period, the Republic of Korea naturally considered her relationship with the United States the most important. In a real sense, most of the ROK's diplomacy was with the United States, and the administrative aspect of the two-nation relationship worked satisfactorily. Government activities were transferred smoothly and expeditiously from the U.S. occupation authorities to the Korean government. By the spring of 1949, embassies representing the two countries in each other's capitals were in full operation, and the official recognition by the United States of the new republic was made on the first day of the new year. In addition, the United States made a genuine effort to achieve recognition of the new nation at the United Nations. However, beyond this rather mundane administrative level, Korean–American relations in the realm of the development of democratic practices, security, and welfare experienced much strain and many difficulties. The United States faced a moral dilemma in siding with an autocratic government to fight the Cold War. Through his many years of education and life in the United States, President Rhee must have truly understood the principles of democratic institutions, but once he began to govern his own country, his style was more authoritarian than democratic. His rough dealings with the National Assembly perplexed many Americans. Along with some other Koreans, he argued that Korea was going through a time of crisis and that such an idealistic ideology as democracy would not work during times of emergency. This contention might have had some truth in it, but in the long run, democratic idealism would be most important, and President Rhee and other Koreans should have made a much more serious effort to build a sound democratic system. The two nations experienced serious difficulties in the area of security for the republic. Under normal conditions, the withdrawal of the U.S. occupation troops would have been carried out as part of the usual procedures accompanying the establishment of a new nation. But Korea was not in a state of normality during this period; she was fighting the Cold War, and the United States was one of the two leaders in this war. Partly because of this leadership and partly because of their past relationship, South Korea asked for as much help from the United States as her Cold War adversary was getting from the leader of the other camp. Despite the real military and economic needs of the Republic of Korea for her very survival and for fighting the Cold War, the United States ignored them and withdrew its troops according to a somewhat delayed schedule and sat tight with a limited amount of aid. All told, the Acheson and Connally statement, the troop withdrawals, and the reluctance to provide military and economic aid gave South Koreans a great sense of disappointment and an equally great sense of encouragement to the other Korea.

Why did this happen? First, the U.S. military erred in several ways in fighting the Cold War. The block-and-gap approach was an incorrect application of the containment policy, because the communist expansionist force was constantly looking for the weakest point, and creating a gap was an invitation for them to take action. Also, Korea had long been attractive to the Russians since the imperial period. Another error, corrected later, was to concentrate too much on the global war and neglect taking measures against small-scale conventional wars. It has been said that the main reason for the block-and-gap approach adopted by the military was the shortage of manpower and money. The United States had a large manpower base and was at the peak of economic prosperity, and it could have mobilized adequate resources to fight the Cold War under appropriate political leadership. The failure to provide such resources before it was too late was a definite failure of the Truman administration. One additional point to be made is that, as some U.S. congressmen pointed out during the debate for economic aid, the moral responsibility of the United States for Korea could be neglected only with grave consequences. Soon the time came to account for all of the mistakes and the unaccomplished deeds, and the nation had to stand for judgment through fire on the battlefield.

NOTES

1. Postpresidential memoirs, interview with Acheson, February 18, 1955, p. 13, Truman Library; Frank J. Pace, Jr., oral interview transcript, p. 97, Truman Library; William H. Draper, oral interview transcript, p. 76, Truman Library; Shepley to C. D. Jackson or others, October 18, 1952, Eisenhower Library, Ann Whitman File, Campaign Series, box 7; John J. Muccio, oral interview transcript, Truman Library; Niles H. Bond, oral interview transcript, Truman Library.

2. *Seoul Sinmun*, January 15, 1950 (morning edition) no. 1: 1–5; ibid., (evening edition) no. 1: 2–4; Acheson Paper, memorandum of conversation, Truman Library, box 65; Chang Myŏn, oral interview transcript, Princeton University Library; memorandum of conversation by Bond, April 3, 1950, *FRUS, 1950*, 7: 42.

3. Vladimir Petrov, "Soviet Role in the Korean War Confirmed; Soviet Documents Declassified," *Journal of Northeastern Studies* 13 (Fall 1994): 51; Evgueni Bajanov, "Assessing the Policies of the Korean War," *Cold War International History Project Bulletin* 6–7 (Winter 1995–1996); Kathryn Weathersby, "The Soviet Role in the Early Phase of the Korean War: New Documentary Evidence," *The Journal of American–East Asian Relations* 24 (Winter 1995): 26. Also consult Dobbs,

The Unwanted Symbol, pp. 181–183; Ernest R. May, *"Lessons" of the Past: The Use and Misuse of History in American Foreign Policy* (London: Oxford University Press, 1973), p. 66; Richard Nixon, *The Real War* (New York: Warner Books, 1980), p. 254; Cho Soon-sung, *Korea in World Politics*, p. 260; Buhite, *Soviet-American Relations in Asia, 1945–1954*, p. 169; Cumings, "Introduction," pp. 45–48; Gaddis, "The Strategic Perimeter," pp. 61–62, 65, 106, 112, 115–116; idem, *Long Peace*, pp. 72, 75, 96, 101–102; idem, "Korea in American Politics," p. 285.

4. Rusk to Webb, May 2, 1950, *FRUS, 1950*, 7: 65–66; *U.S. News and World Report*, 28 (May 5, 1950): 30; Drumright to the Secretary of State, May 3, 1950, NA, RG 59, Numerical File, box 4299; Drumright to the Secretary of State, May 5, 1950, *FRUS, 1950*, 7: 78; Drumright to the Secretary of State, June 19, 1950, NA, RG 59, Numerical File, box 4299; *Kyŏnghyang Sinmun*, May 6, 1950, 1: 1–7.

5. John Muccio, oral interview transcript, p. 28, Truman Library; Muccio to Rusk, June 1, 1950, *FRUS, 1950*, 7: 97; Rusk to Muccio, June 15, 1950, welcome address for Dr. and Mrs. Jessup, by P. H. bid., p. 106.

6. Shinicky, Chairman of National Assembly, January 12, 1950, NA, RG 59, Numerical File, box 2882A; notes on conversation with Korean officials, ibid.; memorandum by Jessup, January 14, 1950, *FRUS, 1950*, 7: 1–7; Muccio to the Secretary of State, January 28, 1950, ibid., pp. 18–23; *Kyŏnghyang Sinmun*, January 11, 1950, 1: 1–4; *Seoul Sinmun*, January 11, 1950, 1: 1–5; ibid., January 13, 1950, 1: 5–8; *Chosŏn Ilbo*, January 15, 1950, 1: 1–5; *New York Times*, January 13, 1950, 3: 8; ibid., January 13, 1950, 1: 6–7; ibid., January 13, 1950, 15, 2: 2; ibid., February 2, 1950, 3: 7.

7. Department of State Press Release, July 7, 1950, Princeton University Library, Dulles Papers, box 48; Dulles Speech, September 17, 1952, ibid., box 61; *Department of State Bullletin* 23 (July 3, 1950): 12–13; memorandum of conversation by the Director of the Office of Northeastern Affairs (Allison) with Rhee, Dulles, Muccio, and Im Pyŏng-chik, June 19, 1950, *FRUS, 1950*, 7: 107; Dulles Statement, Seoul, June 20, 1950, Princeton University Library, Dulles Papers, box 48; Dulles to the Department of State, June 23, 1950, ibid; oral interview transcript with Chang Myŏn, ibid.

8. Rhee to MacArthur, June 20, 1950, MacArthur Library; Im, *Im Pyŏng-chik hoekorok*, p. 350; Bertrand to Felix, June 29, 1950, Princeton University Library, Dulles Papers, box 48; "Visit to Korea of John Foster Dulles," June 23, 1950, ibid.; "Peking NCNA in English Morse to North American 1652 12/7," ibid., box 49; *Seoul Sinmun*, June 16, no. 1: 1–7; idem, June 18, no. 1: 1–8; idem, June 22, 1950, no. 1: 1–9; *Kyŏnghyang Sinmun*, June 17, 1950, 1: 1–7; *Chosŏn Ilbo*, June 18, 1950, 1: 1–7; *New York Times*, June 20, 1950, 20: 3, 26: 2; Cumings, "Introduction," p. 49; Cho Soon-sung, *Korea in World Politics*, p. 263.

PART III

WAR AND DIPLOMACY
IN KOREA

CHAPTER 9

The Nature of and Responsibility for the Outbreak of the War

Sunday, June 25, 1950 began calmly in Seoul. Soon, however, the morning quiet was shattered by the news of the invasion from the north, and the capital city of South Korea was suddenly like a beehive rudely poked with a big stick. The invasion did not come as a total surprise for the average citizens of South Korea. For years, they had lived with the nervous expectation that someday they would be awakened with the news of a North Korean invasion. The only thing they did not know was exactly when it would occur. Most South Koreans had a fairly accurate picture of the respective military strengths of the two Koreas and of the aggressive intentions of the communists in the north. They thought that as soon as the invasion came they would have to dash to Pusan at the southern tip of the peninsula to save their lives. When the invasion came, the communist army moved too swiftly, and on the third day of the war, communist troops were already in the capital city. Most of the city's residents were trapped behind the battle lines. It was later learned that the invasion had begun at four o'clock in the morning, and soon an all-out northern offense was under way along the 150 miles of the 38th parallel. Thus, the Korean War, which lasted a little over three years, began.[1]

Because of the complexity of its nature, the perception of the Korean War has been varied among observers. Some contemporaries immediately recognized the significance of the war and called it the post–Second World War Pearl Harbor, while others thought it was the most powerful phase of the Cold War or a "new chapter in history."[2] Still others thought the war was an irritating, frustrating, and cruel "tragedy." And, even before the war ended, some already began to call it a "forgotten war."[3] Later observers' views on the Korean War were not much different from those of contemporaries. Some authors readily recognized the magnitude of the war; to others the war was "bitter and bloody," "meaningless," an "uncomfortable episode," or a "sour little war."[4] Callum A. MacDonald in his book on the Korean War said that in the United States, it became a "forgotten war." Bruce Cumings firmly stated that the Korean War was called a forgotten war because "it actually was forgotten."[5] Probably the truth is that many Americans, like many others, wished to forget the unpleasant experience of the war, but these people also may remember more as they try hard to forget it.

For the Koreans, it was an entirely different story; this was a war they could not and should not forget. The war for them was a great tragedy, one of the greatest the nation had ever experienced since its establishment as a unified nation in the seventh century A.D. The nation had undergone the experience of being invaded by outsiders from the north and the south and sometimes had been caught in the midst of two contending powerful neighbors at the same time, but the peninsula had never experienced the disaster of being involved in a civil and an international war at the same time. The war was also a total war for the Koreans; the nation and its population were totally involved and suffered nearly complete destruction.

One of the most important and most difficult questions about the Korean War, or any other war or great historical event, is the question of its causes. Because of the complexity of this question, many authors avoid attempting to find causal linkages and simply try to clarify the origins or explain the background of the war. Thousands of pages have been written on the causal factors and background of the Korean War. Yet, until all the testimonies of those who were directly involved in the war making can be examined (many of them are no longer in this world, and some of the evidence may have already been destroyed) and all the archives of the major countries that were involved in the process leading to the war are fully opened, all attempts, including this one, to try to explain why the war began can be only partial and temporary.

A question to be raised first is who started the invasion. There have been debates over this fundamental question, and to some the answer still may not be clear. But for millions of Koreans who personally witnessed the rolling out of the formidable North Korean military machine across the 38th parallel and the quick occupation of the capital city of South Korea in late June 1950, the debate is a luxurious verbal exercise.[6] A more important question concerns the motives and the reasons behind the roles of those who were responsible for the invasion. By this time, it seems clear that Kim Il Sung, the leader of the North Korean regime, was the person who initiated the planning for the invasion and led at least the beginning of the war and definitely was the one most responsible for the war. Only Kim himself could give the final word about exactly why he conceived the idea of launching the war, and someday, when the North Korean governmental archives are fully opened, we may find more direct evidence for his reasoning about the invasion. The seemingly most obvious motivational factor for the venture was Kim's desire to achieve the reunification of the Korean peninsula. Since the division of the peninsula, reunification has been the ambition of all Korean leaders, not only Kim's. When we turn to the question of whether this national goal should be achieved through war, it becomes a philosophical debate, and most people argue that however noble the goal, it should not be achieved through violence. Another motivational factor for Kim's venture must have been revolutionary zeal. As a communist political leader, he wished to "liberate" the South Korean "comrades" who were suffering under the capitalist yoke. However strong Kim's desire for independence in the prewar period, we can at least hypothesize, in view of his attitude toward Mao in the spring of 1950, which some considered to be "arrogant" or even "deceptive," that his desire for Korean independence from friends as well as enemies was powerful. Other than these three more obvious motives, Kim must have had a host of special reasons for the adventure. In addition to his high-minded motivation, he also needed certain resources for the invasion; and with the exception of well-mobilized manpower, he lacked the necessary resources for war, such as military equipment, arms, and ammunition. For these essential resources, he had to turn to Stalin and Mao, who thus inevitably played significant roles in the outbreak of the Korean War.[7]

Presently available Russian sources indicate that Stalin began to provide Kim with the necessary approval and support for launching the war in the spring of 1950. Stalin, who had been skeptical about Kim's plan for the invasion of the south and had kept a cautious posture throughout 1949, changed his position early in the following year and began in February to supply North Korea with military hardware and advisers. Finally, in April, when Kim visited the Soviet leader to obtain approval for military action, Stalin gave him the green light, but with the condition that Kim also obtain the consent of Mao. Stalin also promised Kim logistic and other necessary support for the invasion. In the following month, Kim traveled to Beijing to obtain Mao's consent for his venture. Mao, busy with his own plans and problems and with reservations about Kim's plan, nevertheless gave Kim his consent and promised his support. Once Stalin decided to give approval to Kim, he moved swiftly to send the necessary military equipment and supplies and a group of military advisers who drew up an operational directive for the invasion. Thus, by mid-May of 1950, both Stalin and Mao gave their consent for the northern invasion, and soon Soviet logistical and advisory support and one division from China with Korean personnel began to arrive in Korea, setting the stage for the Korean War.[8]

The Soviet and Chinese roles in the outbreak of the Korean War have been a subject of much study and speculation for many years by both contemporaries and later observers. Some have taken the extreme position that either Kim was solely responsible for initiating the war and that Stalin and Mao were not involved at all in the planning stage and were caught by surprise just like the Westerners or that the two powers, especially the Soviet Union, played key roles in the decision to launch the war, and the North Koreans were simply executing their plans. Many others have taken the middle position that all three had roles to play and share the responsibility for initiating the war. Presently available Russian and Chinese sources, which explain the roles of the three leaders, support the middle position more than the extreme ones. There has also been much speculation that, even though China played less of a role than did the Soviet Union, approval of the plan and a promise of assistance was given to North Korea for the invasion.[9]

Quite obviously, Stalin and Mao would not have consented in the spring of 1950 to a North Korean invasion of South Korea simply to satisfy Kim's personal ambitions or the Korean people's wish for reunification; they must have had their own set of objectives as the bases for their consent and commitment. If Kim's "persuasion" or success in "breaking the Russian leader" with the argument that the operation would be quickly finished before the United States could intervene, and that as many as 200,000 South Koreans would rise up for the north when the invasion was launched, were factors, they should not be given much weight. Sergei N. Goncharov and others identify three major factors for Stalin's decision to approve and support Kim's plan. These include his desires to create a buffer zone on the Korean peninsula, a springboard for action against Japan, to intensify the hostility between China and the United States, and to test American resolve. Other important contributing factors behind his decision were his view that the United States would not intervene, given U.S. policy toward the war in China and the statements made by responsible Americans like Acheson in Washington in the spring of 1950. If all the benefits could be reaped with a limited amount of logistical support and without direct military intervention, the invasion certainly was a good deal for the Soviet Union. Some seem to think that Mao was simply "outmaneuvered" and even "cheated" by Kim and was used by Stalin to achieve Soviet goals, but it is very likely that Mao also had his own reasons for his consent and support of Kim's plan. Beyond his sympathy for Kim's venture and his sense of obligation to go along with Stalin in exchange for the Soviet assistance for China's plan for an invasion of Taiwan, Mao must have had his eyes on benefits like the creation of a security zone, which would be even more important for China than for the Soviet Union, and a long-term improvement of China's international and leadership position in East Asia.[10]

If the responsibility of Kim, Stalin, and Mao for the outbreak of the Korean War can be at least tentatively established, the question of how important each role was remains. Of course, it is true that without Kim's initiation there would have been no war, and in that sense Kim's role was essential. At the same time, it is also the case that without the approval and support of Stalin and Mao, there also would have been no war. In this regard, Stalin and Mao's approval and support was necessary. Each of the three leaders played different but important and essential roles for the outbreak of the war; together, they created the necessary and sufficient conditions for the initiation of the war. Each of the three must have thought that he was getting the best of the deal.

It seems unfair to assign guilt to the victim in criminal cases. Quite often, however, the victims provide criminals with an opportunity by creating conditions in which the crime can take place. When international wars of the past are examined carefully, we often find guilty victims. It is the unfortunate case that the Korean War was one such war, and in an examination of the responsibility of the opposite side, we have to turn first to the role played by South Korea. Some South Koreans argued that the northern invasion was a preemptive attack. To the degree that a desire for unification of the divided Korea was concerned, President Rhee did not fall behind anyone, including Kim Il Sung. Indeed, it is a good hypothetical question to ask as to whether he could have successfully restrained himself from undertaking a venture similar to that undertaken by Kim if the South Korean military forces had been much stronger than those of the north, especially if that differential was close to 2 to 1. Even given the actual difference in military strength between the north and south, he still sometimes suggested that he would march north to unify the Korean peninsula immediately. Most probably, he tried to convey a sense of confidence to his own people and their American friends and a sense of caution to his enemies in the north and elsewhere. To a certain extent, he achieved his objective because his declarations gave a sense of security to a good part of his own people and some sense of relief to his American friends. Probably, his tactic was less effective with regard to his enemies, but even in this sector the now-available Soviet documents show that his statements had some effect on the enemy camp, or in the very least, Stalin used President Rhee's strong words as a reason for caution. However, President Rhee's tough talk also had its negative side. It provided the American government with a rationale for hesitancy in the building of a larger defense force in South Korea. A similar mistake was made by other ROK government officials, who exaggerated the strength of the enemy. Their intention was to alert their American friends, but when the warnings were overdone, it hurt their credibility. Indeed, the much more serious problem for the South Koreans was their weakness. Like poverty for an individual, weakness for a nation may not be a sin in and of itself. However, it attracts the fist of a stronger nation, just as poverty tends to lead aggressors to undertake ruthless actions. Probably the biggest part of the Korean share of responsibility for the outbreak of the Korean war was their weakness after the division of the Korean peninsula. The division was in a sense the price the Koreans paid for liberation, which came to them as a gift and without their contribution.[11]

The last country to be considered in this analysis of responsibility for the outbreak of the Korean War is the United States. It is very difficult to determine exactly how much weight to assign this country for the outbreak of the Korean War. One way to gauge its importance is to look at the picture from the invader's viewpoint. From the perspective of the North Korean leaders, it must have been fairly clear that what the United States would or would not do in the war would be decisive. If there was a good possibility that the Americans would intervene, then the Soviet Union and China would not consent to start the war, and even if they did, and the war began, the chance of North Korean victory would be uncertain. If an exact weighting of the U.S. role in the outbreak of the Korean War is not feasible, at least a close examination of the components of the role played by the United States is possible.

The responsibility of the United States for the Korean War has long roots, which developed through a series of actions. The 1945 division of the Korean peninsula, the 1945 to 1948 military occupation, the 1947 decision to refer the Korean problem to the United Nations, the 1949 troop withdrawal, the 1948 to 1950 reluctance on the part of the United States to provide adequate military and economic aid for the Republic of Korea, the candid Acheson–Connally statements of U.S. policy toward Korea in case of crisis in the spring of 1950, and finally the later outbreak in that year of the war— all these actions and events were cumulatively and causally related. In terms of weight, the earlier acts tended to be more significant because of their impact upon later events. Some reexamination of these actions and an examination of the linkage between them will perhaps further clarify the role of the United States in the outbreak of the Korean War.

The U.S. decision in favor of the division of the Korean peninsula in the summer of 1945 was definitely the most important step in the series of actions and events leading to the Korean War. If there had been no division, there would have been no war. The importance of this fateful decision comes both from the magnitude of the action of dividing a nation with thirteen centuries of history and the fact that it identified a series of decisions which established the direction for subsequent actions and events. The decision was made by the U.S. government between August 10 and 15, 1945, primarily because of military expediency. The small number of American troops that could be used for the occupation of Korea were far away, and the much larger Soviet force was nearby. Later, when Congressman Walter H. Judd questioned the American government's decision to divide the Korean peninsula, although at the time of the decision there was not a single Russian soldier in Korean territory, the military's response was that, even though Soviet troops were not physically present in Korea, they could have moved in at any time. Further, the American government defended its decision by indicating that the Russians had entered the war in the Far East according to the Yalta Agreement and that a price had to be paid for this contribution. Both arguments seem to have firm bases, but it is questionable whether they were sufficient to justify the division at the 38th parallel. If the Soviet Union needed a reward for its small contributions, it certainly did not deserve to have a half of the peninsula, and if the division was done for the purpose of receiving the Japanese surrender, as it has been explained, the division of Korea would not in fact be a reward for the Russians or for any other nation involved. Further, the decision indicates clearly that those who participated in the policy-making process did not seem to have thought through the implications of the division. It is historically true that defeated countries have been divided without any hesitation by the victorious powers, but such divisions have brought ample harmful results in the long run.

The decisions to divide countries at the end of World War II were no exception (Germany, Austria, and Korea). Moreover, the division of a national territory against a people's will under any circumstances should be considered a serious offense against a national right. International society is by no means an amoral society, and in order to maintain order and peace within this society, national rights, like human rights, should be respected. Once a commitment is made that violates this right, it is impossible for the nation involved to escape its responsibility.[12]

The military occupation of the southern part of Korea by the U.S. Army between 1945 and 1948 was a natural, if illogical, action following the division of Korea. Some may even argue that the occupation was the real objective of the division. Once the division was made, the occupation was very difficult, though not impossible, to avoid. There were alternatives, however. Had both the U.S. and the Soviet armies withdrawn from Korea as soon as the Japanese had surrendered their troops, the U.S. government could have avoided making a further commitment to occupy the south. Chaotic conditions and even a conflict could have developed on the Korean peninsula, but not a full-scale war. Had the situation in Korea been allowed to work itself out, the outcome might not have been exactly what the United States wished, but it would certainly not have resulted in the development of a Soviet-style communist society on the Korean peninsula. If this course had been taken, the next serious step—American disengagement by shifting the burden to the United Nations—could have been avoided. Another alternative, which could at least have lessened the bad effect of the occupation, was expanding the occupation powers from two to four by inviting participation from Great Britain and China.[13]

The U.S. decision to turn South Korea over to the United Nations in 1947 resulted from its failure to unify the divided nation through cooperation with the other occupying power, the Soviet Union. The consequence was the creation of two antagonistic nations, or two half-nations, on the peninsula at a time when the world organization was too young to handle such a volatile situation. In addition to becoming a link in the causal chain leading to the war, the U.S. action in 1947 also internationalized the Korean problem. Internationalization created a situation in which the young and still weak collective security institution took over a job which was beyond its capability. Later, when the war broke out, the United States used this internationalization of the conflict as a framework for its intervention. In short, the decision to transfer the Korean problem to the United Nations was probably an expedient action for the United States, which wished to dump unwanted baggage into the lap of the infant organization. Nonetheless, it certainly hastened the coming of the war by creating two antagonistic half nations.

The U.S. troop withdrawal of mid-1949, the single most important step leading to the war since 1945, was closely related to the 1945 division, the occupation of 1945 to 1948, and the U.N. takeover and establishment of two Koreas in 1947 and 1948. The division brought the Cold War to Korea; the occupation brought the occupation forces to the Korean peninsula; and the independence of the Republic of Korea provided a legal basis for the withdrawal if the United States chose to use it as a reason or pretext. Ultimately, the withdrawal of U.S. troops in 1949 meant the removal of the only existing deterrent against a hot war which might come as a part of the Cold War in Korea. At the very end of the century, U.S. troops in South Korea still remain like a "thorn in the eyes" of North Korea; the U.S. troop withdrawal in 1949 must have been greeted with rejoicing by the North Korean authorities. Many—then and later—have been critical about this action on the part of the United States, which took place exactly a year before the outbreak of the war in Korea.[14]

Even after the troop withdrawal was completed, with all of its implications and dangers, if the U.S. government had taken compensatory actions by strengthening the South Korean defense force with adequate military and economic aid, the damage would have been lessened and either the war would have been avoided or at least postponed, thus allowing South Korean security forces time to improve their readiness. But as it turned out, the U.S. government, that is, both Congress and the administration, were very reluctant and would not provide South Korea with even minimal necessities to deter the invasion from the north. This reluctance and negligence was well revealed by the actions and inactions in the Congress and the executive branch during the year between the troop withdrawal and the outbreak of the war. This must have conveyed an unmistakable impression to the North Korean leaders and their comrades that the troop withdrawal was an action signifying that the United States was abandoning the republic to its fate. After the removal of the token U.S. troops, constructing a substantial defense force and a viable economy in South Korea were the only remaining possibilities for deterring a hot war in Korea. But the chance was lost, and many—Americans and Koreans, Democrats as well as Republicans, legislators and administrators—were alarmed then, and all were critical later.[15]

One of the most important questions for Kim Il Sung and Stalin in 1949 was what the United States would do when the North Korean invasion plan was carried out. By 1950 both Kim and Stalin must have inferred from the

U.S. troop withdrawal and the weak U.S. military and economic aid policies for South Korea that U.S. intervention was very unlikely in the case of a North Korean invasion. If there was any amount of uncertainty left about this judgment, it was soon clarified by the statements of the two responsible officials in Washington—Secretary of State Acheson and the Senate Foreign Relations Committee Chairman Connally. Through these public declarations even the benefit of doubt was lost, and South Korea lay open for the Northern invasion.[16]

One of the controversies regarding the North Korean invasion concerns the question of intelligence: Why did the South Korean and American intelligence agencies fail to detect beforehand the preparations for the invasion and the movements which immediately preceded it? Though it is doubtful whether the American government could have changed the decision of its policy quickly and substantially enough to prevent the coming war in the spring of 1950, implied in this question is the suggestion that if these agencies had early on successfully detected the North Korean preparations for the invasion, something could have been done to prevent it or at least to lessen the effect of surprise attack. In a real sense, the intelligence failure was closely related to the general policy of the United States, a failure that seems to have been difficult to avoid. The problem involved in this failure was not lack of information, but the management of the information obtained. The Korean and American intelligence agencies had enough information about North Korean preparations and troop movements in the spring of 1950. Information about the North Korean military build-up, its training program, the transfer of Korean units in the Chinese Communist Army to the North Korean defense force, and troop movements to the 38th parallel on the eve of the invasion was gathered by the Korean intelligence agencies and sent to the highest levels of Korean and American military authorities. But because of the gap between the working level and the policy-making level both in the Korean and the American government and between the Korean and American information-processing authorities, this intelligence information failed to provide meaningful input for policy making in Washington and Seoul. Acheson thought MacArthur's intelligence people were quite "schizophrenic" in giving information on North Korean military movements. The policy makers in Washington, who already had a well-established policy regarding the Korean situation, were able to see only what they wanted to see, not what they should have seen, in the somewhat confusing situation. Thus, because of flawed communication between various government levels and a breakdown in information processing, the intelligence failure regarding the outbreak of the Korean War seems to have been most unfortunate but almost impossible to prevent.[17]

The American policy of engagement and disengagement in the Korean peninsula has been subjected to examination and criticism for decades. Both the decisions to engage and disengage were criticized by observers. If one direction was wrong, the other direction should have been right; but both directions have been criticized. The logic seems to be that the excessive zigzagging process itself was the problem; perhaps, once a wrong commitment had been made, correction was difficult, and more errors were made in the process of correction. Once the choice was made to bring the Cold War to the Korean peninsula, the Americans should have stuck to a commitment to keep the Cold War cold.[18]

Of course, there were good reasons behind the U.S. troop withdrawal and the lukewarm aid policy. Cited often as most important were troop shortages and a lack of money. But in fact the problem facing the United States in the post–World War II years was not lack of money and manpower. Lacking instead were foresight and political leadership. The Truman administration failed to mobilize adequate human and material resources for the security needs of the free world. The far-too-small defense force and the fiscal conservatism of the Truman administration made the block-and-gap approach in the containment strategy almost inevitable. The United States certainly had at this point a large manpower basis for an adequate defense force, and the nation also had equally large economic resources that could be mobilized for national security purposes. What the nation needed were leaders with more foresight and plenty of courage. Perhaps the situation the United States faced in the Korean peninsula in the late 1940s can be described best in the words of Quincy Wright, who was speaking in a more general context: "Democracies tend to be fluctuating in policy, slow in defense preparation, and hesitant in making international commitments for long-run objectives, and to become involved in war through encouraging aggression by others through their own passivity."[19]

An issue closely related to that of the responsibility for the outbreak of the Korean War has been the question of whether the war was a civil war or an international war. First it should be pointed out that the argument that it was a civil war is based on the view that there was only one country on the Korean peninsula in 1950. If this is factually erroneous, then the civil war argument loses its basis. If we set aside this technicality for the moment, everyone who has some understanding of the Korean War has to admit that it had elements of both a civil and an international war. The war began as a war between the two parts of the Korean peninsula, and to its end, these two parts remained to play key roles in the conduct of the war and the peacemaking process. It is also factually correct to say that from the very beginning to the end of the war, the two Koreas were involved in the fighting, in addition to the two great powers and a substantial number of other countries. In terms of location and sacrifice, the war was definitely Korean. On the other hand, in terms of resources—both human and material—and the control–command factor, the war was international. If one step further is taken, then the international component can be narrowed down to two major antagonists, the United States and the Soviet Union. The Russians provided supplies and equipment and an element of control. In contrast, the Americans provided a fighting force, in addition to supplies, equipment, and an element of control. As a result, the war was essentially a struggle between these two great powers. The Korean War as such is thus wrongly named. Korea provided the stage for the action and the sacrifice, and the two great powers were the major actors; therefore, it should be called the Korea War. The Korean War was much less Korean than the Vietnam War was Vietnamese.[20]

In retrospect, it seems that the Korean War, part of the Cold War which impregnated the whole world in the latter part of the twentieth century, was very difficult to avoid, and a special mechanism and some very special efforts were needed for its avoidance. Since Soviet leaders had a clearer idea about the peculiar geopolitical characteristics of the Korean peninsula as a buffer zone, if the American leaders had had an equally adequate understanding of the special nature of the peninsula, the unfortunate division at the 38th parallel might have been avoided. Once a dynamic entity such as a nation was artificially divided, a natural force began to operate for its restoration. The fusion, however, did not have to be violent; it could have been a peaceful one. To monitor the process peacefully, power equilibrium or a moderating mechanism was necessary. But instead of such a mechanism, the world provided Korea with a fierce ideological struggle between communism and liberal democracy. To overcome the added difficulty, a special human effort was necessary. Fortunately Stalin had been cautious in handling the Korean question and had been successfully resisting Kim Il Sung's prodding for a green light for his risky venture, and if even one of the series of mistakes—the U.S. troop withdrawal, the failure to build an adequate deterrent force in the south, and the unfortunate statements of the two responsible U.S. government officials in the spring of 1950—which were made between 1945 and 1950 had been avoided, the war could have been prevented.

NOTES

1. For the outbreak of the Korean War, see *Chŏson Ilbo*, June 25, 1950, 1: 1; *New York Times*, June 25, 1950, 1: 1; Acheson to the Seoul Embassy, June 24, 1950, National Archives (NA), RG 59, box 4262; Sebald to the Department of State, June 29, 1950, ibid., box 4263; Ohn Ch'ang-il, "Cho-ch'ongryŏkchŏn kŭriko chehanchŏn: 6.25 Chŏnchaengŭi suhaeng kwachŏng" (A super total war and a limited war: The process of the Korean War), in *Hankuk Chŏnchaeng ŭi yŏksach ŏk koch'al* (Historical consideration of the Korean War), ed. Hankuk Chŏngch'ioekyosa Hakhoe (Seoul: Pyŏngminsa, 1991), p. 199.

2. John J. Muccio, speech, May 30, 1952, *Department of State Bulletin* 26 (June 16, 1952): 941; Robert Taft, remarks, *Congressional Record*, 81st, 2d sess., vol. 96, pt. 7, p. 9320; *New York Times*, July 3, 1953, 14: 2; John Foster Dulles, remarks, August 7, 1950, *Department of State Bulletin* 23 (August 7, 1950): 207;

Matthew B. Ridgway, *The Korean War: How We Met the Challenge* (Garden City, N.Y.: Doubleday, 1967), p. v; Cho Ŭi-sŏl, "Hankuk chŏnchaengŭi sekechŏk ŭii" (The meaning of the Korean War in world history), *Kukche P'yŏngnon* 3 (1959): 62.

3. Omar N. Bradley, remarks, March 2, 1953, *Department of State Bulletin* 28 (March 6, 1953): 413; John Foster Dulles, remarks, July 27, 1953, ibid., 29 (August 10, 1953): 175; "Reconstruction of Korea," Edgar A. E. Johnson Papers, Truman Library; *New York Times*, October 25, 1952, 8: 2–8; *Seoul Sinmun*, June 25, 1951, no. 1: 1–10.

4. Burton I. Kaufman, *The Korean War: Challenge in Crisis, Credibility, and Command* (New York: Knopf, 1986), pp. 338, 356; Calum A. MacDonald, *Korea: The War before Vietnam* (New York: Free Press, 1986), pp. 205, 220, 262; David S. McLellan, *Dean Acheson: The State Department Years* (New York: Dodd, Mead, 1976), p. 316; William Stueck, "The Korean War as International History," *Diplomatic History* 10 (1986): 291–292; Sin Ki-hyŏn, "Hankuk Chŏnchaengŭi hyŏntaesachŏk ŭii: kuknae mit kukchesachŏk ch'awŏn" (The modern historical meaning of the Korean War: Domestic and international dimensions), *Kukche Chŏngch'i Nonch'ong: Hankuk Chŏnchaengŭi yŏksachŏk Chaech'omyŏng* (International Politics Forum: Historical reclarification of the Korean War) (Seoul: Hankuk Totŏk Chŏngch'i Yŏnkuso, 1990), pp. 333–411; Kim U-sang, "6.25 ŭi imi" (The meaning of the Korean War), in *Hankuk Chŏnchaeng ŭi yŏksachŏk chomyŏng* (Historical examination of the Korean War), ed. Hankuk Totŏk Chŏngch'i Yŏnkuso (Seoul: Hankuk Totŏk Chŏngch'i Yŏnkuso, 1990), pp. 63–69; Lee Myŏng-yong, "6.25 Sapyŏn, ŏtŏke bolkŏtinka" (The June 25 incident: How should we characterize it?), ibid., pp. 11–20; Lee Sang-sik, "Hankuk Chŏnchaeng ŭi sŏngkyŏkkwa pansŏng" (The nature of and reflection on the Korean War), ibid., pp. 75–83; Ra Jong-il, *Kŭtnachi anŭn chŏnchaeng: Hanpantowa kangtaekuk chŏngch'i, 1950–1954* (Unended war: The Korean Peninsula and the strong-power politics, 1950–1954) (Seoul: Chŏnyewŏn, 1994), pp. 11–44.

5. Bruce Cumings, *The Origins of the Korean War*, vol. 2, *The Roaring of the Cataract, 1947–1950* (Princeton, N.J.: Princeton University Press, 1990), p. 267; MacDonald, *Korea: The War before Vietnam*, p. 262.

6. For documentation and a discussion of this subject, see, "Reconnaissance Order #1, issued by Operations Section, 4th Infantry Division, 0512 24 June (1950)" (translation), attached to Research Supplement Documentary Evidence of North Korean Aggression, October 30, 1950, MacArthur Library, RG 6, Far Eastern Command, box 15; Kim Chŏm-kon, *The Korean War: The First Comprehensive Account of the Historical Background and Development of the Korean War, 1950–1953* (Seoul: Kwangmyŏng, 1973), pp. 422–423; Kim Chull-baum, ed., *Chinsilkwa chŭngŏn: 40-nyŏnmane palkyŏchin Hankuk Chŏnchaengŭi chinsang* (The truth and testimony: The fact of the Korean War revealed after forty years) (Seoul: Ŭlyu Munhwasa, 1990), pp. 113–125, 144–147; Pak Myŏng-lim, "Nuka Hankuk Chŏnchaengŭl sichak hayŏnnŭnka?: Namch'im-pukch'im nonchengŭi chongkyŏlŭl ŭihan charyowa sasilŭi kŏmt'owa haesŏk" (Who did start the Korean War?: An examination and interpretation of source materials and facts for ending the controversy of the northern or southern invasion), *Hankuk Chŏngch'ihak Hakpo* 28 (1994): 79–105; *Facts Tell* (P'yŏngyang: Foreign Language Publishing House, 1960), pp. 11–199; Ra Jong-il, *Kŭtnachi anŭn chŏnchaeng*, p. 40.

7. For the North Korean initiative, see the *Department of State Bulletin* 24 (May 21, 1951): 828–830; *New York Times*, May 3, 1951, 6: 3–6; ibid., May 29, 1951, 3:

2; Stueck, *The Road to Confrontation*, p. 192; idem, "The Korean War as International History," p. 293; idem, *The Korean War: An International History* (Princeton, N.J.: Princeton University Press, 1995), p. 31; Sergei Goncharov, John W. Lewis, and Xue Litai, *Uncertain Partners: Stalin, Mao, and the Korean War* (Stanford: Stanford University Press, 1993), pp. 137–139; Kim Chull-baum, "A Triangle of Kim, Stalin, and Mao in the Korean War" (manuscript, July 1995), pp. 2–3; Kim Hakjoon, "Russian Foreign Ministry Documents on the Origins of the Korean War" (manuscript, July 1995), pp. 5–7; Valeri Denissov, "The Korean War of 1950–1953: Thoughts about the Conflict's Causes and Actors" (manuscript, July 1995), p. 13; Ra Jong-il, *Kŭtnachi anŭn chŏnchaeng*, pp. 49–50. See also Vladimir Petrov, "Soviet Role in the Korean War Confirmed," *Journal of Northeast Asian Studies* 13 (Summer 1994): 63; Kathryn Weathersby, "New Findings on the Korean War," *Cold War International History Project Bulletin* 3 (Fall 1993): 14.

   8. *Chŏson Ilbo*, July 25, 1994: 14–15; ibid., July 26, 1994: 22–23; ibid., July 27, 1994: 18–19; *Hanguk Ilbo*, July 22, 1994: 4–7; ibid., July 25, 1994: 4; Stueck, *The Korean War*, pp. 31–46; Goncharov, Lewis, and Xue, *Uncertain Partners*, pp. 136–154; Kim Chull-baum, "A Triangle," pp. 2–5; Kim Hakjoon, "Russian Foreign Ministry Documents," pp. 5–24; Denissov, "Korean War of 1950–1953," pp. 1–13.

   9. Michael C. Sandusky, *American Parallel* (Alexandria, Va.: Old Dominion Press, 1983), p. 66; I. F. Stone, *The Hidden History of the Korean War* (New York: Monthly Review Press, 1952), p. 66; Bruce Cumings, "Introduction: The Course of Korean–American Relations, 1943–1953," in *Child of Conflict: The Korean–American Relations, 1943–1953*, ed. Bruce Cumings (Seattle: University of Washington Press, 1983), p. 50; Stueck, *The Road to Confrontation*, p, 192; Rosemary Foot, *The Wrong War: American Policy and the Dimensions of the Korean Conflict, 1950–1953* (Ithaca, N.Y.: Cornell University Press, 1985), pp. 58, 61; McLellan, *Dean Acheson*, p. 275. See also Nikita S. Khrushchev's memoir, "Kareiskaya bonina," (The Korean war), *Oganiok*, January 1991, pp. 27–28; *Department of State Bulletin* 23 (July 17, 1950): 89; ibid., 24 (January 8, 1951): 64; ibid., 24 (February 19, 1951): 295; *Military Situation in the Far East: Hearings before the Committee on Armed Services and Committee on Foreign Relations*, U.S. Senate, 82d Cong., 1st sess., part 1, p. 173. For the Chinese involvement, see "Former North Korean Gen. Says Kim Started War," *Korea Newsreview* 19, no. 45 (November 10, 1990): 7; "How War Started in Korea," ibid., 20, no. 30 (July 27, 1991): 30; "Kim Il-Sung, Stalin, Mao Agreed to Start Korean War," ibid., 22, no. 27 (July 3, 1993): 6; MacDonald, *Korea: The War before Vietnam*, p. 28; Nixon, *The Real War* (New York: Warner Brothers, 1980), p. 281; Pak Du-bok, "Chungkukŭi Hankuk Chŏnchaeng kaipe kwanhan yŏnku" (A study on the reasons for the People's Republic of China's intervention in the Korean War), in Hankuk Chŏngch'ioekyosa Hakhoe, ed. *Hankuk Chŏnchaengŭi chŏngch'ioekyosachŏk koch'al*, pp. 113–143. See also Goncharov, Lewis, and Xue, *Uncertain Partners*, p. 130.

   10. Goncharov, Lewis, and Xue, *Uncertain Partners*, pp. 141–142, 152; Denissov, "Korean War of 1950–1953," p. 11; Xue Litai, "State Interest and Realpolitik in the Decision-Making Process" (manuscript, July 1995), p. 5.

   11. Goncharov, Lewis, and Xue, *Uncertain Partners*, pp. 136, 142, 145–146, 163–154, 209; Chen Jian, *China's Road to the Korean War: The Making of the Sino-American Confrontation* (New York: Columbia University Press, 1994), p. 203. Regarding South Korean intentions for a forceful unification, see the memorandum

of conversation, Muccio to Acheson, December 20, 1948, NA, RG 59, Decimal File 1945–49, box 2111; memorandum by Kenneth Royall, February 8, 1949, *Foreign Relations of the United States (FRUS), 1949*, 7: 957; memorandum for the President, February 18, 1949, Truman Library, President's Secretary's File, box 220; Rhee to MacArthur, May 22, 1949, MacArthur Library; Muccio to Acheson, November 4, 1949, *FRUS, 1949*, 7: 1093; Hickerson to Acheson, November 5, 1952, NA, RG 59, 795.00/11–552; "Basic Factors in the Korean Situation," NA, RG 59, Records of Policy Planning Staff, box 20; *New York Times*, March 2, 1950, 20: 4–5; ibid., June 27, 1950, 13: 3.

12. For the decision-making process behind the division at the 38th parallel, see Dean Rusk's statement, *FRUS, 1945*, 6: 1039. For the comments that relate the division to the war, see *Congressional Record*, 81st Cong., 2d sess., vol. 96, pt. 21, p. 16914; ibid., 82d Cong., 1st sess., vol. 97, pt. 7, pp. 9160, A4309; "Military Situation in the Far East," hearing before the Committee on Armed Services and the Committee on Foreign Relations, U.S. Senate, 82d Cong., 1st sess., pt. 3, p. 2167; *New York Times*, August 27, 1952, 15: 3; *Chŏson Ilbo*, November 5, 1952, 1: 1–6; John Merrill, "Internal Warfare in Korea, 1948–1950: The Local Setting of the Korean War," in Cumings, *Child of Conflict*, p. 161.

13. For comments on the occupation by relating it to the war, see Pelz, "U.S. Decision on Korean Policy, 1943–1950," in Cumings, *Child of Conflict*, p. 105; Stueck, *The Road to Confrontation*, p. 31.

14. Muccio to Acheson, November 12, 1948, *FRUS, 1948*, 6: 1325; Muccio to Acheson, May 26, 1949, ibid., *1949*, 7: 1035; *Congressional Record*, 81st Cong., 2d Sess., vol. 96, pt. 7, p. 9320 (Senator Taft's comment) pt. 12, p. 16915 (Senator Morse's comment); "Military Situation in the Far East," pt. 1, pp. 242–243 (Senate Morse's comment), pt. 3, p. 2010 (Senator Byrd's comment); "Withdrawal from Korea," August 1952, Princeton University Library, John Foster Dulles Papers; Postpresidential Memorandum, interview with Dean Acheson, February 18, 1955, Truman Library.

15. Merchant to Bruce, February 16, 1950, NA, RG 84, Seoul Embassy, Top Secret Records, 1950–54, box 1; CINCFE to the Department of the Army, June 30, 1950, MacArthur Library, RG 9, Far Eastern Command, box 9; "The North Korean Pre-Invasion Build-up," ibid., RG 23B, Papers of C. A. Willoughby; Military History Situation in the Far East, pt. 3, p. 1993 (Acheson's remarks); *Congressional Records*, 81st Cong., 1st sess, vol. 95, pt. 7, p. 9533 (Senator Lodge's comment); vol 96, pt. 7, pp. 9158, pt. 9, 12600–12601 (Senator Knowland's comment), pt. 9, p. 10536 (Senator Douglas's comment); "Military Situation in the Far East," pt. 1, p. 234 (Senator Morse's comment), p. 1052 (Senator Knowland's comment); ibid., pt. 3, p. 2013 (Senator Byrd's comment), p. 2115 (Senator Green's comment); "Press Conference of President Syngman Rhee, December 4, 1950," in Drumright to the Secretary of State, December 5, 1950, NA, RG 59, Decimal File 1950–54, box 4303; "Acheson Princeton Seminar," Paul H. Nitze's comment, Truman Library, box 76; Ridgway, *The Korean War*, pp. 11, 17; Im P'yŏng-chik, *Im P'yŏng-chik hoekorok: Kŭntae oekyo imyŏnsa* (Im P'yŏng-chik memoirs: The inside history of modern diplomacy) (Seoul: Yŏwŏnsa, 1956), pp. 326–328; Niles Bond, Truman Library, oral history interview transcript, pp. 37–38; *New York Times*, November 4, 1952, 1: 2–3. See also Nam Chu-hong, "Mikukŭi ch'amchŏn" (Participation of

the United States in the war), in Hankuk Chŏngch'ioekyosa Hakhoe, ed., *Hankuk Chŏnchaengŭi chŏngch'ioekyo sachŏk koch'al*, pp. 25–94.

16. Military Situation in the Far East, pt. 3, p. 1741 (Acheson's remarks); *Congressional Record*, 81st Cong, 2d sess., vol. 96, pt. 4, p. 4321, pt. 9, p. 12185 (Senator Knowland's comment); Ernest R. May, *"Lessons" of the Past: The Use and Misuse of History in American Foreign Policy* (London: Oxford University Press, 1973), p. 66.

17. For the Korean handling of Korean–American intelligence, see Donald S. MacDonald to John Edward Wiltz, April 3, 1978, Miscellaneous Historical Documents, Truman Library; Im P'yŏng-chik, *Im P'yŏng-chik hoekorok*, pp. 327, 348–350; Kim Chong-pil, "Tongnan chŏnya nanŭn yukpon tangchik changkyoyŏtta" (I was an officer on duty at the Korean Army Headquarters on the eve of the war), *Wŏlkan Chungang* (June 1968): 170–173, 174, 176–177; Kim Chŏm-kon, *The Korean War*, pp. 29, 289–290. For the handling of intelligence information on the American side, see Military Situation in the Far East, pt. 3, pp. 1990–1991 (Acheson's remarks); Acheson Papers, Princeton Seminar, Truman Library, box 76; CINCFE to the Department of the Army, June 12, 1950, MacArthur Library, RG 9, Radiograms, box 75; Current Capabilities of the North Korean Regime, ORE 18-50, June 19, 1950, Truman Library, President's Secretary's File, Intelligence File, box 157; The North Korean Pre-Invasion Build-Up, MacArthur Library, RG 23B, Papers of C. A. Willoughby, box 3; Military Situation in the Far East, part 1, pp. 239–241 (comments by General MacArthur and Senator Morse); *New York Times*, May 11, 1950, 14: 5; Ridgway, *The Korean War*, p. 12.

18. For criticisms on U.S. policy toward Korea, see Stueck, *The Road to Confrontation*, pp. 170–171, 173, 251; idem, *The Korean War: An International History*, pp. 41–44; Charles M. Dobbs, *The Cold War and Korea, 1948–1950* (Kent, Ohio: Kent State University Press, 1981), pp. 191, 193, 195; John Merrill, *Korea: The Peninsula Origins of the Korean War* (Newark: University of Delaware Press, 1989), p. 188; Cho Soon-sung, *Korea in World Politics, 1940–1950: An Evaluation of American Responsibility* (Berkeley and Los Angeles: University of California Press, 1967), pp. 271–273, Ohn Chang-il, "The Joint Chiefs of Staff and U.S. Policy and Strategy Regarding Korea, 1945–1953," Ph.D. diss., University of Kansas, 1983, pp. 351–352; Robert T. Oliver, *Syngman Rhee and American Involvement in Korea, 1942–1960: A Personal Narrative* (Seoul: P'anmun, 1978), p. 287.

19. For comments on the failure of the U.S. security and foreign policies of the Truman administration, see *Congressional Records*, 81st Cong., 2d sess., vol. 96, pt. 6, p. 10537 (Senator Douglas's comments), pt. 9, p. 12540 (Representative Coudart's comments), p. 16914 (Senator Morse's comments); Military Situation in the Far East, pt. 3, p. 2375 (General Wedemeyer's comments); Drumright to Wiltz, June 10, 1978, Miscellaneous Historical Documents, Truman Library; *New York Times*, September 5, 1952, 12: 2–7 (General Eisenhower's comments); John Foster Dulles, speech, September 17, 1952, Princeton University Library, Dulles Papers. For the later comments, see Stueck, *The Road to Confrontation*, pp. 112, 168; idem, *The Korean War: An International History*, pp. 41–44; Gaddis, "Korea in American Politics," pp. 247–248, 286–288; MacDonald, *Korea: The War before Vietnam*, pp. 217, 220; Peter Lowe, *The Origins of the Korean War* (London: Longman, 1986), pp. 59, 145, 214; Kaufman, *The Korean War*, p. 24; McLellan, *Dean Acheson*, p.

400; Pelz, "U.S. Decision," p. 118; Quincy Wright, "American Policy toward Russia," *World Politics* 2 (1950): 462.

20. Stueck, *The Korean War*, pp. 3–5; Lowe, *The Origins of the Korean War*, p. 68; Robert R. Simmons, *The Strained Alliance: Peking, P'yŏngyang, Moscow and Politics of the Korean Civil War* (New York: Free Press, 1975), p. 103; Okonogi Masao, "The Domestic Roots of the Korean War," pp. 299–300, 302, 306; John Merrill, *Korea: The Peninsula Origins of the Korean War*, pp. 181, 189; MacDonald, *Korea: The War before Vietnam*, p. 3; Kaufman, *The Korean War*, p. 1.

CHAPTER 10

The War

The last six days of June 1950, probably the most important six days in the entire history of the Korean peninsula, were also important for the United States and many other countries in the world. Because of the conditions existing on the Korean peninsula, the North Korean invasion was hardly a surprise for those who had taken an interest in Korea. There was a reasonable expectation of what would happen on the battlefield once the war began. When the curtain rose, the war proceeded much as had been anticipated. The pressing question was what the United States, which had a special relationship with the Republic of Korea since 1945, would do. Many people definitely thought that the Americans would repeat what they had done in China and that they would watch to see how the dust would settle on the Korean peninsula. They were surprised. How and why did the United States decide to intervene?

The first three days of the attack were critical for the outcome of the Korean War. The South Korean Army was not without a defense plan against a northern attack but had not anticipated an attack at this time and was caught completely by surprise. In the west, the war began with an assault against the ROK 17th Regiment on the Ongjin Peninsula and an attack against the regiments of the ROK First Division in the area of Kaesŏng City. Facing superior enemy forces with large artillery pieces and tanks, the ROK regiments had to give up the ancient city and retreat to the Imjin River line. The next day, the ROK regiment evacuated the Ongjin Peninsula but managed under division commander Colonel Paik Sŭn-yŭp a defensive stand at Munsan. To the east, the ROK 7th and 2d divisions had a much tougher time defending the important Ŭijŏngbu corridor against the invader's main offensive force (the 3d and 4th divisions) and gave up Tongduch'ŏn and P'ŏch'on before the end of the first day of the war. The next day, with reinforcements from the rear, the ROK forces in this region executed a counteroffensive and briefly took Tongduch'ŏn back. Soon, however, they had to abandon the city and were evacuated to Ŭijŏngbu. This important spot also soon fell into the hands of the enemy force. The ROK forces did much better in the central and east coast regions. The ROK 6th Division held the Ch'unch'ŏn area until June 27, and the ROK 8th Division also managed to defend the Kangnŭng and Samch'ŏk areas against the enemy forces (the 5th Division and the amphibian special forces) until June 27.

The North Korean invasion was not confined to the ground. On the first day, the North Korean Air Force not only covered the landing operation in the P'ohang area on the east coast, it also attacked fuel tanks at the Seoul and Kimp'o airports. Five North Korean planes strafed Seoul City in the afternoon, and the next day North Korean airplanes repeatedly attacked the Kimp'o and Yŏido airports.[1]

Muccio in Seoul promptly and accurately reported to Washington the outbreak of war in Korea. His Dispatch 925, sent from Seoul at 10:00 A.M., received by the State Department at 9:26 P.M. on June 24, opened with the statement, "According [to] Korean army reports which [are] partly confirmed by KMAG field advisor reports, North Korean forces invaded ROK territory at several points this morning." He calmly and factually reported what had happened by midmorning on the first day: The attack had begun at 4 A.M. with artillery fire; at about 6 A.M., North Korean infantry had commenced crossing the 38th parallel at Ongjin, Kaesŏng, and Ch'unch'ŏn areas; and an amphibious landing was made by the North Korean forces near Kangnŭng on the east coast. Tanks were participating in the invasion, Kaesŏng was already captured, and the invaders were closing in on Ch'unch'ŏn. He added that the invasion appeared to him to be an all-out attack. In his 7 P.M. telegram, he reported the activities of the North Korean Air Force—a total of three sorties against the Kimp'o and Seoul airports, with some damage.

In facing the North Korean tanks, heavy artillery, and airplanes, one of the most serious problems the South Korean Army confronted from the very beginning was the need for more and better arms and equipment. In his first meeting with Ambassador Muccio after the outbreak of the war, President Rhee talked about the urgent need for more arms and ammunition for the ROK defense forces. In his early telegram of June 26, which reached Washington in the midafternoon (3:46 P.M.) of the same day, Muccio reported the specific requests of President Rhee: ten F-51s, thirty-six 105-mm Howitzers, thirty-six 75-mm antitank guns, and thirty-six 155-mm Howitzers. Muccio made an earnest effort to appeal for ammunition and equipment; in his 7 P.M. telegram of June 25, he said, "I can only express hope that some positive and speedy action can be taken at this late date to remedy this deficiency which is extremely serious threat and handicap to gallant ROK forces who are otherwise capable of putting up most effective opposition." He added, "As Department doubtless aware, Rhee and other Korean officials will look to US for air assistance above all else." The Korean government appealed also through its representative in Washington. Ambassador Chang saw President Truman and Secretary Acheson and conveyed to them the messages requesting arms and equipment from the government in Seoul. The Korean National Assembly also appealed to President Truman and Congress. In addition, American military advisers dispatched an urgent telegram asking for a ten-day supply of arms and ammunition to Pusan.[2]

Based on the urgent dispatches from Seoul, the foreign-policy makers in Washington began immediately to act, telephoning key State and Defense Department officials. On the initiative of Assistant Secretary of State Dean Rusk and Assistant Secretary of State for U.N. Affairs John D. Hickerson, it was agreed that the case should be referred to the U.N. Security Council. Acheson called President Truman in Independence, Missouri to report the crisis and get approval for taking the case to the U.N. Security Council. The following morning, high-level State and Defense Department officials met again at the State Department, and it was there that the military representatives stated that Korean appeals for supplies had been promptly met and that the ten days of emergency supplies were already being flown under air escort to Korea. This statement indicates clearly that the first action to aid Korea during the Korean War was taken by General MacArthur. The military also brought up several other measures, including sending military equipment to Korea and using U.S. air and naval power to establish a protective zone in the Seoul–Kimp'o air base and Inch'ŏn areas for the dual purpose of protecting the evacuation of U.S. nationals and gaining time for the U.N. Security Council to take political measures. The group met again in the afternoon to discuss possible courses of military action open to the United States. After these two preparatory meetings, Acheson called the president to ask him to return to Washington. Truman left the Kansas City Airport a little after 2 P.M. and went directly to Blair House immediately after arriving at the Washington National Airport at 7:40 P.M. In the meantime, the State Department took the crisis to the U.N. Security Council, and the proposed resolution passed shortly before 6 P.M. on June 25. It called upon the North Koreans to withdraw their troops to the 38th parallel and for all members of the United Nations to render "every assistance" to the world organization in the execution of the resolution.[3]

Philip Jessup took careful notes during the June 25 Blair House meeting, and we know much about the discussion during the three-hour dinner meeting. The president asked Secretary Acheson to speak first, and then other representatives from the two departments had a chance to express their views on the measures that should be taken in response to the Korean crisis. Summarizing the matters to be considered by the president, Acheson pointed out the desirability of authorizing MacArthur to send military supplies and equipment above that provided by the MDAP program and to provide air cover for the evacuation of U.S. nationals. He also recommended sending the 7th Fleet to Formosan waters and the stepping-up of aid to Indochina. All of these measures were approved by the president, and instructions were accordingly sent to Tokyo. MacArthur was also instructed to send a survey group to Korea to collect firsthand information. While expressing their views at this meeting, the top military authorities—Secretary of Defense Louis Johnson, Secretary of the Army Frank Pace, Jr., and Chairman of the Joint Chiefs of Staff General Omar N. Bradley—questioned the desirability of sending ground forces to Korea. The Army Chief of Staff General J. Lawton Collins reported that General MacArthur was shipping mortars, artillery, and so on with ammunition. He also indicated that F-51 fighter planes were ready in Japan to be flown to Korea by Korean pilots. Other equipment was also on its way to Korea. The request for supplies from Korea included a ten-day supply of ammunition for 105-mm M3, 81-mm mortar, 60-mm mortar, and carbine caliber 30. In addition, ten F-51s, thirty-six 105-mms, thirty 57-mms, and thirty-six 155-mms were on the list of requested equipment. No civilian leader raised any question regarding the military's decision to send these supplies and equipment to Korea. Apparently, the action was within the range of the actions they would be willing to recommend to respond to the crisis in Korea.[4]

On the second day of the war, Muccio's early morning message to Washington began with a slightly more optimistic tone. He apparently had recovered from the initial shock. He said in his 9 A.M. telegram to Rusk, "After being taken surprise and knocked off balance yesterday morning by overwhelming North Korean armor and artillery aided in afternoon by aircraft, hard fighting ROK ground forces made gallant comeback by midnight and seem to have stabilized situation." He even praised the ability of the Korean soldiers, pointing out that it would be essential for the United States to give them adequate and sustained aid. Apparently, he was encouraged by the ROK counteroffensive in the northern section of Ŭijŏngbu and the determination of the ROK chief of staff to take a firm stand against the invading forces. But ROK effort and determination were not enough to stem the march of the far superior invading forces, and a disappointing deterioration in the battlefield was unavoidable. By the end of the day, Muccio sounded very pessimistic. In his 11 P.M. telegram, he reported that in view of the deterioration and disintegration of the ROK defensive forces, he would immediately start an evacuation operation. The White House had a good intelligence summary of the day's situation in Korea. "After considerable stabilization," the report stated, "along the main line of defense 25 miles north of Seoul" and "several minor offensive actions" by the ROK force, an enemy column was now only nine miles from Seoul. The report also indicated that the morale of the ROK government was reasonably good, the

Korean National Assembly had a reasonably calm spirit, and President Rhee had been upset and "deeply perturbed." The Joint Chiefs of Staff summary of the events in Korea on June 26 was even more succinct: North Korean tanks were in Seoul, and it appeared that the North Korean Army would take the city within twenty-four hours; ammunition and other supplies were being loaded in Japan, but none had arrived in Korea; the ROK forces had not succeeded in halting the advance of the North Korean forces; and, the ROK government had fled to Taegu.[5]

The second Blair House meeting after the outbreak of the Korean War was held on the evening of June 26. Participating were the president and his top military and foreign policy advisors, including Defense Secretary Johnson and the chairman of the Joint Chiefs of Staff General Bradley, both of whom had just returned from their trip to the Far East. Once again, Acheson took the leading role. First he suggested that the United States should go "all-out" and give its "fullest" air and naval support to the ROK force; second, he recommended that the Seventh Fleet be ordered to the Formosan waters to prevent an attack on the island; finally, he recommended that U.S. military forces in the Philippines be increased and that U.S. aid to the Philippines and Indochina be accelerated. All were approved by the president. When the president asked if any of the military representatives had any objection to what Acheson had outlined, no one spoke. General Collins commented that the military situation in Korea was bad and noted that the Korean chief of staff had no fight left in him, saying that he did not know how much good U.S. aid would do. Acheson responded by stating that it was important for the United States to do something, even if the effort were not successful. Defense Secretary Johnson supported Acheson by saying that, even if we lost Korea, the "action would save the situation." Then the president stated that he had done everything he could for five years to prevent this kind of situation in Korea, but the crisis had come anyway. He added, "We must do what we can do to meet it." The president next raised the question of mobilizing the National Guard by asking General Bradley if it would be necessary. The general pointed out that if the United States wanted to commit ground forces, then mobilization would be necessary, but he added that it would be preferable to wait a few days. Acheson also suggested putting the possibility of mobilization "in reserve." The president concluded this discussion by asking the Joint Chiefs of Staff to think about it and let him know their opinion within a few days. The U.S. government decided to take a big step toward intervention at the second Blair House meeting. When the president sounded out his advisers' views on the commitment of ground forces through the mobilization of additional military forces, they hesitated. Nonetheless, both the president and Secretary Acheson demonstrated determination by stating that the United States should do everything possible to meet the communist challenge. After the Blair House meeting, the president told George M. Elsey in a private conversation that

Korea was the "Greece of the Far East," arguing that if the United States stood firm as it had done three years earlier, the enemy would not take any additional steps. Elsey got the impression that the president was sincerely determined to go much further than the measures he had approved on the previous evening.[6]

As had been feared, the U.N. Security Council resolution of June 25 did not have any effect upon the North Korean authorities, and the North Korean military machine kept rolling toward the capital city of the Republic of Korea. The government of the United States, which had emphasized from the beginning the importance of working through the United Nations to meet the communist challenge, decided to ask for a step-up operation of the collective security system, and it worked hard to line up support from members of the Security Council. The U.S.-proposed resolution was approved by the Security Council late in the afternoon of June 27. It recommended that members of the United Nations furnish such assistance to the Republic of Korea as might be necessary "to repel the armed attack and to restore international peace and security in the area." The words were vague, probably purposely, which later caused many different interpretations. But they were much stronger than those of the resolution of June 25, and provided a necessary legal framework for future action to deal with the crisis.[7] Thus, important steps were taken in three days toward U.S. intervention in the Korean crisis, and a legal base was established for future action by members of the collective security system.

In Korea, by early morning on June 28, the defense of the capital city was practically over. At about 2 A.M. North Korean tanks began to come into the city, news which terminated the Miari Combat Operation; at the same time, the Han River bridge was blown up by an ROK engineering corps, a deed which prematurely pushed the battle front to the south bank of the river. The 1st ROK division, which had continued its defensive fighting at Kŭmch'ŏn, northwest of Ŭijŏngbu, also gave up its position as soon as it learned during the early morning of June 28 the fate of Seoul and the Han River bridge and retreated to Sihŭng. Under the leadership of Major General Kim Hong-il, the ROK forces gave up fighting to the north of Seoul and regrouped as effectively as they could. They built a defensive line along the south bank of the Han River and kept fighting until July 3, when North Korean tanks began to cross the river. The six days of time earned by this operation became extremely valuable for the American intervention, thus saving the Republic of Korea from communism. American military advisers encouraged the defending forces by saying that because it would take at least three days for the American forces to reach the battle front, the survival of the republic depended on holding the battle line for three days. The "rifle divisions," or more accurately the remnants of the divisions, managed to sustain the line for at least twice as long as the time needed for the Americans to enter the war with the ground forces. The news of the "U.S.

intervention" with air forces reached some ROK combat forces as well as the personnel at the ROKA headquarters during the early afternoon of June 27 and greatly boosted Korean morale. But most of the average citizens of Seoul and some ROK soldiers did not know the good news of the American intervention. Nevertheless, they had heeded the president's radio message to trust the ROK defense forces and to remain calm in the city, but now were trapped behind the battle lines and soon were gripped by confusion, disillusionment, and fear.[8]

The news about the Korean situation which arrived in Washington during the four-day period between June 26 and 30 was overall grim and very disappointing, and there was little hope to be found in it. In the early afternoon of June 27, MacArthur's headquarters reported to Washington that the South Korean forces were unable to resist the determined Northern offensive and that South Korean casualties, taken as an index to fighting, did not demonstrate a great capacity for resistance or the will to fight. Accordingly, a complete collapse was thought to be imminent. On June 28, however, the assessments by Ambassador Muccio and the CIA appeared a little brighter. Muccio reported that the military situation was a little firmer and that morale was improving. The CIA argued that action by the U.S. Air Force would provide a tremendous psychological boost to the South Korean government, its armed forces, and the people and that chances of maintaining organized resistance were improving. Military intelligence for the following day, however, was gloomier: "Koreans from President Rhee dispirited by [the] course of hostilities and [the] lack of concrete evidence of U.S. aid." Late on the afternoon of June 30, Far Eastern Headquarters, through a teleconference, reported to Washington the state of affairs in Korea, indicating that the ROK Army had suffered 60-percent casualties, that it had been reduced to about 30,000 men who faced a North Korean force of 100,000, that the civilian population was very pessimistic, and that the government was in a disorganized state.[9]

The decision to commit ground forces was definitely the most important step taken by the United States to meet the communist challenge in Korea during the summer of 1950. On June 26, the president raised the question of mobilization, sounding out the possibility of committing U.S. ground forces in Korea. At the June 29 State–Defense meeting in the White House, Defense Secretary Johnson pointed out that the Joint Chiefs of Staff believed it was essential to establish the beachhead in Korea. Secretary Acheson bluntly stated that he was willing for U.S. ground troops to go into Korea. In short, by this time, the ground was prepared in Washington for the dispatch of U.S. ground troops to Korea. A concrete step toward the decision was MacArthur's survey trip to Korea and his resulting recommendations. Instructions for the survey trip had already been given him on the very first day of the war, but he did not find an opportune time to do so until June 29. On that day, he also received General Collins's request for an evaluation of current U.S. efforts in Korea and his recommendation for additional or even different measures to be taken by the United States. Because of North Korean air activities, his trip to Korea involved considerable risk, but his visit with ROK troops defending the south bank of the Han River greatly encouraged the Korean soldiers. After the trip, MacArthur sent Washington a lengthy telegram reporting on what he had observed in Korea and recommending further steps for the United States to take. Only about 25,000 soldiers were left in the ROK force, and the rifle divisions lacked artillery, mortars, and antitank guns. The only hope for the troops was to retard the march of the enemy. The civilian population, according to MacArthur, was rather tranquil and orderly and retained a high degree of national spirit and maintained a firm belief in the Americans. Then he observed that unless provisions could be made for the full utilization of the Army–Navy–Air team in the shattered areas, the U.S. mission would at best be needlessly costly in life, money, and prestige. He concluded that the only assurance of holding the existing line and of regaining lost ground would be the introduction of U.S. ground combat forces. He added that if authorized he would send a regimental combat team as the spearhead of two divisions from Japan. During the early morning teleconference of June 30 between Washington and Tokyo, the Washington authorities were inclined to consider the Joint Chiefs of Staff instruction, which gave enough authority to MacArthur to send the regimental combat troops to Korea, but they decided also to get tacit approval from the president before sending troops. That approval came early that same morning. When the president was about to take his morning walk (4:57 A.M.), Secretary of the Army Frank Pace called and informed the president that MacArthur had called and wanted to send a regimental combat troop to Korea as the spearhead of two American divisions. The president gave the authorization instantly. MacArthur's headquarters were informed immediately of the presidential approval for the use of ground forces. The last message from Washington said, "Congratulations and best wishes." Later that morning, at 9:30 A.M., the president met with representatives of the State and Defense Departments and approved the commitment of two divisions to the war in Korea. Step by step, the U.S. decision to intervene in the Korean War had been made in a period of a little over five days. The question of how and why this happened is worth exploration.[10]

Like many other large-scale policy decisions, many people were involved in the steps leading up to American intervention in the Korean crisis in that summer of 1950. Certainly, the president was the most important among those, as scholars agree.[11] Among the president's many advisers who had meaningful roles in reaching this decision, Acheson and MacArthur may be considered to have played the most important roles. As the chief foreign policy adviser for the president, Acheson, who acted more like a prime minister, was much more than one among equals. He quite often spoke on behalf of the whole group of the president's advisers. Because of the nature of events, military advisers naturally played an important role. Among them, MacArthur's part was especially important. He was the one who took the very first step—that of sending emergency military supplies—even before obtaining tacit instructions from Washington. One may try to discount the importance of this act by pointing out that the United States had been providing all of the supplies for the ROK forces and that there was thus no need for special approval for the continuation or even the stepping-up of the supplies, but its inclusion in the first Blair House decision indicates its importance as a first step. Indeed, given the incremental nature of the decision-making process in this case, this first act was very important. MacArthur's role in the decision to commit ground forces was also important. It is true that by June 29, the preparatory actions for sending U.S. ground troops to Korea had already been taken. It is likewise the case that during the teleconference, the Washington group, not the Tokyo group, considered that the instructions already given MacArthur were sufficient for dispatching a regimental combat troop to Korea and that Washington authorized the survey trip and gave additional instructions regarding the possibility of additional U.S. responses to the Korean crisis. But, MacArthur was the one who perceived the urgent need for U.S. ground forces on the battle field and recommended sending the troops. Had he not done that, it is doubtful that Washington would have made the decision to commit ground troops.

Both policy makers and later observers consider various other factors important in making the decision to intervene. All of them concerned U.S. national interests. These include the value of the Korean peninsula for U.S. national interests, the saving of the United Nations, the preservation of American prestige and credibility, the impact of the Korean crisis elsewhere in the world, the prevention of a Third World war, and the lessons of recent history. As many recognized, when the North Korean invasion began, the Korean peninsula suddenly became not only politically but also strategically important for the United States. Truman expressed the changed outlook clearly: "More seriously, a Communist success in Korea would put Red troops and planes within easy striking distance of Japan, and Okinawa and Formosa would be open to attack from two sides." The collective security system of the United Nations was not Truman's creation, but the president—and many others in Washington—were quite serious about the importance of the United Nations as a factor in the U.S. decision to take action in the Korean crisis. "It was also clear to me," Truman recalled later, "that the foundations and the principles of the United Nations were at stake unless this unprovoked attack on Korea could be stopped." The factor of prestige was also significant in the decision-making process. Whether right or wrong, the fall of Kuomintang China in 1949 had created a general feeling of unease among the nations of Asia, and Korea became a testing ground in the eyes of the Asian people. Acheson clearly recognized this and later wrote, "To back away from this challenge, in view of our capacity for meeting it,

would be highly destructive for the power and prestige of the United States."
The president and his advisers did not think Korea was an isolated case and
believed that whatever the United States did would have an impact elsewhere in the world. On June 26, as previously noted, the president told
Elsey that Korea was the Greece of the Far East. "If we are tough enough
now, if we stand up to them like we did in Greece three years ago, they
won't take any next step. But, if we just stand by, they'll move into and
they'll take the whole Middle East," he said. Diplomatic historians also
point out that the "lessons" of past experience became an important influence on the American decision to intervene in the Korean War. Truman
wrote, "I recalled some earlier instances: Manchuria, Ethiopia, Austria. I
remembered how each time that the democracies failed to act it had encouraged the aggressors to keep going ahead." He continued, "Communists
were acting in Korea, just as Hitler, Mussolini, and the Japanese had acted
ten, fifteen, and twenty years earlier." Whether he was properly using the
lessons of history is a different question.[12]

Alongside the factors relating to American national interests, still other
considerations influenced those making the U.S. decision to intervene in the
Korean crisis. These included the perception of the Soviet role in the crisis,
the realities of domestic politics, the positions of the countries involved in a
world society, and the personality factor. From the very beginning of the
crisis, one very important assumption made by President Truman and his
advisers was that the Soviet Union was the major force behind the North
Korean invasion. Soon, a second assumption was made: If the United States
took a firm stand, then the Soviet Union would not be openly involved with
combat troops and would try to manage a war by proxy. These two assump-
tions were extremely important for U.S. intervention, and the U.S. Ambassador in Moscow Alan G. Kirk played an important role in convincing
others to accept them.[13]

Domestic or party politics played two different roles in the American
decision to intervene in late June 1950. Republican criticism of the Truman
administration for the Chinese catastrophe strengthened the government in
its decision to make a strong response in the Korean crisis. Moreover, the
strong bipartisan support for the Truman administration's early response to
the Korean crisis must have provided further encouragement for the government. It should also be pointed out that on June 28 the draft extension
bill passed the Congress and was sent to the White House.[14]

Once it decided to act through the United Nations, the United States
became sensitive to the responses of the member nations. This was a time
when the United States possessed strong leadership in the world organization, expecting and receiving the solid support of members from the beginning. It is doubtful whether the United States would have gone as far as
sending ground forces if it had not received this support. The nations which
gave encouragement to the United States in those early days may be divided

into different groups according to the manner and the degree of the support. The first group, those that gave unquestioned and enthusiastic support from the beginning, represented most of the nations in Europe and the Western Hemisphere and the relatively few nations elsewhere in the world who had strong ties with the United States or felt threatened by communism: The Netherlands, Belgium, the United Kingdom, France, Spain, Portugal, Denmark, Sweden, Norway, Greece, Turkey, Canada, Cuba, Brazil, Argentina, Uruguay, Australia, New Zealand, Taiwan, Thailand, Indochina, and Pakistan. A second group of nations was composed of those who had problem with giving full support from the beginning because of their physical proximity to the Soviet Union or their neutral position: Finland, Yugoslavia, India, and Indonesia.[15]

In almost every case of foreign policy making, it is not easy to gauge accurately the degree of importance of personalities involved in leadership. The American decision to intervene in the Korean crisis is no exception. But it is not too difficult to surmise at least that President Truman's personality played a key role in this case. Analyzing the factors in favor of U.S. intervention in the Korean case, Ernest R. May wrote, "Part of the answer doubtless lies in Truman's style, temperament, and mental make-up." After describing Truman's early life, May continued, "Handicapped also by shortness and extreme near-sightedness, he developed a style in which graciousness and good humor were combined with an appearance of quickness, tough self-assurance, and decisiveness." Together with his conscious and unconscious efforts to make up for his handicaps, it seems that his midwestern background had much to do with his toughness, decisiveness, and sense of righteousness that influenced his decision to intervene in Korea. If someone else had occupied the White House in June 1950, the decision on how to respond to the Korean crisis could have been quite different. Furthermore, the personality of the strong and self-confident Acheson must have supplemented Truman's as a factor in the Korean decision. Beside these two, many other personalities played a significant role in making the Korean decision, especially General MacArthur and Secretary of the Army Pace, as well as Army Chief of Staff Collins, all of whose strong personalities and active temperaments seem to have played important roles in the decision in favor of sending ground forces.[16]

If these two groups of factors can explain a fairly large portion—at least more than half, perhaps even 75 or 80 percent—of the reasons behind American intervention, any analyst, including this one, should be satisfied. Why then should we look for more reasons? Ernest May puts his finger on this question: "Even taking account of Truman's personal style, the logic of containment and deterrence, signals coming from Europe, and domestic political considerations, one still cannot pull together a fully plausible explanation of why he acted as he did." Two other factors may be suggested and tentatively explored: accelerating pressure for quick escalation and human moral consciousness. As discussed already, MacArthur's decision, and Truman's approval of it, to send ammunition and equipment to Korea was in a sense a continuation of what the United States had been doing in an limited way and was not a new or groundbreaking decision. However, in the context of the urgent needs of the Koreans, its importance was that of a first step taken, and as the situation began to deteriorate quickly, Korea's needs escalated. As needs escalated, the United States was under pressure to escalate its support. Thus, once the war broke out, events began to move according to their own logic and momentum. Combined with a sense in the military profession that when a challenge is presented it should be met, this factor of spiraling incremental needs seems to have produced a process of escalation that shaped decision making in a crisis condition.

Last, the moral factor seems to have played a familiar role in the decision for American intervention in the Korean crisis. It often plays a role in human decision making, and the Korean case was no exception. It is true that Korea was not much known to the average American before the outbreak of the war. Even for those who knew something about the significance of Korea in American foreign policy, it was more of a symbol than a real national entity; but it soon became more than a symbol. On June 29, President Truman wrote to the Korean Ambassador in Washington, "While I commend the heroic resistance of the Korean defenders I am deeply grieved by the terrible suffering of your people because of loss of life and destruction from the brutal Communist attack." He and probably a good number of other Americans must have felt some sense of obligation to the Koreans who had been the victims of a series of U.S. actions since 1945. It is a very interesting irony that the very person, Dean Rusk, who was personally involved in the decision to divide the Korean peninsula at the 38th parallel was quite responsible for the intervention decision five years later as assistant secretary of state for Far Eastern affairs. It might have been a sheer coincidence, but it seems to be more than that. Acting Secretary of State Robert Lovett stated, "No matter how State Department squirms—Berlin, Vietnam, and now in Korea—it can't escape the consequences of its own and its predecessors' mistakes."[17]

So far, we have concentrated on Washington. Now, we turn to Seoul to see how Syngman Rhee and his government approached the U.S. government and how Ambassador Muccio handled the crisis in relation to President Rhee and his government. Essentially, the Rhee government faced two tasks in late June 1950: First, to stop the North Korean onslaught and to push them back to the 38th parallel; second, to minimize the damage, human as well as material. The Koreans could not do the job without outside help. Hence, they must get immediate American assistance in halting the North Korean invasion. However, American policy toward Korea on the eve of the war appeared to advocate letting the Koreans work out their own fate with a very limited amount of American help.

When President Rhee received the war news, it was about 10:30 A.M. on June 25, some six and a half hours after the attack began. According to the recollections of Kim Chong-pil, one of the officers on duty at the ROKA headquarters, the G-2 ROKA received the information of the North Korean attack at about 5:15 A.M. and immediately delivered the information to the ROKA Chief of Staff General Chae Pyŏng-dŏk, who must have received it by about 5:30 A.M. While President Rhee was fishing at Kyŏnghoeru after a late Sunday breakfast, the news was brought to him by Defense Minister Sin Sŏng-mo. Both communications and channels of command had problems at this critical time. Immediate efforts were undertaken to communicate with MacArthur, Dulles (in Tokyo at this point), Acheson, and Ambassador Chang Myŏn, but telephone communication was completed only with Chang on that day (about 10:30 A.M. on June 24 in Washington). When Chang had gone to the Department of State at 11:00 A.M.on June 24, he already had information from the Associated Press (AP), the United Press (UP), and Korea. He delivered President Rhee's urgent request to Rusk for more arms and ammunition. Yet, the effort to appeal to MacArthur in Tokyo did not go through until the early morning of June 26 (3:00 A.M.). MacArthur must have had plenty of information and time to think about the possibilities of handling the crisis by this time; he immediately promised President Rhee that he would send ten fighter planes and thirty-six each of 105-mm and 155-mm and some 57-mm guns. Late on the afternoon of June 26 (4:00 P.M.), Chang visited President Truman and Acheson and made the same request for arms and ammunition. By this time, he had received three telephone calls from Seoul about the urgent need on the battlefield. President Truman informed the Korean ambassador that he had already issued orders to General MacArthur to supply all necessary ammunition and equipment for the South Korean troops. The decision for the United States to supply ammunition and equipment was made relatively quickly and without any difficulty, and the Rhee government seems to have done its job in making the appeal to MacArthur and President Truman. But what the effect of the Korean appeal was in the making of this decision is questionable. In both Tokyo and Washington, President Rhee's messages arrived after the decision had already been made.[18]

The evacuation of President Rhee and his cabinet and the questionable way the Korean government handled the evacuation of other important and not-so-important people in Seoul has long been controversial in Korea. The fact is that the president and his cabinet members left Seoul on June 27, on the third day of the war, and that others, including half of the members of the National Assembly, other important people, and most of the common people were trapped behind the battle line. All of them suffered, and many died or were taken captive by the North Koreans. According to military plans, the Han River bridge was to be blown up right before North Korean troops could cross it, but due to confusion and communication problems, the ROKA engineering corps destroyed the bridge much too early, at 2 A.M. on June 28 and trapped most of Seoul's citizens north of the river. Even after the destruction of the single Han River bridge, some Seoul citizens crossed the river using small boats, but most listened to the president's voice when he asked them to remain calm and to endure for a little while because the United States had decided to aid the Koreans with arms and ammunition, and the enemy would soon be expelled from the city. Later, the people learned that the voice of the president was coming from a tape played by the Korean Broadcasting Service (KBS), while the president himself was in Taejŏn. Had the citizens been told the truth by the president, great chaos must have ensued as people tried to leave the city. Nevertheless, the people later felt they had been betrayed by their own leaders.

Ambassador Muccio in Seoul performed his duties well when the war broke out. Late in the evening of June 25 (10:00 P.M.), when Muccio went to President Rhee's residence, he found the president in a state of emotional strain and was told that the cabinet had decided to evacuate Seoul and move to Taejŏn. Muccio tried to persuade the president to keep the government in Seoul to encourage the people; when he failed to change the evacuation plan of the Korean government, he told the president that, even if the ROK government moved to Taejŏn, he would stay in Seoul. President Rhee was much troubled by the evacuation problem. When he was advised by Defense Minister Sin early in the morning of June 27 to leave immediately, he was still very reluctant to take the advice and insisted that he wanted to stay in the capital. Muccio also had to leave the city before the Han River bridge was blown up. It certainly would have been foolish for the president and his cabinet members to fall into enemy hands, and their safety was imperative for the continued functioning of the government. However, their failure to give proper warning to other important people in the government, including members of the National Assembly, and to control carefully the destruction of the Han River bridge were clearly unfortunate mistakes. The premature destruction of the bridge trapped not only Seoul citizens but also half of the ROK Army with its heavy equipment. President Rhee's radio message was later subjected to much criticism. When a similar situation arose in January of the following year, a great part of the people chose to leave the city.[19]

In retrospect, of the two main tasks the Rhee government faced, of stopping the invading forces and obtaining necessary assistance for this task, only one was handled properly. President Rhee and his assistants made a prompt appeal to MacArthur and President Truman for arms and ammunition. They came, and brought more than the Koreans asked for—U.S. air and naval assistance and even ground troops. Furthermore, the Americans had decided to send aid even before the appeal messages were received. Nevertheless, the appeal was made properly, even if it was not needed. At this point, there is another question to be raised: Could the Rhee government have done something more than simply asking for arms and ammunition? The answer is probably not. To ask or not to ask is often not much of a choice for the one who has to make an appeal. And, often the style of asking usually does not seem to influence greatly the decision of the giver, as was the case in the Korean situation in late June 1950. If nothing could be done at that point about the condition of the South Korean defense force, at least the top military leadership could be changed. This was done, following the suggestion of General MacArthur, and General Chŭng Il-kwŏn replaced General Chae on June 30. But, President Rhee's move to replace the defense minister was blocked by Ambassador Muccio.[20]

Muccio managed his job well in Korea in those early days of the war. He acted effectively in handling communications with both the governing authorities in Seoul and Washington. Very quickly he reported the crisis to Washington and maintained effective communication throughout the crucial period. His request to Washington for a quick supply of badly needed arms and ammunition in Korea was done effectively. Moreover, there were about 2,500 Americans in Korea when the war broke out, and he efficiently handled their evacuation, with the exception of military advisers and others who were needed for the war effort, and was later highly commended by his superiors in the State Department. By far the most important task in the early days of the Korean crisis was giving encouragement and hope to the drowning people, and Muccio did it well. He was quite brave in wanting to stay even longer in Seoul after the Korean government's evacuation from the city. Instructed by Acheson not to expose himself to danger beyond necessity, he moved first to Suwŏn, the temporary location of the ROKA headquarters, and then to Taejŏn, where the Korean government was located. He did an excellent job of staying close to President Rhee and his advisers in those most uncertain and darkest days and in trying to keep morale high for the Korean leaders by promptly providing information from Washington. His dedicated service in those days was appreciated by President Rhee and many others who knew of it.[21]

Of the little more than three years the Korean War lasted, the first one-third, from early July 1950 to late July 1951, was most critical. The main part of the war was waged during this period. In addition, the war went through a number of dramatic changes during these thirteen months: from the difficult and frustrating two and a half months for the U.N. forces, followed in the next month and a half by the exciting Inch'ŏn landing and the march to the Yalu–Tuman border line; to the Chinese intervention, the retreat by the U.N. forces, the counterattack by the U.N. forces, and the establishment of the battle line along the 38th parallel in the spring of 1951. After the United States decided upon full intervention in the war, the eyes of the whole world turned to the Korean peninsula to see how the U.S.–U.N. forces would handle the North Korean forces.

In the midst of great hopes and expectations, an American ground combat unit arrived in Korea in early July. The Smith special unit, the 1st Battalion of the 21st Regiment of the 24th Division, landed at Pusan harbor on the first of the month and reached the battlefield at Chukmilyŏng, a few miles north of Osan, on July 5. Supported by an artillery battalion with 4.2 inch mortars, six bazooka teams, and one 75-mm platoon, the Smith Battalion immediately took up a position against an overwhelming number of North Korean forces in the early morning of July 5. The coming of the American combat unit was thought to be almost a miracle by most Koreans, but a miracle did not occur on the battlefield; there was no way for the lightly armed and greatly outnumbered American unit to stop the march of the North Korean troops. T-34 enemy tanks, which continued to march forward ignoring the explosions of 2.36-inch rocket shells, looked like a "gunboat" to the observers. Fortunately, the 105-mm Howitzer was effective against the tanks, but all of the six shells the American troops had were quickly exhausted. The American unit lost about a third of its 540 men in this first combat, and evacuated to Ch'ŏnan, about thirty-five miles to the south. The enemy (the 4th Division) suffered losses of 127 men and 4 of 33 tanks. To many, especially the Koreans, the first performance by an American combat force in the war was very disappointing. But for those who knew the relative strengths of the two forces in this first small battle, the outcome was not surprising; the two sides were just too unequal in strength. The outcome must have also been expected by those at Far Eastern Headquarters in Tokyo. Perhaps the Smith special force was dispatched too hastily to the battlefield for psychological rather than military reasons. Nevertheless, to the Koreans and others, the Smith unit, only the first of many more Americans to come, had great assuring symbolic value.[22]

After the initial contact at Chukmilyŏng, delaying tactics were used by the U.S. Army, yielding territory to gain time to build up adequate forces for an offensive operation. First, MacArthur was appointed the commander of U.N. forces in Korea, and the whole ROK Army was also placed under his command. Ch'ŏnan, Choch'iwŏn, and Taejŏn—the major regional centers along the Seoul–Pusan highway—were given up successively on July 8, 12, and 20. Meanwhile, the U.S. 1st Cavalry and the U.S. 25th Infantry Division arrived in Korea. The retreat was also carried out in the central and eastern sector of the peninsula; Yŏngdong, Sangju, Andong, Yŏngdŏk were all evacuated between July 28 and August 1. By the first day of August, the U.N. forces built the 100-by-50-mile Naktong River defense line, where the defensive force managed to maintain its position until mid-September, when the Inch'ŏn landing took place, and the counteroffense began.[23]

The entire month of July was a difficult time for U.S. forces in Korea. MacArthur, reporting to the Joint Chiefs of Staff on July 9, said, "The situation in Korea is critical. We are endeavoring by all means now avail[able] here to build up the force nec[cessary] to hold the enemy, but to date our efforts against his armor and mechanized forces have been ineffective." Then, he candidly praised the enemy: "His armored equip[ment] is of the best and the service thereof, as reported by qualified observers, as good as any seen at any time in the last war." Further, the report stated that the enemy infantry was "thoroughly first class quality." Commenting upon his own troops, MacArthur added that they were "fulfilling expectations" and were "fighting with valor against overwhelming odds of more than ten to one." A journalist's description of the situation in the battlefield was more expressive: "The American soldiers . . . appeared weary, grim, nervous and mad. They cursed the absence of heavy artillery, tanks and aircraft." But the situation began to improve during the second and third weeks of the month: Tanks began to appear on the American side, two divisions of reinforcements came, and General Walton Walker, a well-known World War II hero, arrived in Taegu as the commander of the 8th Army. With superb air and very good navy support, the situation improved for the U.N. forces by the end of the month, and stabilization of the defense line was achieved.[24]

The Walker (Defense) Line, about one-hundred miles south along the Naktong River from Waegwan, eighteen miles northwest of Taegu, and about fifty miles to Yŏngdŏk on the east coast, was the last and the best defensive line for the U.N. forces. The time they had bought with the space yielded was certainly useful for the arrival of reinforcements, and the U.N. force was able to line up, from the south to the north, the U.S. 25th, 2d, 24th Divisions and the 1st Cavalry Division against four enemy divisions (the 6th, 4th, 10th, and 3d Divisions) and, from west to east, the ROK 1st, 6th, 8th, the Capital, and 3d Divisions against six North Korean divisions (the 15th, 13th, 1st, 8th, 12th, and 5th) to Yŏngdŏk on the east coast. Helping the Americans and the South Koreans were excellent air and naval support and the geographical advantages of the river and mountains. Nonetheless, the month and a half defensive operation was described as "a defensive improvisation" against the enemy's offensive "nibbling campaign." With the additional strength that came from the realization that this was the last defensive line and that there was nowhere else to go except into the sea, the U.N. forces were able to defend the perimeter against five separate offensive campaigns in August and the last big North Korean assault in September. Journalist Hugh Bailie reported on September 15 from "somewhere in Korea," praising what Americans and other U.N. forces "have accomplished in Korea, holding the present perimeter, inflicting casualties at the rate of five to one, destroying the enemy's strongest troops and setting the stage for an eventual counter offensive to end the existing stalemate."[25]

The bravely conceived, carefully planned, and masterfully executed Inch'ŏn landing began early on the morning of September 15 and was completed by the early afternoon of the following day. This epic-size operation was an extremely delicate and difficult one because of the very high tide at Inch'ŏn, the port of Seoul. Accordingly, if one could manage the technical problem of overcoming the tide, the invading force was not expected to encounter much resistance. Such was the case with MacArthur's venture.

The huge operation, which involved a 75,000-man force and over 260 ships from seven countries, was met by a resistance force of only about 6,500 defenders. Indeed, the most difficult part of the operation was persuading the chiefs at the Pentagon and assembling the necessary forces for the operation. Between early July and early August, MacArthur successfully impressed upon Washington the urgent need for four additional divisions to halt and then hurl back the powerful aggressor forces, and by late July he came forward with a clear request for two more divisions—one infantry and one marine—for the mid-September amphibious operation in Korea. The most crucial point in MacArthur's effort occurred early in August. When presidential representative W. Averill Harriman came to Tokyo with General Lauris Norstad and General Ridgway to assess his grand scheme, MacArthur succeeded in convincing them of the feasibility of his plan with a "brilliant" two and a half hour presentation. Upon his return to Washington, Harriman reported to the president, and Truman immediately (on August 9) requested the Joint Chiefs of Staff to consider MacArthur's plan. Within twenty-four hours the Joint Chiefs decided to approve the Inch'ŏn plan. After one more visit by representatives from Washington, by General Collins and Admiral Sherman this time, the Joint Chiefs gave on August 28 the final approval for MacArthur's plan. Even with MacArthur's record and prestige, Washington still went through the process of very carefully examining all the factors involved in the operation. When the operation was completed, the Joint Chiefs of Staff, not penurious in recognizing MacArthur's contribution, said in their September 29 message, "The Joint Chiefs of Staff are proud of the great success you have achieved."[26]

As soon as the landing operation was completed by the early afternoon of August 16, the troops under the U.S. 10th Corps began to move toward Seoul. The U.S. 1st Marine and the U.S. 7th Division together with the ROK Marine Corps and the ROK 17th Regiment carried out a week-long sweeping campaign in the areas surrounding the capital city and four days of street-fighting in Seoul against a defending force of 20,000, operations which were completed by August 28. The 8th U.S. Army on the Naktong defense line also commenced an all-out offensive operation; the 1st ROK Corps (the 3rd and Capital Divisions) on the east pushed through the coastal region and reached the 38th parallel on the last day of September. Meanwhile, the 2d ROK Corps (the 6th and 8th Divisions) marched through the central part of the peninsula and captured Ch'unch'ŏn on October 2. The U.S. 1st Corps (the U.S. 1st Cavalry, the U.S. 24th Division, and the ROK 1st Division) on the west moved along the Pusan–Seoul main road and reached the 38th parallel by the October 5. Except for some 40,000 North Korean soldiers who were left behind the fast-moving front line, all of the invading forces were thrown across the 38th parallel by the end of September. Now the big question was what to do at the parallel: to cross or not to cross the line.[27]

The question of the 38th parallel became (or remained) the most important issue in Korea and Washington during the summer of 1950. It was closely related to several other issues, including the possibility of Chinese intervention, the question of whether to fight a general or a limited war, and the nature and the objectives of war for the Republic of Korea and the United States, and it was in a real sense one of the most important issues of the Korean War. The subject has drawn much attention from scholars. Many of them have been very critical of the decision to cross the line, calling it a "gamble," "an ill-advised venture," and "the most disastrous decision of the Truman Administration," pointing out that it brought on Chinese intervention, a terribly high price for little gain. Some have also pointed out that, on the contrary, there was a great opportunity to unify Korea. It was difficult for the policy makers in Washington to resist taking that chance. Many hindsight comments seem to have given too much weight to the place of rational calculation in the decision-making process.[28]

July was a dark month for U.S. troops in Korea. The question of whether the troops should cross the 38th parallel to the north came up for the first time in the middle of the month. On July 13, when the question was raised during his press conference, President Truman said that he would make a decision when it became necessary to do so. A few days later, the president instructed the National Security Council to study the subject, and the State and Defense Departments began to give it consideration. In general, the military view was that from a military perspective the line had no significance. On June 29, when the question was raised whether U.S. air activities should be confined to the south side of the parallel, the president indicated that Commander-in-Chief MacArthur should be allowed the discretion to make his own assessment, and Acheson stated that if the Air Force spotted North Korean tanks it should not worry whether they were located on the southern or northern side of the parallel. Two different views emerged from the State Department. The Policy Planning Council, under the leadership of George Kennan and Paul Nitze, thought that a crossing was not advisable because of the risk involved. In contrast, the Far Eastern Division under Rusk and Allison took the position that the U.S. government should not make any announcement on the issue until the battle situation became much clearer.[29]

On July 31, the Defense Department came forward with a clear and firm view on the issue in a memorandum, in which it reviewed first the military and political factors in the war and then concluded that the 38th parallel, in and of itself, has "no military significance" and that the unification of Korea would square with historical necessity, Korean aspirations, U.S. obligations and policies, and objectives of the United Nations. By the end of August, the State Department reached the viewpoint that the U.N. commander be given authority to conduct operations without regard to the parallel if neither Chinese nor Soviet forces were then involved in the conflict and linked the issue with the Security Council's resolutions. The interdepartmental views on the issue of the parallel were consolidated in early September through the National Security Council's action, which was documented in NSC 81/1. The conclusion stated that the U.N. forces had a legal basis for conducting operations north of the 38th parallel and added that such operations would take place with presidential approval and after prior consultation with and approval of members of the United Nations. Further, the operation would be carried out only if there were no Soviet or Chinese occupation of North Korea nor any announcement or threat of such action. The directive for crossing the 38th parallel received the president's approval on August 27, and on the same day the Joint Chiefs of Staff transmitted to MacArthur the directive, through which the field commander was authorized to conduct military operations north of the 38th parallel in Korea. After NSC 81/1, it took another month for the United States to work out the international dimensions of the issue. The U.S. government decided to let another member nation of the United Nations come forward with a proposal on the issue of the parallel, and it was not until October 7, when the eight-power proposal passed the General Assembly with a toned-down simple, vague statement that the assembly recommended that "all appropriate steps be taken to ensure conditions of stability throughout Korea." With the long and complicated approval process over, the 38th parallel was crossed by ROK troops on October 1 and a week later by other U.N. troops.[30]

The U.S. government's decision in favor of the crossing of the 38th parallel by U.N. forces was essentially a compromise, first, between two groups within the Department of State—Allison, Dulles, Rusk, and their supporters in the department who advocated crossing the parallel, and Nitze and his supporters in the Policy Planning Council who argued against the action—and, second, between the State, which took a weak position on the issue, and the Defense Department, which took a strong position favoring crossing the parallel. For the proaction group in the State Department, first Dulles, the consultant to the secretary, came forward and strongly asserted that the 38th parallel was no longer a political line and that the line should be obliterated to achieve security and peace in Korea. Allison, in his July 15 memorandum, argued that the line should be crossed to carry out the June 27 U.N. Security Council resolution, both to punish an aggressor and not to compromise with justice and to prevent the loss of the Korean people's confidence in the United Nations. Through two memoranda of July 22 and 25, the Policy Planning Council argued against crossing the parallel on the grounds that such an action might not receive support from U.N. members, that there was a risk of Soviet and Chinese intervention, that there was no commitment to unify Korea by force, and that there was a need to balance military strength and commitment. Soon, both Allison and Dulles indicated that, although they did not like the arguments of the Policy Planning Council, they favored the recommendation to defer the decision of crossing or not crossing the parallel until the military and political situation had become clearer, which was the original position of the two.[31]

Then eloquent and powerful words advocating crossing the parallel came from the Defense Department on the last day of month. After stating that, from the perspective of military operations, the 38th parallel had no more significance than any other meridian, and that the 38th parallel was "a geographical artificiality violating the natural integrity of a singularly homogeneous nation," it pointed out that in Korea the United States and the free world had the first opportunity to set the stage for the noncommunist penetration into an area of Soviet influence, and that the political value to the United States of establishing a free, united, and stable Korea and of carrying out the resolve of the United Nations would justify the cost in military forces, as long as the assumption held that the United States would mobilize adequate forces to do the job in Korea and that there would be no Soviet or Chinese intervention. The document concluded that the unification of Korea would square with historical necessity, Korean aspirations, U.S. obligations and policies, and the objectives of the United Nations. These words must have impressed officials in the State Department; Allison even began to use the now popular word "rollback" to describe the U.S. policy in Korea and the only change made to the expression of the Defense Department's view was the addition of the United Nations to the approval process. An argument based on "justice," "faith," and legality had triumphed over an argument based on the danger of Soviet and Chinese intervention, the fear of losing support from U.N. members, and the need to balance military strength and commitment. In short, U.S. military logic and moral argument prevailed over the opinions of civilian leadership. An additional strength of the military argument was the long-range view that their suggestion would solve once and for all a Korean problem which otherwise would remain a source of trouble for many years to come. Not to let the military view prevail, the civilian leadership would have needed more and tighter reasoning as well as tremendous courage. Of course, the most important concern for the policy makers in Washington was the possibility of Soviet and Chinese intervention, and a built-in regulatory mechanism was set up to guard against the danger, but just how this mechanism would work was a big question. Again, the war and events moved according to their own logic and momentum.[32]

Following the 3d ROK Division, the first troops to cross the 38th parallel and march north, all the U.N. troops (with the exception of the U.S. 2d and 25th Divisions, which remained behind to handle the North Korean forces which had failed to flee across the parallel) crossed the parallel in the early part of October and moved toward the Yalu–Tuman border. The 1st ROK Corps took the east coast; the central mountainous region was taken by the 2d ROK Corps which was joined later by the 10th U.S. Corps; and the 8th Army advanced in the western section of the peninsula. Because of the surprise effect of the Inch'ŏn landing, the retreating North Korean troops dashed for the border without offering much resistance, and the U.N. troops literally raced north, sometimes at the speed of sixteen miles a day. On the east coast, the ROK 3d and Capital Divisions occupied Wŏnsan on October 10 and continued to march north, reaching Hamhŭng on October 17. The Capital Division continued its march along the coast, arriving in Ch'ŏngjin on November 26. In the center, the ROK 6th and 8th Divisions marched ahead, crossing the Ch'ŏngch'ŏn River, toward the Yalu, and the ROK 6th Division entered Ch'osan on October 26 and on the same day reached the Korean–Manchurian border. In the west, the U.S. 24th Division went through Pakch'ŏn (the 25th), Chŏngju (the 30th), Sŏnch'ŏn (the 31st), and reached Ch'ŏngch'adong on November 1, just seventeen miles from Siniju on the Yalu River.

Meanwhile, the 1st ROK Division marched toward the Yalu border, reaching it on November 1, 110 miles north of Kusŏng. The 10th U.S. Corps was switched to the east after completion of the Inch'ŏn landing and landed at Wŏnsan on October 26, when the 2d ROK Corps already had begun to have contact with the Chinese troops in the central sector. But, because the Chinese delayed action in the eastern section, the 10th Corps was able to continue fighting until the early part of December. The 1st U.S. Marine Division meanwhile had an action in the Ch'ŏngjinho area, and the 7th U.S. Division occupied Hyesanjin on November 21, becoming another U.N. unit to stand on the Korean–Manchurian border. By late October, the war seemed to be approaching its end with great success by the U.N. forces.

But then came another surprise, one which could be matched only by the U.S. intervention of late June—the Chinese intervention. Chinese communist troops, which quietly had begun to cross the Yalu River in mid-October, launched their main initial thrust through the central mountainous area, and the ROK 6th Division began to clash with them on the 25th and, as a result of heavy pressure, began to retreat on the following day. In the west, the 1st U.S. Corps also came into contact with the Chinese troops, and Chinese intervention became a reality by the end of October. The first major Chinese advance began on the first day of November and lasted for a week.[33]

MacArthur declared that he had a new war on his hands, and, faced with an enemy possessing much larger numbers of troops and using tactics that were very effective in the mountainous area, he ordered the U.N. forces to retreat to the Ch'ŏngch'ŏn River line. After little more than two weeks of quiet, during which both armies prepared for the next move, MacArthur ordered a counterattack on November 24. It was responded by the Chinese premature campaign on the following day, which lasted until mid-December. At the end of this round of the campaign, the U.N. forces found themselves back on the 38th parallel, which they had crossed three months earlier. While the swift but orderly U.N. retreat was taking place in the west and center, the operation in the east was more dramatic. Because of delays by the Chinese in this region, the 10th U.S. Corps and the 1st ROK Corps were still moving north, while the 8th Army was quickly retreating to the south. When the communist attack came to this region, U.N. troops found the road for a retreat already cut off and faced the danger of being surrounded and destroyed. The only possible escape route was evacuation by sea. The U.N. forces—the 1st U.S. Marine, the 7th U.S., and the ROK Capital Divisions—together with about 220,000 civilians were evacuated successfully from Hŭngnam in ten days beginning on December 14. This successful operation was a wonderful Christmas present for the U.N. forces.[34]

Toward the end of the year, an important change in the leadership of the U.N. forces in Korea took place. General Walker was killed in an automobile accident on December 23, and General Matthew Ridgway arrived in Korea on December 27 to replace him as commander of the 8th Army at this critical time. After much soul searching, the leaders in Washington confirmed their decision to stay and continue the fighting in Korea. Meanwhile, the Chinese launched their second offensive operation on the last day of the year and continued it until late January, forcing the U.N. forces to retreat to the P'yŏngt'aek-Samch'ŏk line by January 25. In response, General Ridgway launched a counterattack on February 15 and took Suwŏn. This operation continued until the middle of June. Despite the Chinese February 11 to 18 offensive, U.N. troops succeeded in pushing the enemy back to the 38th parallel by the end of March. Ridgway declared that his aim was not gaining real estate but killing the enemy, and U.N. fire power and mobility inflicted heavy losses on the enemy forces. The Chinese made two more attempts, the April 22 to 30 offensive and the May 16 to 22 offensive, but U.N. troops rolled them back to the Wyoming Line, about twenty miles north of the estimated cease-fire line, by the middle of June.[35]

After this brief survey of the changes on the battlefield during the early part of the Korean War, we notice that the changes took place periodically and with a certain rhythm. Three months after the North Korean invasion forces crossed the 38th parallel, at the end of September, an invading force once again crossed the line, but this time it was moving in the opposite direction; after another three months, toward the end of December, the two opposing armies crossed the line again and moved south; after another three months, toward the end of March of the following year, the two armies again crossed the line moving north; it took another three months to settle down for peace talks. The war itself took three years: The battle line started on the parallel in late June 1950; a year later, the two armies were back to the line; and two years were necessary to negotiate an end to the war. There seem to be many different kinds of cycles of different lengths in the world, and this is one of those. There is nothing systemic about the number "three" in this case except for the size of the peninsula, the size of the two armies, and the strength of the will to fight on both sides, which seems to have been the major determining factors for this number. Along with this rhythm, there also seems to have been pressure toward equilibrium in the process of intervention–counterintervention and attack–counterattack in the war. Dynamic equilibrium may be a mechanism through which fairness or justice operates. Now, we have to return to a more concrete question: Why did the Chinese decide to intervene, and what were the dynamics in the U.S.–U.N. response to the Chinese attack?

Just as the matter of U.S. intervention in the Korean conflict has attracted much attention from scholars, so has the question of Chinese intervention. Some have argued that Chinese security was the main reason underlying the Chinese decision to intervene; the Chinese did not think, so goes this thesis, that they could afford to have the Americans on the other side of the Yalu–Tuman River border.[36] Others contend that the Soviet Union was definitely involved in the intervention; according to these scholars, there must have been a prior agreement between the Russians and the Chinese for Soviet support of Chinese combat forces in Korea.[37] In addition to these two factors, there must have been others at play. One possibility is ideology. Right after the Chinese communist forces victory over the nationalist Chinese forces, the Chinese Communist Party leadership was proud and vigorous, and they could not just sit idly by and watch the collapse of communist North Korea and a victory by the capitalist nations. Another possible factor was a tradition of historical ties between Korea and China: In the past, the Chinese had maintained a brotherly relationship with Korea, and the Chinese might have perceived some sense of obligation to help a younger brother nation confronting a serious crisis. A Chinese scholar advances the argument that Mao's determination to beat the "American arrogance" of power was the key factor behind the PRC's intervention in the Korean War. Emotion often plays an important role in diplomatic and military decisions, and it is a convincing argument that Mao, proud and vigorous after the defeat of the Koumintang force, was eager to challenge the proud and powerful Americans. However, it is very difficult, if not impossible, to gauge accurately exactly how much of a role this and other factors played in the Chinese decision.[38]

The now available Chinese and Russian documents and some recent studies indicate that communist China went through several stages of policy making in the three and a half months between early July and mid-October of 1950. The first stage of the initial preparation began on July 7, twelve days after the outbreak of the war in Korea, when the Central Military Committee (CMC) made a decision to send the crack units of the Fourth Field Army to the northeast of the country, near the Korean peninsula. The units took up the post by the end of the month. On July 13, the CMC issued an order to establish the Northeastern Defense Army (NEDA), which was used later for the intervention. Thus, communist China began to take the first step to prepare for the probable intervention in the Korean War almost immediately after the outbreak of the war. The next stage of further mobilization, training, and strategic planning followed during the months of August and September. In early August, the Chinese Communist Party (CCP) leadership gave consideration to the issue of intervention and Mao ordered on the same day Premier Chou Enlai to set up a contingency plan for the probable military action. In early September—two weeks before the Inch'ŏn landing operation and a month before the U.N. forces crossing the 38th parallel to the north—the CCP leaders concluded that the intervention would be inevitable and began an extensive mobilization of some 300,000 of the best CCP troops with 400,000 reserve forces for the expedition.

October began with a formal appeal by Kim Il Sung for both Soviet and Chinese intervention in Korea. Immediately, the Chinese communist leaders took up the final stage of decision making for the intervention. First, Mao's determination to intervene was firmed; and, his forceful leadership in persuading the other key CCP leaders continued through July 7, the day on which Mao's consensus building for the decision was completed and the final national policy decision was made to intervene. With his strong will and the support of the prominent field commander Peng Dehuai, Mao was successful in persuading the still reluctant CCP leaders to go along with the intervention. However, during the following six days, he had difficulty in securing the Soviet leader's support for the operation. It is still not clear whether the discrepancy between the two powers' views on the Soviet air cover came from sheer intercultural miscommunication and misunderstanding or from Stalin's actual reneging, as some have claimed. Through his emissary Chou Enlai, Mao learned that the Soviet air cover would not be available for his troops' border crossing; but Stalin promised Mao immediate delivery of all necessary military equipment and supplies and air cover to be provided later to the Chinese troops in Korea. Mao swallowed the pill and decided to initiate the military action without the Soviet air cover. The final decision for the intervention was made on October 18 and the next day the "Chinese People's Volunteers" (CPV) began to cross the Yalu River. Throughout the whole period, the Soviets prodded the Chinese to intervene. However, it was not necessary. The communist Chinese leaders had an indomitable concern for China's security and strong ideological zeal to see the triumph of communist North Korea. In addition, Mao had a keen sense of the value of external military action to promote internal cohesion as well as some sense of sympathy for the crisis in Korea, China's long-traditional special neighbor.[39]

Many historians have argued that Chinese intervention was not inevitable, that it could and should have been avoided, and that American mistakes helped cause it. Some have even argued that it was "the greatest disaster for the Truman administration." Many turn to American intelligence for an explanation, assuming, as is the case with many other historical events, that the possession of accurate information about the possibility or likelihood of Chinese intention would have assisted policy makers in avoiding it. These scholars also contend that American intelligence did not do the job and that there was a "massive intelligence breakdown." Others have thought that there were simple misjudgments in the process, and some have pointed their fingers at the "arrogance" of Acheson and others involved in the policy-making process. How information is received, processed, interpreted, and acted upon is an important matter, and the process in this case needs to be studied closely.[40]

During the MacArthur hearings, when General Bradley was asked about the intelligence the Joint Chiefs of Staff had regarding Chinese intervention, he stated, "We had no intelligence that they were going to enter the war. We had the intelligence that they were concentrating in Manchuria. You can only then consider their capabilities." During the same hearings, Secretary Acheson summarized the status of intelligence estimates between the outbreak of the war and late September 1950 in two words: "intervention improbable." We can clarify these words describing the inadequate state of intelligence in Washington by tracing the background story. A concern about the probability of Chinese intervention began quite early, in fact, as soon as the U.S. intervention began, and on June 30 Jessup said that the main danger of intervention came from the Chinese communists. In early July, the State Department had exaggerated information that 200,000 Chinese communist troops were massing in the Autung area at the mouth of the Yalu River. By early August, the British government had received information that Chinese troops were moving north to a location between Hankow and Beijing and that a substantial part of Lin Piao's 4th Army was garrisoned along the Korean border. Toward the end of August, the U.S. Army had information that 246,000 Chinese troops were in Manchuria and that 80,000 of them were in the Tantung area. In early September, Washington received information from Hong Kong that Chou Enlai had made a statement on August 23 that if the North Korean Army were pushed back to the Yalu–Tuman border, then the Chinese would fight. On September 27, Washington received a communication that V. M. Panikkar, Indian ambassador in Beijing, had reported to Nehru his September 21 conversation with Chou, in which the Chinese foreign minister gave him an impression of taking an "aggressive policy" line in dealing with the war in Korea. In early October, a clear message came from China: On the first of the month, London reported Chou's statement that the Chinese would not "stand idle" if North Korea were to be invaded. Two days later (October 3), an even clearer message came from Chou. He called in the Indian ambassador and informed him that if the U.N. forces crossed the 38th parallel, China would send troops across the border to defend North Korea and that this intervention would not take place if only South Korean forces crossed the line. The Chinese warning was repeated on October 10.[41]

At the end of July, after the information about the massing of as many as 200,000 Chinese troops right across from Shinuiju, the major border Korean city at the mouth of the Yalu River, had been received, a memorandum prepared by the Defense Department stated, "On the basis of available intelligence, the North Korean forces will not be reinforced by any large number of Chinese Communist troops, Soviet ground forces, or Soviet air forces as long as the ground fighting is confined to the area south of the 38th parallel." A day after receiving additional information that 246,000 Chinese troops were in Manchuria and that 80,000 of them were located in the Tantung area, the State Department declared that Chinese intervention was not likely. During the two-week period after the Inch'ŏn landing, the view that Chinese intervention was not likely still persisted in Washington, with the exception of Oliver Edmund Clubb, director of the Office of Chinese Affairs, who pointed out on September 27 the possibility of Chinese intervention given the movement of troops into Manchuria. Three Chinese warnings were issued in early October—on October 1, 3, and 10—and still the possibility of Chinese intervention was considered "unlikely" in Washington. On October 12—even after all three Chinese warnings—the CIA still did not think that intervention was likely; on October 14 MacArthur expressed the same view and repeated it on the next day to the president at Wake Island; on October 30, four days after the 6th ROK Division was attacked by Chinese communist forces at Chosan, MacArthur still did not want to acknowledge that the intervention had taken place. But Washington became uneasy, and the Joint Chiefs of Staff directed MacArthur to continue to fight in case the Chinese intervention was a reality. The State Department said that if the Chinese declaration was not a bluff, then the (right) time for intervention had passed already.[42]

What General Bradley stated during the MacArthur hearings regarding intelligence was correct: the Joint Chiefs of Staff had information about the troop concentrations, but there was no indication that these troops would be used across the border. This is almost a repetition of the situation in North Korea before the outbreak of the war: The troop concentrations and troop movements north of the 38th parallel were known to American intelligence, but the American analysts concluded that a Northern invasion was "possible but not probable." This misinterpretation was made in June, and three months later the same mistake was repeated. Let us suppose that Bradley was correct in doubting that Chinese troops concentrated in Manchuria would be ordered across the border. In early October, after two clear warnings from Chou—statements that China would use the troops in Manchuria to intervene under certain circumstances—the Joint Chiefs of Staff decided to ignore the warnings and processed through the secretary of defense and the president a directive to MacArthur to continue to fight if major Chinese communist units intervened anywhere in Korea so long as there was a "reasonable chance of success." Clearly, lack of intelligence was not a problem; there was plenty of intelligence, but the warnings were ignored or, more accurately, the Chinese were not taken seriously. Then and later, there was much discussion concerning the trustworthiness of the messenger Panikkar, the Indian ambassador in Beijing, who brought Chou's messages. In view of the nature of the messages, the circumstances under which the messages were given, and his official position, the messages should not have been taken lightly unless one were looking for a reason to ignore the messages.[43]

Had the Pentagon slightly modified its position and looked into alternatives to avoid Chinese intervention, especially since Chou had clearly indicated that it would happen if only the South Koreans crossed the parallel—an event that had already taken place by the time of this statement—then there was a possibility that the Koreans themselves could have decided their own fate between the 38th parallel and the Yalu–Tuman border, with both the U.N. and Chinese forces watching and cheering but staying outside of these two boundary lines. It is doubtful whether South Koreans could have destroyed the North Korean Army or chased them across the Yalu–Tuman border line, but at least one advantage this side had, which was of course a disadvantage for the other side, was that the battlefield would have been north of the parallel. The Americans then would not have been able to erase the line they had drawn, but the South Koreans might have drawn a new line probably at P'yŏngyang and Wŏnsan or even between Anju and Hŭngnam, which would have been more proportional to the population of the two half Koreas. Of course, this would not have solved the Korean unification problem, which was feared by Allison and his colleagues, but it would have made it somewhat easier for the Koreans to solve the problem.

Once the decision was made to ignore the Chinese warnings and after the massive intervention began, U.S. military leaders realized the Chinese–North Korean force was too formidable and ordered the U.N. forces to retreat quickly. Some have wondered why the Americans retreated so rapidly; in fact some Korean War veterans still today say they do not understand why the Americans with such superior fire power gave up so quickly and so easily once the Chinese came in. MacArthur, one of the most confident Americans, began to claim that he would not be able to handle the Chinese forces with the troops he had and that he would either have to step up the war by bombing Manchuria or get out of Korea and the war. He was told by the Pentagon that he would not have any more reinforcements until the following March. When one examines the manpower and budget situation in the United States at this time, one realizes that MacArthur's confidence did not have much basis and that it was for the most part sheer vanity. Too much confidence and pride can be harmful; when they are combined with an inadequate basis, the outcome can be serious.[44]

The policy makers in Washington went through a trying period in the summer and winter of 1950 as they debated what to do with the Chinese intervention in Korean situation. Two groups emerged with extreme views: One, which was led by Nitze and Kennan and later joined by Jessup, argued that U.S. troops should get out of Korea as soon as possible; the other, which was headed by MacArthur, thought that hitting the enemy's sanctuary in Manchuria and taking other necessary measures against China would lead to victory in the war. To Washington this meant a general war with China, and policy makers there wanted to avoid a general war by limiting the war to the Korean peninsula. In mid-August, when U.N. troops were trying desperately to hold to the last beachhead in Korea, Jessup expressed his view that the peninsula had no strategic value and that the nation should be extricated from the situation. A week later, Kennan said that the United States would not be able to keep Korea out of the Soviet orbit, and it would be better for the nation to let the Soviets have it until the Japanese came back to take it over! In early November, when the Chinese intervention was under way, Frank E. Lowe, who had made a trip to Korea as a special representative of the president, recommended that the United States should get out of Korea. On November 10, the Joint Chiefs of Staff expressed the same view, and at the end of the month, the secretary of defense expressed a slightly modified view: He favored getting out of Korea with honor. But during the same month, some in Washington began to think about the psychological impact of the U.S. withdrawal. Toward the end of the month Acheson felt that if the United States withdrew from Korea, it would "lose face," and the consequences would be disastrous for the country. Throughout December the idea of evacuation lingered in the minds of some of the policy makers in Washington, but a position gradually emerged and became firm indicating that the United States would not get out voluntarily; it would stay and fight. In January, MacArthur came forward with his idea of a stepped-up war or a withdrawal. By this time, however, Washington's decision not to withdraw was firm, and moreover, Ridgway had taken over command of the fighting in Korea and saved the difficult situation with his strong will to fight. Unable to swallow, or adjust to, Washington's line, MacArthur had to leave the scene. In a sense, Washington took once again a sensible, easy middle position, rejecting both extremes. In January, the U.S. government drew up detailed plans for evacuation to Cheju Island with a certain number of Koreans, each of whom had a priority number on his neck. Indeed, leaders in Washington needed considerable courage to decide to stay in Korea in the winter of 1950. In the course of adjusting the U.S. military strategy to the changing situation, the United States also adjusted its national objective. Through October, when the war was going well, Washington interpreted the key phrase of the June 27 U.N. Security Council, "restoration of international peace and security," to mean that unification of Korea was the war aim; after November, when the Chinese intervention came, Washington began to assert that the action prescribed in the resolution was a "permissive" but not "required" one and to claim that the unification of Korea by force had never been the U.S. objective. The interpretation of a legal document may change given different time periods or circumstances, and there is no legal problem with such changes. In this case, however, it is more a matter of maintaining confidence and dependability, and some critics have had difficulty accepting the changes in the interpretation of the U.N. document and in the policy of the United States government. In a sense, both the Chinese intervention and the U.S. policy decision to stay in Korea had the function of restoring the balance of power in the area. A sense of justice may have favored the restoration of an equilibrium.[45]

NOTES

1. Yukkun Sakwan Hakkyo, *Hankuk Chŏnchaengsa* (History of wars in Korea) (Seoul: Ilshinsa, 1987), pp. 219–244; Taehanminkuk Kukpangpu, Chŏnsa P'yŏnch'an Wiwŏnhoe, *Hankuk Chŏnran ilnyŏnchi, April 1, 4283–June 30, 4284* (Annual Record of the Korean War, 1950–1951) (Seoul: Ilyŏngsa, 1951), pp. B11–B13; Paik Sŭn-yŭp, *Kunkwa na: 6.25 Hankuk Chŏnchaeng hoekorok* (The Army and me: The Korean War memoirs) (Seoul: Daeryuk Yŏnkuso, 1989), pp. 28–29; Yu Chae-hŭng, "Hoeko: Park Chŏng-hi, Chŭng Il-kwŏn, kŭriko Chŏng In-suk sakŏn" (Memoir: Park Chŏng-hi, Chŭng Il-kwŏn, and Chŏng In-suk incident), *Donga Ilbo*, March 3, 1994, 7: 5–6; ibid., March 4, 1994, 7: 1–6; ibid., March 5, 1994, 7: 1.

2. Muccio to the Secretary of State (925), (929), (935), June 25, *Foreign Relations of the United States (FRUS), 1950*, 7: 125–126, 129, 130, 132; (944), (951), June 26, 1950, ibid., pp. 147–148, 167; Subject: Acheson's phone call to the President, June 24, 1950, Truman Library, Elsey Papers, box 71.

3. Acheson to Muccio, June 24, 1950, *FRUS, 1950*, 7: pp. 126–127, 143–144; editorial notes, ibid., p. 131; Subject: Korea, with representatives of certain members of the United Nations, memorandum of conversation by Charles P. Noyes, June 25, 1950, ibid., pp. 144–147; June 25 U.N. Security Council resolution, ibid., pp. 155–156; Truman Library, Elsey Papers, box 71 (for June 25, 1950); teleconference, participating Washington and CINCFE, 252330Z June 50, Douglas MacArthur Memorial Archives (MacArthur Library), RG 9, Radiograms, box 113.

4. Subject: Korean Situation, Memorandum of conversation by the Ambassador at Large (Jessup), June 25, 1950, *FRUS, 1950*, 7: pp. 157–161; Subject: Blair House Meeting, JCS Instruction to MacArthur, June 25, 1950, Truman Library, Elsey Papers, box 71; teleconference, 252330Z June 50, MacArthur Library, RG 9, Radiograms, box 113.

5. Muccio to the Secretary of State (946), (957), June 26, 1950, *FRUS, 1950*, 7: 165–166, 170; memorandum for the President, June 26, 1950, Truman Library, Records of the NSC, CIA file box 1; Seoul ROB 004, 261630Z 50, National Archives (NA), RG 59, Numerical File, box 4262; Subject: Events in Korea, June 26, 1950, Truman Library, Elsey Papers, box 71.

6. Subject: Korean Situation, memorandum of conversation by the Ambassador at Large (Jessup), participants: the President, Acheson, Johnson, Matthews, Rusk, Hickerson, Jessup, Pace, Finletter, Bradley, Sherman, Vandenberg, and Collins, June 26, 1950, *FRUS, 1950*, 7: 178–183; President Truman's conversation with George M. Elsey, June 25, 1950, Truman Library, Elsey Papers, box 71; Teleconference, participating hqs.: Washington and CINCFE, 270217 Z June 50, MacArthur Library, RG 9, Radiograms, box 113.

7. Subject: Korean Situation, memorandum of conversation by the Ambassador at Large (Jessup), participants: the President and the representatives of the State and Defense Departments, June 25, 26, 1950, *FRUS, 1950*, 7: 158, 178, 181, 183;

Muccio to the Secretary of State, June 26, 1950, ibid., pp. 167–168; the Secretary of State to the Embassy in Yugoslavia, June 26, 1950, ibid., pp. 177–178; the Secretary of State to the Embassy in the United Kingdom, June 27, 1950, ibid., pp. 186–187; the U.S. Representative in the United Nations (Austin) to the Secretary of State, June 26, 1950, ibid., pp. 188–193; the Ambassador in the United Kingdom (Kirk) to the Secretary of State, June 27, 1950, ibid., pp. 187–188; Subject: Notes on Meeting in the Cabinet Room at the White House, memorandum of conversation by the Ambassador at Large (Jessup), participants: the President, representatives of the State and Defense Departments, and congressional leaders, June 27, 1950, ibid., p. 201; the Ambassador in India (Henderson) to the Secretary of State, June 27, 1950, ibid., pp. 204–206; the Secretary of State to the Embassy in India, June 27, 1950, ibid., p. 206; the Ambassador in the Netherlands (Chapin) to the Secretary of State, June 27, 1950, ibid., pp. 206–207; editorial notes, ibid., p. 207; resolution adopted by the U.N. Security Council, June 27, 1950, ibid., p. 211.

8. Taehanminkuk, Kukpangpu, Chŏnsa P'yŏnch'an Wiwŏnhoe, *Hankuk Chŏnchaengsa*, vol. 2, pp. 234–293. Yukkun Sakwan Hakkyo, *Hankuk Chŏnchaengsa*, pp. 228–229, 234–237, 250–255; Taehanminkuk, Kukpangpu, Chŏnsa P'yŏnch'an Wiwŏnhoe, *Hankuk Chŏnran Ilnyŏnchi*, pp. B12–B13; Paik Sŭn-yŭp, *Kunkwa na*, pp. 40–46.

9. CINCFE to Department of State (CX-56820), June 27, 1950, NA, RG 59, Numerical File, box 4263; memorandum for the President from the CIA Director, June 28, 1950, Truman Library, Records of the National Security Council, box 1; from 0001/29 (June 1950) to 2200/29 (KT), Truman Library, Intelligence File, Army Intelligence–Korea, Sitrep 1; note on June 30, 1950, 8:05 A.M., teleconference between CINCE and the Department of the Army, *FRUS, 1950*, 7: 255.

10. Draft memorandum of the conference, June 29, 1950, with assistants, Truman Library, Elsey Papers, box 71; G-2 CSUSA to SSR, Tokyo, personal, from Collins to MacArthur, June 29, 1950, MacArthur Library, RG 6, FECOM, box 9; DA to CINCFE, June 30, 1950 (JCS 84681), ibid., RG 9, Radiograms, box 43; CINCFE to DA, 30 June 1950 (C56942), ibid.; teleconference, participants: Washington and CINCFE, 300740Z, June 30, 1950, ibid., box 113; Chŭng Il-kwŏn, *Chŭng Il-kwŏn hoekorok: 6.25 pirok; chŏnchaengkwa hyuchŏn* (Chŭng Il-kwŏn memoir: Confidential record of the Korean war; the war and the armistice) (Seoul: Donga Ilbosa, 1986), pp. 32–34. See also Clay Blair, *The Forgotten War: America in Korea, 1950–1953* (New York: Time Books, 1987), pp. 82–86; D. Clayton James, *Refighting the Last War: Command and Crises in Korea 1950–1953* (New York: Free Press, 1993), pp. 141–143.

11. Ernest R. May, *"Lessons" of the Past: The Use and Misuse of History in American Foreign Policy* (London: Oxford University Press, 1973), pp. 72–75; Calum A. MacDonald, *Korea: The War before Vietnam* (New York: Free Press, 1986), p. 34; Steven Pelz, "U.S. Decision on Korean Policy, 1943–1950: Some Hypotheses," in *Child of Conflict*, ed. Bruce Cumings, p. 128; James, *Refighting the Last War*, p. 15.

12. Harry S. Truman, *Memoirs*, 2 vols. (Garden City, N.Y.: Doubleday, 1956), vol. 2, pp. 332–334, 337; Dean Acheson, *Present at the Creation: My Years in the State Department* (New York: Norton, 1969), p. 405; Subject: President Truman's conversation with George M. Elsey, June 26, 1950, Truman Library, Elsey Papers, box 71; the Department of State to SCAP, Tokyo, June 29, 1950, MacArthur Library, RG 9, box 90; intelligence estimate by the Estimate Group, Office of Intelli-

gence Research, Department of State, June 25, 1950, *FRUS, 1950*, 7: 151–154. See also William W. Stueck, Jr., *The Road to Confrontation: American Policy toward China and Korea, 1947–1950* (Chapel Hill: University of North Carolina Press, 1981), pp. 6–7, 173, 186; Burton I. Kaufman, *The Korean War: Challenge in Crises, Credibility, and Command* (New York: Knopf, 1986), p. 39, May, *"Lessons" of the Past*, pp. 51, 69, 71–72, 80–85, 115, 172; John Lewis Gaddis, "Korea in American Politics, Strategy and Diplomacy, 1945–50," in *The Origins of the Cold War in Asia*, ed. Y. Nagai and I. Akira (New York: Columbia University Press, 1977), p. 288.

13. The Secretary of State to the Embassy in the United Kingdom, June 27, 1950, *FRUS, 1950*, 7: 186–187; Austin to the Secretary of State, June 28, 1950, ibid., p. 224; the Ambassador in France (Bruce) to the Secretary of State (for Kennan), June 26, 1950, ibid., p. 174; Kirk to the Secretary of State, June 25, 27, 1950, ibid., pp. 139, 169, 199; editorial notes, ibid., p. 143.

14. *Congressional Record*, 81st Cong., 2d sess., vol. 96, pt. 7, p. 9158 (June 26, 1950, by Senators Knowland and Connally), p. 9625 (June 27, 1950, by Senator Douglas), p. 9231 (June 27, 1950, by Senator Morse), pp. 9533–10537 (June 30, 1950, by Senators Lodge, Byrd, Wiley, Wherry, Knowland, Stennis, Millikin, Saltonstall, Connelly, and Douglas); *New York Times*, June 28, 1950, 1: 7; ibid., June 28, 1950, 6: 3. See also May, *"Lessons" of the Past*, pp. 74, 78, 82, 115; Stueck, *The Road to Confrontation*, p. 256.

15. Memorandum of conversation by Charles P. Noyes, Adviser on Security Council Affairs, United States Mission at the United Nations, with some representatives of U.N. member nations, June 25, 1950, *FRUS, 1950*, 7: 144–146; the Ambassador in France (Bruce) to the Secretary of State, June 26, 1950, ibid., p. 175; the Ambassador in The Netherlands (Chapin) to the Secretary of State, June 26, 1950, ibid., p. 185; the Secretary of State to the Embassy in Yugoslavia, June 26, 1950, ibid., p. 177; Austin to the Secretary of State, June 26, 1950, ibid., pp. 189–192; the Ambassador in Belgium (Murphy) to the Secretary of State, June 27, 1950, ibid., p. 207; the Ambassador in Greece to the Secretary of State, June 27, 1950, NA, RG 59, Numerical File, box 4263; the Embassy in Denmark to the Secretary of State, June 27, 1950, ibid.; the Ambassador in Spain to the Secretary of State, June 27, 1950, ibid.; the Ambassador in Finland to the Secretary of State, June 27, 1950, ibid.; the Ambassador to the Secretary of State, June 27, 1950, ibid.; Kirk to the Secretary of State, June 27, 1950, ibid.; the Ambassador in Turkey to the Secretary of State, June 27, 1950, ibid.; the Secretary of State to all diplomatic missions and certain consular officers, June 29, 1950, *FRUS, 1950*, 7: 231; the Secretary of State to all diplomatic missions and certain consular officers, June 30, 1950, ibid., pp. 255–257; the Ambassador in India (Henderson) to the Secretary of State, June 30, 1950, ibid., pp. 266–267; World Reaction to Korean Development, no. 3, Office of Intelligence Research, the Department of State, June 30, 1950, NA, RG 59, Numerical File, box 4267. See also Stueck, *The Korean War: An International History* (Princeton, N.J.: Princeton University Press, 1995), pp. 23–27.

16. May, *"Lessons" of the Past*, p. 75; Blair, *The Forgotten War*, pp. 82–84.

17. Draft, Truman to John Chang, enclosure in Acheson to Truman, June 29, 1950, NA, RG 59, Numerical File, box 4263; Lovett to Muccio, September 24, 1950, ibid., box 3828.

18. Francisca Rhee, "6.25wa Rhee Syngman Taet'ongryŏng" (The Korean War and President Syngman Rhee), *Chungang Ilbo*, June 24, 1983, p. 3; Chang Myŏn,

Han alŭ mili chukchiankonŭn: Chang paksa hoekorok (Unless a grain of wheat is sacrificed: Dr. Chang's memoir) (Seoul: Kidok kyo Ch'ulp'ansa, 1967), pp. 99–104; Han P'yo-wook, *Han-Mi oekyo yoramki* (The early years of the Korean–American diplomatic relationship) (Seoul: Chungang Ilposa, 1984), pp. 69–88; Im Pyŏng-chik, "Rhee Paksawa tŏpulŏ Pusankachi" (To Pusan with Dr. Rhee), *Sindonga* (June 1970): 175–177; Kim Chong-pil, "Tongnan chŏnya nanŭn yukpon tangchik changkyoyŏtta," (I was an officer on duty at the Korean Army headquarters on the eve of the war) *Wŏlkan Chungang* (June 1968): 175–177; memorandum of conversation, the President with Chang Myŏn, Han P'yo-wook, and Acheson, June 26, 1950, Truman Library, Elsey Papers, box 71.

19. Muccio to the Secretary of State, June 26, 1950, *FRUS, 1950,* 7: 141; Francisca Rhee, "6.25wa Rhee Syngman Taet'ongryŏng," June 24, 1983, p. 3; Im Pyŏng-chik, "Rhee Paksawa tŏpulŏ Pusankachi," pp. 173–177; Kim Chae-myŏng, "Rhee Syngman Seoul t'alch'ulki" (A story of Rhee Syngman's escape from Seoul), *Wŏlkan Kyŏnghyang* (June 1987): 201–221.

20. Rhee, "6.25wa Rhee Syngman Taet'ongryŏng," *Chungang Ilbo*, June 24, 1983, p. 3.

21. Muccio to the Secretary of State, June 26 (940), and 27 (unnumbered), (966), (967), 1950, *FRUS, 1950,* 7: 142, 173, 176; CINCFE to the Department of State, June 27, 1950, MacArthur Library, RG 59, Radiograms, box 83.

22. CINCFE, Tokyo, Japan to CG 8th Army, Yokohama, Japan, June 30, 1950, MacArthur Library, RG 6, Radiograms, box 28; Tokyo to Secretary of State, June 30, 1950, NA, RG 59, Decimal File 1945–49, box 4313; Joint Morning Sitrep 6, 0001/03 to 2200/04(KT)/July 1950, Truman Library, Military Intelligence File, Military Intelligence–Korea, box 262; Joint Morning Sitrep 6, 0001/2 to 2200/2(KT)July 1950, ibid.; *New York Times*, July 5, 1950, 1: 8; ibid., July 7, 1950, 1: 5–8; Taehanminkuk, Kukpangpu, Chŏnsa P'yŏnch'an Wiwŏnhoe, *Hankuk Chŏnchaeng ilnyŏnchi*, pp. A35–A36; idem, *Hankuk Chŏnchaengsa*, vol. 2, pp. 359–367; Yukkun Sakwan Hakkyo, *Hankuk Chŏnchaengsa*, pp. 260–264. See also Ohn Chang-il, "Cho-ch'ong-ryŏkchŏn kŭriko chehanchŏn: 6.25 Chŏnchaengŭi suhaeng kwachŏng" (A super total war and a limited war: The process of the Korean War), in *Hankuk Chŏnchaengŭi yŏksachŏk koch'al* (Historical consideration of the Korean War), ed. Hankuk Chŏngch'ioekyosa Hakhoe (Seoul: P'yŏngminsa, 991), p. 21.

23. Department of the Navy to the Department of State, July 7, 1950, NA, RG 59, Decimal File, box 4264; Joint Daily Sitrep 20, July 20, and Joint Daily Sitrep 21, July 18, both 1950, Truman Library, Military Intelligence File, Military Intelligence File–Korea, box 262; Drumright to Allison, July 30, 1950, NA, RG 59, Decimal File, box 4266; *New York Times*, July 10, 1950, 1: 4–8; ibid., July 10, 1950, 2: 2; ibid., July 11, 1950, 30: 1; ibid., July 26, 1950, 1: 4; Taehanminkuk Kukpangpu, Chŏnsa P'yŏnch'an Wiwŏnhoe, *Hankuk Chŏnchaeng ilnyŏnchi*, pp. B15–B22; idem, *Hankuk Chŏnchaengsa*, vol. 2, pp. 368–780; Yukkun Sakwan Hakkyo, *Hankuk Chŏnchaengsa*, pp. 264–316; Ohn Chang-il, "Cho-ch'ongryŏkchŏn kŭriko chehanchŏn," pp. 210–213.

24. CINCFE to the Joint Chiefs of Staff, July 9, 1950, NA, RG59, Decimal File, box 4264; Joint Daily Sitrep 16, July 12, Joint Daily Sitrep 20, July 17, and Joint Daily Sitrep 21, July 18, all 1950, Truman Library, Military Intelligence File, Military Intelligence–Korea, box 262; Drumright to Allison, July 30, 1950, NA, RG 59, Numerical File, box 4266; *New York Times*, July 11, 1950, 1: 4.

25. CINCFE to the Department of the Army, September 1, 1950, NA, RG 59, Numerical File, box 4268; *New York Times*, August 2, 1950, 5: 1–2; ibid., August 6, 1950, IV, 5: 1–2; ibid., August 20, 1950, IV, 5: 1–2; ibid., September 5, 1950, 1: 6–7; ibid., September 6, 1950, 1: 4–8; ibid., September 7, 1950, 1: 5–8; ibid., September 15, 1950, 3: 2–3; Taehanminkuk, Kukpangpu, Chŏnsa P'yŏnch'an Wiwŏnhoe, *Hankuk Chŏnchaeng ilnyŏnchi*, pp. A37–A39; idem, *Hankuk Chŏnchaengsa*, vol. 3, pp. 17–304, 385–528; Yukkun Sakwan Hakkyo, *Hankuk Chŏnchaengsa*, pp. 320–362.

26. CINCFE to the Department of the Army, July 7, 14, 23, 1950, MacArthur Library, RG 9, Radiograms, box 43; Collins to MacArthur, August 4, 1950, ibid., RG 10, Personal Correspondence, VIP file; memorandum of conversation with MacArthur, Harriman, Norstad, Ridgway, and Almond, August 8, 1950, ibid., RG 9, Far Eastern Command, General Files, box 1; Joint Chiefs of Staff to CINCFE, August 28, September 29, 1950, NA, RG 218, Geographic File 1948–1950, 383.21 Korea; Taehanminkuk Kukpangpu, Chŏnsa P'yŏnch'an Wiwŏnhoe, *Hankuk Chŏnchaeng ilnyŏnchi*, p. A39; idem, *Hankuk Chŏnchaengsa*, vol. 3, pp. 529–616; Ohn Ch'ang-il, "Cho-ch'ongryŏkchŏn kŭriko chehanchŏn," pp. 214–216.

27. CINCFE to the Department of Army, September 16, 1950, MacArthur Library, RG 9, Radiograms, box 113; CIA Director's memorandum for the President, September 27, 1950, Truman Library, Records of the National Security Council, CIA file; *New York Times*, September 23, 1950, 1: 8; ibid., September 30, 1950, 1: 5–8; Taehanminkuk, Kukpangpu, Chŏnsa P'yŏnch'an Wiwŏnhoe, *Hankuk Chŏnchaeng ilnyŏnchi*, A39–A40; idem, *Hankuk Chŏnchaengsa*, vol. 3, pp. 617–802; Ohn Ch'ang-il, "Cho-ch'ongryŏkchŏn kŭriko chehanchŏn," pp. 216–217; Yukkun Sakwan Hakkyo, *Hankuk Chŏnchaengsa*, pp. 380–391.

28. Stueck, *The Road to Confrontation*, pp. 233–234, 253; idem, *The Korean War: An International History*, pp. 89–111; MacDonald, *Korea: The War before Vietnam*, pp. 37, 47–49, 56; Rosemary Foot, *The Wrong War: American Policy and the Dimensions of the Korean Conflict, 1950–1953* (Ithaca, N.Y.: Cornell University Press, 1985), pp. 68–70; Gaddis, *The Long Peace*, p. 98. See also Joyce Kolko and Gabriel Kolko, *The Limits of Power: The World and United States Foreign Policy, 1945–1954* (New York: Harper and Row, 1972), p. 596; Lowe, *The Origins of the Korean War*, p. 198.

29. Allison to Rusk, July 15, 1950, NA, RG 59, Decimal File, box 4265; Acheson to Muccio, July 20, 1950, ibid.; "Crossing the 38th Parallel," NA, RG 59, 55D 388, box 3; Rusk to Matthews, Nitze, Hickerson, and others, July 22, 1950, NA, RG 59, Decimal File, box 4265; draft of memorandum prepared by the Policy Planning Staff, July 22, 1950, *FRUS, 1950*, 7: 449–452; Allison to Nitze, July 24, 1950, NA, RG 59, Decimal File, box 4265; Acheson, *Present at the Creation*, pp. 451–452.

30. Draft memorandum prepared in the Department of Defense, July 31, 1950, *FRUS, 1950*, 7: 502–510; draft memorandum prepared in the Department of State, August 31, 1950, ibid., pp. 671–679; report by the National Security Council to the President, NSC 81/1, September 9, 1950, ibid., pp. 712–721; memorandum prepared in the Department of State, September 14, 1950, ibid., 726–727; memorandum prepared by John Foster Dulles, Consultant to the Secretary of State, to the Secretary of State, September 22, 1950, ibid., p. 751; minutes of the sixth meeting of the U.N. Delegation to the U.N. General Assembly, September 25, 1950, ibid., pp. 768–773; the Acting Secretary of State to the Secretary of State, at New York,

September 26, 1950, ibid., pp. 782–783; minutes of the ninth meeting of the U.N. Delegation to the U.N. General Assembly, September 28, 1950, ibid., pp. 799–808; the U.S. Representative at the United Nations (Austin) to the Secretary of State, September 29, 1950, ibid., pp. 826–828; editorial note, ibid., p. 903; Resolution 376 (V), adopted by the U.N. General Assembly, October 7, 1950, ibid., pp. 904–906; Joint Chiefs of Staff to CINCFE (JCS 92801), September 27, 1950, NA, RG 218, Geographic File 1948–1950, 383.21 Korea; Marshall to MacArthur, September 29, 1950, RG 59, Radiograms, box 43; "Crossing the 38th Parallel," NA, RG 59, 55D 388, box 3; Acheson, *Present at the Creation*, pp. 451–454.

31. Memorandum by the Director of the Office of Northeast Asian Affairs (Allison) to the Assistant Secretary of State for Far Eastern Affairs (Rusk), July 13, 1950, *FRUS, 1950*, 7: 373; memorandum by John Foster Dulles, Consultant to the Secretary of State, to the Director of the Policy Planning Staff (Nitze), July 14, 1950, ibid., pp. 386–387; Allison to Rusk, July 15, 1950, ibid., pp. 393–395; draft memorandum prepared by the Policy Planning Staff, July 22, 1950, ibid., pp. 449–454; Allison to Nitze, July 24, 1950, ibid., pp. 459–461; draft memorandum prepared by the Policy Planning Staff, July 25, 1950, ibid., pp. 469–473; Allison to Rusk, July 27, 1950, ibid., pp. 480–481.

32. Draft memorandum prepared by the Department of Defense, July 31, 1950, *FRUS, 1950*, 7: 502–510; Dulles to Nitze, August 1, 1950, ibid., p. 514; Allison to John K. Emerson of the Office of Northeast Asian Affairs, ibid., pp. 617–623; draft memorandum prepared in the Department of State for National Security Council Staff consideration only, August 23, 1950, ibid., pp. 635–638; memorandum prepared in the Department of State, ibid., pp. 653–654; draft memorandum prepared in the Department of State for National Security Council Staff study only, August 30, 1950, ibid., pp. 660–666; draft memorandum prepared in the Department of State, August 31, 1950, ibid., pp. 671–679.

33. Joint Daily Sitrep 96, October 1, 1950, Truman Library, Military Intelligence File, Military Intelligence–Korea, box 262; CINCFE to the Joint Chiefs of Staff, October 2, 1950, MacArthur Library, RG 9, Radiograms, box 43; *Department of State Bulletin* 24 (January 1, 1951): 43; *New York Times*, October 2, 1950, 1: 8; ibid., October 15, 1950, IV, 5: 1–2; ibid., October 21, 1950, 1: 8; ibid., October 22, 1950, IV, 1: 1; ibid., October 23, 1950, 1: 6–8; ibid., October 24, 1950, 7: 1; Taehanminkuk Kukpangpu, Chŏnsa P'yŏnch'an Wiwŏnhoe, *Hankuk Chŏnchaeng ilnyŏnchi, 1950–1951*, pp. A41–A42; Chŭng Il-kwŏn, *Chŭng Il-kwŏn hoekorok*, pp. 162–214; Paik Sŭn-yŭp, *Kunkwa na*, pp. 83–128; Taehanminkuk, Kukpangpu, Chŏnsa P'yŏnch'an Wiwŏnhoe, *Hankuk Chŏnchanegsa*, vol. 4, pp. 291–690; Ohn Chang-il, "Cho-ch'ochongryŏkchŏn kŭriko chehanchŏn," pp. 218–220; Yukkun Sakwan Hakkyo, *Hankuk Chŏnchaengsa*, pp. 411–452; Sergei Goncharov, John W. Lewis, and Xue Litai, *Uncertain Partners: Stalin, Mao and the Korean War* (Stanford: Stanford University Press, 1993), pp. 168–199; Zhang Shugung, "China's Military Strategy during the Korean War" (manuscript, July 1995). See also Chen Jian, *China's Road to the Korean War: The Making of the Sino-American Confrontation* (New York: Columbia University Press, 1994), p. 206.

34. Joint Daily Sitrep 127, November 3, 1950, Truman Library, Military Intelligence File, Military Intelligence–Korea, box 263; Joint Sitrep 114, November 29, 1950, ibid.; Muccio to the Secretary of State, November 27, 1950, *FRUS, 1950*, 7: 1235; SCAP to the Department of the Army, November 29, 1950, MacArthur Li-

brary, RG 9, Radiograms, box 83; CINCFE to the Department of the Army, December 17, 1950, ibid., RG 6, FECom, box 9; CIA Director's memorandum for the President, November 28, 1950, Truman Library, Records of the National Security Council, CIA file; *Department of State Bulletin* 24 (March 19, 1951): 470; *New York Times*, November 2, 1950, 4: 2–4; ibid., November 21, 1950, 1: 6–8; ibid., December 5, 1950, 1: 4–8; ibid., December 8, 1950, 1: 5; ibid., December 24, 1950, 1: 7; ibid., December 25, 1950, 1: 8; ibid., December 26, 1950, 22: 1; Taehanminkuk Kukpangpu, Chŏnsa P'yŏnch'an Wiwŏnhoe, *Hankuk Chŏnchaeng ilnyŏnchi, 1950–1951*, pp. A43–A44; Chŭng Il-kwŏn, *Chŭng Il-kwŏn hoekorok*, pp. 221–277; Paik Sŭn-yŭp, *Kunkwa na*, pp. 116–143; Taehanminkuk, Kukpangpu, Chŏnsa P'yŏnch'an Wiwŏnhoe, *Hankuk Chŏnchengsa*, vol. 5, pp. 57–313; Yukkun Sakwan Hakkyo, *Hankuk Chŏnchaengsa*, pp. 453–511.

35. Joint Daily Sitrep 158, January 4, 1950, Truman Library, Military Intelligence File, Military Intelligence–Korea, box 263; Joint Daily Sitrep 186, January 30, 1950, ibid.; memorandum of conversation by Rusk with Hurbert Graves of the British Embassy, February 12, 1951, *FRUS, 1951*, 7: 169; Muccio to Rusk, February 12, 1951, ibid., p. 168; *Department of State Bulletin* 24 (April 30, 1951): 710; ibid., 24 (May 7, 1951): 755; Subject: Briefing of Ambassadors on Korea, memorandum of conversation by Windsor G. Hackler, May 4, 1951, *FRUS, 1951*, 7: 414–415; *New York Times*, January 4, 1951, 1: 8; ibid., March 8, 1951, 1: 8; Taehanminkuk, Kukpangpu, Chŏnsa P'yŏnch'an Wiwŏnhoe, *Hankuk Chŏnchaeng ilnyŏnchi, 1950–1951*, pp. A45–A48; Chŭng Il-kwŏn, *Chŭng Il-kwŏn hoekorok*, pp. 143–200, 277–321; Taehanminkuk, Kukpangpu, Chŏnsa P'yŏnch'an Wiwŏnhoe, *Hankuk Chŏnchaengsa*, vol. 5, pp. 323–862, vol. 6, pp. 9–15; Ohn Chang-il, "Choch'ochongryŏkchŏn kŭriko chehanchŏn," pp. 220–226; Yukkun Sakwan Hakkyo, *Hankuk Chŏnchaengsa*, pp. 511–563.

36. Stueck, *The Korean War: An International History*, p. 295; Lowe, *The Origins of the Korean War*, pp. 157, 215; Kaufman, *The Korean War*, p. 93; Ohn Chang-il, "The Joint Chiefs of Staff and U.S. Policy and Strategy Regarding Korea, 1945–1953," Ph.D. diss., University of Kansas, 1983, p. 237.

37. Lowe, *The Origins of the Korean War*, p. 198. See also a postpresidential memorandum, interview with Bradley, March 30, 1955, Truman Library.

38. Chen Jian, "Why and How China Entered the Korean War: In Light of New Evidence" (manuscript, July 1995). See also Chen, *China's Road to the Korean War*, pp. 125–190; Goncharov, Lewis, and Xue, *Uncertain Partners*, pp. 168–199; Stueck, *The Korean War: An International History*, pp. 111–126.

39. Li Xialing and Glen Tracy, annot. and trans., "Mao's Telegram During the Korean War, October–December 1950," *Chinese Historians* 5.2 (Fall 1992): 67–69; Alexsandre Mansurov, "Stalin, Mao, Kim and China's Decision to Enter the Korean War, September 16–October 15, 1950: New Evidence from the Russian Archives," *Cold War International History Project Bulletin* 6–7 (1995–1996): 95, 98, 100–103, 104, 114, 119; Vladimir Petrov, "Mao, Stalin, and Kim Il Sung: An Interpretative Essay," *Journal of Northeast Asian Studies* 13 (Summer 1994): 27; Kathryn Weathersby, "New Russian Documents on the Korean War: Introduction and Translation," *Cold War International History Project Bulletin* 6–7 (Winter 1995–1996): 44; Chen, *China's Road to the Korean War*, pp. 133, 136, 143, 156–157, 182–184, 186, 188, 200, 202, 204, 206, 208; Goncharov, Lewis, and Xue, *Uncer-

tain Partners, pp. 152, 159, 160–162, 168, 171, 176, 182, 194; Evgueni Bajanov, "Assessing the Policies of the Korean War," pp. 9–14.

40. MacDonald, *Korea: The War before Vietnam*, pp. 52–53, 57, 62; Foot, *The Wrong War*, pp. 79–81; Stueck, *The Road to Confrontation*, pp. 211, 228–229, 231, 237; Lowe, *The Origins of the Korean War*, pp. 176, 200; Kaufman, *The Korean War*, p. 89.

41. "Military Situation in the Far East," Hearings of the Committee on Armed Service and the Committee on Foreign Relations, U.S. Senate, 82d Cong., 1st sess., pt. 2, p. 759, pt. 3, p. 1832; memorandum of conversation by Frederick E. Nolting with Matthews, Jessup, Bohlen, Hickerson, June 30, 1950, *FRUS, 1950*, 7: 258; the Secretary of State to certain diplomatic and consular officers, July 6, 1950, ibid., p. 309; Douglas to the Secretary of State, August 11, 1950, ibid., p. 883; memorandum of teletype conference prepared by the Department of the Army, August 30, 1950, between Major General A. R. Bolling in Washington and Major General C. A. Willoughby in Tokyo, ibid., pp. 659–660; Consul General at Hong Kong (Wilkinson) to the Secretary of State, September 5, 1950, ibid., p. 698; memorandum of conversation by Merchant, September 27, 1950, with Herbert Graves, Counselor of the British Embassy, ibid., pp. 793–794; Chen, *China's Road to the Korean War*, pp. 164, 180; *New York Times*, October 2, 1950, 3: 1; Holes (London) to the Secretary of State, October 3, 1950, ibid., p. 839; Editorial Note, *FRUS, 1950*, 7: 914; *New York Times*, October 12, 1950, 5: 1–2.

42. Draft memorandum prepared by the Department of Defense, August 31, 1950, *FRUS, 1950*, 7: 673; memorandum of Club for Rusk, September 27, 1950, ibid., p. 795; Bradley to the Secretary of Defense, October 6, 1950, NA, RG 330, Office of Administrative Secretary, Defense File, July–December 1950, box 180; Deputy Undersecretary of State (Matthews) to Special Assistant to the Secretary of Defense for Military and Assistance (Burns), October 19, 1950, *FRUS, 1950*, 7: 980; CIA Director's memorandum for the President, October 30, 1950, Truman Library, Records of the National Security Council, CIA file, box 3; Truman, *Memoirs by Harry S. Truman*, vol. 2, p. 366.

43. "Military Situation in the Far East", part 2, p. 759, part 3, p. 1832; Bradley to the Secretary of Defense, October 5, 1950, NA, RG 330, Office of the Administrative Secretary, Defense File, July–October, 1950, box 180; the Deputy Secretary of Defense (Lovett) to the President, October 7, 1950, *FRUS, 1950*, 7: 911–912; the Joint Chiefs of Staff to the Commander in Chief, Far East (MacArthur), October 9, 1950, ibid., p. 915; Holes (London) to the Secretary of State, October 3, 1950, ibid., p. 839; the Acting Secretary of State to the Embassy in India, October 4, 1950, ibid., pp. 875–876; MacDonald, *Korea: The War before Vietnam*, p. 53.

44. The Joint Chiefs of Staff to the Commander in Chief, Far East (MacArthur), January 9, 1951, *FRUS, 1951*, 7: 41–43; the Commander in Chief, U.N. Commander (MacArthur) to the Department of the Army, January 10, 1951, ibid., 55–56; memorandum of a telephone conversation by Lucius D. Battle, Special Assistant to the Secretary of State, between Acheson and Marshall, January 11, 1951, ibid., pp. 57–60; memorandum by Rusk to Acheson, January 12, 1951, ibid., pp. 66–67. See also Truman Library, President's Secretary's File, Subject File, Cabinet, box 156, March 16, 1946, August 22, 1950; memorandum for the President, November 24, 1950, National Security Council, 73d meeting, Truman Library, President's

Secretary's File, box 220; Truman to Marshall, March 21, 1951, ibid., President's Secretary's File, Subject File, Cabinet, box 156; Robert G. Nixon, oral history interview transcript, Truman Library, p. 729.

45. Memorandum by the Ambassador at Large (Jessup) to the Deputy Undersecretary of State (Mathews), August 17, 1950, *FRUS, 1950*, 7: 595; memorandum by the Counselor (Kennan) to the Secretary of State, August 21, 1950, ibid., 624–625; Frank E. Lowe to Truman, November 4, 1950, MacArthur Memorial Library, RG 37; draft memorandum by John P. David of the Policy Planning Staff, November 7, 1950, *FRUS, 1950*, 7: 1082–1083; memorandum by James S. Lay for the National Security Council, November 10, 1950, NA, RG 59, Records of the Policy Planning Council 1947–1954, box 20; the Department of the Army to CINCFE, November 24, 1950, MacArthur Library, RG 9, Radiograms, box 43; memorandum for the President, November 24, 1950, National Security Council, 73d meeting, Truman Library, President's Secretary's File, box 220, NSC Meetings; memorandum of conference by Jessup with the Vice President and members of the State and Defense Departments, November 28, 1950, *FRUS, 1950*, 7: 1245–1247; memorandum of conversation by Jessup with members of the State and Defense Departments, December 3, 1950, ibid., p. 1327; memorandum of conversation with Acheson, Webb, Jessup, Kennan, Mathews, and others, December 4, 1950, Truman Library, Acheson Papers, box 65; minutes of the first meeting of President Truman and Prime Minister Atlee, December 4, 1950, *FRUS, 1950*, 7: 1364; memorandum of conversation by Jessup with Acheson, Jessup, Rusk, and Oliver Franks, December 4, 1950, ibid., 1374; memorandum of conversation by W. J. McWilliams with senior State Department staff, December 5, 1950, ibid., 1383; memorandum by Rusk for the Secretary of State, January 12, 1951, *FRUS, 1951*, 7: 66–67; memorandum by the Joint Chiefs of Staff to the Secretary of Defense, January 12, 1951, ibid., pp. 70–72; memorandum of conversation with Acheson, Collins, and Vandenberg, January 19, 1950, NA, RG 59, Numerical File, 795.00/1–1951. See also Chen, *China's Road to the Korean War*, p. 160.

CHAPTER 11

Wartime Diplomacy

In a sense, every historical unit of time is important; but some are more important than others, at least from the historical perspective. The year from July 1, 1950 was just such an important time for the Korean–American relationship. Of course, this was not the first wartime relationship for the two nations. They had been involved during the Sino–Japanese (1894–1895), the Russo–Japanese (1904–1905), and the American–Japanese (1941–1945) wars. Every one of these experiences had its own uniqueness and commonalties with other wartime experiences. However, in 1950, the United States was for the first time a full-fledged participant in a Korean war—actually much more than just a participant—and at the same time, the war was the first test case for the United Nations to see if its collective security system would work. The relationship between the two nations during this period developed through stages or subperiods: the first, from early July to mid-September; the second, from mid-September to the end of October; and the third, from late October to early July of the following year.

The first two and a half month period was difficult for both Koreans and the Americans. The general military strategy was to sacrifice space for the time needed to prepare for an offense, but there was not much space to sell, and the simple physical problem of too many people in too small an area in a crisis condition created frustration, irritation, and unnecessary quarrels. Nonetheless, President Rhee and the American diplomats managed the situation relatively well. Conditions on the battlefield were extremely difficult during this period, but more American troops and supplies were arriving every week, and there was hope that the situation would improve. More than anything else, the Koreans were thankful that the Americans had come to the rescue in a time of crisis, and they expressed their feelings of gratitude whenever the opportunity presented itself. One of the ways President Rhee found to do so in the early period was by putting the ROK Army under MacArthur's command. On July 15, the president wrote General MacArthur that he was happy to assign to the general command authority over all land, sea, and air forces of the republic during the war. This measure enabled U.N. commanders to use the available forces more effectively. At the same time, however, it had complicating legal and diplomatic implications.[1] Ambassador Muccio continued to make special efforts to keep the morale of the Koreans high in this depressing time. He remained involved in the domestic politics of the Republic of Korea throughout this period. This delicate subject of American involvement in Korean domestic matters forced Muccio to walk a thin line between the necessity of being involved in Korean domestic politics because of the concern by U.N. members who were making contributions to the war and the traditional American policy of nonintervention in other nations' domestic politics. Muccio did not hesitate to make suggestions to President Rhee to replace certain cabinet members, and he tried to reduce the conflict between the executive and legislative branches in South Korea.[2]

The most important issue for the South Korean government in this period was crossing the 38th parallel. It seemed almost ridiculous for the Koreans to think seriously that they could abolish the 38th parallel and achieve the reunification of the nation in those dark days. But, for them, especially for President Rhee, this was the most important concern. In his July 19 letter to President Truman, President Rhee recalled that the Korean people were divided against their will as a result of military decisions in 1945, "to which no Korean was a party," and he stated that when the North Korean troops invaded South Korea, the parallel ended as a political or military dividing line. In the same letter, President Rhee stated also that any future agreement or understanding regarding Korea by other states or groups of states without the consent and approval of the government of the Republic of Korea would not have any binding effect on the Korean government. He expressed the same view in an interview given early in September: "We never recognized the legality of the country's division at the thirty-eighth parallel." The president also conveyed his views on the issue through Ambassador Chang in Washington. The response of the American government to this expression of Korean anxiety was caution. It must have recognized the importance of the issue but decided that it was a little too early to decide what to do with it. John M. Allison, the director of the Office of Northeast Asian Affairs, in his memorandum to Rusk, expressed his view that President Rhee should not make an open statement on the issue, but that the Korean position on the issue was understandable, adding that it would be "folly" for the American government to make any negative statement at that point. On September 11,

Acheson cautioned the Americans dealing with President Rhee to carefully avoid expressing views on the issue.[3]

Soon after the Inch'ŏn landing operation, a new issue emerged for Korean–American relations—how to manage the land conquered in North Korea. Because of the brief period the U.N. forces spent in the north, this concern did not last long. Nevertheless, the Korean and the U.S. governments developed different views on the issue. The Korean government's position with regard to the jurisdiction over land that had been conquered or was to be conquered in North Korea was clear: The government of the Republic of Korea was the only legitimate government which was organized under the supervision and guidance of the United Nations, and its authority should extend automatically to the Northern territory. If the north had failed to elect representatives under U.N. supervision in 1948, it was their own fault, and they could do so now and fill the seats in the National Assembly in Seoul which had been saved for that purpose. In late September, Rusk and Allison argued against the ROK government's position that their authority automatically extended to the north. The U.N. General Assembly also took up the issue and in its October 7 resolution recommended that "all constituent acts be taken, including the holding of elections" under the auspices of the United Nations for the establishment of a unified, independent, and democratic government in Korea. It further resolved to establish the United Nations Commission for the Unification and Rehabilitation of Korea (UNCURK) to represent the United Nations in bringing about the establishment of a government for a unified Korea. The assembly also resolved to establish, pending the arrival in Korea of the UNCURK, an interim committee at the United Nations to advise the United Nations. President Rhee immediately stated that the resolution was acceptable and that he would work with the commission. Throughout the month, President Rhee held the same view on the U.N. resolution. Meanwhile, Muccio and Drumright in Seoul were cautioned not to undercut the authority of the ROK government and were told that the elections should be held only in North Korea. By the end of the month, a new situation had developed in the battlefield, and there was no need to pursue these matters further.[4]

The two and a half months between late October and mid-January of the following year were critical not only for the U.N. forces in Korea, but also the most difficult period for Korean–American relations. The most important issue was how to respond to the Chinese intervention. The Koreans showed their determination to resist the onslaught with every resource at their disposal. In early December, President Rhee called upon his people to resist the Chinese invaders by gathering whatever arms they could and by transforming every village into an armed camp. President Rhee also proposed to arm a half million Korean youths and put them in the field to repel the Chinese forces and to deploy 50,000 nationalist Chinese troops against the communist Chinese forces. The first proposal received some attention in

Washington, but it reached a dead end when MacArthur suggested arming additional Japanese policemen with the arms the United States could have used to arm the Koreans; the second proposal did not get any response at all from the American government. The matter of the 38th parallel was another key issue during this period. In the winter of 1950, ideas were discussed for all sorts of lines on the Korean peninsula, and the Koreans feared that Korea might be left divided at the end of the war at the 38th parallel or some other line. The Americans, on the other hand, thought that the issue would be decided on the battlefield, whatever the preferences of the Koreans, and consequently did not take it very seriously as a matter needing a decision.[5]

Two new issues for Korean–American diplomacy that arose during this period concerned the question of the withdrawal of U.N. forces from Korea and the treatment of POWs by the ROK government. It is true that when the situation on the battlefield was going poorly, the idea of an evacuation occurred to some Americans, and an evacuation list was drawn up, but just how seriously this option was considered by policy makers in Washington is questionable. On December 3, when the matter was brought up during a conference President Truman had with his top advisers—Acheson, Marshall, and Bradley—all agreed that Korea would not be abandoned. The Koreans, however, feared that the Chinese intervention would test the resolve of the United States and the United Nations to fight, and through Ambassador Chang in Washington, they repeatedly brought up their serious concern about this issue for American assurance. Wars that involve ideologies are inherently cruel, and the issue of atrocities became important during this period. Atrocities were committed on both sides, although the behavior of the communist side was much more cruel. When the British and other participants of the U.N. member nations brought up this issue, the Americans showed their understanding of the issue, while the Koreans responded by moderating their actions.[6]

When the battle line was approaching the 38th parallel in early February 1951, the question again arose concerning the crossing of the line. Rusk thought the U.N. forces should stop at the line and wait until it became clear what the enemy would do. If it indicated that it favored peace, the U.N. forces should stop. If on the other hand the enemy brought in reinforcements the U.N. forces should not hesitate crossing the line. Meanwhile, the Koreans came up with the clever idea of making a "tactical crossing." President Rhee returned to his old theme that the 38th parallel was nonexistent. The Americans treated this "explosive" issue very cautiously, but in mid-April, Acheson warned that if Korean troops pushed to the Yalu, the U.N. forces would withdraw altogether from the peninsula. All these words were close to rhetorical game playing, or were "hypothetical" questions, according to Rusk. The military leadership wished to gain more real estate for tactical reasons, and the Korean troops made a "tactical" crossing to the north on March 26. President Rhee again brought up the idea of raising a 500,000-man new force to annihilate the Chinese, but it failed to draw much attention from the Americans.[7]

For slightly more than a year, between late June 1950 and early July 1951, the war dominated the life of Koreans, and Korean–American relations changed significantly. If we view the major statements of the United Nations and the U.S. government, we find the June 27 U.N. Security Council resolution "recomm[ending] that the Members of the United Nations furnish such assistance to the Republic of Korea" as necessary to repel the (North Korean) attack. On the same day, President Truman ordered U.S. Air and Naval Forces to "assist the Republic of Korea," and three days later, he also committed ground forces to accomplish the same purpose. On the battlefield, the war began on June 25 as a Korean war but remained one only until the early part of the following month. Then, the nature of the war began to change, first with the participation of the U.S.–U.N. force on July 5 and then with President Rhee's assignment on July 15 of command authority over the ROK Army to General MacArthur, the commander of the Unified Command since July 7. In brief, the war changed from a war between the two Korean nations to a war between North Korean forces and the U.N. forces. As the nature of the war changed, the position of the ROK forces also changed. First, they were one of the two parties fighting the war, but then they voluntarily gave up this independent position and became a part of the U.N. forces. Further, when we look at the composition of the U.N. forces, we find in late October 1950 that U.S. ground forces equaled 54 percent of the total U.N. ground forces, that U.S. air and naval forces had an even larger share, and that the United States was solely responsible for all U.N. war expenses. Hence, the war in Korea was a Korean war for only the first ten days; it then became a U.N.–North Korean war. In a real sense, however, it was a U.S.–North Korean war, and when the Chinese intervened, it became a U.S.–Communist Chinese war. Because of its dominating position in the war, the United States was naturally in a position to dominate its relationship with the Republic of Korea. An understanding of the positions of the two nations in the war is thus essential to understanding correctly the two-nation relationship. If we look at the Korean–American relationship during this early war period from this perspective, we will realize that it went relatively smoothly. There was more cooperation than conflict. But whether this relationship would continue for two more years becomes a serious question.[8]

NOTES

1. *New York Times*, July 2, 1950, 4: 8; Sebald to the Department of State, July 4, 1950, National Archives (NA), RG 59, Decimal File, box 4264; SCAP to the Department of State, for Rhee to Chang, July 4, 1950, Douglas MacArthur Memorial Archives, (MacArthur Library), RG 9, Radiograms, box 83; Drumright to the Secretary of State, July 14, 1950, Truman Library, Control no. 5763, box 1305; press release, General Headquarters Far Eastern Command, July 19, 1950, MacArthur Library, RG 7, UNC, box 1; Taegu to the Secretary of State, July 18, 1950, NA, RG 59, Decimal File 1950–54, box 4303.

2. Muccio to the Secretary of State, July 1, 1950, *Foreign Relations of the United States (FRUS), 1950*, 7: 272–274; Drumright to the Secretary of State, July 14, 1950, ibid., p. 388; Muccio to the Secretary of State, July 9, 10, 14, September 2, 15, 1950, ibid., pp. 336, 344, 389, 694–695, 729–730.

3. The President of the Republic of Korea to President Truman, July 19, 1950, *FRUS, 1950*, 7: 429; *New York Times*, September 2, 1950, 3: 1; Astin to the Secretary of State, July 10, 1950, NA, RG 59, Decimal File, box 4265; memorandum of conversation by the Officer in Charge of Korean Affairs (Emmons) with Chang and Rusk, September 8, 1950, ibid., pp. 709–711; memorandum by Allison for Rusk, July 13, 15, 1950, ibid., pp. 373, 394; Acheson to Muccio, September 11, 1950, ibid., p. 723.

4. Minutes of the sixth meeting of the U.S. Delegation to the U.N. General Assembly, September 25, 1950, *FRUS, 1950*, 7: 770; Allison to Austin, September 27, 1950, ibid., p. 790; memorandum of conversation by John C. Ross of the U.S. Delegation to the U.N. General Assembly with Chang Myŏn, September 28, 1950, ibid., 812–813; CINCFE to the President, October 16, 1950, Truman Library, Naval Aide Files, box 15; *New York Times*, October 18, 1950, 11: 1–4; ibid., October 22, 1950, 1: 5; Joint Chiefs of Staff to CINCFE, October 20, 1950, Truman Library, Naval Aide Files, box 15; Muccio to the Secretary of State, October 10, 1950, ibid., p. 920; Drumright to the Secretary of State, October 13, 30, ibid., pp. 941, 1015.

5. Memorandum of conversation by Emmons with Chang Myŏn, and Rusk, November 20, 1950, *FRUS, 1950*, 7: 1198; *New York Times*, December 3, 1950, 4: 1; memorandum of conversation by Emmons with Chang, Rusk, and others, December 4, 1950, *FRUS, 1950*, 7: 1351; memorandum of conversation by Emmons with Chang and Rusk, December 6, 1950, NA, RG 59, Numerical File, box 4270; memorandum of conversation by Emmons, December 6, 11, 1950, *FRUS, 1950*, 7: 1423, 1513; Muccio to the Secretary of State, January 6, 1951, Truman Library, Selected Documents Related to the Korean War, Department of State.

6. Memorandum of conversation by the Deputy Director of the Executive Secretariat (Shepard) with the President, Marshall, Bradley, and others, December 3, 1950, *FRUS, 1950*, 7: 1337; memorandum of conversation by Johnson with Emmons and members of the Defense Department, December 7, 1950, NA, RG 59, Numerical File, box 4270; Muccio to the Secretary of State, January 18, 1951, ibid; *Korean War Atrocities: Report of the Committee on Government Operations*, 83d Cong., 2d sess., 1954, p. 15; *Korean War Atrocities: Hearings before Subcommittee on Korean Atrocities of the Permanent Subcommittee on Investigations of the Committee on Government Operations*, 83d Cong., 1st sess., December 2, 1953 (1954), pp. 5, 11.

7. Memorandum by Rusk, February 11, 1951, *FRUS, 1951*, 7: 167; Muccio to the Secretary of State, February 11, 1951, NA, RG 84, Seoul Embassy, Top Secret Records, 1950–1954, box 1; Acheson to Marshall, February 23, 1951, *FRUS, 1951*, 7: 192; memorandum of conversation by Emmons with Rusk, Han P'yo-wook, and others, March 15, 1951, ibid., p. 230; memorandum of conversation by Emmons with Im Pyŏng-chik (ROK foreign minister), Rusk, and others, March 22, 1951, ibid., p. 260; memorandum of conversation by Emmons, April 16, 1951, Truman Library, Selected Papers Related to the Korean War, Department of State; the Secretary of State to the Korean Chargé (Kim Sesŏn), April 16, 1951, *FRUS, 1951*, 7: 390.

8. Joint Daily Sitrep 122, October 27, 1950, Truman Library, Military Intelligence File, Military Intelligence–Korea, box 263.

PART IV

PEACEMAKING AND DIPLOMACY

CHAPTER 12

Armistice Negotiations

Making peace is usually harder than making war. This is especially true when there is a stalemate on the battlefield. The involvement of different nations, cultures, and ideological orientations make the situation even more complicated. The peacemaking process in the Korean War had all of these aspects, and it was difficult and complex. For Korean–American relations, the two years were another—and probably the most severe—testing period. While the fighting was going on, the two nations buried all their minor differences as they pursued the common objective of winning the war. But once the peace negotiations began, all kinds of differences began to surface, and a struggle began between the forces of divergence and convergence. Often, the power of the former seemed to be more formidable than that of the latter. Accordingly, worth asking are questions about how the human capacity for patience, understanding, perspective, wisdom, and even courage could be mobilized throughout the extremely difficult process of peacemaking by two unequal partners in crisis. Able scholars have analyzed the policy-making process within the United States and among the nations involved in making peace on the Korean peninsula. The focus of this study will therefore fall mainly on relations between the Republic of Korea and the United States during this arduous two-year period.[1]

Efforts to stop the war early began as soon as the fighting broke out in the summer of 1950. Many countries, especially India, the United Kingdom, Norway, Russia, Byelorussia, Poland, and Czechoslovakia—neutrals, allies, and communist countries—tried to bring the unfortunate conflict to an early end. But whether there were real missed opportunities for peace for

Korea and the United States is debatable. Since the United States did not want to negotiate for peace from a position of weakness, and since it also resisted negotiating for peace when it was in a dominant position, it was extremely difficult to catch the right moment for peace negotiations. In retrospect, probably the one real missed opportunity was the one proposed in early October 1950 by Russia and three other communist countries. They called for the withdrawal of all foreign military forces from the Korean peninsula and the holding of an all-Korea election under U.N. supervision, proposals which could have achieved the major objectives of both the Republic of Korea and the United States in unifying Korea, repelling the armed attack, and restoring peace and security in the area. However, the idea of a "roll back," or ending war with victory, was too attractive for both the United States and Korea, and the opportunity was lost. Hence, until the two sides had expended a large amount of energy and reached a point of rough equilibrium on the battlefield, neither would be willing to come to the negotiating table. This point at last arrived in the early summer of 1951.

The communist sources reveal that by the early summer of 1951 North Korea and communist China were ready to end the fighting. The casualties and destruction, especially those of North Korea, were too great. In June of that year, two prominent communist emissaries—Kim Il Sung and Kao Kang—traveled to Moscow to persuade Stalin to take steps to end the war. Stalin seemed to have realized by this time that there would be no victor in the war and was easily persuaded by the two. By June, both sides were ready to initiate a negotiation to end the war. In late June, peace initiatives were made through George Kennan's initial talk with Jacob Malik and Malik's radio talk of June 24, and arrangements were quickly made for armistice talks to begin on July 10 at Kaesŏng, an ancient capital city of Korea. The negotiations were carried by General Nam Il, the North Korean delegate, and Fang Hsieh, the delegate of the Chinese Volunteer Army, on the communist side and Admiral C. Turner Joy representing the U.N. side. Once the location had been agreed upon, at least for the beginning of the talks, the next order of business was the adoption of an agenda. Immediately differences of opinions emerged. The U.N. side wanted to confine the agenda strictly to procedural matters so as not to prejudice later discussions and wanted to consider only military issues during the armistice negotiations. In contrast, the communist side wanted to insert content items into the agenda and to take up political problems during the negotiations for an armistice. The communist side wanted the 38th parallel as the line of demarcation and included the subject of the withdrawal of foreign troops from Korea as agenda items. The U.N. command opposed the communist proposals on the ground that they were beyond the scope of discussion for military matters. The communists agreed to drop the first of the two on July 16 and the second on July 25. In exchange, the U.N. side agreed to include on the agenda an item providing an issue not strictly military in nature—recommendations to the governments concerned. On July 26, after two weeks and two days of discussion, the agenda was agreed upon: (1) adoption of the agenda; (2) fixing a military demarcation line with a demilitarized zone; (3) arrangement for the realization of a ceasefire and an armistice, including the composition, authority, and function of a supervising organization; (4) arrangements relating to prisoners of war; and (5) recommendations to the governments of the countries concerned.[2]

The second item, fixing a military demarcation line, was more complicated than the first, and the difficulty was enhanced because while this item was discussed, the location of the conference became a vexing problem. Even though earlier, during the time of the MacArthur hearings in May and June 1951, American military strategists had considered ending the war at the 38th parallel as a "victory" for the U.N. forces, by the time the military demarcation line was discussed in the late summer of the same year, U.S. policy makers had changed their position and opposed the communist idea of using the 38th parallel as the military demarcation line. The 38th parallel would be politically undesirable and militarily indefensible from the U.N. side's viewpoint, and the U.N. negotiators took the initially high position of asking for the so-called "neck line" (sometimes called a "waistline") between P'yŏngyang and Wŏnsan. This was much more territory than the U.N. forces had at the time of discussion, and a communist negotiator called the U.N. demand "naive and illogical." But on August 20, the communists suggested their idea of substituting the military contact line for the 38th parallel, which was a concession of major proportions for them. When the communists proposed to fix the demarcation line at the existing military contact point, the U.N. side could not accept it because the U.N. forces then would not be able to use military pressure for the settlement of important remaining items of the agenda. On August 23, the communists suspended the deadlocked discussions, alleging that U.N. forces had bombed and strafed the conference site. Discussions did not reconvene until October 24.[3]

During the five months of talks in the summer and fall of 1951, the U.N.-U.S. side developed a negotiating strategy and tactics. The American military, especially General Ridgway in Tokyo, was very confident about the superior position of the U.N. forces on the battlefield and believed that military pressure would be effective in forcing the U.N. position on the opposite side at the conference table. As a consequence, heavy ground and air operations were carried out during the summer and the fall. While these operations were underway, the American military did not see any reason for hurrying to agree upon a cease fire, and Ridgway's "intransigence" and slow pace of negotiation were the results. However, the State Department was politically sensitive to the views of the major U.S. allies and to those of Congress and public opinion in the United States, which had a moderating influence upon the military's "combative" posture. Either because of U.N. military pressure or because of their own needs—probably some of both—

the communists agreed on September 20 to resume the talks and to switch the conference site to P'anmunjŏm. After the resumption of the armistice talks on October 24, the issue of who would control the city of Kaesŏng emerged, but except for the Koreans on both sides, whose views did not count very much anyway, no one cared much about which side would get the city, and the matter was put aside to be decided by the location of the demarcation line, the second item on the approved agenda. The U.N. team did not see much of a problem in reducing the width of the demilitarized zone from the original twenty miles to four kilometers, and under pressure from the Joint Chiefs of Staff, Ridgway sent on November 17 instructions to the negotiators at P'anmunjŏm to agree to fix the demarcation line at the contact point with a thirty-day time limit. Fixing the demarcation line was finally agreed to on November 27 after four months of discussion on the subject. But *uti positetis* was not a real fixing of the cease-fire line; rather, it was an open-ended measure, and the agreement was to continue to fight indefinitely. The fighting lasted for over a year and a half.[4]

The winter of 1951 and early spring of 1952 was the most productive period for the peace talks. At one time, discussions on all three of the remaining items were taking place, and by the end of the period, agreements were reached on all remaining issues except the exchange of prisoners. Following the agreement on agenda item 2, discussions began on items 3 and 4, on arrangements for the implementation of the armistice and the disposition of prisoners of war. While discussions were continuing on these two items, on February 3, the communist delegation agreed to hold concurrent discussions on the last item regarding recommendations to the governments concerned. Washington's original stance was to avoid making a commitment to holding a political conference and to keeping the language general, while the communists' initial proposal was for a political conference that would cover a whole range of Far Eastern problems. Avoiding such a political conference after the armistice was impossible for the United States, but the communist proposal for a conference that would consider political issues affecting the whole region was rejected by the U.N. command on the ground that the military delegation did not have power to deal with political matters. However, the United States agreed to make a procedural recommendation for a conference to handle Korean political problems after the conclusion of an armistice. An agreement was reached on February 19 to recommend that within three months after the armistice became effective a political conference would be held on a high level to settle questions such as the withdrawal of foreign forces from Korea and the peaceful settlement of the Korean question, "et cetera." Admiral Turner Joy, the chief negotiator of the U.N. command, issued a statement that "foreign forces" meant "non-Korean forces" and the word "et cetera" did not relate to matters outside of Korea. The agreement was reached swiftly and without much difficulty because the language was vague, and it was only a recommendation, without any binding power on any nation.[5]

The third item dealing with arrangements for the implementation of the armistice was a largely technical one and not much difficulty was initially expected. However, the question of the degree of inspection needed to prevent violation of the armistice inevitably reflected the orientation of the two different political systems. Of the five requirements of the U.N. side for supervisory arrangements—(1) the cessation of hostilities within twenty-four hours following the signing of the armistice; (2) the withdrawal of all armed forces from the demilitarized zone; (3) no increases in the armed strength of either side; (4) the withdrawal of all armed forces from the territory controlled by the other side; and (5) the establishment of an organ to supervise the execution of the terms of the armistice, a supervisory organ with observation teams that would have access to the territory controlled by both sides—the first two and the fourth items would not cause any problems, but the other two—especially the last item establishing the supervisory organ—caused considerable difficulty.

The United States—especially the Pentagon—considered the inspection and prevention of the reinforcement of military units and their equipment, allowing a limited degree of rotation and replacement of worn-out equipment very important. Soon after the talk on these items began, it was discovered that they were not a concern for the communist side. Their main concern was the withdrawal of troops to the correct side of the cease-fire line and the withdrawal of foreign troops from Korea. Gaps were found on several issues: The U.N. delegation wanted broad access to all parts of Korea to prevent the reinforcement of military forces after an armistice, but the communists wanted to limit such inspection; the U.N. side considered the rotation of troops and the replacement of worn-out equipment important, but the communists opposed the measure; the U.N. command proposed a ban on the construction of new military airfields and a limit on rehabilitation of civilian airfields; and there were also disagreements over the nature of supervisory organs.

Narrowing these gaps did not seem easy in the early weeks of the negotiations. However, a breakthrough came after North Korean representative Nam Il's proposal on December 3 for inspection by inspection teams from neutral nations at agreed ports of entry and the prohibition of military forces, weapons, and ammunition into Korea. The pressure from the American public and major American allies for flexibility in the negotiations and Frank Pace's idea of yielding on relatively trivial matters while standing firm on essentials in the negotiations were helpful in mitigating the U.N. command's posture in the winter of 1951 and early spring of 1952. By the end of December 1951, the communists lifted a 5,000-man limit on the rotation of troops, and the U.N. side reciprocated by accepting the limitation on troop rotation. By late February of the following year, the two sides agreed on a figure of 35,000 for troop rotation, about half the U.N. side's original offer and seven times greater than the initial communist figure—and five ports of entry, a little less than half of the U.N. side's initial figure and a little less than half more than the communists' starting point. Encouraged by the U.N. delegation to suggest a supervisory organ, the communists first suggested Switzerland, Sweden, Norway, Denmark, Poland, or Czechoslovakia, later adding the Soviet Union to the list. The inclusion of the Soviet Union in a neutral nation's organ was certainly not acceptable to the United States government. The talks continued, however, and the two sides reached by March an agreement on item 3, with the exception of two issues, that of the composition of the neutral supervisory organ and the reconstruction of airfields. They agreed upon a cease fire within twelve hours of the signing of an armistice and withdrawal of all forces from the demilitarized zone within twenty-four hours and from rear areas and the coastal islands and Korean waters within five days after the signing of an armistice. They also agreed that both sides should cease introducing into Korea reinforcements of military personnel and combat aircraft, armed vehicles, weapons, and ammunition, but the rotation of 35,000 military personnel a month should be permitted; that the Military Armistice Commission, composed of military officers of both sides, would supervise the implementation of the armistice and deal with alleged armistice violations; and that the Neutral Nations Supervisory Commission with four senior officers, two each of whom will be nominated by the two sides, would supervise, observe, inspect, and investigate the introduction into Korea of reinforcing military personnel and equipment.[6]

By far the most difficult part of the peace talks during the Korean War concerned item 4, which dealt with prisoners of war. This item became the focus of the truce talks from April 1952, and it consumed up to two-thirds of the two years of negotiation. From the very beginning of the war, the POW issue had been a problem, largely because there were great differences between the treatment of prisoners by the U.N. command and by the communists. Once the talk had begun, difficult problems plagued the negotiations, including the contrasting styles and approaches of the two sides, the problem of the numbers of prisoners held by the two sides, and the thorny issue of voluntary repatriation. An important question to be raised is whether the whole matter of the exchange of the prisoners of war was handled properly by both sides at the end of the Korean War.

During the war, the U.N. command carefully adhered to the principles of the humane treatment of prisoners of war specified in the Geneva Convention. It sent lists of captured enemy personnel to the International Committee of the Red Cross (ICRC). It also allowed and facilitated the ICRC's inspection and reporting on its treatment of the prisoners of war. The humane treatment of prisoners by the U.N. forces was noteworthy, and the very few instances of violation were promptly corrected. In contrast, the communist side, while proclaiming that it was abiding by the Geneva Convention, failed to carry out any one requirement of the convention. Except for a token number of 110 names, they failed to report to the ICRC the identities of captured personnel. They rejected efforts by the ICRC to inspect its prisoner-of-war camps. They refused the exchange of relief packages; they even refused until later the exchange of mail; they failed to report on the health conditions of the prisoners and to provide the accurate location of their prisoner-of-war camps; and they purposely located their camps near military targets. These communist failures were harmful in that they prevented the development of a sense of trust and confidence in the minds of the U.N. command, two of the basic conditions for the successful negotiation of all peace treaties.[7]

When the prisoner-of-war question began to be considered in December 1951, the U.N. command still had not received a list of the U.N. and ROK prisoners in communist hands, except the few already mentioned, while the communist side had received through the ICRC a list of 170,000 names from the U.N. command. Later, it was discovered by the U.N. command that 37,500 of them were refugees who had been erroneously categorized as prisoners; still later 11,000 more persons were reclassified as civilian internees, leaving about 121,000 prisoners. The list provided by the communists had only 11,500 names, although they earlier had broadcast that they had captured 65,000 persons within the first nine months of the war. The ROK and U.S. missing numbered 88,000 and 11,500, respectively. The U.N. command's later adjustments of the number of prisoners in custody and the small number of prisoners in the hands of the communists caused difficulties throughout the negotiation process.[8]

In early spring of 1952, the two delegations reached an agreement on the less controversial or noncontroversial matters of the prisoner exchange. Among its provisions were the following: Sick and injured prisoners would be repatriated first; prisoners of war, when released from custody, would not be engaged again in war activities during the Korean War; a committee of officers from the two sides would supervise the exchange of the prisoners of war; this committee would be assisted by joint Red Cross teams composed of representatives of the U.N. Red Cross and the communist Red Cross societies; Korean civilians would be permitted to return to their homes on either side of the demarcation line; and foreign civilians would also be permitted to return to their homes.[9]

The nonforceful repatriation of prisoners was definitely the most important and difficult issue raised during discussions about the exchange of war prisoners. According to Article 118 of the Geneva Convention, all prisoners of war were supposed to "be released and repatriated without delay after cessation of hostilities," and the initial plan of the U.N. command was to adhere to this principle, but as an increasing number of enemy personnel deserted to the U.N. side, it became evident that a substantial number of war prisoners would suffer heavy punishment if they were returned to the communist side and that many of them would resist repatriation. To repatriate these prisoners against their will would be contrary to humanitarian principles and the spirit of the Geneva Convention. Some policy makers in Washington also saw the potential for a propaganda coup in the nonforceful repatriation policy. Both the humanitarian and psychological appeal of the idea of nonforceful repatriation were powerful enough to convince President Truman and some of his key advisers in Washington, while the American public, Congress, and key allies were also persuaded by the principle. Once adopted, the moral force and the strategic value of the policy line were too great to be challenged.[10]

However, the magnitude of the difficulty presented by the nonforceful repatriation principle was not realized until April 1952, when interviews were begun at U.N. prisoner-of-war camps to find out the number of prisoners who wished to be repatriated and who would resist it. In early April, it was found that of 106,000 prisoners who had consented to be interviewed only about 70,000, or 60 percent of those who were interviewed and 58 percent of all the prisoners in U.N. hands wanted repatriation. Subsequent screening raised the number to 83,000, 69 percent of all prisoners of war in U.N. camps. When the communists were notified that only 70,000 prisoners would be repatriated, they insisted firmly that all prisoners of war should be repatriated according to Article 118 of the Geneva Convention. To break the deadlock on the repatriation issue, the U.N. command took the initiative by making a "firm and final offer" on April 28, a package proposal that included two other relatively minor unresolved issues: (1) There shall not be forced repatriation of prisoners of war; (2) the U.N. command would not insist on prohibiting the reconstruction and rehabilitation of airfields; and (3) the U.N. command would agree to accept Poland and Czechoslovakia as members of the Neutral Nations Supervisory Commission if the communists would agree to accept Sweden and Switzerland (withdrawing their demand for inclusion of the Soviet Union). Apparently, the communists did not think that the U.N. concession on the rehabilitation of airfields was important enough to trade, and they made a "firm and final" counteroffer on May 2 accepting the last two items but leaving the first—the forced repatriation issue—to be resolved. Through this agreement on two final proposals, at least the negotiations was narrowed down to one major issue, that of repatriation, by the spring of 1952.[11]

After the exchange of the package proposals, a year-long lull followed in the truce negotiations. Until the following April, when the exchange of sick and wounded captured personnel was agreed upon, no progress was made in the negotiations. However, during this period of wasted time, important personnel changes took place that would affect the negotiations, and meanwhile the battlefront was not quiet. The U.N. side experienced a change among policy makers in Washington and among those responsible for the negotiations in Tokyo and P'anmunjŏm: General Ridgway was replaced by General Mark Clark in Tokyo and Admiral Turner Joy was replaced by General William Harrison at P'anmunjŏm in the spring of 1952; in the following January, Eisenhower became president, replacing Truman in the White House in Washington. During the same time an important change took place on the communist side, when Stalin died in March of 1953. These changes, especially the death of Stalin, had a significant impact on the negotiations in Korea.

After stabilizing the battleline at about ten to twenty miles north of the 38th parallel, called the Kansas-Wyoming line on the U.N. side, both sides refrained from taking any major offensive which might disrupt the peace negotiations. At the same time, both sides tried to improve their positions on the battlefield by taking higher terrain, and each also tried to use their forces to gain advantages at the negotiating table. This process continued to the end of the negotiations.

In May, soon after the new team was in place in Tokyo and P'anmunjŏm, Harrison and Clark recommended to the authorities in Washington completion of the screening of the prisoners of war, and the release of 27,000 civilians and of a new count of prisoners willing to be repatriated. In case the communists would not accept the April 26 U.N. proposal, Harrison and Clark recommended that the U.N. side recess the negotiations until the communists accepted the proposal or broke off the negotiations entirely. Contact would be maintained through liaison officers. By the middle of the following month, Washington approved the Harrison–Clark proposal for infrequent meetings with recesses, the completion of the screening process, and the release of detained civilians. After unproductive meetings in July and frequent recesses in September, Washington approved at the end of September an indefinite recess if the communists failed to accept the U.N. command's new alternative method of dealing with the matter of prisoners opposing repatriation. On October 8, the U.N. delegate announced an indefinite recess of the negotiations pending acceptance of one of the U.N. proposals or the submission by the communists of an "acceptable" counterproposal. The recess lasted until the following spring.[12]

While the stalemate continued in P'anmunjŏm, the battleline became more active. There was action in the eastern section during the summer months, while the central section of the battleline was most active in the fall. The communists tried to take strategically located hills and mountain ranges along the Wyoming Line, located north of Kŭmhwa and Ch'ŏlwŏn and south of Kŭmsŏng, from early September to late October. The fighting on the Paekma Koji (Hill 395) was especially fierce, and its possession changed hands as many as twenty times, showing the degree of determination on both sides to hold on to a strategic piece of territory. The divisions under 9th U.N. Corps and ROK 2d Corps defended the hills, and the two important points of the "Iron Triangle"—Ch'ŏlwŏn and Kŭmhwa—were firmly held by U.N. forces. Kŭmsŏng, an important enemy base located northeast of the Iron Triangle, was under the practical control of U.N. forces. The cost of these battles was high on both sides.[13]

In the fall of 1952, at the seventh meeting of the U.N. General Assembly held in New York, one of the key concerns was breaking the stalemate in the armistice negotiations in Korea. When V. K. Krishna Menon, the chief delegate from India, offered a proposal for the resolution of the POW issue in the armistice negotiations, Acheson expressed concern. Especially troubling was the proposal's lack of an affirmation that force would not be used against prisoners of war to prevent or effect their return to their homelands and of a provision calling for the turning over of the prisoners who refused repatriation after ninety days to some other organization (e.g., political conference) without any time limit. But the Indian proposal, which was officially introduced on November 17, received wide support from the U.N. members, including the United Kingdom and other British Commonwealth nations, and the only choice left for the United States was to amend the Indian proposal according to its general line of principles and policies. However, the amended proposal met with rejection by the Soviet delegate. It may be argued that the United States could claim at least a diplomatic victory through the passage of the amended proposal by the General Assembly by a vote of fifty-four to five on December 3.[14]

The change which had by far the most significant impact on the negotiations in Korea between the fall of 1952 and the following spring was the change of heads of states in the United States and Soviet Union. Especially important was Dwight Eisenhower's ascent to the American presidency in early 1953. As some analysts have pointed out, the conditions surrounding the negotiations remained the same, and the new president did not have any specific plan to bring the negotiations to a successful conclusion of the negotiations beyond a strong desire to end the war, but his impressive military background gave people on both sides the expectation that he would somehow end the stalemate. Furthermore, the death in March of Stalin, ending his presence as a commanding figure in the communist camp, was an equally important factor for the conclusion of the peace negotiations.[15]

The opposed forces favoring forcefulness or flexibility in the peace negotiations continued to operate under the new administration in Washington in the spring of 1953. There were expectations both in the United States and elsewhere in the world that the Eisenhower administration would take a more forceful step, but the new president had also to accommodate the wishes of the allies for a more flexible posture during the peace negotiations. Eisenhower's trip to Korea, which he had promised to take during the election campaign, may have given him strong impressions in how to develop his peacemaking strategy. If nothing else, he concluded that no small measure would solve the problem and that a more decisive step would be necessary for the successful conclusion of the negotiations.[16]

When General Clark proposed on February 22 an immediate exchange of sick and wounded prisoners, the communists responded promptly, indicating not only that they were willing to exchange the sick and wounded but also that they were ready to resume peace negotiations. The Eisenhower administration thought that the firm American stance and military pressure had been the deciding factors in bringing the communists back to the negotiating table, but some analysts think that communist political and economic forces did it. Presently available Russian sources indicate that Stalin began to provide Kim with the necessary approval and support for launching the war in the spring of 1950. Stalin, who had been skeptical about Kim's plan for the invasion of the south and who kept a cautious posture throughout 1949, changed his position early in the following year and began in February to supply North Korea with military hardware and military advisers. In fact, it was probably a combination of these factors that made the communists willing to conclude the negotiations. In any case, it is impossible to assign exact weights to each of these factors.[17]

On March 28, 1953, a month after Clark's proposal for an exchange of the sick and wounded, the communists agreed to the exchange and proposed a resumption of negotiations. Quick and decisive steps followed. The U.N. command replied three days later by proposing an early meeting of liaison officers for the exchange and an arrangement for the resumption of negotiations. But a big step came when Chou En-lai and Kim Il Sung made broadcasts on March 30 and 31 proposing handing over those who resisted repatriation to a neutral state. For the first time, the communists recognized the existence of nonrepatriates, which was a big concession for them, and what was now left were the detailed arrangements. The less difficult part was the exchange of the sick and wounded, and arrangements were made during the first ten days of April with an agreement signed on April 11. "Operation Little Switch" was executed between April 20 and the May 3. The communists returned 684 prisoners, while the U.N. command handed over 6,670.[18]

The more complicated and difficult part of the exchange was the question of what to do with the nonrepatriates. On April 2, the contents of the March 30 and 31 Chou–Kim statements were communicated to the U.N. delegates. Three days later, the U.N. command presented to the communists detailed suggestions on the proposal for settling the entire question of repatriation of the POWs. The communists responded three weeks later with a six-point program to implement the Chou–Kim statements. The communists proposed to transport within three months of the signing of the armistice the nonrepatriates to a neutral state and to place them in the custody of the neutral state for six months. Harrison, in his three-points response, attacked the idea of physically transporting the POWs to a neutral state, and he condemned the communist plan for keeping the nonrepatriates for six months in the hands of a neutral state, stating that sixty days would be sufficient. Ten days later, on May 6, the communists came up with an eight-point proposal, which was similar to the Indian proposal which the United States had supported previously in the U.N. General Assembly. It conceded that the POWs would not have to be transported physically to a neutral state and suggested a five-nation repatriation commission consisting of Switzerland, Sweden, Czechoslovakia, Poland, and India. In this proposal, the communists planned to turn over to a neutral state the remaining nonrepatriates after four months—a reduction of two months from the previous proposal.[19]

After over a month of efforts, the U.N. command managed to find out the contents of the late March Chou–Kim statements, but there was a considerable gap between the detailed communist position and that of the U.N. command. The revised communist proposal for a four-month period of custody for the nonrepatriates in the hands of a neutral nation was still too long for the U.N. command, which maintained that two months would be adequate; the U.N. command was much concerned about the lack of a time limit for POWs in the hands of the political conference. Another concern for the U.N. side was the manner in which the decisions would be made in the Neutral Nations Repatriation Commission. The fear of the U.N. command was that the communists still held firm to its principle of the repatriation of all POWs and that they would try to prolong the process endlessly to keep the nonrepatriates in their hands. However, by May 18, the U.N. command moderated certain aspects of its position: Instead of demanding the immediate release of Korean nonrepatriates when the armistice came into effect, it would agree to turn them over, like the Chinese prisoners, to the custody of the commission; it would agree to keep the nonrepatriates for three rather than two months in the custody of the commission and to release the remaining nonrepatriates within 120 days after custody of the commission; and it would agree to majority rule instead of unanimity in all matters of decision by the commission. Further, General Clark proposed presenting the revised position to the communists with the proviso that if they were not accepted by the communists within a week, the negotiations would be terminated rather than recessed, and all Korean and Chinese POWs opposed to repatriation would be released immediately. The Clark proposal was approved by the Joint Chiefs and the president.[20]

Almost parallel with the negotiation process, a more fundamental question of how to deal with the Korean situation was discussed among the policy makers in Washington. On April 2, 1953, two days after the Chou–Kim statements, the National Security Council Planning Board submitted a report on the subject to be considered by the council during its April 8 meeting. The board presented six alternative courses of action, ranging from a continuation of the present level of military pressure (A) to a coordinated, large-scale offensive in Korea with a naval blockade and air and naval attack directly against Manchuria and China (F). The first three alternatives (A, B, C) could be carried out by maintaining the restrictions on military operations against Manchuria and Communist China; the latter three alternatives (D, E, F), however, could not be carried out without lifting the restrictions. Furthermore, President Eisenhower expressed his view that an atomic weapon should be considered simply another weapon, and its use could be considered seriously in the last three alternatives. The Joint Chiefs of Staff were asked by the National Security Council to recommend their choice among the alternatives, which was reported on May 19. After consideration of the risks and costs of each alternative, the Joint Chiefs of Staff recommended to the council to "extend and intensify military action against the enemy, to include air and naval operations directly against China and Manchuria," a combination of the last three alternatives. On the following day, the National Security Council agreed that "if conditions arise requiring more positive action in Korea, the course of action recommended by the Joint Chiefs of Staff should be adopted as a "general guide." Even though the president and his advisers worried about the possibility of Soviet intervention, for the reasons of economy and efficiency, the American government decided to step up the war if the last "final" offer was not accepted by the communists.[21]

By late May, the American government was ready to make a final offer to the communists, and if it was rejected, then stepped-up military operations would take place. On May 25, Harrison presented the final proposal, and the two sides agreed to meet again a week later, which was postponed to June 4 at the request of the communist side. When the two delegations met, the communists made a counterproposal, which accepted most of the provisions of the U.N. proposal of May 25. The communists' continuing insistence on ten explains per thousand POWs in the custodian's hands was a minor matter; much more important was their language regarding the remaining nonrepatriates, for whom no other disposition has been agreed upon by the political conference. They would be released to civilian status within 120 days after the Neutral Repatriation Commission had assumed their custody. This was beyond the "most optimistic expectations" of Washington, and the POW issue was finally resolved by this communist offer. On June 8, Harrison and Nam Il signed the agreement which established the Terms of Reference for the Neutral Nations Repatriation Commission, culminating eighteen months of negotiation on the issue.[22]

Thus, in the spring of 1953, both the U.N. and communist sides made concessions, and by early June the armistice negotiations in Korea were practically over. Why were the two sides able to agree at this particular time? Between the allies' pressure for a more relaxed posture and the South Korean position urging a strong stand, the Eisenhower administration had managed to find a way to solve the POW issue. The concessions the communists made in both late March and early June were certainly more significant than the ones the U.N. side made, and analysts' views have varied regarding the reason for the communist decisions. American policy makers naturally thought their policy of added pressure on the battlefield was effective. However, some analysts argue that the effect of military pressure has been exaggerated and that political and economic conditions within China and North Korea were much more important factors. Without doubt, both the military pressure and domestic problems in communist China and North Korea were significant, but recently available Soviet archival material and analytical studies show that the single most important factor for the conclusion of the armistice negotiation was the death of Stalin, who had been prolonging the armistice talks.[23]

NOTES

1. Rosemary Foot, *A Substitute for Victory: The Politics of Peacemaking at the Korean Armistice Talks* (Ithaca, N.Y.: Cornell University Press, 1990); Burton I. Kaufman, *The Korean War: Challenge in Crisis, Credibility, and Command* (New York: Knopf, 1986), pp. 183–358; William Stueck, *The Korean War: An International History* (Princeton, N.J.: Princeton University Press, 1995), pp. 308–347.

2. Papers of Dean Acheson, Princeton Seminar, Synopsis, Truman Library, pp. G8–H2; Foot, *A Substitute for Victory*, pp. 42–46; Kaufman, *The Korean War*, pp. 192–198; Taehanminkuk, Kukpangpu, Chŏnsa P'yŏnch'an Wiwŏnhoe, *Hankuk Chŏnchaeng hyŭchonsa* (History of the Korean War armistice negotiations) (Seoul: Taehanminkuk, Kukpangpu, Chŏnsa P'yŏnch'an Wiwŏnhoe, 1989), pp. 49–86. See also Evgueni Bajanov, "Assessing the Policies of the Korean War" (manuscript, 1995), p. 91; Kathryn Weathersby, "New Russian Documents on the Korean War," *Cold War International History Project Bulletin* 6–7 (Winter 1995–1996): 13, 26.

3. Papers of Dean Acheson, Princeton Seminars, Synopsis, Truman Library, pp. H2–H3; Foot, *A Substitute for Victory*, pp. 45–50.

4. Papers of Dean Acheson, Princeton Seminars, Synopsis, Truman Library, pp. H8–H9, I1–I4; Foot, *A Substitute for Victory*, pp. 51–69; Taehanminkuk, Kukpangpu, Chŏnsa Py'ŏnch'an Wiwŏnhoe, *Hankuk Chŏnchaeng hyuchŏnsa*, pp. 87–100.

5. Papers of Dean Acheson, Princeton Seminars, Truman Library, Synopsis, I3; Foot, *A Substitute for Victory*, pp. 74–76.

6. Papers of Dean Acheson, Princeton Seminars, Synopsis, Truman Library, pp. H3–H5; Foot, *A Substitute for Victory*, pp. 76–87; Taehanminkuk, Kukpangpu, Chŏnsa P'yŏnch'an Wiwŏnhoe, *Hankuk Chŏnchaeng hyuchŏnsa,* pp. 147–168.

7. Papers of Dean Acheson, Princeton Seminars, Synopsis, Truman Library, p. H5.

8. Papers of Dean Acheson, Princeton Seminars, Synopsis, Truman Library, pp. H5–H6; Foote, *A Substitute for Victory*, pp. 87–99; Kaufman, *The Korean War*, p. 238.

9. Papers of Dean Acheson, Princeton Seminars, Synopsis, Truman Library, p. H6.

10. Papers of Dean Acheson, Princeton Seminars, Synopsis, Truman Library, p. H6; Foote, *A Substitute for Victory*, pp. 87–93.

11. Papers of Dean Acheson, Princeton Seminars, Synopsis, Truman Library, pp. H7–H8; "State of Armistice Negotiations when General Clark Assumed Command," the Citadel Archives, Mark W. Clark Papers, box 8, folder 5, p. 1; Foote, *A Substitute for Victory*, p. 102; Kaufman, *The Korean War*, pp. 245, 268–269.

12. The Commander in Chief to the Joint Chiefs of Staff, October 8, 1952, *Foreign Relations of the United States (FRUS), 1952–1954*, 15, part 1: 554–557; "Status of Armistice Negotiations when General Clark Assumed Command," pp. 1–4. See also Foote, *A Substitute for Victory*, pp. 149–152.

13. Ministry of National Defense, Republic of Korea, *Korea in War, July 1952–July 1953* (Seoul: Ministry of Defense, Republic of Korea, 1954), pp. A33–A35;

Taehanminkuk, Kukpangpu, Chŏnsa P'yŏnch'an Wiwŏnhoe, *Hankuk Chŏncheng hyuchŏnsa*, pp. 239–244; Yukkun Sakwan Hakgyo, *Hankuk Chŏnchaengsa* (History of wars in Korea) (Seoul: Ilshinsa, 1987), pp. 587–588; Ohn Chang-il, "Choch'ongryŏkchŏn kŭriko chehanchŏn: 625 Chŏnchaengŭi suhaeng kwachŏng," (A super total war and a limited war: The process of the Korean War), in *Hankuk Chŏnchaengŭi yŏksachŏk koch'al* (Historical consideration of the Korean War), ed. Hankuk Chŏngch'ioekyosa Hakhoe (Seoul: P'yŏngminsa, 1991), pp. 226–230.

14. The Secretary of State to the Department of State, November 14, 15, 17, 24, 1952, *FRUS, 1952–1954*, 15, part 1: 623–625, 628–633, 645–647, 676; the Secretary of State to the President, November 15, 20, 21, 26, 1952, ibid., pp. 662–663, 663–664, 683–686; Resolution 610 (VII), adopted by the U.N. General Assembly, December 3, 1952, ibid., pp. 702–705. See also Kaufman, *The Korean War*, pp. 296–300.

15. Foot, *A Substitute for Victory*, pp. 159, 212–213; Kaufman, *The Korean War*, pp. 293–295.

16. See Foot, *A Substitute for Victory*, pp. 159–160, 173–175; Kaufman, *The Korean War*, pp. 292–231. See also John Gittings, "Talks, Bombs, and Arms: Another Look at the Korean War," *Journal of Contemporary Asia* 5, no. 2 (1975): 205–217; Pierce Brerdor, *Ike: His Life and Times* (New York: Harper and Brothers, 1986), p. 236.

17. "Armistice Negotiations 22 Feb–27 July 1953," the Citadel Archives, Mark W. Clark Papers, box 8, folder 5, p. 1; Foot, *A Substitute for Victory*, pp. 146–147, 166.

18. "Armistice Negotiations 22 Feb–27 July 1953," the Citadel Archives, Mark W. Clark Papers, box 8, folder 5, pp. 1–3; memorandum by the Secretary of State, *FRUS, 1952–1954*, 15, part 1: 857; Chou En-lai's statement of March 30, *Department of State Bulletin* (1953): 526–527.

19. Memorandum of a telephone conversation between the President and the Secretary of State, March 30, 1953, *FRUS, 1952–1954*, 15, part 1: 824; memorandum by the Secretary of State to the President, April 1, 1953, ibid., p. 833; the Secretary of State to certain diplomatic offices, April 28, 1953, ibid., pp. 951–952; the Commander in Chief, U.N. Command (Clark) to the Joint Chiefs of Staff, ibid., pp. 979–981; "Armistice Negotiations 22 Feb–27 July 1953," the Citadel Archives, Mark W. Clark Papers, box 8, folder 5, pp. 1–4.

20. The Commander in Chief, U.N. Command (Clark) to the Joint Chiefs of Staff, May 8, 11, 14, 16, 1953, *FRUS, 1953–1954*, 15, part 1: 987–992, 999–1002, 1020–1022, 1033–1036; the Chief of Staff, U.S. Army (Collins) to the Commander in Chief, Far East (Clark), May 9, 1953, ibid., pp. 997–999; the Joint Chiefs of Staff to the Commander in Chief, Far East (Clark), May 15, 1953, ibid., p. 1027; memorandum by the Acting Secretary of State to the President, May 18, 1953, ibid., pp. 1046–1048.

21. Enclosure, note by the Executive Secretary (Lay) to the National Security Council, April 2, 1953, *FRUS, 1952–1954*, 15, part 1: 839–856; memorandum of discussion at the 143rd meeting of the National Security Council, May 6, 1953, ibid., pp. 975–978; memorandum of discussion at the 144th meeting of the National Security Council, May 13, 1953, ibid., pp. 1012–1017; memorandum by the Joint Chiefs of Staff to the Secretary of Defense (Wilson), ibid., pp. 1059–1062; memorandum of discussion of the 145th meeting of the National Security Council, May 20, 1953. ibid., pp. 1064–1068.

22. Editorial note, *FRUS, 1952–1954*, 15, part 1: 1096–1097, 1137, 1151; memorandum by the Secretary of State to the President, June 4, 1953, ibid., p. 1138; text of the agreement on prisoners of war, *Department of State Bulletin* (1953): 866–868.

23. Foot, *A Substitute for Victory*, pp. 171–175; Kaufman, *The Korean War*, pp. 310–311; Kathryn Weathersby, "The Soviet Role in Prolonging the Korean War, 1951–53" (manuscript, July 1995); idem, "New Findings on the Korean War," *Cold War International History Project Bulletin* 6–7 (Winter 1995): 15; idem, "New Russian Documents, p. 80; Natalia Bajanova, "Assessing the Conclusion and Outcome of the Korean War" (manuscript, July 1995); Bajanov, "Assessing the Policies of the Korean War," pp. 17–18.

CHAPTER 13

Korean Reaction and
the Armistice

By early June 1953, the POW issue was resolved, and although it seemed that the end of the long drawn-out armistice negotiations were imminent, the war continued until the end of the following month. There was still a remaining task for the United States—to deal with reactions of the Republic of Korea. To understand the role played by this nation in the peace negotiations, our story has to go back to its beginning point. In December 1950, when the thirteen-power draft resolution for a cease fire in Korea was introduced at the U.N. General Assembly meeting, the ROK government expressed its concern and its desire to be involved in the process of searching for a way to end the war. This same concern and desire were expressed again in June of the following year, when the truce talks were about to begin. In January of the new year, 1951, President Rhee expressed mixed reactions to the peace moves. He said there would be no question about his cooperation with the United States, but he also indicated that he had to register "a protest in the court of world opinion" against the peace moves in the United Nations. In June and early July 1951, when the negotiations for a cease fire in Korea became a reality, the ROK government showed both skepticism about the peace moves as a whole and fear of a settlement which would leave the country divided at the 38th parallel. Furthermore, the Korean people began to march in the streets against an armistice in June, demonstrations which were at least encouraged by the government. Most important, by late June, the ROK government announced a definite position that it was against ending the war with Chinese troops on Korean soil and without unification. It presented five conditions for a cease fire which it insisted must be met: (1) withdrawal of Chinese forces from Korea; (2) disarmament of North Korea; (3) a guarantee against any third power providing military or financial assistance to North Korea; (4) full participation of the ROK in any international conference considering the Korean problem; and (5) opposition to any agreement conflicting with the sovereignty of the Republic of Korea. Thus, by the time the armistice negotiations began in early July, the Koreans had expressed fully their concerns and fears about the possibility of ending the conflict in the middle of the war and had presented also the minimum conditions for a cease fire which should be met from their viewpoint.[1]

The Korean reaction to the starting of peace negotiations in early July 1951 initially generated a cautious posture in the American government. In early June, Ambassador Muccio reported home that he had told the Koreans that the United Nations had never committed itself to unification by force and that the objective of the U.N. force was the defeat of aggression. He also tried to assure the anxious Koreans that the political objective of Korean unification had not been abandoned and that the armistice would leave a "reasonable assurance" against the resumption of war. These vague words were not enough to soothe the troubled Koreans, and Muccio asked the State Department for some "suggestions" on how to calm them down. Acheson responded to Muccio's request and toward the end of the month gave Muccio six suggestions or guidelines. First, the Koreans should be told that they did not possess any authority beyond the 38th parallel; second, the United States and United Nations had never taken a position in favor of achieving unification by force; third, the June 25, 27, and October 7 U.N. resolutions "authorized but did not require" pacification of North Korea; fourth, the ROK must realize that an outbreak of a Third World War would be a disaster for its people; fifth, the nation's future hopes would rest on the free world; and sixth, postwar reconstruction of Korea would depend upon the resources and the will of the United States. Finally, Acheson added that "intransigent and inflammatory statements and provocative or violent actions" would jeopardize the peace settlement, and reckless and foolish actions by the Koreans could not be tolerated. The practical value of these legal and formal arguments mixed with a mild threat is open to question, but the secretary's statement clearly revealed the posture of the Truman administration in dealing with the Koreans regarding the cease-fire negotiations. A week later, Acheson promised Muccio that he would do all he could to help him in handling the situation in Korea. While receiving these instructions from Washington, Muccio was warning the Koreans against hasty decisions and anticease-fire statements. He also clearly pointed out to the Koreans that their cooperation for the common goal was an "absolute necessity."[2]

When the negotiation began at Kaesong on July 10, Muccio observed the concern and fear of the Korean leaders that a possible arrangement leading to cessation of the conflict and withdrawal of the U.N. troops would leave the republic undefended and unsupported. They felt powerless to influence this turn of events which might decide the fate of the nation and were annoyed by the role Kim Il Sung was playing in the cease-fire movement. This sense of disappointment and fear was soon translated into action when tens of thousands of demonstrators marched in the streets of Pusan and other major cities. As had happened in the prenegotiation period, more rational calculation soon prevailed, and the ROK government came forward with more clearly defined positions and assertions. From late July, the theme of no cease fire without unification and the withdrawal of Chinese troops dominated the Korean view. In late September, the government presented four minimum conditions for the resumption of peace talks: (1) the withdrawal of all Chinese troops from Korean territory; (2) the disarming of North Korean communists; (3) the representation of the North Koreans in the National Assembly through a U.N. observed election; and (4) a time limit for the truce talks, after which they should be terminated.[3]

During the six-month period between late October 1951 and late April 1952, when three items of the negotiations—the demarcation line, recommendations of postarmistice measures for the governments concerned, and arrangements for implementation of the armistice agreement—were discussed and agreed upon at P'anmunjŏm, President Rhee and his assistants continued to follow the dual line of persisting with the Korean position regarding the truce talks and at the same time trying to cooperate with the Americans. In early November, about two weeks after the resumption of the talks at P'anmunjŏm, Muccio noticed resignation on the face of Rhee, and when the demarcation line was agreed upon late that month, the Korean leaders, both the head of the executive branch and the members of the National Assembly, indicated regret about the exclusion of Kaesŏng from South Korean territory, but otherwise the reaction was rather mild. Late in November, the tough words concerning the expulsion of Chinese troops from Korea and the insistence upon the idea of no truce without unification returned and remained until the following spring. Meanwhile, demonstrations against peace talks in spite of the Korean desire for cooperation with the United States continued during the winter and spring. While repeating old lines and familiar actions, there was one new idea the Koreans brought up during this period: the idea of a security pact with the United States. In a sense this follows the Korean sense of resignation evident in the fall of 1952. If not earlier, by the early spring of 1951, Korean leaders began to think that if an armistice was inevitable then some assurance from the United States would be needed for the future security of the republic, and a security pact seemed best for this purpose. On March 21, President Rhee wrote President Truman, "A mutual security pact between our two nations, I sincerely believe, is an essential thing. Since your desire has been, as we all know, to defend Korea against red aggression, there can be no reason for objecting to such a pact which alone would give the Korean people the supporting assurance they would badly need during a hazardous armistice."[4]

The American reaction to the Korean attitudes and actions hardened during this period; the military took the initiative of formulating a policy for dealing with the Korean antitruce activities. Late in February, Ridgway indicated his concern about the Korean activities and told the Joint Chiefs of Staff that unless the ROK government's antitruce activities were promptly reversed, he believed that the Koreans might "gravely endanger" the attainment of an armistice. He suggested consideration at the highest government levels of countermeasures. The Joint Chiefs of Staff responded immediately to Ridgway's suggestion and on February 27 proposed firm guidelines which remained in effect until the last day of the negotiations. These became the single most important guide for the U.S. government in dealing with the Koreans: intensifying efforts to keep the ROK in line during the armistice negotiations, presenting the ROK with an armistice as a *fait accompli*, and then taking the strongest measures to assure ROK compliance. In early March, President Truman, in his letter to President Rhee, indicated a "mounting concern" with the Korean leader's expression of open opposition to the armistice negotiations, pointing out the importance of an "outstanding unity of purpose" on the part of all nations participating in the U.N. action and stressing that unity must be maintained at all cost. This emphasis on unity was repeated many times by U.S. government leaders in their effort to keep the Koreans in line during the negotiations. Truman also tried to tie good behavior on the part of the Korean leaders to U.S. assistance during and after the war.[5]

The eleven-month period between April 28, 1952, when a package deal was offered by the U.N. negotiators to the communists, and the end of the following March, when Chou En-lai and Kim Il Sung came forward with a proposal to end the deadlock on the POW issue, was an empty period for Korean–American interactions regarding the matter of truce talks. Much of the spring and early summer of 1952 was occupied by Korean domestic issues in the relations between the two nations. The Koreans just managed to register during the fall and winter of the year their protests against any kind of armistice and their desire to march north for unification. Naturally, there was little need during this period for American action or reaction to Korean initiatives regarding the armistice negotiations; the only item the American government had to handle was providing a late answer to President Rhee's letter of March 4 which had formally requested the conclusion of a bilateral security treaty. Acheson suggested to Truman that making such a security pact with the Koreans would be against American interests.[6]

Korean reactions to the armistice negotiations again became important during the following two months from late March to early June 1953, when the difficult POW issue was resolved. The Koreans were relatively reserved in the early part, but then they turned to a more business-like thrust and ended with a "shock." On April 15, Ambassador Ellis Briggs, who replaced Muccio in Seoul, reported that President Rhee declared that he did not want to rock the boat and expressed his desire for having a genuine Korean government representative attached to the negotiating team. In April, the Korean leaders again turned to the persistent themes of the expulsion of Chinese troops and of no armistice without Korean unification. Moreover, the Koreans added a new angle to the Chinese troop theme; they said that if the withdrawal of only Chinese troops was a problem, they would rather see the withdrawal of all foreign troops. This revision seemed to show the seriousness of their assertion regarding the Chinese troops. Late in April, President Rhee repeated his five minimum conditions for an armistice. Throughout April, demonstrations in major Korean cities took place. Finally, on May 25, when President Rhee learned the terms of the final U.S. proposal, which would leave Chinese troops in Korea, he expressed his disappointment with "burning sincerity and unshakable conviction" to General Clark and Ambassador Briggs: "Withdraw UN forces and terminate economic aid—do that tomorrow if you must," but he added, "even so we shall go forward."[7]

For the United States and the United Nations, the seventy-day period between March 30 and June 8 was the critical final stage in the negotiations, and Washington took a firm stand toward both the communists and the ROK government and gave consideration to extreme measures to deal with them. President Eisenhower adopted the view that the atomic bomb was simply another weapon, and placing President Rhee in temporary custody was seriously considered to remove the danger of a last-minute disruption of the conclusion of the truce negotiations. Since March, however, the issue of a security pact had become a central concern of Korean–American relations, and by the middle of April, Ambassador Briggs had formulated the view that the real ROK objective was a security pact with the United States and that the security pact in addition to military and economic aid would give maximum satisfaction to the nation. However, this view soon proved to be a little too optimistic. In his letter of April 30 to General Clark, President Rhee asked not only for a security pact before the truce, but also for the simultaneous withdrawal of all foreign troops if the Chinese troops could not be withdrawn from the Korean peninsula. Four days later, General Taylor, commander of the 8th U.S. Army, came up with an outline of Operation Everready, a plan to take President Rhee into personal custody.[8]

When the U.N. command offered its final proposal on May 25, President Rhee declared that the proposal, which would leave Chinese troops in the nation and the Korean peninsula divided, was not acceptable and that he would consider making his own proposal which would include the simultaneous withdrawal of all foreign troops and the release of all Korean nonrepatriate POWs. In his May 29 communication to the Joint Chiefs of Staff, General Clark speculated about what President Rhee could possibly do to block the armistice—release of the Korean nonrepatriate POWs, offer a separate ROK proposal to the communists, and withdraw ROK troops from the U.N. command. On the same day, the Washington policy makers considered three alternatives in dealing with the ROK leaders: a security pact, custody of the ROK president, and pulling the U.N. troops out of Korea. General Collins expressed his personal view that the U.S. government should be ready to take Rhee into protective custody rather than try to sweeten him up with a security pact. Collins telegraphed Tokyo late in the evening of May 29 and revealed his concern about the situation in Korea created by dissatisfaction with the armistice terms and instructed to take all precautionary measures to secure the U.N. command. Collins also authorized Clark to make oral assurances that the secretary of state was strongly recommending the security pact to the president if it was necessary to avert "a grave emergency." On the afternoon of the following day, May 30, Collins informed Clark that the president had authorized Clark and Briggs to tell President Rhee that the United States was prepared to undertake immediate negotiations for a mutual defense treaty with the ROK government if that government would refrain from opposition to an armistice, cooperate in the implementation of an armistice agreement, and keep the ROK defense force under the Commander in Chief, United Nations Command (CINCUNC). Fifteen minutes later, at 3:31 P.M., Collins sent another telegram to Tokyo ordering that no action be taken to implement Operation Everready.[9]

In his letter of May 30 to President Eisenhower, which was sent to Washington on June 2, President Rhee stated that a cease fire with Chinese troops left in Korea would be a "death sentence" for the Korean people and expressed his preference for the simultaneous withdrawal of all foreign troops as an alternative. General Clark thought President Rhee's idea of simultaneous withdrawal worthy of consideration. On June 5, a day after the communist acceptance of most of the final U.N. proposal, President Rhee told Clark and Briggs that the Chinese withdrawal was still important to him, but he also promised not to take any unilateral action against the armistice negotiations without prior consultation, which was taken by Dulles as "a promising sign." Clark and Briggs agreed that since President Rhee could not be satisfied with anything short of the withdrawal of foreign troops from the Korean peninsula, they would not offer the security pact to him, a decision later approved by Collins. Thus, when the POW issue was resolved and the truce negotiations practically ended, the U.S. alternatives for dealing with the unhappy ROK leaders were narrowed to two: the security treaty or an exit from Korea. But for President Rhee, the security pact was not an adequate assurance for the survival of the Korean people in the postarmistice era as long as Chinese troops remained on the Korean peninsula. In short, there remained a wide gap between what the United States was prepared to do and what Republic of Korea wanted the United States to do, and it took almost two more months to close this gap.[10]

To deal with President Rhee, the American policy makers came up with two devices in the early part of June: They hastened to conclude the truce talks and try to soften Rhee up by meeting with President Eisenhower in

Washington. On June 10, Clark thought the best American strategy would be to avoid giving the Koreans more time to formulate doubts and apprehension by completing the armistice negotiations as quickly as possible. Washington supported the idea. On the same day, Dulles telegraphed Briggs that the president wished to sit down with President Rhee and explain the actual possibility, not just a mirage, of finding peaceful means for unification of Korea. President Rhee thanked Dulles for the invitation but said that it was not feasible for him to leave Seoul even for a short while and expressed his preference for the secretary to make a trip to Korea. Dulles also could not leave Washington, and the outcome of the sweetening tactic was Assistant Secretary Walter S. Robertson's three-week trip to Seoul in late June and early July. Thus, in mid-June, when both the Koreans and the Americans were wondering what alternatives and moves the other side would choose to reach the point of resolution, President Rhee made his first dramatic move and showed his determination and seriousness: He released nonrepatriate Korean POWs. This Korean move, while on one hand not a total surprise to some Americans but still a drastic step, still shocked many Americans, and the American leaders reacted strongly. An important question then was how the leaders of the United States would manage the damaging incident and proceed to conclude the peace negotiations successfully.[11]

President Eisenhower and Secretary Dulles reacted forcefully to President Rhee's action. Eisenhower told Rhee bluntly on June 18 that his order for the release of North Korean POWs had been carried out by the use of open violence by South Korean elements against the authority of the U.N. command. Then he went to the heart of his message: "Your present order and the action thereunder constitutes a clear violation of these assurances and creates an impossible situation for the UN Command." Threatening words followed: Unless the Korean leader was prepared immediately and energetically to accept the authority of the U.N. command to conduct the present hostilities and bring them to a close, it would be necessary to effect "another arrangement." On the same day, the White House made a public statement that the ROK's unilateral and premature release of the North Korean prisoners was a violation of the U.N. command to which the Korean government had agreed. Writing to Dulles on the same day, however, Eisenhower pointed out that dissension among the allies would only benefit the communists and that the safety and reunification of Korea could be assured only through the entirety of free nations and by strengthening the collective structure. When, in the afternoon of June 18, ROK Prime Minister Paik Tu-chin, who happened to be in Washington at this time, and Ambassador Yang Yu-ch'an, who replaced Chang Myŏn in Washington, came to see the secretary of state, Dulles told them that the unilateral action by the ROK had violated several assurances given by President Rhee to Clark during the past few weeks, specifically that the two nations must be unified and cooperative under the U.N. command or "some new arrangement" would be found because the two governments fighting the same enemy should do so together rather than apart. On the same day, President Eisenhower told members of the National Security Council that he would not tell Rhee that the U.S. forces would get out of Korea but that he would bluntly tell him that another arrangement would be made unless the Korean leader would agree to go along with the United Nations and the United States.[12]

In a conversation with Ambassador Briggs on the following day, June 19, which was conducted by President Rhee in "more sorrow than in anger," he reacted to President Eisenhower's letter of the previous day by saying that Korea was "permanently and profoundly grateful" to the American government and people for aid and comradeship in arms, but that he could not accept an armistice leaving Chinese communists in Korea because that would be a "death warrant." He told the American ambassador, "If it becomes necessary for your country to go your way while I go mine, then let us at all events part as friends." Regarding the "broken promises," President Rhee remarked that the only assurance he had given to General Clark was that if he contemplated removing the ROK forces from the U.N. command he would inform the general in advance. On the same day, but a few hours after the reception of Brigg's telegram in Washington reporting his meeting with President Rhee, President Eisenhower and congressional leaders met to discuss the Korean situation. At this meeting the leaders of the two branches agreed that the United States would not get out of Korea, and the congressional leaders expressed clearly their view that the United States should not take any action against Rhee. Representatives of the Joint Chiefs of Staff and the State Department also met on the same morning to consider the alternatives open to the United States in Korea, but did not reach any clear-cut consensus.[13]

On the following day, June 20, Ambassador Briggs, in his telegram to General Clark, reacted angrily by stating that Rhee's principal aim was to torpedo an armistice which failed to provide for the withdrawal of Chinese troops, that a showdown with Rhee would be unavoidable, and that the only alternative left for the United States would be to bring Rhee into line or remove him. Two days later, General Clark gave a clear and firm message to President Rhee that it was the "firm determination" of his government to secure an armistice under honorable terms and that the Korean government must accept the fact that the U.S. government was not prepared to eject the Chinese troops from Korea by force nor would it attempt to inject this issue into the terms of the armistice. On the following day, President Rhee announced the conditions for acceptance of the armistice by the ROK government. The two major conditions were that (1) if the ninety-day period for the political conference expired without finding a means for evacuating Chinese troops from Korea and without effecting the unification of Korea, then the ROK army would advance north with American air and naval support; and (2) that before signing the armistice, the United States would enter into a mutual defense pact with the Republic of Korea. If these conditions were met, the ROK government would not withdraw its armed forces from the U.N. command, and it would refrain from taking action against the armistice.[14]

Thus, by June 23, within a week after the release of the nonrepatriate North Korean POWs, the anger and sorrow simmered down in Washington and Seoul, and the leaders of the two countries entered the last stage of interaction to try to find a meeting point between the optimum goals of the two nations: for the United States, successful conclusion of the truce negotiations with the support of the ROK government for the United States; and for Korea, ejection of the Chinese troops from the Korean peninsula and the unification of Korea with U.S.–U.N. support for the Republic of Korea. Fortunately, the leaders of both countries saw the value of high-level face-to-face talks, and the three-week Robertson mission to Seoul played an important role in finding the point of resolution for the two countries.

Assistant Secretary of State for Far Eastern Affairs Walter S. Robertson, who carried out special missions for President Eisenhower and Secretary of State Dulles, was a capable and patient negotiator and the right choice for the difficult and important mission. He left Washington on June 22 with General Collins and his assistants and did an excellent job in Seoul. On the way to the South Korean capital, on June 24 and 25, Robertson's group met in Tokyo with General Clark and Robert D. Murphy, General Clark's political adviser. The group reached the positions that the armistice should be signed as soon as possible, that if Rhee remained "intransigent," Robertson should be authorized to inform him that U.N. forces would withdraw from Korea, and that if Rhee could be convinced that the United States was really determined to withdraw U.N. troops from Korea, then he might change his attitude. Early in the evening of June 25, the Joint Chiefs of Staff instructed Clark that he should not make any commitment or agreement or take action which would require total U.N. withdrawal. Nevertheless, the chiefs also stated that Clark should not be prevented from taking any action which might lead ROK leaders to believe that the United Nations would be prepared to withdraw the troops from Korea if ROK compliance was not forthcoming.[15]

On the morning of June 26, Robertson had his first meeting with President Rhee for a general exchange of views. President Rhee expressed his opposition to the armistice terms, especially with regard to prisoners, the failure to provide an armistice instrument to require withdrawal of the Chinese communist forces, and his fear that the political conference would involve endless futile discussions. Robertson presented the American views, emphasizing the benefits accrued by the ROK from American assurances already given, the secretary of state's intention to collaborate with the ROK in the political conference to attain the objective of uniting Korea, and the allied forces unwillingness to continue fighting to unify Korea by force. In his private conversation with Robertson, President Rhee indicated that he would accept the truce with the following modifications to his *aide memoire* of June 23: (1) Moving the remaining 8,600 nonrepatriates Korean POWs to the demilitarized zone so they could be transferred to the NNRE; (2) getting a ninety-day time limit on the political conference; (3) providing economic and military aid for twenty divisions of ROK forces; and (4) offering an immediate guarantee of a mutual defense pact. President Rhee also indicated that division between the nations was unthinkable and that he would make every effort for continued cooperation. President Eisenhower and Secretary Dulles in Washington thanked Robertson for the "encouraging" report. Dulles indicated that the imposition of a time limit upon other countries would not be possible but that he would be ready to withdraw jointly with the ROK representative if the political conference failed to make progress or was abused by the communists for propaganda purposes. President Eisenhower also agreed that economic and military aid would be possible if it were logistically feasible and that the guarantee of a mutual defense pact was of course subject to the advice and consent of the Senate.[16]

Thus, on the first day, the two sides stated their respective positions in a somewhat reserved and moderate manner. In the following two days, when the two sides exchanged *aide memoires*, the two sides' positions became clearer. On the afternoon of June 27, Robertson and Clark delivered to President Rhee the American government's view on the four items the president had brought up during the previous day's conversation based on the answers given in the departmental telegram of June 26. After receiving them, President Rhee remarked, "Well, the President has met all of my views" and requested confirmation in writing. In his *aide memoire* of June 27, Robertson had stated (1) that the U.S. government would be willing to have at a certain point a high-level conference with representatives of the ROK government to discuss the common objectives of the two nations to be pursued at the political conference, (2) that the U.S. government would be prepared to retire jointly with the ROK government at the end of ninety days of the political conference if there was no progress or if the conference was exploited by the communists, and (3) that the U.S. government was prepared to begin immediate negotiations to conclude a mutual defense treaty along the lines of the treaty between the United States and the Philippines. Robertson pointed out in the *memoire* that these U.S. government assurances were dependent upon the agreement of the ROK government to accept the authority of the U.N. command to conduct and conclude the hostilities; to support the armistice and pledge to collaborate in the execution of the armistice; and to keep ROK forces under the operational control of CINCUNC until the two governments agreed that the arrangements were no longer necessary.[17]

Clark noticed on the evening of June 27 that President Rhee seemed to be disturbed over the Robertson–Clark *aide memoire* of that day, indicating that the *memoire* did not fully express all the thoughts he had in his mind. In his *aide memoire* of the following day, June 28, President Rhee fully revealed his thoughts. The *memoire* began with the statement: "This *Aide-*

Memoire is intended to convey the understanding reached in the course of conversation between President Rhee and Assistant Secretary of State Walter Robertson." On the topic of economic and military assistance, President Rhee referred to President Eisenhower's letter of June 7, with the specification that the main purpose of strengthening the ROK military force would be the defense of democracy against communism and the goal of economic aid would be self-sufficiency and logistical support of the defense force. With regard to the mutual defense pact, the *memoire* indicated that it was the hope of the Republic of Korea government to conclude it prior to the signing of the armistice. And, with regard to the postarmistice measure, President Rhee stated that if the political conference failed to achieve the common objective of reunifying Korea "under its only legal government" and evacuating the Chinese communist forces from Korea, the delegates of the two nations would withdraw together from the conference and "immediately resume the military operations" without consulting with any other nation or organization for the purpose of accomplishing the original objective by military means." He wrote that the government of the Republic of Korea would cooperate with the U.N. command in moving the communist Korean and Chinese prisoners of war to the demilitarized zone, and the loyal Korean prisoners would be interrogated in the presence of U.N. command and ROK representatives.[18]

Robertson and Clark's reaction to President Rhee's memoire was critical and firm. In their telegram of late the evening of the same day, they characterized Rhee's message as "dilatory" and they stated that the *memoire* did not represent the understanding reached between the two sides. Whether President Rhee intended to be dilatory is questionable, but Robertson and Clark were right in claiming that President Rhee's *memoire* went beyond the understanding the two sides had reached on the first day of the meeting. In a sense the Korean leader was returning on June 28 to his position of June 23; why he did not mention his position regarding postarmistice measures at the meeting of June 26 is questionable. Probably he had tried to be modest in his demand at this first meeting with Robertson, although the expulsion of the Chinese communist forces and the unification of Korea were two basic concerns firm in his mind during the entire war. Robertson and Clark believed that President Rhee was still not convinced that the U.N. troops would withdraw from Korea and that the only chance of obtaining Rhee's cooperation depended upon convincing him that the United States had gone as far as it could go to meet his position. On the following day, Robertson went over each point at a meeting with President Rhee and returned the *memoire* to the President, saying that it was unacceptable. Thus, by June 28 the two sides had clearly revealed their positions. Now the question was how much they would give and take to reach the point of resolution.[19]

In his July 1 letter, President Rhee told Robertson that he would accept the latter's position in the *memoire* of June 27 with the following exceptions: Indian troops should proceed directly to the demilitarized zone without landing on Korean soil, and the United States should pledge to resume fighting for the unification of Korea, or at least provide air and naval support for ROK forces. Perhaps this did not look like much of a concession as long as fighting would resume after the armistice, but at least he moderated his demand for all-out U.S. military action to air and naval support. During the following week, some of the content and procedures for the mutual defense treaty-making process were clarified, and President Rhee further moderated his position on the issue of postarmistice measures. In this game of maximizing gains and minimizing losses, each side had aces as well as trumps to play. The United States could threaten to withdraw its troops from the Korean peninsula, while the ROK government could say that it might withdraw its troops from the U.N. command. They were questionable cards and entailed considerable risk. Once Washington decided not to get out of Korea, it did not deviate from this policy, but it signaled Tokyo to use the possibility as a bargaining chip. But when this little trick was put into practice in Korea by creating an impression in the minds of the Koreans that the U.N. force was getting ready to withdraw, President Rhee showed immediate indignation. The reverse worked a little better: Robertson was firmly convinced that President Rhee was not bluffing when he threatened to withdraw ROK troops from the U.N. command.[20]

Robertson emphasized to President Rhee that after the signing of the armistice, high-level conferences would be held to consider all aspects of the U.S.–ROK objectives at the political conference and that after the political conference, immediate consultation would take place to determine what action should be taken "in light of circumstances then existing to seek unification of Korea." By July 6, the Americans agreed to use in the defense treaty some of the terminology used in a similar treaty with Japan and informally cleared approval of the mutual defense pact with the Senate leadership to alleviate President Rhee's fear of Senate rejection of the treaty. With these concessions on relatively minor matters, the Americans stood firm on the major issue of the possibility of a postarmistice resumption of hostilities on the grounds that only Congress had the prerogative of initiating war according to the U.S. constitution. On the Korean side, President Rhee made a further concession in his July 7 *memoire* on the major issue of postarmistice measures by reducing his request for U.S. air and naval support to moral and material support for ROK postarmistice military action. On July 9, in his letter to Robertson, President Rhee repeated his request for U.S. assurances of moral and material support in case of the failure of the political conference and stated that the ROK representative would not sign the armistice but would not obstruct it. He also indicated that he understood the difficulty of immediate "ratification" (approval) of the mutual defense pact by the U.S. Senate and that he realized that approval might be obtained in the following session of the Congress. Washington recognized this as "great progress," and Robertson was happy with the concessions President Rhee had made.[21]

Thus, by July 9, the U.S. government had obtained a pledge from President Rhee not to obstruct the armistice, but as Robertson saw, still awaiting resolution were a number of issues: U.S. commitments for action to follow the political conference; an ROK agreement to leave ROK forces under U.N. command; and the narrowing of the gap between the Korean and U.S. drafts of the mutual defensive pact. Robertson decided that he had achieved the main objective of his mission by obtaining President Rhee's assurance not to obstruct the armistice. He returned to Washington on July 13, leaving the remaining issues to be resolved later. A joint statement noting the agreements reached was prepared on July 11, and two days later Robertson left Korea, completing his three-week mission. The Robertson mission was good for both the ROK and the U.S. governments: Both gained a better understanding of each other's positions through face-to-face negotiations, and both took major steps forward toward agreement. In his letter to President Eisenhower, President Rhee expressed his feelings regarding the Robertson mission: "As Mr. Robertson is now about to depart from Korea, I want you to know how pleased I have been with the fine spirit of consideration and understanding he has shown in all our talks together." "Even if we have differed on certain matters," he continued, "I have never found him lacking in a most sympathetic spirit of accord which has helped us to keep clearly in mind the fundamental and vital unity." He added that he had decided not to obstruct, in any manner, implementation of the armistice.[22]

After the Robertson mission, two relatively minor incidents arose between Seoul and Washington. The content of the joint statement on the mission was prematurely leaked in Seoul by an American journalist who interviewed President Rhee, which disturbed officials in Washington. In addition, General Harrison's statement at the truce negotiation regarding the maintenance of the armistice by U.N. command in case of any violation of the terms of the armistice by the Republic of Korea irritated Koreans. Two major issues still waiting to be resolved before the truce were whether the United States would come with "immediate and automatic military support" in case the Republic of Korea was attacked by an external force. The second issue was whether the United States would join the Republic of Korea in resuming military efforts to drive the Chinese troops out of Korea and to achieve the objective of the unification of Korea and whether, if such military action was not possible, the United States would provide moral and material support for an ROK effort, in case the political conference failed to achieve the objective of unification.

When Secretary Dulles called President Eisenhower on July 24 regarding these two issues, the president responded positively to the first but negatively to the second item. On the same day, Secretary Dulles explained to President Rhee that he could count upon an "immediate and automatic U.S.

reaction" in case of an unprovoked attack in violation of the armistice, but that moral and material support for ROK military efforts in the case of the failure of the political conference was not possible because President Eisenhower could not give a "blank commitment in advance" for postarmistice Korean military efforts to achieve the unification of Korea.[23]

In his letter of July 26 to Secretary Dulles, the last communication before signing the armistice document, President Rhee expressed his satisfaction with the American government's assurance of immediate action in the case of an unprovoked attack upon the Republic of Korea. On the second issue, that of a U.S. promise of military or moral and material support for ROK military efforts to achieve unification in the case of the failure of the political conference, he had no choice but to accept the final negative word of President Eisenhower and fell back on the July 3 U.S. offer of consultation to determine the course of action to be taken in the light of the future circumstances for the unification of Korea. Thus, the two issues between the two nations were settled through a compromise two days before the armistice; President Eisenhower went as far as he could by promising the Koreans an immediate and automatic military response in the case of another communist attack, and President Rhee accepted U.S. assurances of the nation's security against future communist threats and abandoned the demand for U.S. assistance to unify Korea by force.[24]

By early July, when the POW issue was resolved, and the truce negotiations were practically over, the main problem left to be solved for the U.S. government was how to obtain the cooperation of the ROK government for the implementation of the armistice. In contrast, the ROK government, which must have seen that the armistice was an unavoidable fact, wished to obtain the necessary U.S. assurances for the security, and indeed the survival, of the nation. Of the three alternatives the United States considered—a mutual defense pact, the removal of President Rhee from office, and the evacuation of all U.S. troops from Korea—the second alternative was dropped by the end of May and the third was not an alternative with much practical value. Accordingly, the only real and practical alternative was the mutual security treaty. For President Rhee, there were three national goals—a mutual defense pact with economic and military aid, withdrawal of the Chinese troops, and unification of Korea by force. For him, the presence of Chinese troops on Korean soil was the most serious single problem, but whether he actually thought he could gain U.S. support for their removal is questionable. He even proposed the radical alternative of the withdrawal of all foreign troops, including the U.S. troops. It is also doubtful that President Rhee really expected U.S. support for an ROK effort to achieve unification by force in the spring of 1953. If withdrawal of the Chinese troops was an absolute necessity for the survival of Korea, and unification was an ideal no Korean could give up, both of them were mere wishes, with little hope of realization at this point. The only feasible alternative left for President Rhee to take was the assurance of the maximum security of the republic through a mutual security treaty with the United States. President Eisenhower stood firm on the twin issues of the withdrawal of Chinese troops and unification of Korea by force, but showed maximum flexibility in giving assurances for Korean security by promising the Korean leader an immediate and automatic intervention of U.S. forces in the case of an unprovoked attack by an outside forces. President Rhee did his best in obtaining the necessary security assurance from the United States, but he was realistic in abandoning the other two assertions, which were in fact more wishes than policy objectives. Both sides did well in finding an optimum conversion point in the spring of 1953, mainly because of the firm but flexible management capabilities of Syngman Rhee and Dwight D. Eisenhower.

Once the U.S. government obtained word from President Rhee on July 9 that he would not obstruct the signing of the armistice, the U.N. delegation at P'anmunjŏm used this promise to try to satisfy the communists by stating that it had a "suitable assurance" from the ROK government for the execution of the armistice agreement. Although not completely satisfied with the assurances given by the U.N. delegation, the communists decided by July 19 to accept the assurances of the U.N. command and to proceed with the final arrangements for the armistice. Since the matters of the demarcation line and the demilitarized zone had already been settled, and the procedure for turning over the nonrepatriate prisoners to the Repatriate Commission and the functioning of the Military Armistice Commission had also been agreed upon, the only remaining task to work out was the signing of the final armistice document. The two delegations finally agreed on the afternoon of July 26 on the procedures for the signing ceremony; the senior delegates would sign the document at P'anmunjŏm at 10:00 A.M. of the following day and immediately thereafter the military commanders would sign in their respective headquarters. President Rhee declined General Clark's invitation to send an ROK representative to the signing scene, alleging that he had not yet received satisfactory assurances from the American government. The signing took place according to the agreement, and the fighting which had lasted a little over three years formally stopped at 10:00 P.M., July 27, 1953. President Rhee immediately wrote to President Eisenhower to thank him for assistance in the days of desperation and congratulated him on the statesman-like vision that had enabled him to bring a powerful nation and a weak nation together. President Eisenhower responded, thanking President Rhee for agreeing not to obstruct the implementation of the armistice despite his misgivings about the final outcome of the conflict.[25]

The cease-fire agreement, which was a product of more than two years of negotiation and a large amount of blood and iron, is an elaborate document with five articles and an annex. The preamble stated that the armistice will insure a complete cessation of hostilities and of all acts by armed forces in Korea until "a final peaceful settlement is achieved." The first article stipulated that the military demarcation line would be fixed, and the two sides would withdraw two kilometers from this line to establish a demilitarized area as a "buffer zone." The second article specified the concrete arrangements for the cease fire and armistice. The cease fire would become effective within seventy-two hours after the signing of the agreement, and within ten days the two sides would withdraw their military forces, supplies, and equipment from the rear of the other sides of the demarcation line. In addition, the two armies would cease introducing military reinforcements and equipment into Korea except for the rotation of a limited number of military personnel and the replacement of restricted equipment through specified Korean ports. The second article also specifies the establishment of two commissions to execute the cease-fire agreement: the Military Armistice Commission, with five members from each side and ten observer teams, to supervise the implementation of the armistice agreement; and the Neutral Nations Supervisory Commission, with four senior officers from Sweden, Switzerland, Poland, and Czechoslovakia with the support of twenty Neutral Nations Inspection Teams, to carry out the functions of supervision, observation, inspection, and investigation of the execution of the armistice agreement.

The third article of the armistice agreement dealt with the arrangements relating to prisoners of war, the most thorny subject during the negotiation. Within sixty days after the effective date of the armistice agreement, each side would repatriate in groups all prisoners of war who wished to return to their home country. The remaining prisoners would be turned over to the Neutral Nations Repatriation Commission. Joint Red Cross teams would also be established to assist the repatriation process on both sides. All civilians would also be permitted to return to their homes. A special provision was established for the Neutral Nations Repatriation Commission to follow while handling the nonrepatriated prisoners. The nonrepatriated prisoners would be turned over to the commission within sixty days after the effective date of the agreement, and the commission would immediately make arrangements for the nation from which the prisoners came to exercise, within ninety days after the prisoners came into the commission's custody, freedom of "explanation" to the POWs. The number of the representatives permitted to make these explanations would be between five and seven per thousand. At the expiration of the ninety days from the initiation of the commission's custody, any prisoners left in the hands of the commission would be submitted to the political conference, and any prisoners left without any provision by the conference within 120 days from the date of the commission's assumption of the custody would be released to go to a neutral nation or to become civilians.[26]

According to Article IV, the military commanders of both sides recommended to the governments of the countries concerned that within three months after the armistice became effective, a political conference be held to settle the question of withdrawal of all foreign troops from Korea and the peaceful settlement of the Korean question. When the Big Switch took place, 75,823 prisoners were turned over by the U.N. command to the communist side in exchange for 12,773 U.N. command POWs, which included 7,862 Koreans and 3,597 Americans. Over 22,600 communist and 359 U.N. command nonrepatriates were turned over to the Neutral Nations Repatriation Commission. From this number, 137 communist prisoners and 10 U.N. command nonrepatriates, including 8 Koreans and 2 Americans, were persuaded by the explanation process to return to their home countries, and the rest were released in January 1954, thus completing the exchange of the prisoners.

No matter what one's perspective, the peace negotiations to end the Korean War lasted too long—about twice as long as the fighting—and the cost was high on both sides. It should be pointed out that the person most responsible for the delay was Stalin, who had purposively prolonged the war because of the advantages for the Soviet Union and the People's Republic of China. As soon as death removed him from the scene, the new Russian leadership was willing to end the war, and the final stage of the negotiations began. Another factor behind the delay was the U.S. policy of the nonforceful repatriation of prisoners. Underlying it, of course, were both humanitarian principles and strategic elements, but the price for adhering to these principles and strategy was high. The third factor causing the delay was Syngman Rhee; at least a month of delay at the end of the negotiations resulted from his obstinacy. Although Rhee's delay was probably less harmful than the other two, it was still a delaying factor. Fortunately, however, despite these delaying forces, there was a strong desire to end the war on both sides, and the armistice was signed after a number of compromises. Altogether, it was an unfortunate peacemaking process for an unfortunate war.

NOTES

1. Editorial note, *Foreign Relations of the United States (FRUS), 1950*, 7: 1524–1525; memorandum of conversation, Rusk with Chang Myŏn and Emmons, December 12, 1950, Truman Library, Truman Papers, Selected Records Relating to the Korean War, Department of State, box 6; Muccio to the Secretary of State, June 9, 1951, *FRUS, 1951*, 7, pt. 1: 526; Rusk to Acheson, June 20, 1951, National Archives (NA), RG 59, Decimal File, 795.00/6-2051; Weekly Political Review for week ending June 2, 1951, NA, RG 59, Decimal File, 795B.00/6-551, 1950–1954, box 4300; Lightner to Emmons, June 18, 1951, ibid., 795.00/6-1851; Chang Myŏn to Truman, January 19, 1951, in Rusk to William D. Hassett, Secretary to the President, February 13, 1951, Truman Library, Truman Papers, box 1305; Muccio to the Secretary of State, June 13, 24, 1951, NA, RG 59, 795.00/6-1351, 795B.00/6-2451; memorandum of conversation by the Officer in Charge of Korean Affair (Emmons), June 30, 1951, *FRUS, 1951*, 7, pt. 1: 601–604; Lightner to the Secretary of State, July 8, 1951, NA, RG 59, Decimal File, 1950–54, box 4300; Intelligence Brief, no. 1393, April 21, 1953, NA, RG 84, Seoul Embassy Classified General Records, 1953–55, box 6.

2. Muccio to the Department of State, June 9, 30, and July 7, 1951, *FRUS, 1951*, 7, pt. 1: 526–527, 604–605, 635–636; Acheson to Muccio, ibid., pp. 588–590, 623. See also memorandum of conversation by the Office in Charge of Korean Affairs (Emmons) with Rusk, Yu Chan Yang, and Han P'yo Wook, June 30, 1951, ibid., pp. 601–604.

3. Muccio to the Secretary of State, July 10, 1951, *FRUS, 1951*, 7, pt. 1: 644–645; Muccio to the Secretary of State, July 19, August 9, 1951, NA, RG 59, Decimal File, 795.00/7-1451, 795.00/8–951; Rhee to Truman, July 28, 1951, Truman Library, White House Central File, Confidential File, box 22; Muccio to the Secretary of State, July 20, 28, 1951, *FRUS, 1951*, 7, pt. 1: 710, 745; Muccio to the Secretary of State, July 29, August 21, September 21, 1951, NA, RG 59, Decimal File, 1950–54, box 4300; ibid., Decimal File, 795B.00/8–2151; ibid., Decimal File, 795.00/9–2151; *Seoul Sinmun*, September 22, 1951, no. 1: 1–2.

4. Muccio to the Secretary of State, November 6, 1951, *FRUS, 1951*, 7, pt. 1: 1091–1092; Muccio to the Secretary of State, November 26, 27, 1951, and February 6, December 14, 18, 1952, NA, RG 59, Decimal File, 795.00/11-2651, 795.00/11-2751, 795B.11/2-652, 795.00/12-1452, 795.00/12-1852; President Rhee to President Truman, March 21, 1952, *FRUS, 1952-1954*, 15, pt. 11: 114–116; Briggs to the Secretary of State, February 25, 1952, NA, RG 84, Seoul Embassy Top Secret Records, 1950–54, box 1.

5. Ridgway to the Joint Chiefs of Staff, February 25, 1952, *FRUS, 1952-1954*, 15, pt. 1: 59–61; the Joint Chiefs of Staff to Ridgway, February 27, 1952, ibid., pp. 69–70; Truman to Rhee, March 4, 1952, ibid., 74–76.

6. U.S. Embassy in Pusan to the Department of State, NA, RG 59, Decimal File, 795.00/10-452; *Chosŏn Ilbo*, January 16, 1953, 1: 1–11; *Seoul Sinmun*, January 16, 1953, 1: 1–7; memorandum by the Secretary of State to the President, April 30, 1953, *FRUS, 1953*, 15, pt. 1: 185–186.

7. Briggs to the Department of State, April 15, 1953, *FRUS, 1952-1954*, 15, pt. 1: 910–912; Briggs to the Secretary of State, April 1, 1953, NA, RG 84, Armistice Negotiations, 1953, 822402, box 9; President Rhee to President Eisenhower, April 9, 1953, Dwight D. Eisenhower Library, Eisenhower Papers, Whitman File; Briggs to the Secretary of State, April 26, May 25, 1953, *FRUS, 1952-1954*, 15, pt. 1: 938, 1097–1098; Rhee to Eisenhower, May 30, 1953, ibid., pp. 1124–1125; *Seoul Sinmun*, April 3, 15, 1953: 1–2; ibid., April 15, 1953, 1: 1–6; *Chosŏn Ilbo*, April 23, 1953, 1: 1–5; Briggs to the Secretary of State, June 2, 1953, NA, RG 84, Seoul Embassy Classified General Records, 1953–55, box 9; Intelligence Brief, no. 1393, April 21, 1953, ibid., box 6; Briggs to Deussles, April 10, 1953, NA, RG 84, Armistice Negotiations, box 9; CG KOMZ to CG AFFC, April 23, 1953, NA, RG 84, National Assembly, 822402 box 114; Dulles to Briggs, April 25, 1953, ibid., RG 84, Armistice Negotiations, 822402, box 9.

8. Memorandum of a discussion at a special meeting of the Security Council, March 31, 1953, *FRUS, 1952-1954*, 15, part 1: 825–827; Briggs to the Department of State, April 14, 1953, ibid., pp. 906–907; Rhee to Clark, April 30, 1953, ibid., 955–956; paper submitted by the Commanding General of the United States Eighth Army (Taylor), May 4, 1953, ibid., pp. 965–968.

9. Briggs to the Department of State, May 25, 30, 1953, *FRUS, 1952-1954*, 15, pt. 2: 1097–1098, 1121–1122; Clark to the Joint Chiefs of Staff, May 29, 30, 1953, ibid., pp. 1112–1114, 1120–1121; memorandum of the substance of a discussion at

a Department of State–Joint Chiefs of Staff meeting, May 29, 1953, ibid., pp. 1114–1119; Collins to Clark, May 30, 1953 (DA 940241, DA 940242), ibid., pp. 1122–1123, 1123–1124.

10. Rhee to Eisenhower, May 30, 1953, *FRUS, 1952–1954*, 15, pt. 2: 1124–1126; Clark to the Joint Chiefs of Staff, June 2, 1953, ibid., pp. 1132–1133; Briggs to the Department of State, June 3, 5, 1953, ibid., pp. 1134–1135, 1144–1146; Collins to Clark, June 5, 1953, ibid., pp. 1146–1147.

11. Clark to the Joint Chiefs of Staff, June 10, 1953, *FRUS, 1952–1954*, 15, pt. 2: 1163–1164; the Secretary of State to the Embassy in Korea, June 10, 1953, ibid., p. 1164; Rhee to Dulles, June 14, 1953, ibid., p. 1168.

12. Eisenhower to Rhee, in the Secretary of State to Briggs, June 18, 1953, NA, RG 59, Records of the Policy Planning Staff, box 71; press release, June 18, 1953, the White House, Eisenhower Library, John Foster Dulles Files, Subject Series, box 9; memorandum of conversation by the Director of the Office of the Northeast Asian Affairs (Young), June 18, 1953, *FRUS, 1952–1954*, 15, pt. 2: 1206–1210; memorandum of a discussion of the 150th meeting of the National Security Council, June 18, 1953, ibid., pp. 1201, 1204–1205.

13. Briggs to the Department of State, June 19, 1953, *FRUS, 1952–1954*, 15, pt. 2: 1221–1223; memorandum of the substance of a discussion at a Department of State–Joint Chiefs of Staff meeting, June 19, 1953, ibid., pp. 1213–1221.

14. Briggs to Clark, June 20, 1953, *FRUS, 1952–1954*, 15, pt. 2: 1225–1227; Clark to the Joint Chiefs of Staff, June 22, 23, 1953, ibid., pp. 1231–1232, 1240–1242.

15. Memorandum of a discussion of a meeting held at Tokyo on the Korean Situation, June 24, 25, 1953, *FRUS, 1952–1954*, 15, pt. 2: 1265–1269; the Joint Chiefs of Staff to Clark, June 25, 1953, ibid., pp. 1271–1272.

16. Robertson to the Department of State, June 26, 1953, *FRUS, 1952–1954*, 15, pt. 2: 1276–1277; the Secretary of State to the Embassy in Korea, June 26, 1953, ibid., pp. 1277–1278.

17. Robertson to the Department of State, June 27, 1953, *FRUS, 1952–1954*, 15, pt. 2: pp. 1279–1280.

18. Clark to the Joint Chiefs of Staff, June 28, 1953, *FRUS, 1952–1954*, 15, pt. 2: 1280–1282; *aide memoire* from the President of the Republic of Korea (Rhee) to the Assistant Secretary of State for Far Eastern Affairs (Robertson), June 28, 1953, ibid., pp. 1282–1284.

19. Clark to the Joint Chiefs of Staff, June 28, 1953, *FRUS, 1952–1954*, 15, pt. 2: 1280–1282; Robertson–Clark to Rhee, June 28, 1953, the Citadel Archives, box 8, folder 5.

20. Rhee to Robertson, July 1, 1953, *FRUS, 1952–1954*, 15, pt. 2: 1292–1295; the Deputy Secretary of Defense (Kyes) to Clark, June 29, 1953, ibid., pp. 1286–1288; memorandum of the substance of a discussion at a Department of State–Joint Chiefs of Staff meeting, July 3, 1953, ibid., pp. 1317–1323; memorandum of a discussion at the 152nd meeting of the National Security Council, July 2, 1953, ibid., pp. 1300–1312; Clark to the Secretary of State, July 5, 1953, ibid., pp. 1332–1333; Robertson to the Department of State, July 7, 9, 1953, ibid., pp. 1337–1338, 1355–1356.

21. Robertson to Rhee, July 2, 1953, NA, RG 84, box 9; Robertson–Clark–Rhee, the Citadel Archives, box 8, folder 5; the Acting Secretary of State to the

Embassy in Korea, July 5, 1953, *FRUS, 1952-1954*, 15, pt. 2: 1331-1332; the Secretary of State to the Embassy in Korea, ibid., 1340; Rhee to Robertson, July 9, 1953, ibid., pp. 1357-1359; Robertson to the Department of State, July 8, 10, 1953, ibid., pp. 1350-1352, 1361-1362.

22. Robertson-Clark-Rhee, the Citadel Archives, box 8, folder 5; Rhee to Eisenhower, July 11, 1953, *FRUS, 1952-1954*, 15, part 2: 1369.

23. Briggs to the Department of State, July 21, 1953, *FRUS, 1952-1954*, 15, pt. 2: 1404-1406; Robertson to Rhee, July 21, 1953, ibid., pp. 1411-1412; Rhee to the Secretary of State Dulles, July 24, 1953, ibid., pp. 1428-1429; memorandum of a telephone conversation between the President and Secretary of State, July 24, 1953, ibid., p. 1429.

24. Rhee to Dulles, July 26, 1953, *FRUS, 1952-1954*, 15, part 2: 1439-1441. See Yang Tae-hyŏn, "Hankukŭi hyuchŏn hoetamkwa Mikukŭi tae Han chŏngch'aek—hyŏpsang chonryakŭl chungsimŭro" (The Korean armistice negotiations and the U.S. policy toward Korea: with an emphasis on the negotiation strategies), *Kukche Chŏngch'i Nonch'ong* 23 (1983): 321-345. The author is critical about the U.S. strategy in the armistice negotiations, but highly praises President Rhee's diplomatic skill in dealing with the U.S. leaders in the last phase of the negotiations. See also Robert H. Ferrell, *The Eisenhower Diaries* (New York: Norton, 1981), p. 148, July 24, 1953 entry; Barton J. Bernstein, "Syngman Rhee: The Pawn as Rook—The Struggle to End the Korean War," *Bulletin of Concerned Asian Scholars* 10, no. 1 (1978): 45.

25. Clark to the Joint Chiefs of Staff, July 11, 15, 17, 25, 26, 1953, *FRUS, 1952-1954*, 15, pt. 2: 1377, 1380-1383, 1432-1436, 1438-1439, 1441; editorial note, ibid., pp. 1403-1404, 1443-1444; Rhee to Eisenhower, July 27, 1953, ibid., pp. 1444-1445; Eisenhower to Rhee, July 27, 1953, ibid., 1445.

26. Armistice Agreement, vol. 1, Text of Agreement, NA, RG 59, Lot 608 D330, Lot 56 D225, and D256, box 10; Kaufman, *The Korean War*, pp. 340-341.

CHAPTER 14

Aid Diplomacy and
Korean Domestic Politics

The Korean War was one of most destructive wars in modern times, and there were considerable difficulties in coping with the problem of relief, rehabilitation, and reconstruction during and after the war. First of all, surviving the destruction and destitution created by the war was a problem for the Koreans themselves; they had to do everything possible to save themselves from the calamity, and after the exhaustion of self-help, they had to turn to others for help. One question worth exploring is whether they did what they should have done for their own relief and rehabilitation. A second question concerns the proper management of aid received from others. On the giving side, the United States bore most of the burden, as it had during the war. Some of the questions to be raised regarding the U.S. role in the relief and rehabilitation efforts related to the Korean War included the following: Did the United States formulate appropriate policies in its efforts to meet the needs for relief and rehabilitation in Korea during the first year of the war and during the following two years when armistice negotiations were underway? How well were these policies carried out over the three-year period? How well was the multilateral and bilateral approach managed?

As soon as the war broke out, tens of thousands of Koreans fled to the south, and widespread suffering began. Many stayed with relatives and friends until they were able to return home, if their home still existed. Others had little choice other than going to refugee camps, and they became the main recipients of relief. Because of the chaotic condition of the time, an accurate and comprehensive figure of the number of refugees is virtually impossible to obtain. But according to reliable sources, there were fifty-eight refugee camps by late July 1950, and almost 3 million refugees soon after the Inch'ŏn landing operation. The U.N. command's winter evacuation operation from the North Korean border to the south produced still more refugees, and by the spring of 1951, when the front line had been stabilized along the 38th parallel, 3.5 million refugees were reported. The most comprehensive set of figures, which were presented during the U.S. Congressional Committee hearings in the fall of 1953, indicates that there were 2.75 million registered refugees, 4.1 million destitute persons, and 3.6 million war victims—this total of over 10 million was about half the population of South Korea. Even though these numbers are large, they cannot be comprehensive, and it may more properly be said that practically every Korean suffered in one way or another during the tragic war and that those who needed the most help were those in the refugee camps.[1]

The quantity of aid needed by the Korean civilian population during the war is even harder to document. For the refugees, food, clothing, and housing came first. Medical care was also very important for those in the refugee camps, but vaccinations and other preventive measures were needed by the entire civilian population. In early August 1950, 20,000 metric tons of rice and 10,0000 metric tons of barley were provided by the U.N. command; 20,000 metric tons and 30,000 metric tons of grain were expected to be distributed, respectively, in September and October of the year. A little over $5 million of relief supplies were brought in July and August. One source reported that by the spring of 1951, 100,000 tons of grain had been brought in for the refugees, and 12 million civilians were vaccinated against smallpox, 13 million against typhoid, 9 million against typhus, and 3 million against cholera. Medical relief was extensive, and by the summer of 1953, 94 hospitals and 573 dispensaries were treating on a daily basis about 7,000 patients in all the provinces of South Korea.[2]

These extensive relief efforts notwithstanding, it is difficult to discover if the minimum daily needs of the Korean civilian population were met during the war years. Without doubt, food is the most important element in any relief operation. Accordingly, an examination of the figures provided by the Food Administration Bureau of the Korean Agricultural Ministry reveals much about the situation in which many Koreans found themselves. Total food consumption in Korea during 1951 was only 40 percent of that in 1949; it increased to 69 percent in the following year and in 1953, Koreans consumed 25 percent more than they did in the year before the war. Imports of grain for the three years after 1950 were 16 percent of the total consumption for the first two years and 24 percent for the last year. Such figures clearly indicate that the food situation in Korea in 1951 was certainly bad, but gradually improved during the following two years; they also indicate that the import of relief grain played a significant role. A tentative conclusion concerning the effectiveness of relief work during the Korean War indicates that a sincere and serious effort was made, but it was not adequate to meet the basic needs of the civilian population.[3]

During the war, the Korean government, like any government in a time of crisis, had the responsibility for doing everything possible to reduce the suffering of its people by providing an adequate supply of food, clothing, housing, medicine, and other basic needs and for restoring health to the economy. In addition to its domestic duties, the government was also responsible for keeping the U.S. government as well as other governments and the concerned U.N. agencies informed regarding the needs of the civil population which could not be met by the Koreans themselves, for thanking donors for the aid, and for utilizing efficiently the goods and services provided. It is evident that President Rhee made timely appeals to the U.S. government for aid, expressing his views on how the relief work had been done, and properly thanking donors for their generosity. There is much more room for debate when questions about cooperation and the efficient use of the aid are raised. In this area, President Rhee also showed his candor and toughness and did not hesitate to disagree with the donors as to the kind of aid the Koreans needed. He also insisted that rehabilitation as well as relief should be provided in the later period of the war and refused to yield to the U.S. government in dealing with issues like the U.N. command's use of Korean currency, the *won*–dollar exchange rate, and the control of the foreign exchange fund. The president at the same time did his duty of cooperating with the Americans through the Meyer Agreement of May 1952 and other measures. On the Korean side, the best performance was accomplished by the people. They showed their basic strength in enduring hardships, and they never lost their basic goodness and humanity. Not only did they open their homes and share their possessions in times of crisis with their less fortunate relatives and friends, but they also helped strangers.[4]

The American side of the story is much more complicated to relate, and careful examination is necessary. In the early months of the war, the Americans exhibited a great amount of good will and enthusiasm for alleviating the suffering of the civilian population in Korea. After the Chinese intervention, when the war became much difficult to manage, the civilian aid program began to face difficulties. On June 29, 1950—only four days after the outbreak of the war—President Truman allocated $50 million to the Economic Cooperation Administration, the organization which had handled Korean economic aid during the prewar years, thus showing quickly his serious concern for the suffering of Koreans. Dean Acheson was also enthusiastic: In his memorandum of October 11, 1950 to the president, he presented estimates of an annual need of $200 to $300 million for relief and rehabilitation work in Korea for about three years. And, on December 1, the United Nations Korean Reconstruction Agency (UNKRA) was established under the auspices of the United States to carry out relief and rehabilitation work in Korea. All these efforts clearly indicated that the U.S. government took very seriously the task of relief and rehabilitation in Korea. However, the initial American enthusiasm and good intentions did not last long. One reason for this change in attitude was the Chinese intervention, which changed the original assumption that the war would soon end and that rehabilitation work would begin. Another reason for the demise of the original plan was the nature of the policy or the lack of a clear-cut policy on the part of the American government regarding relief and rehabilitation in Korea during the two-year period from the summer of 1951 to the armistice.[5]

According to a report to a congressional committee, the U.S. government spent $299 million for relief and rehabilitation in Korea between June 26, 1950 and June 30, 1952. These expenditures amounted to a monthly average of a little over $12 million, which was about half of what Dean Acheson had estimated in the fall of 1950 for the needs of the Korean civilians. Part of the reason for the relatively small amount spent is that the work was mainly relief, and very little work was done for rehabilitation during the entire period. Why was the relief provided not larger? During the following one-year period, 1952 to 1953, the United States spent $323.25 million, for a monthly average of close to $27 million—slightly more than twice the per-month expenditure of the previous year. The main reason for the increase during the last year of the war was the fact that Korean economic aid was then closely tied to the Korean military build-up.[6]

When the war broke out in Korea, the U.S. government acted through the intermediary of the United Nations, and it was logical for the government to take the same multilateral approach in its relief and rehabilitation work. Steps were taken to organize these efforts through the United Nations. For example, the U.N. Security Council added to its July 7, 1950 resolution an "other" category besides that of providing military aid when it requested U.N. member nations to assist the Republic of Korea to repel the North Korean invasion. In early October, the U.N. General Assembly passed a resolution to recommend that the U.N. member nations take, along with the works for reunification of Korea, "all necessary measures" to accomplish the economic rehabilitation of Korea. It established the United Nations Commission for the Unification and Rehabilitation of Korea, and requested the Economic and Social Council to expedite the study of long-term measures to promote the economic development and social progress of Korea. On December 1, the General Assembly established the United Nations Korean Reconstruction Agency to carry out relief and reconstruction work in Korea.[7]

The U.S. government made every effort to ensure that the multilateral organization worked. The original plan of the Truman administration was to assign the relief work to the U.N. command, and it provided that the rehabilitation work would be transferred first from ECA to the U.N. command and then to UNKRA. This division of tasks created problems. Relief and rehabilitation were separate but related works, and unless a certain amount of rehabilitation accompanied the relief work, it was likely that the whole civilian aid program would have considerable waste and would have difficulty in achieving its objective. Especially during the armistice negotiation period, which lasted for two-thirds of the whole three-year war period, this division was a considerable hindrance. In addition, the complicated organizational scheme and the problem of the transfer of responsibility from one organization to another caused difficulties: The transfer from the ECA to the U.N. command was done at the end of June 1951, but the other transfer, from the U.N. command to the UNKRA, was not worked out until the end of the war. Muccio suggested that the transfer should be made directly from the ECA to the UNKRA, but his proposal was not accepted in Washington. During the uncertain period of the negotiations, the UNKRA, through agreements between the U.N. command and the U.N. agency, had the job of handling long-term recovery planning and highly technical works, but even this limited job assignment was not permitted to be carried out. Some contemporaries and later observers have claimed that this multilateral scheme failed because the U.N. command asserted the role of the military in relief and rehabilitation work during wartime, and the policy makers in Washington, especially those in the State Department, failed to exercise their responsibility in the policy-making process. An examination of the expenditures by UNKRA reveals the problems faced by the U.N. agency. UNKRA began operations with a $250 million budget approved by the Advisory Committee in early 1951. The U.S. government pledged to contribute $162.5 million—65 percent of the total budget—and the Truman administration requested an appropriation of $112.5 million and the transfer of $50 million in unexpended ECA money from Congress. The U.S. Congress responded by cutting the requested amount by about 90 percent from $112.5 million to $11.25 million and agreeing to the transfer of the ECA fund, but the approved fund was never appropriated. The total U.S. contribution to the UNKRA to the end of 1953 was only $50.78 million; additional contributions received by the agency from other U.N. member nations was $23.01 million plus $32,193,074 of in-kind contributions. In short, UNKRA never had the kind of money needed for rehabilitation operations during the war in Korea.[8]

If the multilateral approach existed only as an ideal during the Korean War, the bilateral approach, with the participation of Republic of Korea, did not work out much better. The Koreans were the recipients in the operation, and they did not have much to say about how much they wanted. As recipients, however, they probably had an obligation to specify what they needed, and their participation would certainly have been helpful for a successful operation of the aid program. Korean participation was a part of the original plan, but, in fact, the Koreans did not play much of a role in the whole operation, and some thought this negligence of their role came from the donors' "distrust and disrespect" for the recipients. When, however, matters such as the advance of Korean currency for the U.N. command, the *won*–dollar exchange rate, and the control of the foreign currency fund became important issues related to the aid program, the two governments had to settle them through negotiations. The outcome was the Meyer Agreement of May 1952, which gave the Koreans a part to play in the aid program through their participation in the Combined Economic Board. Progress was also made, through the agreement, on exchange rates, and U.S. payment for the Korean currency advanced.[9]

The issues of the mobilization of Korean manpower for the Korean War and the expansion of the Republic of Korea's Army, important issues by themselves for Korean–American relations, were also important because they were related to the economic aid program during the war. After the military disaster the ROK Army had experienced at the outbreak of the war, the matter of how to rebuild and strengthen the army so it could play its role in the war became an important concern of both Koreans and Americans. Especially after the massive intervention of the Chinese Army, the manpower problem became acute for the United States. President Rhee, who was well aware of this fact and was very conscious of the role of the Korean Army in the war, broached the idea of arming a large number of Korean young men to balance the Chinese numbers, and requested from the American government enough arms for 250,000–500,000 men. Although the request was considered by the State and Defense Departments, the American government decided not to respond positively. This decision was based on General MacArthur's view that he would rather arm the Japanese militia with the small arms and use Korean manpower resources for replacing the losses suffered by regular ROKA troops. Both the Truman and the Eisenhower administrations agreed that the expansion of the ROK Army was needed to replace American troops on the frontline and make the withdrawal of American troops possible. When General James Van Fleet replaced General Ridgway in the spring of 1951 as the commander of the 8th U.S. Army, he launched a training program and soon expanded the ROK force from 65,000 to 200,000 and to fourteen divisions by the fall of 1952. He also made plans for its expansion to twenty divisions, each with a strength of 14,000 men. This expansion seems to have had at least two effects on the aid program in Korea. Total economic aid was more than doubled between FY 1952 and FY 1953 to provide an economic basis for the expanded Korean military force, but this increase hindered the UNKRA multilateral program which began with a $70 million budget plan. Further, the emphasis on the development of heavy industry to support the expanding ROK military forces distorted to certain extent the aid program in meeting the Korean people's consumer needs.[10]

In sum, the Americans took the relief and rehabilitation program during the Korean War very seriously and sincerely. The more than one-half billion dollars contributed to the aid program saved millions of Korean lives and much suffering. However, much more aid was needed and was indeed possible, but it was minimally provided because of the weight given military needs and because a unilateral approach prevailed through the whole war period instead of bilateral or multilateral approaches. In a broad sense, this was one of the cases in which idealism and realism collided and in which human interests and national interests competed as national priorities. The victory of realism and national interests was unfortunate but understandable.

Korean–American relations during the three-year war period of 1950 to 1953 were pretty much subsumed by the war and peacemaking with one exception: American involvement in the domestic politics of the Republic of Korea. The matter was of course not unrelated to the war. Nevertheless, American involvement in the internal politics of Korea has a long history. This ongoing process of involvement in Korean–American relations received different degrees of emphasis in various periods. In the spring of 1952, the issue suddenly became explosive and critical during a ten-day period in late May and early June. In a larger sense, the crisis was symbolic of Korean–American relations as a whole, especially for this period. In the late 1940s and early 1950s, the world was going through an important transitional period in which international relationships shifted from independence–dependence to interdependence. In the Korean case, it is interesting to see how American and Korean leaders handled the problem of a powerful nation's involvement with a weak semi-independent partner's internal politics during this transitional period. In another sense, this case deserves special attention: It also exemplifies the struggle between idealism and realism in foreign policy-making processes both in Washington and in Seoul.

The year 1952 was an election year in the Republic of Korea. Because of his heavy-handed style of governing, President Rhee was unpopular with the more educated sector of the Korean people, and his reelection was far from certain. A man with a great sense of mission, he was confident that Korea needed his leadership at this critical time of crisis, and he must have thought that if he were not popular, it was the people's fault, not his own defects or shortcomings. As part of the preparations for reelection, he organized the Liberal Party in 1951, and the process was diligently reported to Washington. Late in May, after martial law was promulgated in Pusan without consulting U.N. military authorities, the Korean Assembly was prevented from having meetings, and some of its members were arrested. The Americans became alarmed by Rhee's actions. On May 27, General Van Fleet met with President Rhee, and on the following day, Ambassador Muccio advised President Rhee to moderate his actions so as not to lose the world's support for the Korean cause. Rhee remained adamant, and John M. Allison, Louis A. Johnson, and Kenneth T. Young in the State Department all perceived signs of "clear and real danger" in Korea and suggested decisive action. By May 28, they even began to consider the desirability of taking military action against President Rhee. On May 29, Muccio received from President Rhee the explanation that his actions were necessary because communist elements had infiltrated the National Assembly, but Washington rejected this explanation as unsatisfactory. On the following day, Acheson instructed Muccio to point out to the president the grave danger that increased political instability would harm the success of military operations in

Korea and to register strong objections to his failure to lift martial law. On the same day, Clark was instructed to use the "strongest terms" in his talk with President Rhee, but he was also told there would not be an "open threat or an ultimatum." Three days later, on June 2, President Truman sent strong words to the Korean leader: "I am shocked at the turn of events during the past week reported to me by many official sources." The letter continued: "It would be a tragic mockery of the great sacrifices in blood and treasure which the peoples of the United States and the free world have invested in Korean leadership and the Korean democratic institutions." The letter ended with a request: "Therefore I urge you most strongly to seek acceptable and workable ways to bring this crisis to an end." The turning point in this domestic crisis came on June 2. In his meeting with the UNCURK people and General Van Fleet, General Clark stated clearly his view that the political situation in Korea "did not endanger military operations or maintenance of order in the rear area." He held firmly to this view, and General Van Fleet, who had a more sympathetic understanding of the Korean political situation, agreed with him on this issue. The people in the State Department were not quite satisfied with the rigidity of the military on the problem, but they did not have much choice but to moderate their position. On June 4, they informed Muccio that the persuasion approach had been adopted for the Korean political crisis.[11]

Once this crisis ended in Seoul, the American government's involvement in Korean domestic politics was over, at least for this season. When the dust settled in Seoul, it was a compromise. The constitution was amended on July 4 to switch the power to elect the president from the National Assembly to the people, a change which was considered a victory for President Rhee. The opposition gained by the introduction of some of the features of a cabinet system with a strengthened prime minister and a bicameral National Assembly. The structural change made the Korean government look more democratic, and Americans were pleased with the outcome. Martial law was not lifted until late July, and when the presidential election was held on August 5, President Rhee was reelected with a great majority. But the Americans were happy with the way in which the election was held in a free atmosphere and a "dignified and restrained" manner. They also thought their pressure had produced the compromise, which seems to be partially, if not totally, true.[12]

Initially, the Americans had tried to take a neutral position regarding the Korean elections, but when they saw President Rhee's determination to use all available means, including the use of military force, to secure reelection, they modified their position and considered various options, ranging from advice to military intervention. The American decision to use only persuasion was based on two main considerations: President Rhee's use of ROK force to achieve his political objective might affect the combat capabilities of the U.N. command, and his repressive and crude methods would affect the support of U.N. member nations contributing to the war effort. The latter reason was well founded. The British and other key governments expressed their concern, and the press in Holland and in other allied nations was loud in criticizing President Rhee's antidemocratic moves. The first reason, however, was somewhat less credible: It is true that President Rhee had a plan to pull some ROK forces from the front, but it is doubtful whether it would have been necessary for him to do so, and even had it been necessary, it is not certain that he could have done so. In any case, General Clark and General Van Fleet discounted the military factor of the U.S. policy as grounds for strong action, and their professional perspective was decisive in preventing the United States from embarking upon the questionable course of military intervention in the domestic affairs of even a nominal ally during wartime. As part of the policy-making process during this crisis, full communication took place between Seoul and Washington. Authorities in Washington wisely allowed a full expression of views by American diplomats and military commanders in Korea and took these views into serious consideration when making the final decision of not intervening militarily. Had the military intervention taken place, then the U.S. government would have faced the difficult burden of occupying an allied nation, which most likely would have resulted in the demoralization of the Korean armed forces and reduced support from the allied nations for the Korean cause. It should be added that even though Edwin A. Lightner and probably a fair number of others in Seoul and Washington thought this was a good opportunity to dump President Rhee, there were others, including important decision makers, who saw that there was no realistic alternative to President Rhee's capabilities and leadership. This appraisal must have influenced the final decision. In the course of diplomatic relations between two unequal allies, there are definite limits on what the strong partner can do to the weaker. In this instance, it was fortunate that the U.S. government did not try to push its privileges beyond such limits. A struggle between idealism and realism took place in both Washington and Seoul, and it is likely that a good number of State Department people, especially Allison, Johnson, and Young, were unhappy at not being able to take stronger action during the Korean political crisis, but they retreated when the military came forward with a realistic assessment of the situation. In Seoul, Chang Myŏn and others were equally unhappy to see the dictatorial political leader left unpunished. President Rhee's problem was how to stay in power with very inadequate and diminishing support from the National Assembly, which had the constitutional authority to elect the head of the state. His weakness was well revealed in mid-January 1952, when his proposal of a constitutional amendment to switch the power of election of the president from the National Assembly to the people was defeated by 19 to 143. He turned to a crude method of staging the people's demonstrations and promulgating martial law in the temporary capital of Pusan to intimidate the members of the National Assembly. Soon, as many as forty-seven assembly members were arrested, and nine of them were jailed. When the executive–legislative conflict was resolved, at least temporarily, on July 4, the assembly conceded that the president be elected by popular vote. As a compromise measure, this deal strengthened the prime minister's position by giving him the power to make appointments of his cabinet members with the approval of the president. The excitement of the crisis passed away, but the incident, which resulted in a more democratic Korean election process, was significant because of the democratic principles involved.

Up to the spring of 1951, the Republic of Korea and the United States faced the common problem of fighting the North Korean and the communist Chinese forces. Even though the Chinese intervention in the winter of 1950 brought changes to this joint task, the fact remained that while fighting was the main concern for both nations, it was not too difficult for them to cooperate. Once the truce negotiations began during the summer of 1951, the gap between the two nations interests began to widen, and by the time the truce negotiations were approaching closure, it was less certain whether the two nations were still friends. The main problem during the two-year period was how they would find a reconciliation point for two diametrically opposed sets of national interests.

A key juncture arrived when the U.S. government perceived that without expansion of the war, victory against China was not be possible, and that if the war was expanded, there was a risk of starting another world war. On the basis of this judgment, the United States decided to make peace and withdraw its military forces from Korea. President Rhee agreed with the Americans on the first but not on the second part of their assessment. He firmly believed that stepped-up fighting with the Chinese would prevent, not cause, a third world war. There was another reason behind the U.S. decision to fight a limited war and to make peace in Korea. Americans reasoned that if another world war was inevitable, the Far East was the wrong place to fight it, and the Chinese were the wrong enemy. Europe was the right place, and the Soviet Union was the right enemy for such a war. President Rhee could not agree with the Americans here. His view was that if the war could be lost in the Far East, then it could also be lost in Europe; if the United States could not beat the Chinese, then it would not have an opportunity to beat the Soviet Union. However, the differences between the two nations rested on more than a problem of perception and strategy. For the Koreans, the U.S. policy change meant the abandonment of the original objective of the war—restoration of "international peace and security," which could not be achieved without Korean reunification. Even worse, the Koreans believed that they would be abandoned with a huge Chinese military force remaining on the Korean peninsula, a situation which President Rhee called a "death sentence" for the Korean people, and a view which was candidly recognized by President Eisenhower.

In mid-June 1951, through NSC 48/5, the U.S. government defined its current task as bringing about a settlement of the Korean problem, or a truce, while maintaining the ultimate political objective of establishing a unified, independent, and democratic Korea. The national objectives remained the same during the period of the truce negotiation. The only question was how this could be achieved given the two key obstacles: the enemy's unwillingness to have a speedy conclusion of the truce negotiation and the Korean unwillingness to go along with the American policy line. Both the Truman and Eisenhower administrations adopted a strategy of adding pressure on the front line and threatening the enemy with an expansion of the war. Causal factors are not always easy to pin down, but because conditions on the battlefield usually control peace negotiation, it is hard to argue that the military threat, including the possible use of atomic weapons, was not effective at all. To be sure, both Chinese and North Koreans must have had the domestic or psychological reasons pushing them to the negotiating table, but this does not eliminate the possible influence of a military threat. Persuading the reluctant ally that an armistice would be beneficial was not easy. When the promise of large-scale, postconflict military and economic aid was not sufficient to bring the unhappy Koreans around, the Eisenhower administration decided to provide a sense of security by initiating negotiations for the mutual security treaty President Rhee proposed. At the same time, they rejected the idea of resuming the war to unify Korea by force in case negotiations failed to achieve unification. Thus, the United States, after long and trying negotiations, achieved its immediate objective of ending the war. As a minor consideration, it is interesting to note how idealistic concerns entered into the midst of the very crude and realistic game of peacemaking with the communists: Beginning in mid-June 1953, policy makers in Washington seriously considered an alternative of creating a "unified permanently neutral" Korea. Because of the military judgment that the arrangement of establishing unified neutralized Korea would be disadvantageous to U.S. strategic interests, the discussion did not go further. It is also unlikely that either of the two half Koreas would have bought into this idealistic notion at this point.[13]

For the Koreans during the two years of truce negotiations, there was not much they could do in dealing with both formidable enemies and the reluctant friends. They fought and suffered in dealing with the enemies; and they protested and threatened in dealing with friends. In early March 1951, Pak Cong-jŏng, a member of the National Assembly, complained that Rhee's government lacked judgment, long-range vision, and a proper national policy. None can claim that President Rhee was weak and incapable; he understood both his enemies and his friends better than any one else in Korea did, and he was strong enough to protest when treated improperly, to demand when there was a danger of not getting what he thought the Koreans were entitled to get, and to threaten when he saw a possibility of its utility. None of these tactics worked, not because they were the wrong tactics or carried out improperly, but because they were tactics of the Republic of Korea, a weak nation. Everyone recognized that he was a tough fighter against communism, and some were not hesitant to recognize his idealism and realism. Fortunately, he had the Eisenhower–Dulles team instead of the Truman–Acheson team in Washington. Eisenhower understood him much better than Truman did, and he and Dulles formed a lasting friendship. Clark and Van Fleet also understood the old, tough fighter. President Rhee insisted to the last moment on the expulsion of Chinese troops from the Korean peninsula and for the resumption of fighting for the reunification of Korea with American assistance. In his mind, although he knew the demands were unrealistic, they represented the earnest wishes of the Korean people, and as their leader he could not help voicing them loudly. The true tragedy of the war and the peacemaking process in Korea between 1950 and 1953 was that the Koreans, who had paid for their "liberation" with the division of their land, also paid for its redemption with enormous suffering through the war, but still not enough to restore the nation's unity.

NOTES

1. *New York Times*, July 26, 1950, 4: 1; ibid., March 1, 1951, 3: 1; "Significant Political and Economic Development in Korea, September 5–21," ORI report no. 5360.1, September 21, 1950, NA, RG 469, Records of U.S. Foreign Assistance Agencies, 1948–61, Division of Korea Program, Office of the Director, Korea Bulletin, 1950; *Relief and Rehabilitation in Korea: Hearings before a Subcommittee on Government Operations*, 83d Cong., 2d sess., October 13, 14, and 16, 1953, p. 36.

2. ECA Administrator Foster to SCAP, August 4, 1950, Truman Library, Selected Records Relating to the Korean War, Department of State, box 7; "Status of Korean Non-Military Assistance of the Programs as of October 5, 1950," ibid.; *New York Times*, March 6, 1951, 3: 1; "Relief and Rehabilitation in Korea," p. 37.

3. Chu Sŏk-kyun, "Why American Aid Failed," *Korean Quarterly* 4 (1962): 64.

4. Rhee to MacArthur, September 1, 1950, National Archives (NA), RG 469, Records of U.S. Foreign Assistance Agencies, 1948–61, Division of Korean Program, Subject Files, 1948–51, box 64; Drumright to Johnson, February 28, 1951, NA, RG 59, lot 54 D278, lot 58 D529, box 1; Rhee to Muccio, March 23, 1951, NA, RG 59, Decimal File, box 5689; Barry Bingham, "The Best Thing about Korea Is the Spirit of Its People," in *Congressional Record*, 83d Cong., 1st sess, vol. 99, pt. 4, pp. 4378–4380.

5. Truman to Paul G. Hoffman, June 29, 1950, Truman Library, Edgar A. J. Johnson Papers, box 1; memorandum for the President, October 11, 1950, NA, RG 469, Records of Foreign Assistance Agencies, 1948–61, Division of Korea Program, Subject Files, 1948–51, box 82.

6. *Relief and Rehabilitation in Korea: Twenty-Third Intermediate Report of the Committee on the Government Operations*, 83d Cong., 1st sess, House Report no. 2574, 1954, p. 4; Gene Martin Lyons, *Military Policy and Economic Aid: The Korean Case, 1950–1953* (Columbus: Ohio State University Press, 1961), pp. 159–160.

7. *The United States and the Korean Problem, Documents 1943–1953* (Washington, D.C.: U.S. Government Printing Office, 1953), pp. 38, 41–43, 46–47.

8. Acheson to Muccio, January 24, March 23, 1951, Truman Library, Truman Papers, Selected Records Relating the Korean War, Department of State; CINCFE to the Department of the Army, February 24, 1951, NA, RG 469, Records of U.S. Foreign Assistance Agencies, 1948–61, Division of Korean Program, Subject File, 1948–51, box 82; Muccio to the Secretary of State, February 17, 1951, Truman Library, Truman Papers, Selected Records Relating to the Korean War, Department of State, box 82; draft of a letter from the President to Acheson, Marshall, and ECA Administrator Foster, n.d., NA, RG 469, Records of U.S. Foreign Assistance Agencies, 1948–61, Division of Korean Program, Subject Files, 1948–51, box 82; *New York Times*, January 18, 1952, 2: 6; ibid., October 3, 1952, 1: 2; Gene Martin Lyons, *Military Policy and Economic Aid: The Korean Case, 1950–1853* (Columbus: Ohio State University Press, 1953), pp. 83, 114, 149, 151, 172–173.

9. Allison to the Secretary of State, April 2, 1952, NA, RG 59, Decimal File, 1950–54, box 4312; *Department of State Bulletin* 26 (1952): 943; *Donga Ilbo*, May 29, 1952, 1: 1–7; Young to Allison, September 12, 1952, NA, RG 59, Decimal File, 1950–54, box 4301; CINCFE to Muccio, NA, RG 84, Seoul Embassy Classified General Records, 1953–55, box 16; C. E. Meyer to Acheson, May 24, 1952, NA, RG 59, Decimal File, 1950–54, box 4312; Young to Johnson, August 14, 1953, NA, RG 59, Decimal File, 895.00/8–1453, box 5689; Briggs to the Secretary of State, February 14, 1953, NA, RG 59, Decimal File, 1950–54, box 4313.

10. Memorandum of conversation between Rusk and Ridgway, August 10, 1950, Truman Library, Truman Papers, Selected Records Related to the Korean War, Department of State; Austin to Acheson, December 7, 1950, ibid.; Muccio to the Department of State, December 25, 1950, NA, RG 59, Decimal File, 1950–54, box 4313; the Joint Chiefs of Staff to CINCFE, January 4, 1951, Truman Library, Truman Papers, Selected Records Related to the Korean War, Department of State, box 82; CINCFE to the Department of the Army, January 6, 1951, ibid.; Muccio to the Secretary of State, January 6, 1951, ibid.; Bradley to the Secretary of Defense, January 17, 1951, ibid.; Marshall to Acheson, January 19, 1951, ibid.; Rhee to Truman, March 26, 1951, ibid.; Rhee to Muccio, April 21, 1951, ibid.; circular, October 6, 1951, NA, RG 59, Decimal File, 795.00/10–651; Wilson to Robert Cutler, Eisenhower Library, White House Office, National Security Adviser, NSC Series, Policy Paper Subseries, box 4; Lyons, *Military Policy and Economic Aid*, pp. 157, 160–161, 165, 167–168, 175, 198–199.

11. Muccio to the Secretary of State, August 25, December 27, 1951, NA, RG 59, Decimal File, 1950–54, box 4300; Bruce to Muccio, May 26, 1952, ibid.; Secretary of State to Muccio, May 28, June 2, 1952, Truman Library, Truman Papers, Selected Records Relating to the Korean War, Department of State, box 13; Muccio to Secretary of State, May 28, 1952, NA, RG 59, Decimal File, 795B.00/5–2852; Van Fleet to Muccio, May 29, 1952, NA, RG 84, Seoul Embassy, Top Secret Records, 1950–56, box 1; memorandum by Allison, Johnson, Young, May 29, 1952, NA, RG 59, lot 58 D258, box 9; Muccio to the Secretary of State, May 29, 1952, Truman Library, Selected Records Relating to the Korean War, Department of State, box 13; Johnson to Secretary of State, May 29, 1952, NA, RG 59, lot 58 D258, box 9; Secretary of State to Muccio, May 30, 1952, NA, RG 59, Decimal File, 1950–54, box 4300; Johnson to Acheson, June 1, 1952, NA, RG 59, Decimal File, 795.00/

6–152; Truman to Rhee, June 2, 1952, *FRUS, 1952–1954*, 15, pt. 2: 285–286; Johnson to Acheson, June 2, 1952, Truman Library, Selected Records Relating to the Korean War, Department of State File, box 13; Acheson to Muccio, June 2, 4, 1952, NA, RG 59, Decimal File, 795.00/6–2552, 795B.00/6–452; Lightner to the Secretary of State, June 3, 1952, NA, RG 59, Decimal File, 795B.00/6–352; Young to Acheson and Allison, June 4, 1952, NA, RG 59, Decimal File, 58D 258, box 9.

12. Memorandum of Acheson of his conversation with Truman, June 5, 1952, NA, RG 59, Decimal File, 795.00/6–552; Muccio to Secretary of State, June 25, 1952, NA, RG 59, Decimal File 795B.00/6–2552; Allison to Secretary of State, July 9, 1952, NA, RG 59, Decimal File 795.00/7–952; *Chosŏn Ilbo*, July 14, 1952, 1: 1–6; Muccio to Secretary of State, July 28, 31, September 15, 1952, NA, RG 59, Decimal File, 1950–54, box 4301; Muccio to Secretary of State, August 13, 1952, NA, RG 59, Decimal File, 795.00/8–1352.

13. Memorandum containing the sections dealing with Korea from NSC 48/5, May 17, 1951, *FRUS, 1951*, 8, part 1: 439–442; draft paper for submission to the Planning Board for the National Security Council, June 15, 1953, *FRUS, 1952–1954*, 15, pt. 2: 1180–1183; memorandum by the Joint Chiefs of Staff to the Secretary of Defense, NSC 157, June 30, 1953, ibid., pp. 1288–1291; report by the National Security Council, NSC 157/1, July 7, 1953, ibid., pp. 1344–1346.

CHAPTER 15

Conclusion

An account of postarmistice Korean–American relations belongs to another
study. Hence, a brief discussion of how two major items—the mutual defense treaty and the political conference—both of which originated during
the armistice negotiation and were completed in 1954, will be suffice in this
conclusion. When it became clear to President Rhee that the United States
had determined to end the war through an armistice, he chose the practical
route of assuring Korea's future security with a treaty and military and
economic assistance. The Eisenhower administration made concessions and
began negotiations for the treaty before the armistice negotiations were completed, and Assistant Secretary Walter Robertson, during his special mission in Seoul, settled most of the treaty issues. In early August 1953, Secretary
of State Dulles came to Seoul to discuss several postarmistice issues with
President Rhee, one of which was the mutual defense treaty. During his
five-day stay, the treaty was completed and initialed. It was signed by Foreign Minister Pyŏn Yŏng-t'ae and Secretary Dulles on October 1, 1953. The
treaty was approved by the legislative branches of both nations in mid-
January 1954, the ratifications were exchanged, and the treaty became effective on November 17, 1954. The third article was the heart of the treaty,
stipulating that each of the two parties would recognize that an armed attack
on either of the parties would be dangerous to its own peace and safety and
declared that "it would act to meet the common danger in accordance with
its constitutional process." The two nations also agreed to develop appropriate means to deter armed attack through "self help and mutual help." The
U.S. government retained the so-called Monroe Doctrine formula, and Presi-

dent Rhee did not get the promise of an automatic response in the case of an attack. But he obtained formal assurances of U.S. assistance in the case of a future communist attack, which he had not had prior to the war. In short, the American government under the leadership of Eisenhower and Dulles recognized the importance of deterrence to prevent the recurrence of war on the Korean peninsula.[1]

A political conference for the purpose of resolving the Korean problem and establishing a unified nation through peaceful means also grew out of the war and the cease-fire negotiations. Few Korean and American leaders had an illusion that a political conference would bring about a unification of Korea, which had not been achieved on the battlefield. The unification of Korea through peaceful means was nonetheless one of the key components of American policy toward Korea in the summer of 1953, and Korean leaders had to explore every avenue that might lead to unification, including this one. As a consequence, President Rhee and Secretary Dulles held exploratory discussions on August 5, during Dulles's visit to Seoul, on five points relating to the conference: the date, place, agenda, participants, and duration. Preliminary meetings for the political conference began in P'anmunjŏm in late October 1953 between Arthur H. Dean, the representative of the U.N. side, and his North Korean and communist Chinese counterparts and continued into early February 1954 without accomplishing anything. The U.N. side's objectives were limited to deciding the time and place of the political conference, while the communists wanted to discuss the questions concerning possible participants and substantive matters. As a result, the meetings ended with an exchange of charges and countercharges. Meanwhile, the Berlin Foreign Ministers Conference took up the issue of the political conference for Korean unification, and the P'anmunjŏm meeting folded quietly. However, the preliminary meetings at least served to reveal what might be expected to happen at a future conference, and the Republic of Korea and the United States had the opportunity to gain valuable experience cooperating with each other. President Rhee fully expressed his views on the meetings; he had four to five weekly conferences with Dean during the course of the meetings; and he sent two observers to P'anmunjŏm.[2]

Some think that the Korean political conference died in the womb, but the baby was actually transferred from one womb to another, the latter called the Berlin Foreign Ministers Conference, before its birth at Geneva, so it escaped the fate of being stillborn. But when the conference was held in Geneva in the spring of 1954, world conditions had changed. The Soviet Union had now come to the fore, India would play a much greater role, and the issue of Vietnam was added to the agenda. The Republic of Korea found herself in the very awkward position of having to contend with the active role of the Soviet Union and India, who originally wished not to be present at the conference, but there was also considerable danger of losing the battle with its adversaries on an expanded diplomatic stage. Partly because of persuasion by the United States, but mainly because Korea did not want to miss even a meager opportunity to achieve reunification, President Rhee decided to send a small mission of seven to Geneva. The outcome after near two months of meetings was the same as at P'anmunjŏm—stagnation and no accomplishment. The delegates from the two governments on the Korean peninsula had an opportunity to present their positions to the major powers of the world, but there was such a wide gap between the two that there was no way of narrowing it in two months. Fortunately for South Korea, a loss in the diplomatic battle was avoided, and the South Korean and American governments again managed to cooperate with each other, despite their differences on the approaches and issues involved. However, the most unfortunate outcome of the conference for the Koreans was a recognition that the division of the nation had been even more firmly established by the conference.[3]

In conclusion, an attempt will be made for a final evaluation of the Korean–American diplomatic relations during the critical five-year period of 1948 to 1953, in terms of some key factors in international relations—national interests, power, leadership, culture, ideology, and small and large power relationships. Since its establishment in the early modern period, the nation-state system has been going strong, and in the mid-twentieth century, protection of national interest became the most important task facing any nation. The Republic of Korea, both its leaders and its citizens, felt very insecure with the fanatical communist state to the north. With a sizable population—about twice that of North Korea—the new republic in the south lacked the necessary psychology, such as the crusading spirit of the north, as well as the material resources. Also lacking in the south was strong outside support, such as that which the north had from the Soviet Union. Under these very difficult circumstances, the best the leaders of the Republic of Korea could do was develop a self-help attitude and cooperate with the United States to secure the necessary assistance. The two-year period in Korea between the summer of 1948 and June 1950 was much like the two decades between 1883 and 1904; whether the Korean people would overcome the enormous difficulties facing them was questionable. The Koreans failed in the 1950s, just as had happened at the turn of the century. In the self-help endeavor, we wonder whether the Koreans did everything possible in trying to obtain the necessary help. They should have been able to cultivate a greater sense of trust and confidence in the mind of the Americans. The conditions with which the Koreans worked were certainly not favorable; still, they failed to avoid the coming calamity.

We wonder also whether the United States properly handled their national interests and national policies during these two years of dealing with the Korean problem. First of all, the military judgment that the Korean peninsula had no strategic value for U.S. security in case of a general war was flawed because it was based on the assumption that the nation would fight only general wars. A general war would in fact be a nuclear war, and a nuclear war would never be fought because of the horror it would bring. Therefore, small wars were the only kind of wars fought in the post–World War II world. Another problem with American policy toward Korea was that if the geopolitical position of the peninsula was properly recognized, political concerns should have come first, and military judgment should have been subjected to them, not the other way around. One may also argue, as many have done in the past, that the Americans had limited resources to support their national security policies, that more of them were needed in Europe, and that whatever was left over should have been available for Korea and other countries in Asia. But Europe and Asia were related, and if Korea and Asia fell to communism, then Europe would soon face the whole communist threat. Deciding upon the ends within the limit of the means sometimes, and probably quite often, forces national leaders to mobilize extra resources for essential national objectives and needs. American security needs and resources in the post–World War II period definitely faced this problem. There is an argument that the American government adopted the containment policy in 1947 to fight the Cold War in Korea. If such was the case, then the policy was not executed properly, and the failure of deterrence became one of the key factors in the coming of the war in Korea.

It is not easy at any level of human existence to make sacrifices in the present for future benefits. Because of this tendency, maintaining a balance among the different ranges of national interests and objectives is difficult. Had the Koreans acted according to long-range visionary views in the years between 1945 and 1948, they would have been in a much better situation during the following years and might have avoided the war. For the United States, the long-range national objective of establishing a unified, democratic, and economically viable nation in Korea remained quite consistent. However, the immediate U.S. purpose was withdrawal of the troops and providing a very limited amount of military and economic aid for Korea. There was a gap between these short- and long-range objectives. All nations confront the general problem of giving too much priority to one's own national interests. Although the national interest is always in a dominating position, it is one of many human interests, and the human interests below and above the national level demand their due. While blindly following their national interests, nations tend to sacrifice other interests of the people. The Korean leaders' insistence on the use of nuclear bombs in Korea during the Korean War and the extensive bombing operations by the U.N. forces which almost totally destroyed the Korean peninsula are only two of the many cases which illustrate this problem. The mode or the relationship between two nations interests makes relations between two nations difficult. Depending upon whether nations pursue common, complementary, or conflicting interests, the nations cooperative or conflicting relationship will develop. During the little over two-year period between the summer of 1948 and the late fall of 1950, the Republic of Korea and the United States had more in common than conflicting objectives to pursue; however, from the late fall of 1950 to the summer of 1953, the two nations faced a mixed situation of pursuing divergent concerns regarding the truce negotiations. While still pursuing common objectives against a common enemy, the two nations' interests were also in a sense complementary. If not consciously, at least unconsciously the two nations' leaders successfully managed the changing complex structure of their national interests.

If national interest is a dominating factor for achieving ends, power dominates as means. A key concern regarding power in international relations is the question of who has how much more power and how it is used. The power discrepancy between the Republic of Korea and the United States was definitely one of the most significant factors in the two-nation relationship. Two very unequal nations—a very powerful and rich nation and a very weak and poor nation—contributed to produce a power imbalance, one that did work in at least two different ways. This powerful and rich United States could help the weak and poor Korea when they played a game of cooperation. The powerful and rich nation could also threaten and coerce the other when they came into conflict. During the entire five-year period, the Koreans expected and received military and economic assistance as a junior ally. During the same period, they also received threats when conflicting views emerged between the two countries. In short, the two nations had to go through many unpleasant phases largely because of the asymmetrical power configuration between them. The international system is in a sense a threat system, and without doubt, the Korean–American relationship operated within this general context. A powerful partner can enjoy many advantages in a relationship with a weak partner, including the use of threats. However, there are definite limits on the use of threats, and one example was Operation Ever-Ready, fortunately not executed, at least in part because of the potential damage to the U.S. world image. The weaker partner often enjoys the advantage of weakness, but it too has limits, which can be found in the diplomatic exchanges over military and economic aid.

As in other diplomatic cases, but probably even more so in this case, the leadership factor was significant for the relationship between the Republic of Korea and the United States. Both countries were blessed with capable leaders during the post–World War II period. For South Korea, crisis conditions produced a number of patriot–heroes. Unfortunately by 1948 some of them had been removed from the scene, but there were still enough capable and dedicated people in Korea to serve the nation during these critical times. Syngman Rhee was definitely the most illustrious figure in Korea in those years, and, in a sense, it was fortunate for Korea to have a man of his caliber and capabilities at this difficult time. But at the same time, it was also unfortunate for the nation that it fell under the domination of one man, which denied other Koreans the opportunity to make their full contributions. His excellent education in both Korea and the Unites States

and his half-century of valuable experience in Eastern and Western countries gave him a firm foundation for his work during the fifteen-year period
from 1945. Some have portrayed him as a peculiar product of Oriental
traditions mixed with the influence of Western culture, but his multicultural
background was a strength, not a source of weakness. Probably, with the
added influence of Woodrow Wilson's idealism, his ideal of reunification of
Korea persisted throughout his life. And while living the difficult life of a
semirevolutionary, he had also become a realist, and some have even called
him Machiavellian. He combined extreme idealism with realism and therefore appeared as a queer mixture to most foreigners and even to some Koreans. His personal background and outlook help explain his persistent
assertions for the unification of Korea by any means, while he played at the
same time an extremely crude game of realism, both in domestic and external politics. His toughness and shrewdness often went very far and drew much
criticism from contemporary and later observers. Often he suffered diminishing
returns when he pushed his shrewdness too far. Nonetheless, his astute and
experienced transactional skills were an important asset for the nation. It is
regrettable that other capable Korean leaders like Yŏ Un-hyŏng, Chang
Dŏk-su, and Song Chin-u did not have an adequate opportunity to play their
roles in the early years and that Kim Kyu-sik and Kim Ku's talents and ideas
could not be fully used in the later years. Only Chough Pyŏng-ok and Chang
Myŏn were able to play a limited role in the post–1948 period.

As on the Korean side, it was also true on the American side that personal
backgrounds and outlooks had much to do with the policies and actions
toward Korea under both the Truman and the Eisenhower administrations.
As Ernest R. May and others have pointed out, Truman's personal background and experience had considerable impact upon U.S. policy toward
Korea. Had he been a little more far-sighted in his approach toward Korea
in the prewar years, he would not have had to make the important decision
to intervene in the Korean War in the summer of 1950. But when he encountered the grave situation in Korea, he stood up and gave a decisive
response. For the Europe-first orientation of the United States in dealing
with the Korean situation during the entire five-year period, Acheson's Eastern elitist background had much influence, not to mention the Democratic
Party's traditional unfavorable orientation toward the Far East. His firm
and rigid outlook was often reflected in the State Department's persistently
firm policy toward the tiny East Asian republic. The Eisenhower–Dulles
team had a much different outlook. The Koreans had expected a much more
forceful policy regarding the war from President Eisenhower because of his
military background, and they were disappointed in finding him also determined to end the war without victory. Eisenhower had a special capability
for understanding and warmth, which was revealed in his restraint in dealing with President Rhee's freeing of the Korean POWs and his benevolence
in the Korean relief and rehabilitation problem. If the incident of the release

of war prisoners had happened when the Truman–Acheson team had been in charge in Washington, relations with President Rhee would have been much different. Dulles, though a lawyer like Acheson, had warmer personal feelings toward President Rhee and more understanding for the Korean people. The idealism of some of those in the State Department like Butterworth, Allison, Young, and Bond also seems to have had quite a significant positive impact upon U.S. aid policy for Korea and the policy of U.S. intervention in the Korean domestic politics.

When nations meet, it is much more than a meeting of two states; their cultures also meet. It may also be said that a cultural meeting is more fundamental and basic and that a political encounter is simply part of this meeting of cultures. Because there was little or no understanding of each other's cultures, the Korean–American political relationship experienced many difficulties. Ignorance often brought misunderstanding and even distrust between the two people, and the degree of understanding or misunderstanding tended to be asymmetrical. The Koreans, especially the group in positions of authority, understood American culture better than the Americans understood Korean culture. The Korean who understood the Americans best was President Rhee. Kim Kyu-sik, Chough Pyŏng-ok, Chang Myŏn, and Im Pyŏng-chik, all of whom received their college education in the United States, also had a good understanding of American culture. In contrast, on the other side, none of the American leaders had a similar experience with Korean culture.

In specific instances, cultural factors greatly influence a leader's perception in the process of foreign policy making. Lack of a proper understanding of other cultures creates an arbitrary perception, or a misperception, and policy based on misperceptions or arbitrary perceptions could of course easily become a wrong policy. Quite often, American leaders took almost everything President Rhee and some other Korean leaders did as peculiar, or even wrong, and little could be done to modify or eliminate this misperception problem. On the other hand, the Koreans, who had a reasonable understanding of American culture, understood the American way of thinking and acting. President Rhee understood especially well how the American system operated, and he sometimes took advantage of his knowledge in diplomacy. Many times he made reference to the American and Korean people to persuade the American leaders. International communication is also a difficult aspect of the involvement of culture in international relations. Quite often, distortion or complete misinterpretation of the content of communication occurs. English was usually the diplomatic language for Korean–American transactions. Nonetheless, some misunderstanding of the meaning in communication between the Koreans and the Americans occurred. Cultural diplomacy was very uneven. Even though the American education system and the type of American culture promoted by the U.S. Information Service was introduced to the Koreans, nothing happened in the other direction during these early post–World War II years.

An ideological conflict engulfed the whole world in one way or another for almost a half century after the end of World War II. For Korea and the United States it was impossible to avoid an intensive involvement in the conflict because the former became the battleground of the Cold War and the latter was the leader of the free world in conflict with the communist world. One possibility, taking the ideological conflict in a more relaxed way, was to take a pragmatic approach as the British people did; another possibility was the creation of a neutral state on the Korean peninsula. Of course, there were good reasons why neither alternative was explored seriously. Had Korea been located where the British Isles is located and had the Americans been more like the British, then the pragmatic approach might have had a possibility of success. Had the Koreans—especially Syngman Rhee—been rational enough to listen to Kim Kyu-sik and his associates and had both the Truman and the Eisenhower administrations handled much differently the view of the military that a neutral Korea would become a communist Korea, then a unified and neutral Korea might have had some chance.

Finally, we turn to the war and the peacemaking process, the major events during the five-year period. Although it is difficult to identify the causes or the origins of the war, naming the factors and weighting them on an intuitive basis, using the available sources, some logic, and a little imagination, is probably the best we can do. A large number of contributing factors may be enumerated, but we may have to return to at least the early modern period on the Korean peninsula and the late nineteenth-century American involvement in Korea to trace the origins of the war. It seems that among all events, actions, and inactions of Korea, the United States, and other nations, the division along the 38th parallel stands out as the major cause or origin of the war. The question of who started the war or who was most responsible for the war is not much more than an intellectual exercise at this point. But it seems that, as more and more archival materials, especially those in the former Soviet Union, become available, we return to the view that the Soviet Union played a leading role and that the war was essentially part of the U.S.–Soviet Union struggle. But given the limited and selective documents available, it must be asserted that all these views and conclusions are tentative.

For the question of whether the Korean War was a civil or an international war, it seems that, like so many other historical issues involved in the Korean war, the controversy comes both from a confusion between facts and opinions and a problem of definition. In terms of facts, the war began when one group of Koreans launched an attack on another group of Koreans, and at this point it was a civil war or a war within one nation. However, the civil war lasted only five days, and the international war began with the U.S.–U.N. intervention, which lasted over three years. It is also true that there were two states in one nation; in this sense, the war was an interstate war or a war within a nation. If the war had a dual nature, it seems to be more international than civil. Writing a decade and a half after the war,

Dean Acheson said, "Korea furnished more the locus than the cause of a trial by battle with the Soviet Union." The war should be called the Korea War or the war in Korea rather than the Korean War. There has been a controversy over whether the war was a "wrong" or a "right" war or a "unnecessary" or "necessary" war. The idea of a "wrong war" came from the view that the United States was fighting the wrong war, at the wrong place, and with the wrong enemy. The basic assumption behind this view was the notion that a superpower like the United States would only fight general or global wars, and it should not waste its energy fighting a small war. The assumption was flawed because a general war was a kind of war that nations in the nuclear age would never be able to fight, and the war in Korea was the only kind of war that nations could afford to fight. The controversy over whether the war was unnecessary or necessary is an equally interesting one. Is any war necessary? If one argues that the Korean War was necessary as a substitute for a third world war, it is little more than an after-the-fact consolation. Before arguing that Hiroshima was necessary to save millions of American and Japanese lives, one should ask those souls who perished at Hiroshima. The human race seems to have been spared from a third world war mainly because of the nuclear horror, not because of the small wars in Korea, Vietnam, or Afghanistan.[4]

The central issue of Korean–American relations during the Korea War were the contrasting objectives of the war. War objectives were necessarily tied to conditions on the battlefield, and they remained flexible for both the Koreans and the Americans. Up to the middle of September 1950, the primary objective for both nations was repelling the North Korean invasion. After the successful Inch'ŏn landing operation, the objective became the unification of Korea "to restore international peace and security" on the Korean peninsula. When faced with communist China's intervention in the winter of 1950, the United States switched its primary war objective back to the original one. In contrast, the Koreans insisted upon retaining the second war objective, and the two nations interests began to diverge. The invariable Korean position seems to have been based partly on opportunism, that is, taking advantage of the favorable situation on the battlefield, and partly on the strong desire for national reunification combined with a belief that since the division of Korea had been effected by the great powers, Korean unity should be restored by the same great powers. For the Americans, modification of the war objectives was closely connected to a basic strategy for the nation's security that included not expanding the war but limiting it to the Korean peninsula. For the Koreans, it was almost impossible to abandon the nation's objective of achieving reunification; for the Americans, a general war involving nuclear weapons was to be avoided at all cost. The Korean ideal objective was too far from the reality of the situation. The Americans also found it difficult to limit the war and accept the end of the conflict without victory, but they successfully resisted the temptation to follow the logic of war and allow it to expand. Caught in the situation of being a weak ally of a powerful nation, the Koreans did not have much choice but to yield in the end, and they conceded. During the truce negotiation, the Koreans protested and even threatened to use the tiny leverage they had available—withdrawing the ROK troops from the U.N. command and marching north—but they eventually yielded in exchange for the best possible assurance of future security, a mutual security treaty.[5]

Many consider the Korean War a tragic war. With close to three million casualties, five million refugees, and the nearly complete destruction of Korean cities and villages on the whole peninsula except for a small area around Pusan, the Koreans considered it one of the most destructive wars in modern times. The destruction was not confined to human life and property. The political system in the south became even more authoritarian, anticommunist slogans proliferated after the war, and the government was eventually taken over by the military. Meanwhile, Kim Il Sung's regime in the north became more and more dictatorial in the postwar years. The social impact of the war was also great: The war expedited the decline of the landowning class and a traditional family-centered Confucian value system and encouraged the rise of a spirit of speculation and risk taking along with increased individualism.

Yet the war also had some salutary effects. The destruction of the economic infrastructure made the beginning of an industrial and capitalistic economy much easier, and a new culture, especially in literature and art, grew out of the destruction of the old. The war in Korea had much less impact on American society than it did on Korea. Nevertheless, in the realm of the military, it was significant. The cost of the war for the United States was sizable because it assumed responsibility for all the war expenses of the U.N. war effort. The war also played the important role of catalyst for improving the ability of the American armed forces to fight the Cold War in the following decades. Despite these positive consequences of the war, its tragic nature still remains. As someone said, the events unfolded with "the inexorability of a Greek tragedy."[6]

If we compare the relationship between Korea and the United States at two time points in time—1948 and 1953—we find a marked difference. In the summer of 1948, the Korean situation had deteriorated because of the arbitrary creation of two states within one nation, and the future of the new republic in the south was very uncertain. With the U.S. troop withdrawal and very limited military and economic aid from the United States, the position of the almost defenseless republic, which had only a small security force to maintain domestic order, looked precarious. However, when the invasion from the communist north came, the Americans returned to the scene and pushed the aggressor north of the 38th parallel. When the war ended in the summer of 1953 with the *status quo ante bellum*, the Korean peninsula was still divided, there was a large communist Chinese force in the north, and the situation appeared worse than it had been five years earlier. But this time, the Republic of Korea had a formal commitment from the Americans to return if the communists again invaded, and they were assured of U.S. aid to build a strong ROK security force and to rebuild the shattered economy. Thus the division of the peninsula remained, but South Korea in 1953 enjoyed greater security than it had in 1948. If the Koreans had in 1948 the U.S. assurance they obtained five years later, the tragic war would certainly have been avoided. Both Koreans and the Americans paid a high price for this lesson.

The final, important question is, as two very unequal and different partners, how well did the Republic of Korea and the United States manage their relationship during the five-year period of peace and war from 1948 to 1953? As one of the two superpowers, the United States did not hesitate to use its strength in dealing with the junior partner; the Republic of Korea, as a small and weak nation, naturally tried to minimize her disadvantage and maximize her advantage in relations with her powerful ally. At the same time, both nations were cautious not to push their inclinations too far, and they moderated their power positions. As the leader of the free world, the United States always kept, both in time of peace and war, the whole world as its scope of concern in its relations with other powers. At least partly because of its global perspective, it withdrew its troops from Korea in 1949. Yet although it was penurious in allocating aid to Korea, it intervened in the war in 1950, and limited the war to the Korean peninsula, at last making peace with the communists but without victory. Korea, as a small power, narrowly focused its national goals and at least partly because of this narrow nationalistic focus, hoped the U.S. troops would stay longer in the country and wanted much larger U.S. economic and military aid. They insisted that U.N. forces should continue fighting until Korean unification was achieved. The Americans did not hesitate, however, to recognize the peculiar position of Korea as a nation facing directly the huge communist power bloc; the Koreans for their part recognized the global responsibility of the United States and trimmed their wishes. The Republic of Korea revealed well her sensitivity for her newly obtained sovereignty; the Americans also understood well this Korean sensitivity. Like other small nations, the Koreans tended to take moralistic and normative positions in their diplomacy; the Americans, with a long tradition of a similar inclination, took a tolerant posture toward its small ally. Most important, beyond the differences in size and strength, the two nations recognized the complementary nature of their positions: The Koreans needed help from the great American resources and prestige; the Americans saw clearly the role of the Republic of Korea as a bastion against communism with its eighteen-division fighting force and the people's firm dedication to the free world. On balance, the Republic of Korea and the United States, though very unequal and different, fared well in general in time of peace and war in dealing with each other as good partners.[7]

NOTES

1. Editorial note, *Foreign Relations of the United States (FRUS), 1952–1954*, 15, pt. 2: 1464–1465; memorandum of conversation by the Director of the Office of Northeast Asian Affairs (Young), August 5, 8, 1953, ibid., pp. 1471, 1491; *Mutual Defense Treaty with Korea: Hearings before the Committee on Foreign Relations*, 83d Cong, 2d sess., January 13 and 14, 1954; Syngman Rhee to Dwight D. Eisenhower, January 27, 1954, Eisenhower Library, Eisenhower Papers, Ann Whitman File, box 33.

2. Memorandum of conversation by the Director of the Office of Northeast Asian Affairs (Young), August 5, 1953, *FRUS, 1952–1954*, 15, pt. 2: 1468–1469; Hull to the Joint Chiefs of Staff, October 21, 1953, ibid., p. 1544; Dean to the Department of State, October 24, November 1, December 8, 1953, ibid., pp. 1559, 1578, 1651; editorial note, ibid., p. 1588; memorandum of conversation by Elizabeth A. Brown of the Office of United Nations Political and Security Affairs, ibid., pp. 1666–1672; the Deputy Representative of the Political Conference (Young) to the Department of State, January 23, 26, 1954, ibid., pp. 1730–1733, 1735–1737; Pyŏn Yŏng-t'ae, *Oekyo yŏrok* (Diplomatic memoir) (Seoul: Hanguk Ilbosa, 1959), p. 57.

3. Eisenhower to Rhee, March 20, 1954, Eisenhower Library, Eisenhower Papers, Ann Whitman File, box 6; Rhee to Eisenhower, April 8, 1954, in Seoul to the Secretary of State, April 8, 1954, ibid., Dulles–Herter series, box 2; Geneva to the Secretary of State, May 20, 1954, ibid.; James C. Hagerty diary, June 23, 1954 entry, Eisenhower Library, James C. Hagerty papers, box 1; editorial note, *FRUS, 1952–1954*, 15, part 2: 1750; Pyŏn Yŏng-t'ae, *Oekyo yŏrok*, pp. 58–122; Ra Jong-il, "The Politics of Conference: The Political Conference at Geneva, April 26–June 15, 1954" (manuscript, July 1995).

4. Dean Acheson, *The Korean War* (New York: Norton, 1969), p. 3; Thomas C. Schelling, "The Conventional Status of Nuclear Weapons" (manuscript, April 1995); Melvin Small, *Was a War Necessary?: National Security and U.S. Entry into War* (Beverly Hills, Calif.: Sage, 1980), pp. 269–294; William Stueck, "In Search of Essences: Labeling the Korean War" (manuscript, July 1995).

5. Anatol Rapapport, "The Study of War as an Institution" (manuscript, September 1995); Robert Keohane, "Contested Commitments in United States Foreign Policy, 1789–1989" (manuscript, September 1995).

6. For a systematic study of the consequences of the Korean War, see Son Ho-chŏl and others, *Hankuk Chonchaengkwa Nam-Puk Han sahoeŭi kuchochak pyŏnhwa* (The Korean War and the structural changes of the South and North Korean society), Hankuk yŏnku series, vol. 3 (Seoul: Kyŏngnam Taehakkyo Kŭktong Munche Yŏnkuso, 1991).

7. See R. P. Branson, ed., *The Other Powers: Studies in Foreign Policies of Small States* (London: Allen and Unwin, 1973), pp. 13–28; Maurice A. East, "Size and Foreign Policy Behavior," *World Politics* 26 (1973): 556–576; Annette Baker Fox, *The Power of Small States: Diplomacy in World War II* (Chicago: University of Chicago Press, 1959): Pak Chang-jin, "The Influence of Small States upon the Superpowers: United States–South Korean Republic as a Case Study, 1950–1953," *World Politics* 28 (1975): 97–117.

Bibliography

MANUSCRIPT AND ARCHIVAL COLLECTIONS

The Citadel Archives, Charleston, South Carolina

Clark, Mark W.

Dwight D. Eisenhower Library, Abilene, Kansas

Manuscript

Eisenhower, Dwight D., as President of the United States, 1953–1961 (Ann Whitman File)

Hagerty, James C., White House Office of Special Assistant to the President for the National Security Affairs

Oral History Transcript

Briggs, Ellis
Robertson, Walter

Library of Congress, Washington, D.C.

Alsop, Joseph, and Alsop, Stewart

Douglas MacArthur Memorial Archives and Library, Norfolk, Virginia

Almond, Edward M.
Lowe, Frank E.

MacArthur, Douglas
Willoughby, Charles A.

National Archives, Washington, D.C.

Record Group 59, Records of the Department of State
Record Group 218, Records of the Operations Division, U.S. Army
Record Group 273, National Security Council Policy Papers
Record Group 286, Records of the Agency for International Development
Record Group 319, Records of the Joint Chiefs of Staff
Record Group 469, Records of the U.S. Foreign Assistance Agencies

The Republic of Korea, Ministry of Foreign Affairs, Seoul, Korea

Diplomatic Documents

Harry S. Truman Library, Independence, Missouri

Manuscript

Acheson, Dean
Ayers, Eben A.
Connelly, Matthew J.
Elsey, George M.
Murphy, Charles S.
Pace, Frank K., Jr.
Stein, Harold
Thayer, Charles W.
Truman, Harry S.
Truman, Harry S., President's Secretary's File
White House Central File
Webb, James

Oral History Interview Transcript

Bancroft, Harding F.
Barrett, Robert W.
Bell, David E.
Draper, William H.
Elsey, George M.
Griffith, Paul H.
Harriman, W. Averrell
Hickerson, John D.
Keyserling, Leon H.
Lawton, Frederick J.
Lightner, E. Allan, Jr.
Lovett, Robert
Muccio, John J.
Murphy, Charles
Nixon, Robert G.
Pace, Frank K., Jr.

INTERVIEWS

Chang, Do-yŏng, February 25, 1988
Chŭng, Il-kwŏn, July 18, 1987
Han, P'yo-wook, July 8, 1987
Henderson, Gregory, July 29, 1987
Paik, Sŭn-yŭp, July 14, 1987
Paik, Tu-chin, July 8, 1987
Rhee, Francisca, July 10, 1987

GOVERNMENT AND INTERNATIONAL ORGANIZATION PUBLICATIONS

The Republic of Korea

Shichŏng wŏlpo (Administrative monthly report), January 5, 1949–June 20, 1950.

Kongpoch'ŏ (Public Information Office)

Hankuk Chŏnchaeng: Chŭngŏnkwa charyo (The Korean War: Testimony and documents), 1992.

Oemupu (Ministry of Foreign Affairs)

Hankuk oekyo 30-nyŏn (Thirty years of Korean diplomacy), 1979.
Oekyo t'ongpo (Foreign Affairs Bulletin), 1952–1954.

Yukkun Ponpu (Army)

Hankuk Chŏnchaeng saryo (The Korean War: Historical documents), 9 vols., 1985–1986.
Hankuk Chŏnchaeng saryo, 81–90, chŏnhu myŏngryŏng (The Korean War: Historical documents, 81–90, postwar orders), 1989–1990.
Hankuk Chŏnchaeng saryo, 91–94, chakchŏn ilki (The Korean War: Historical documents, 91–94, operations diary), 1990.

Yukkun Ponpu, Kunsa Yŏnku-sil (The Army, Military History Office)

Hankuk Chŏnchaeng saryo (The Korean War: Historical documents), 1991.

United States

Congress

Congressional Record, 1948–1954 (vols. 94–100).

House of Representatives

Korean Aid. Hearings before the House Committee on Foreign Affairs on HR 5330, 1949.
Relief and Rehabilitation in Korea. Hearings before a subcommittee of the Committee on Government Operations, 83d Cong., 2d sess., 1954.
Relief and Rehabilitation in Korea. 23d Intermediate Report, 1954.

Senate

Military Situation in the Far East. Hearings from the Committee on Armed Services and the Committee on Foreign Affairs, 82d Cong, 1st sess, 1951.
The United States and the Korean Problems, Documents, 1943–1953, 1953.

Department of State

Department of State Bulletin, vols. 9, 12–31 (1945–1954).
Foreign Relations of the United States (FRUS), 1942, vol. 1; *Conferences at Cairo and Teheran, 1943; 1944*, vol. 5; *1945*, vol. 6; *The Conference of Berlin*, 2 vols., 1945; *Conferences at Malta and Yalta, 1945; 1946*, vol. 8; *1947*, vol. 6; *1948*, vol. 6; *1949*, vol. 7; *1950*, vol. 7; *1951*, vol. 7; *1952–1954*, vol. 15, *Korea*.
Korea 1945 to 1948: A Report on Political and Economic Resources with Selected Documents. Publication no. 3305, Far Eastern Series no. 28, 1948.
Korean Problems at the Geneva Conference, April 26–June 15, 1954, 1954.
Moscow Meeting of Foreign Ministers, December 16–26, 1945, 1946.

General Services Administration

Public Papers of the Presidents of the United States: Harry S. Truman, 1948–1953, 1965.
Public Papers of the President of the United States: Dwight D. Eisenhower, 1953–1954, 1960.

United Nations

General Assembly. *Official Records, 1948–1953*.

PERIODICALS

Donga Ilbo, 1948–1954.
New York Times, 1948–1954.

BOOKS AND ARTICLES

Acheson, Dean. *The Korean War*. New York: Norton, 1969.
———. *Present at the Creation: My Years in the State Department*. New York: Norton, 1969.
Alexander, Revin. *Korea, the First War We Lost*. New York: Hippocerene Books, 1986.
Ambrose, Stephen E. *Eisenhower, the President*. Vol. 2. New York: Simon & Shuster, 1984.
Appleman, Roy Edgar. *Eisenhower in Korea: The Chinese Confront MacArthur*. College Station: Texas A & M University Press, 1989.
———. *Ridgway Duels for Korea*. College Station: Texas A & M University Press, 1990.
———. *South to Naktong, North to Yalu, June–November 1950*. Washington, D.C.: Office of Chief Military History, Department of the Army, 1961.
Bacchus, Wilfred. "The Relationship between Conflict and Peace Negotiations." *Orbis* 17 (Summer 1973): 545–574.

Bailey, Sydney D. *The Korean Armistice*. New York: St. Martin's Press, 1992.

Bajanov, Evgueni. "Assessing the Policies of the Korean War." *Cold War International History Project Bulletin* 6-7 (Winter 1995-1996): 54, 87-91.

Baldwin, Franklin, ed. *Without Parallel: The American-Korean Relations since 1945*. New York: Random House, 1973.

Berger, Carl. *The Korea Knot: A Military History-Political History*. Philadelphia: University of Pennsylvania Press, 1957.

Bernstein, Barton J. "New Light on the Korean War." *The International History Review* 3, no. 2 (April 1981): 256-277.

———. "Syngman Rhee: The Pawn as Rook—The Struggle to End the Korean War." *Bulletin of Concerned Asian Scholars* 10, no. 1 (1978): 38-47.

Blair, Clay. *The Forgotten War: America in Korea, 1950-1953*. New York: Time Books, 1987.

Blum, Robert M. *Drawing the Line: The Origins of the American Containment Policy in East Asia*. New York: Norton, 1982.

Bohlen, Charles E. *Witness to History, 1929-1969*. New York: Norton, 1973.

Borg, Dorothy and Waldo Heinrich, eds. *Uncertain Years: Chinese-American Relations, 1947-50*. New York: Columbia University Press, 1960.

Brands, Henry W., Jr. *Cold Warriors: Eisenhower's Generation and American Foreign Policy*. New York: Columbia University Press, 1988.

Brown, William Adams, Jr. *American Foreign Assistance*. Washington, D.C.: Brookings Institution, 1953.

Buhite, Russell D. *Decisions at Yalta: An Appraisal of Summit Diplomacy*. Wilmington, Del.: Scholarly Resources Press, 1986.

———. *Soviet-American Relations in Asia, 1945-1954*. Norman: University of Oklahoma Press, 1981.

Burnham, James. *The Struggle for the World*. New York: John Day, 1947.

Calingaert, Daniel. "Nuclear Weapons and the Korean War." *The Journal of Strategic Studies* 11, no. 2 (June 1988): 177-202.

Caridi, Ronald James. *The Korean War and American Politics: The Republican Party as a Case Study*. Philadelphia: University of Pennsylvania Press, 1968.

Carpenter, William M. "The Korean War: A Strategic Perspective Thirty Years Later." *Comparative Strategy* 2, no. 4 (1980): 335-353.

Chang, Myŏn. *Han alŭi mili chukchiankonŭn: Chang paksa hoekorok* (Unless a grain of wheat is sacrificed: Dr. Chang's memoir). Seoul: Kidokkyo Ch'ulp'ansa, 1967.

Chay, Jongsuk. *Diplomacy of Asymmetry: Korean-American Relations to 1910*. Honolulu: University of Hawaii Press, 1990.

———, ed. *The Problems and Prospects of American-East Asian Relations*. Boulder, Colo: Westview Press, 1977.

Chay, Jongsuk, and Thomas E. Ross, eds. *Buffer States in World Politics*. Boulder, Colo.: Westview Press, 1987.

Chen, Frederick Foo. *The Opening of Korea: A Study of Chinese Diplomacy, 1876-1885*. New York: Shoe String Press, 1967.

Chen, Jian. *China's Road to the Korean War: The Making of the Sino-American Confrontation*. New York: Columbia University Press, 1994.

———. "The Sino-Soviet Alliance and China's Entry into the Korean War." The Woodrow Wilson Center Cold War International History Project, Working Paper no. 1, 1992.

Chin, Dŏk-kyu, and others. *1950-nyŏntaeŭi insik* (The understanding of the 1950s). Seoul: Hankilsa. 1981.

Cho, Soon-sung. *Korea in World Politics, 1940–1950: An Evaluation of American Responsibility.* Berkeley and Los Angeles: University of California Press, 1967.

Choe, Chang-chip, ed. *Haepang chŏnhusaŭi insik* (Understanding of the history of the pre- and postliberation era). Vol. 4. Seoul: Hankilsa, 1989.

Choe, Dŏk-shin. *Naeka kyŏkkŭn P'anmunjŏm* (The P'anmunjŏm I have experienced). Seoul: Samkusa, 1955.

Choe, Sang-ryong. "Mi kunchŏngŭi ch'oki chŏmryŏng chŏngch'aek yŏnku" (A study of the initial policy of the U.S. military occupation). *Kodae Munhwa* 22 (1983): 120–128.

Chŏng, Yong-sŏk. *Mikukŭi tae-Han chŏngch'aek, 1945–1980* (U.S. policies toward Korea, 1945–1980). Seoul: Ilchokak, 1976.

Chough, Pyŏng-ok. *Naŭi hoekorok* (My memoir). Seoul: Minkyosa, 1959.

———. *T'ŭksa UN kihaeng* (Special mission to the U.N.). Seoul: Tokhŭng Sŏlim, 1949.

Chu, Hŏn-su. *Taehanminkuk Imsichŏngpusa* (History of the Korean Provisional Government). Seoul: Toknip Kinyŏmkwan, Hankuk Toknip Undongsa Yŏnkuso, 1989.

Chŭng, Il-kwŏn. *Chŭng Il-kwŏn hoekorok: 6.25 pirok; chŏnchaengkwa hyuchŏn* (Chŭng Il-kwŏn memoir: Confidential record of the Korean War; the war and the armistice). Seoul: Donga Ilbosa, 1986.

Clark, Mark D. *From the Danube to the Yalu.* New York: Harper and Brothers, 1954.

Cohen, Warren I. *Dean Rusk.* Totowa, N.J.: Cooper Square, 1980.

Collins, Joseph Lawton. *War in Peacetime: The History and Lessons of Korea.* Boston: Houghton Mifflin, 1969.

Cumings, Bruce. *The Origins of the Korean War: Liberation and the Emergence of Separate Regimes, 1945–1947.* Princeton, N.J.: Princeton University Press, 1981.

———, ed. *Child of Conflict: The Korean–American Relations, 1943–1953.* Seattle: University of Washington Press, 1983.

———. *The Origins of the Korean War.* Vol. 2, *The Roaring of the Cataract, 1947–1950.* Princeton, N.J.: Princeton University Press, 1990.

Denissov, Valeri. "Korean War of 1950–1953: Thoughts about the Conflict's Causes and Actors." Manuscript, 1995.

Deweed, H. A. "Strategic Surprises in the Korean War." *Orbis* 6 (Fall 1962): 435–452.

Dingman, Roger. "Atomic Diplomacy during the Korean War." *International Security* 13 (Winter 1988–1989): 79–91.

Dobbs, Charles M. "Limiting Room to Maneuver: The Korean Assistance Act of 1949." *Historian* 48 (August 1986): 525–538.

———. *The Unwanted Symbol: American Foreign Policy, the Cold War, and Korea, 1945–1950.* Kent, Ohio: Kent State University Press, 1981.

Esthus, Raymond A. *Theodore Roosevelt and Japan.* Seattle: University of Washington Press, 1967.

Etzold, Thomas H., and John L. Gaddis, eds. *Containment: Documents on American Policy and Strategy, 1945–1950.* New York: Columbia University Press, 1978.

Falk, Richard A. *A Global Approach to National Policy*. Cambridge, Mass.: Harvard University Press, 1975.

Falk, Stanley L. "The National Security Council under Truman, Eisenhower, and Kennedy." *Political Science Quarterly* 79 (September 1964): 403–434.

Farrar, Peter N. "Britain's Proposal for a Buffer Zone South of the Yalu in November 1950: Was It a Neglected Opportunity to End the Fighting in Korea?" *Journal of Contemporary History* 18 (April 1983): 327–351.

Ferrell, Robert H. *Harry S. Truman: A Life*. Columbia: University of Missouri Press, 1994.

Foot, Rosemary. *The Wrong War: American Policy and the Dimensions of the Korean Conflict, 1950–1953*. Ithaca, N.Y.: Cornell University Press, 1985.

———. "Anglo-American Relations in the Korean Crisis: The British Effort to Avert an Expanded War, December 1950–January 1951. *Diplomatic History* 10 (Winter 1986): 43–57.

———. "Nuclear Coercion and the Ending of the Korean Conflict." *International Security* 13 (Winter 1988–1989): 92–112.

———. *A Substitute for Victory: The Politics of Peacemaking at the Korean Armistice Talks*. Ithaca, N.Y.: Cornell University Press, 1990.

Friedman, Edward. "Nuclear Blackmail and the End of the Korean War." *Modern China* 1 (January 1975): 75–91.

Futrell, Robert Frank. *The United States Air Force in Korea, 1950–1953*. Rev. ed. Washington, D.C.: Office of Air Force History, U.S. Air Force, 1983.

Gaddis, John Lewis. *The Long Peace: Inquiries into the History of the Cold War*. New York: Oxford University Press, 1987.

———. *The Strategy of Containment*. New York: Oxford University Press, 1982.

———. *The United States and the End of the Cold War: Implications, Reconsiderations, Provocations*. New York: Oxford University Press, 1994.

———. *We Know Now: Rethinking Cold War History*. New York: Clarendon Press, Oxford, 1998.

Gaenslen, Fritz. "Culture and Decision Making in China, Japan, Russia, and the United States." *World Politics* 39 (1986): 78–103.

Gallop Poll. Vol. 2, *Public Opinion, 1949–1953*. New York: Random House, 1972.

Gardner, Lloyd C., ed. *The Korean War*. New York: The New York Times, 1972.

George, Alexander L. "American Policy-Making and the North Korean Aggression." *World Politics* 7 (1954): 209–232.

———. *The Chinese Communist Army in Action: The Korean War and Its Aftermath*. New York: Columbia University Press, 1967.

———. *Presidential Decision Making in Foreign Policy*. Boulder: Westview Press, 1980.

George, Alexander L., Phillip Fairley, and Alexander Dallin. *U.S.–Soviet Security Cooperation, Achievement, Failures, Lessons*. New York: Oxford University Press, 1988.

Goncharov, Sergei, John W. Lewis, and Xue Litai. *Uncertain Partners: Stalin, Mao, and the Korean War*. Stanford: Stanford University Press, 1993.

Goodrich, Leland Mathew. *Korea: A Study of U.S. Policy in the United Nations*. New York: Council on Foreign Relations, 1956.

Gordenker, Leon. *The United Nations and the Peaceful Unification of Korea: The Politics of Field Operations, 1947–1950*. The Hague: Nijhoff, 1959.

Grey, Arthur L., Jr. "The Thirty-Eighth Parallel." *Foreign Affairs* 29 (April 1951): 482–487.

Gunter, Bischof and Stephen E. Ambrose. *Eisenhower: A Centenary Assessment.* Baton Rouge: Louisiana State University Press, 1995.

Halperin, Morton H. "The Limiting Process in the Korean War." *Political Science Quarterly* 78 (March 1963): 13–39.

———. "Nuclear Weapons and Limited War." *Journal of Conflict Resolution* 5 (1961): 146–166.

Hamby, Aronzo L. *Man of the People: A Life of Harry S. Truman.* New York: Oxford University Press, 1995.

Han, Bae-ho. "Han-Mi pangŏ choyak ch'ekyŏlŭi hyŏpsang kwachŏng" (The process of negotiations for the Korean–American Defense Treaty) *Kunsa* 4 (1982): 163–171.

———. "50-nyŏntae chŏnhuŭi Mi kŭktong chŏngch'aek" (The strategy of the United States in the Far East around the 1950s). *Kotae Munhwa* 22 (1983): 129–137.

Han, P'yo-wook. *Han-mi oekyo yoramki* (The early years of the Korean–American diplomatic relationship). Seoul: Chungang Ilposa, 1984.

Han, Sung-chu. *Che 2 Konghwakukkwa Hankukŭi minchuchui* (The Second Republic and Korean democracy). Seoul: Chongro Sŏchŏk, 1983.

Han, Wan-sang and others. *4.19 Hyokmyongnon I* (Study on the April 19 Revolution I). Seoul: Ilwŏlsŏkak, 1983.

Hankuk Chŏngch'ioekyosa Hakhoe. *Chehan chŏnchaeng ŭrosŏŭi Hankuk Chŏnchaeng* (The Korean War as a limited war). Seoul: P'yŏngminsa, 1989.

Hankuk Chŏngshin Munhwa Yŏnkuwŏn, ed. *Hankuk tongnip untongsa charyochip* (Collection of source materials for the history of the Korean independence movement). Seoul: Pakyŏngsa, 1983.

Hankuk Sahoehakhoe. *Hankuk Chŏnchengkwa Hankuk sahoe pyŏntong* (The Korean War and its social changes in Korea). Seoul: Tolpit, 1992.

Hankuk Totŏk Chŏngch'i Yŏnkuso, ed. *Hankuk Chŏnchaengŭi yŏksachŏk chomyŏng* (Historical clarification of the Korean War). Seoul: Hankuk Totŏk Chŏngch'i Yŏnkuso, 1990.

Hao, Yufun, and Zhai Zhihai. "China's Decision to Enter the Korean War: History Revisited." *China Quarterly* 121 (March 1990): 94–115.

Hastings, Max. *The Korean War.* New York: Simon and Schuster, 1957.

Heller, Francis H., ed. *The Korean War: A 25-Year Perspective.* Lawrence: Regent Press of Kansas, 1977.

Henderson, Gregory. *Korea: The Politics of Vortex.* Cambridge, Mass.: Harvard University Press, 1968.

Hickey, Michael. *The Korean War: The West Confront Communism.* London: John Muray, 1999.

Hickman, Bert G. *The Korean War and the United States Economic Activity, 1950–1952.* National Bureau of Economic Research, Occasional Paper no. 49, 1955.

Hŏ, Man-ho. "Hankuk Chŏnchaengŭi chehan yoindŭlkwa chi-chŏnghakchŏk chakyong" (The reasons for restriction in the Korean War and the role of the geopolitical factor). *Kukpang Ronch'ong* 15 (1991): 120–135.

Hoyt, Edwin P. *The Day the Chinese Attacked.* New York: McGraw-Hill, 1990.

———. "The United States Reaction on the Korea Attack: A Study of the United Nations Charter as a Factor in American Policy-Making." *American Journal of International Law* 55 (January 1961): 45–76.

Hughes, Emmet John. *The Ordeal of Power: A Political Memoir of the Eisenhower Years.* New York: Atheneum, 1963.

Hunt, Michael H. "Beijing and the Korean Crisis, June 1950–June 1951" *Political Science Quarterly* 107, no. 3 (Fall 1992): 453–478.

Huston, James A. *Guns and Butter, Power and Rice: U.S. Logistics in the Korean War.* Selinsgrove, Pa.: Susquehauna University Press, 1989.

Im, Pyŏng-chik. *Im Pyŏng-chik hoekorok: Kŭntae oekyoŭi imyŏnsa* (Im Pyŏng-chik memoirs: The inside history of modern diplomacy). Seoul: Yŏwŏnsa, 1956.

———. "Rhee Paksawa tŏpulŏ Pusankachi" (To Pusan with Dr. Rhee). *Sindonga* (June 1970): 174–178.

Immerman, Richard H. *John Foster Dulles: Piety, Pragmatism, and Power in U.S. Foreign Relations.* Wilmington, Del.: Scholarly Resources Press, 1998.

James, D. Clayton. *Refighting the Last War: Command and Crises in Korea, 1950–1953.* New York: Free Press, 1993.

Jeon, Hyun-su, and Gyoo Kahng. "The Stykov Diaries: New Evidence on Soviet Policy in Korea." *Cold War International History Project Bulletin* 6–7 (Winter 1995): 69, 92–93.

Jervis, Robert. "The Impact of the Korean War on the Cold War." *Journal of Conflict Resolution* 24 (December 1980): 563.

Johnson, U. Alexis. *The Right Hand of Power.* Englewood Cliffs, N.J.: Prentice Hall, 1984.

Joy, C. Turner. *How Communists Negotiate.* New York: Macmillan, 1955.

———. *Negotiating while Fighting: The Diary of Admiral C. Turner Joy at the Korean Armistice Conference.* Stanford: Hoover Institute, 1978.

Kang, Man-kil, ed. *Haepang chŏnhusaŭi insik* (Understanding of the history of the pre- and postliberation era). Vol. 2. Seoul: Hankilsa, 1985.

———. *4-wol hyŏkmyŏngron* (April Revolution theory). Seoul: Hankilsa, 1983.

Kang, Mun-pong. "6.25 chŏnyaŭi Kukkun, Kukkunŭi changpiwa hunryŏnŭl chungsimŭ-ro" (The Korean Army on the eve of the Korean War, with an emphasis on the equipment and the raining). *Chŏnghun* 30 (1976): 20–25.

Kaufman, Burton I. *The Korean Conflict.* Westport, Conn.: Greenwood Press, 1999.

———. *The Korean War: Challenge in Crisis, Credibility, and Command.* New York: Knopf, 1986.

Keefer, Edward C. "President Dwight D. Eisenhower and the End of the Korean War." *Diplomatic History* 10 (Summer 1986): 267–289.

———. "The Truman Administration and the South Korean Political Crisis of 1952: Diplomacy's Failure?" *Pacific Historical Review* 60 (May 1991): 145–168.

Kim, Chae-myŏng. "Rhee Syngman Seoul t'alch'ulki" (A story of Rhee Syngman's escape from Seoul). *Wŏlkan Kyŏnghyang* (June 1987): 194–221.

Kim, Chŏm-kon. *The Korean War: The First Comprehensive Account of the Historical Background and Development of the Korean War, 1950–1953.* Seoul: Kwangmyŏng, 1973.

Kim, Chong-pil. "Tongnan chŏnya nanŭn yukpon tangchik changkyoyŏtta" (I was an officer on duty at the Korean Army Headquarters on the eve of the war). *Wŏlkan Chungang* (June 1968): 168–183.

Kim, Chull-baum. *Chinsilkwa chŭngŏn: 40-nyŏnmane palkinŭn Hankuk Chŏnchaengŭi chinsang* (The truth and testimony: Facts about the Korean War, revelated 40 years later). Seoul: Ŭlyu Munhwasa, 1990.

————. "A Triangle of Kim, Stalin, and Mao in the Korean War." Manuscript, 1995.

————, ed. *Korea and the Cold War*. Claremont, Calif.: Regina Books, 1993.

Kim, Hakjoon. *Hankuk Chŏnchaeng: Wŏnin, kwachŏng, hyuchŏn, yŏnghyang* (The Korean War: The causes, the processes, the armistice, and the impacts). Seoul: Pakyŏngsa, 1989.

————. "Russian Foreign Ministry Documents on the Origins of the Korean War." Manuscript, 1995.

Kim, Myŏng-ki. *The Korean War and International Law*. Claremont, Calif.: Paige Press, 1991.

Kim, Yong-myŏng. "Hankuk chŏngch'i pyŏntongkwa Mikuk" (Political changes in Korea and the United States). *Hankuk Chŏngch'ihak Hoepo* 22 (1988): 97.

Kolko, Joyce, and Gabriel Kolko. *The Limits of Power: The World and United States Foreign Policy, 1945–1954*. New York: Harper and Row, 1972.

Koo, Youngnok. *Hankuk kukka iik: Oekyo chŏngch'iŭi hyŏnsilkwa isang* (The national interests of Korea: The reality and the ideal in international politics). Seoul: Pŏpmunsa, 1995.

Ku, Tae-yŏl. "2 cha taechŏnchung Chungkukŭi Hankuk chŏngch'aek: Kukmintang chŏngkwŏnŭi Imchŏng chŏngch'aekŭl chungsimŭro" (China's Korea policy during the Second World War: With an emphasis on the Koumingtang's policy toward the Korean Interim Government). *Hankuk Chŏngch'i Hoepo* 28 (1994): 747–769.

Kukche Yŏksahakhoe Hankuk Wiwŏnhoe (KYHW). *Han-mi sukyo 100-nyŏnsa* (The 100-year history of Korean–American relations). Seoul: Kukche Yŏksahakhoe Hankuk Wiwŏnhoe, 1982.

Kwak, Tae-hwan, John Chay, Cho Soon Sung, and Shannon McCune, eds. *U.S.–Korean Relations, 1882–1982*. Seoul: Kyongnam University Press, 1982.

La Feber, Walter. "NATO and the Korean War: A Context." *Diplomatic History* 13 (Fall 1989): 461–478.

Langley, Michael. *Inch'on: MacArthur's Last Triumph*. London: Bastford, 1979.

Lee, Chae-jin, ed. *The Korean War: 40-Year Perspective*. Claremont, Calif.: The Kock Center for International and Strategic Studies, Claremont Makennan College, 1991.

Lee, Chong-o, and others. *1950-nyŏntae Hankuk sahoewa 4.19 Hyŏkmyŏng: Hankuk hyŏntaesaŭi ihae II* (The Korean society in the 1950s and the April 19 Revolution: Understanding of the modern Korean history II). Seoul: Taeamsa, 1991.

Lee, Chong-sik. "Ryŏ Un-hyŏngkwa Kŏnkuk Chunpi Wiwŏnhoe" (Ryŏ Un-hyŏng and the Kŏnkuk Chunpi Wiwŏnhoe). *Yŏksa Hakpo* 134–135 (1992): 25–76.

Lee, Hyo-chae. *Hankuk oekyo chŏngch'aekŭi isangkwa hyŏnsil: haepang 8-nyŏn minchok kaltŭngŭi pansŏng* (The ideal and reality of Korean foreign policy: Reflections on the nation's conflict during the eight-year post-liberation era). Seoul: Pŏmmunsa, 1969.

Lee, Hyŏn-hi. *Samil Tokrip Untongkwa Imsi Chŏngpuŭi pŏmt'ongsŏng* (The March 1 Movement and legitimacy of the Korean Provisisonal Government). Seoul: Tongpang Tosŏ, 1987.

Lee, Ki-pong. "Pukhan t'aengknŭn chŏchihalsu isŏtta" (The North Korean tanks could be stopped). *Donga Ilbo* 11 (June 23, 1993): 4–6.

Lee, Wŏn-sŏl. *The United States and Division of Korea in 1945.* Seoul: Kyŏnghi University Press, 1982.

Lee, Yŏng-hwan. "Yalta checheŭi hyŏngsŏngkwa Han Panto puntan yoin" (Formulation of the Yalta system and the reasons for the division of the Korean Peninsula). *Kukche Chŏngch'i Nonch'ong. T'ŭkpyŏlho: Hankuk Chŏnchaengŭi yŏksachŏk chaech'onmyŏng* (1990): 71–119.

Lee, Yul-mo. "The Merits and Demerits of American Assistance to Korea." *Koreana Quarterly* 6 (1964): 40–53.

Lee, Yur-bok. *Diplomatic Relations between the United States and Korea, 1866–1887.* New York: Humanities Press, 1970.

Leffler, Melvin P. "The American Conception of National Security and the Beginning of the Cold War, 1945–1948." *American Historical Review* 89 (April 1984): 346–400.

Li, Hai-wen. "How and When Did China Decide to Enter the Korean War?" *Korea and World Affairs* 18 (Spring 1994): 83–98.

Li, Xialing, and others, trans. "Chinese Generals Recall the Korean War." *Chinese Historians* 7 (Spring and Fall 1994): 123–162.

Li, Xialing, and Glen Tracy, annot. and trans. "Mao's Telegrams during the Korean War, October–December 1950." *Chinese Historians* 5.2 (Fall 1952): 65–85.

Li, Xialing, Wang Yi, and Chen Jian, trans. "Mao's Despatch of Chinese Troops into Korea: Forty-Six Telegrams, July–October 1950." *Chinese Historians* 5 (Spring 1992): 63–86.

Lie, Trigve. *In the Cause of Peace: Seven Years with the United Nations.* New York: Macmillan, 1954.

Lowe, Peter. *The Origins of the Korean War.* London: Longman, 1986.

Lyons, Gene Martin. *Military Policy and Economic Aid: The Korean Case, 1950–1953.* Columbus: Ohio State University Press, 1961.

MacArthur, Douglas. *Reminiscences.* New York: McGraw-Hill, 1964.

MacDonald, Callum A. *Korea: The War before Vietnam.* New York: Free Press, 1986.

Macdonald, Donald Stone. *U.S.–Korean Relations from Liberation to Self-Reliance: The Twenty-Year Record.* Boulder, Colo.: Westview Press, 1992.

Matray, James Irving. *The Reluctant Crusade: American Foreign Policy in Korea, 1941–1950.* Honolulu: University of Hawaii Press, 1985.

———. "Truman's Plan for Victory: National Self-Determination and the Thirty-Eighth Parallel Decision in Korea." *Journal of American History* 66 (September 1979): 314–333.

May, Ernest R. *"Lessons" of the Past: The Use and Misuse of History in American Foreign Policy.* London: Oxford University Press, 1973.

McCoy, Donald, and Benedict K. Zabrist, eds. "Conference of Scholars on the Administration of Occupied Areas, 1943–1955." Manuscript. Independence, Miss.: The Harry S. Truman Library Institute for National and International Affairs, 1970.

McCullough, David. *Truman.* New York: Simon and Schuster, 1992.

McCune, Shannon. "The Thirty-Eighth Parallel in Korea." *World Politics* 1 (1948): 223–232.

McLellan, David S. *Dean Acheson: The State Department Years.* New York: Dodd, Mead, 1976.

Meade, E. Grant. *American Military Government in Korea*. New York: King's Crown Press, 1951.

Meader, Daniel J., ed. *The Korean War Prospect: Lessons for the Future*. Lanham, New York: University Press of America, 1998.

Melanson, Richard A., and David Mayers. *Rethinking Eisenhower: American Foreign Policy in the 1950s*. Urbana: University of Illinois Press, 1989.

Merrill, John. *Korea: The Peninsula Origins of the Korean War*. Newark: University of Delaware Press, 1989.

Millis, Walter, ed. *Forrestal Diaries*. New York: Viking Press, 1951.

Monsourov, Alexandre Y., article and trans. "Stalin, Mao, Kim, and China's Decision to Enter the Korean War, September 16–October 15, 1950: New Evidence from the Russian Archives." *Cold War International History Project Bulletin* 6-7 (1995–1996): 114–119.

Mueller, John E. *War, Presidents, and Public Opinion*. New York: Wiley, 1973.

Nagai, Yonosuke, "The Korean War: An Interpretative Essay." *The Japanese Journal of American Studies* 1 (1981): 151–174.

Nagai, Yonosuke, and Iriye Akira, eds. *The Origins of the Cold War in Asia*. New York: Columbia University Press, 1977.

Nahm, Andrew C., ed. *The United States and Korea: American–Korean Relations, 1866–1976*. Kalamazoo: Center for Korean Studies, Western Michigan University, 1979.

Newmann, Sigmund. "The International Civil War." *World Politics* 1 (1949): 333–350.

Nixon, Richard. *The Real War*. New York: Warner Brothers, 1980.

Noble, Harold J. *Embassy at War*. Seattle: University of Washington Press, 1975.

Ohn, Chang-il. "The Joint Chiefs of Staff and U.S. Policy and Strategy Regarding Korea, 1945–1953." Ph.D. dissertation, University of Kansas, 1983.

Okonoki, Masao. *Hankuk Chŏnchaeng: Mikukŭi kaeipŭi kwachŏng* (The Korean War: The process of the U.S. intervention). Seoul: Chongke Yonkuso, 1986.

Oliver, Robert T. *Syngman Rhee and American Involvement in Korea, 1942–1960: A Personal Narrative*. Seoul: P'anmun, 1978.

———. *Why War Came in Korea*. New York: Fordham University Press, 1950.

Pach, Chester J., and Elmo Richardson. *The Presidency of Dwight D. Eisenhower*. Rev. ed. Lawrence: University of Kansas Press, 1991.

Paige, Glenn D. *The Korean Decision*. New York: Free Press, 1968.

Paik, Sŭn-yŭp. *Kunkwa na: 6.25 Hankuk Chŏnchaeng hoekorok* (The Army and me: The Korean War memoirs). Seoul: Daeryuk Yŏnkuso, 1989.

Pak, Hyŏn-chae, ed. *Haepang chŏnhusaŭi insik* (Understanding of the history of the pre- and the postliberation era). Vol. 3 Seoul: Hankilsa, 1987.

Pak, Myŏng-lim. "Nuka Hankuk Chŏnchaengŭl sichak hayŏtnŭnka?: Namch'im Pukch'im nonchengŭi chongkyŏlŭl ŭihan charyowa sasilŭi kŏmt'owa haesŏk" (Who did start the Korean War?: An examination and interpretation of source materials and facts for ending the controversy). *Hankuk Chŏngch'i Hakhoe Hakpo* 28 (1994): 79–105.

Panikkar, Kavalam M. *In Two Chinas: Memoirs of a Diplomat*. London: George Allen and Unwin, 1995.

Park, Chang-jin. "The Influence of Small States upon the Super Powers: United States–South Korean Relations as a Case Study in 1950–53." *World Politics* 28 (1975): 97–118.

Park, Hong-kyu. "American–Korean Relations, 1945–1953: A Study in United States Diplomacy." Ph.D. dissertation, North Texas State University, 1981.

Paterson, Thomas G. "Presidential Foreign Policy, Public Opinion, and Congress: The Truman Years." *Diplomatic History* 3 (1979): 1–18.

Petrov, Vladimir. "Mao, Stalin, and Kim Il Sung: An Interpretive Essay." *Journal of Northeast Asian Studies* 13 (Summer 1994): 3–30.

———. "Soviet Role in the Korean War Confirmed." *Journal of Northeast Asian Studies* 13 (Fall 1994): 42–67.

Pierpaoli, Paul G., Jr. *Truman and Korea.* Columbia: University of Missouri Press, 1999.

"Pisa oekyo 30-nyŏn" (Confidential history of a 30-year diplomacy). *Seoul Sinmun*, March 16, 1982–March 31, 1983.

Pyŏn, Yŏng-t'ae. *Oekyo yŏrok* (Diplomatic memoir). Seoul: Hankuk Ilposa, 1959.

Ra, Jong-il. "Special Relationship at War: The Anglo–American Relationship during the Korean War." *Journal of Strategic Studies* 7 (1984): 301–317.

———. *Kŭtnachi anŭm chŏnchaeng: Hanpantowa kangtaekuk chŏngch' i, 1950–1954* (Unended war: The Korean peninsula and the strong-power politics, 1950–1954). Seoul: Chŏnyewŏn, 1994.

Reeve, W. D. *The Republic of Korea: A Political and Economic Study.* London: Oxford University Press, 1963.

The Republic of Korea, Ministry of Foreign Affairs. *Relations of the United Nations Organs Relating to Korea (1947–1963).* Seoul: Ministry of Foreign Affairs, n.d.

The Republic of Korea, Ministry of National Defense. *History of the United Nations Forces in the Korean War.* Vol. 6. Seoul: The Republic of Korea, Ministry of National Defense, War History Compilation Commission, 1977.

Rhee, Francisca. "6.25wa Rhee Syngman Taet'ongryŏng" (The Korean War and President Syngman Rhee). *Chungang Ilbo,* June 24, 1983.

Rhee, In-su. *Unnam Rhee Syngman* (Unnam Rhee Syngman). Manuscript, 1987.

Ridgway, Matthew B. *The Korean War: How We Met the Challenge.* Garden City, N.Y.: Doubleday, 1967.

Rose, Lisle. *Roots of Tragedy: The United States and the Struggle for Asia, 1945–1953.* Westport, Conn.: Praeger, 1976.

Roseman, Samuel I., ed. *The Public Papers and Addresses of Franklin D. Roosevelt.* New York: Harper and Brothers, 1950.

Sandusky, Michael C. *American Parallel.* Alexandria, Va.: Old Dominion Press, 1983.

Sawyer, Robert K. *Military Advisers in Korea: KMAG in Peace and War.* Washington, D.C.: Office of the Chief of Military History, Department of the Army, 1962.

Seoul Shinmun T'ŭkpyŏl Ch'uichae Team. *Hankuk oekyo pirok* (Confidential record of Korean diplomacy). Seoul: Seoul Shimunsa, 1984.

Seoul Shinmunsa, ed. *Chuhan Mikun 30-nyŏn* (The 30 years of the U.S. Army in Korea). Seoul: Haenglim Ch'ulpansa, 1979.

Sherwood, Robert E. *Roosevelt and Hopkins: An Intimate History.* New York: Harper, 1948.

Shin, Ki-hyŏn. "Hankuk Chŏnchaengŭi hyŏntaesachŏk ŭii: kuknaechŏk mit kukchechŏk ch'awŏn" (The modern historical meaning of the Korean War: Domestic and international dimensions). *Kukche Chŏngch'i Nonch'ong* (1990): 333–411.

Shin, Sang-ch'o. "Kukchesangŭro pon Hankuk Chŏnchaeng" (The Korean War, seen from an international perspective). *Pukhan* (June 1972): 46–56.

Simmons, Robert R. *The Strained Alliance: Peking, Pyungyang, Moscow and Politics of the Korean Civil War.* New York: Free Press, 1975.

Small, Melvin. *Was a War Necessary? National Security and U.S. Entry into War.* Beverly Hills, Calif.: Sage, 1980.

Snyder, Richard C., and Glenn D. Paige. "The United States Decision to Resist in Korea: The Application of an Analytical Scheme." *Administrative Science Quarterly* 3 (December 1958): 341–378.

Sŏh, Chin-chŏl. "Hankuk Chŏnchaengŭi wŏnin" (The causes of the Korean War). *Chŏngpae* (1966): 90–108.

Son, Ho-ch'ŏl, and others. *Hankuk Chŏnchaengkwa Nam-Pukhan sahoeŭi kuchochŏk pyŏnhwa* (The Korean War and the structural changes of the South and North Korean society). Hankuk yŏnku series, vol. 3. Seoul: Kyŏngnam Taehakkyo Kŭktong Munche Yŏnkuso, 1991.

Song, Kŏn-ho, and others. *Haepang chonhusaŭi insik* (Understanding of the history of the pre- and postliberation era). Vol. 1. Seoul: Hankilsa, 1989.

Stewart. James T. *Air Power: The Decisive Force in Korea.* Princeton: Nostrand, 1957.

Stone, I. F. *The Hidden History of the Korean War.* New York: Monthly Review Press, 1952.

Stueck, William. *The Korean War: An International History.* Princeton, N.J.: Princeton University Press, 1995

———. "The Limits of Influence: British Policy and American Expansion of the War in Korea." *Pacific Historical Review* 55 (February 1986): 65–95.

———. *The Road to Confrontation: American Policy toward China and Korea, 1947–1950.* Chapel Hill: University of North Carolina Press, 1981.

———. *The Wedemeyer Mission: American Politics and Foreign Policy during the Cold War.* Athens: University of Georgia Press, 1984.

Taehanminkuk, Kukpangpu, Chŏnsa P'yŏnch'an Wiwŏnhoe. *Hankuk Chŏnran Ilnyŏnchi, 1950–1951* (Annual record of the Korean War, 1950–1951). Seoul: Munyŏngsa, 1951.

———. *Hankuk Chŏnchaeng hyuchŏnsa* (History of the Korean War armistice negotiations). Seoul: Taehanminkuk, Kukpangpu, Chŏnsa P'yŏnch'an Wiwŏnhoe, 1989.

———. *Hankuk Chŏnchaengsa* (History of the Korean War). 7 vols. Seoul: Taehanminkuk, Kukpanpu, Chŏnsa P'yŏnch'an Wiwŏnhoe, 1967–1974.

———. *Hankuk Chŏnchaengsa: U.N. ch'amchŏnp'yŏn* (History of the Korean War: The U.N. participation). Seoul: Taehanminkuk, Kukpangpu, Chŏnsa P'yŏnch'an Wiwŏnhoe, 1980.

Thompson, Kenneth W., ed. *Korea: A World in Change.* Lanham, New York: University Press of America, 1996.

Truman, Harry S. *Memoirs.* 2 vols. Garden City, N.Y.: Doubleday, 1956.

Truman, Margaret. *Harry S. Truman.* New York: Morrow, 1973.

U.S. Joint Chiefs of Staff. *History of the Joint Chiefs of Staff.* Vol. 3, *The Joint Chiefs of Staff and National Policy: The Korean War.* Edited by James F. Schnabel and Robert J. Watson. Wilmington, Del.: Michael Glazier, 1979.

Van Ree, Erik. *Socialism in One Zone: Stalin's Policy in Korea, 1945–1947.* Oxford: Berg, 1989.

Vatcher, William H., Jr. *Panmunjŏm: The Story of the Korean Military Armistice Negotiations.* New York: Praeger, 1958.

Wainstock, Dennis D. *Truman, MacArthur, and the Korean War.* Westport, Conn.: Greenwood Press, 1999.

Warner, Geofrey. "The Korean War." *International Affairs* 56 (1980): 98–107.

Weathersby, Kathryn. "New Findings on the Korean War." *Cold War International History Project Bulletin* 3 (Fall 1993): 1, 14–18.

———. "New Russian Documents on the Korean War: Introduction and Translation." *Cold War International History Project Bulletin* 6–7 (Winter 1995–1996): 30–40, 42–84.

———. "Soviet Aims in Korea and the Origins of the Korean War, 1945–1950: New Evidence from Russian Archives." The Woodrow Wilson Center Cold War International History Project, Working Paper no. 8, 1993.

———. "The Soviet Role in the Early Phase of the Korean War: New Documentary Evidence." *The Journal of American–East Asian Relations* 24 (Winter 1995): 25–32.

Wedemyer, Albert C. *Wedemyer Reports.* New York: Davin-Adair, 1958.

Weintraub, Stanley. *MacArthur's War: Korea and the Undoing of an American Hero.* New York: Free Press, 2000.

Westad, Odd A., ed. *Brothers in Arms: The Rise and Fall of the Sino–Soviet Alliance, 1945–1963.* Stanford: Stanford University Press, 1998.

Whelan, Richard. *Drawing the Line: The Korean War, 1950–1953.* Boston: Little, Brown, 1990.

Whiting, Allen S. *China Crosses the Yalu: The Decision to Enter the Korean War.* Stanford: Stanford University Press, 1968.

Williams, Phil, Donald M. Goldstein, and Henry L. Andrews, Jr., eds. *Security in Korea: War, Stalemate, and Negotiation.* Boulder, Colo.: Westview Press, 1994.

Williams, William J. *A Revolutionary War: Korea and the Transformation of the Postwar World.* Chicago: Imprint Publications, 1993.

Willoughby, Charles A., and John Chamberlin. *MacArthur, 1941–1951.* New York: McGraw-Hill, 1954.

Wolfers, Arnold. "Collective Security and the War in Korea." *Yale Review* 43 (June 1954): 481–496.

Wŏn, Tong-sŏk. "U.S. Foreign Aid Program in Korea." *Koreana Quarterly* 5 (1963): 95–99.

"World Policy and Bipartisanship: An Interview with Senator Tom Connally." *U.S. News and World Report* 28 (May 5, 1950): 28–31.

Wright, Quincy. "American Policy toward Russia." *World Politics* 2 (1950): 462–481.

Xue, Litai. "State Interests and Realpolitik in the Decision-Making Process." Manuscript, 1995.

Yang, Tae-hyŏn. "Hankuk Chŏnchaengkwa Han-Mi tongmaeng kwanke: Tongmaeng ironŭl chungsimŭro" (The Korean War and Korean–American alliance relationship, with an emphasis on the theory of alliances). *Hankuk Chŏngch'i Hakhoepo* 26 (1992): 401–423.

———. "Hankukŭi hyuchŏn hoetamkwa Mikukŭi tae-Han chongch'aek—hyŏpsang chonryakŭl chungsimŭro" (The Korean armistice negotiations and the U.S. policy toward Korea: with an emphasis on the negotiation strategies). *Kukche Chŏngch'i Nonch'ong* 23 (1983): 321–345.

Yu, Chae-hŭng. "Hoeko: Park Chŭng-hi, Chŭng Il-kwŏn, kŭriko Chŏng In-suk sakŏn" (Memoir: Park Chŭng-hi, Chŭng Il-kwŏn, and Chŏng In-suk incident). *Donga Ilbo*, March 3–5, 1994.

Yukkun Sakwan Hakkyo. *Hankuk Chŏnchaengsa* (History of wars in Korea). Seoul: Ilshinsa, 1987.

Zhang, Shu-gung. *Mao's Military Romanticism: China and the Korean War, 1950–1952.* Lawrence: University Press of Kansas, 1995.

Index

Acheson, Dean: *aide memoire* of April 3, 1950, 107–109; Korean election, 1950, 109; Korean reaction to the armistice negotiations, 254; long-term U.S. objectives in Korea, 88–89; no evacuation from Korea decision, December 1950, 232; outbreak of the Korean War, 193–195; relief and rehabilitation of Korea, 275; role in U.S. intervention in the Korean War, 193–199; role in U.S.-R.O.K. relationship, 293; 38th parallel crossing north, February 1950, 237

Acheson's 1950 Press Club speech: authored by George Kennan, 161; comments on, 163–164; contemporaries' reaction, 163–164; Korea in the speech, 162–163; preapproved by President Truman, 161; the speech, 161–162

Allison, John M.: and Korean election, 1952, 179, 181; and the 38th parallel crossing north issue, 210–211, 230; and U.S. policy toward Korea, 41–42; and U.S.-R.O.K. relationship, 293; and United States taking the Korean case to the United Nations, 46; and U.S. troop withdrawal from Korea, 118

Armistice negotiations, the Korean War: armistice agreement, 267–269; communist side of the beginning, 238; difficulty with the peacemaking, 5, 237; early peace effort, 237–238; factors for reaching the agreement, 249–250; fighting while negotiating, 245; Korean dual line of cooperation and protest, 245; Korean reaction and the United States dealing with the problem, 253–261; POW issues, 242–245, 247–248; process, 238–243, 244–245, 266–267; Robertson Seoul trip, 261–265

Atomic bomb, Eisenhower's view of its being simply another weapon, 257

"Big Switch," 269

Block-and-gap approach, a Cold War strategy, 170

Bond, Niles W.: military aid for Korea and, 152; NSC 8 series, 98; and U.S. Korea policy change, 1948–1950, 145; role in U.S.-R.O.K. relationship, 293; U.S. troop withdrawal and, 117–118, 153

ABOUT THE AUTHOR

Jongsuk Chay is Professor of History Emeritus at the University of North Carolina, Pembroke.